D0874187

59¢ March 1981

The Analysis of Subjective Culture

Comparative Studies in Behavioral Science:

A WILEY SERIES

Robert T. Holt and John E. Turner, *Editors*
Department of Political Science
University of Minnesota

The Logic of Comparative Social Inquiry
    by Adam Przeworski and Henry Teune

The Analysis of Subjective Culture
    by Harry C. Triandis

The Analysis of Subjective Culture

HARRY C. TRIANDIS

University of Illinois, Urbana

in association with

Vasso Vassiliou and George Vassiliou
Athenian Institute of Anthropos
Athens, Greece

Yasumasa Tanaka
Gakushuin University
Tokyo, Japan

A. V. Shanmugam
Indian Institute of Mass Communication
New Delhi, India

and with the assistance of

**Earl E. Davis, Keith M. Kilty, Howard McGuire,
Tulsi Saral** and **Kuo-shu Yang**
University of Illinois, Urbana

WILEY-INTERSCIENCE

A Division of John Wiley & Sons, Inc.

NEW YORK · LONDON · SYDNEY · TORONTO

SERIES PREFACE

The last decade has witnessed the burgeoning of comparative studies in the behavioral sciences. Scholars in specific disciplines have come to realize that they share much with experts in other fields who face similar theoretical and methodological problems and whose research findings are often related. Moreover, specialists in a given geographic area have felt the need to look beyond the limited confines of their region and to seek new meaning in their research results by comparing them with studies that have been made eleswhere.

This series is designed to meet the needs of the growing cadre of scholars in comparative research. The emphasis is on cross-disciplinary studies, although works within the perspective of a single discipline are included. In its scope, the series includes books of theoretical and methodological interest, as well as studies that are based on empirical research. The books in the series are addressed to scholars in the various behavioral science disciplines, to graduate students, and to undergraduates in advanced standing.

Robert T. Holt
John E. Turner

University of Minnesota
Minneapolis, Minnesota

Preface

In the last quarter century indications leading to the view that man has evolved from a species of carnivorous, tool-using apes who lived in Africa a million years ago have been accumulating in the fields of anthropology and paleontology at a rapid rate. Interestingly enough, it seems that most of the major social characteristics of these apes, as far as we can reconstruct them from fossil evidence, can still be found in modern man. Specifically, these apes hunted in packs and used a good deal of cooperation within them while defending their territories in ferocious battles. Within the packs there was a pecking order similar to those we find today among many birds and mammals, including man.

Man's recorded history is but a mere moment on the time scale of evolution—specifically, less than 1% of the time since he started using tools. Culture, which is the man-made part of the human environment, is also relatively recent. Yet, because man is so high on the phylogenetic scale and has such a long maturation period, cultural influences make a major impact on his development.

Modern man's culture for the first time in the last quarter century includes the capacity to destroy all life on earth. Thus we have the paradox of a relatively primitive animal, which only recently killed millions of his own species in wars and concentration camps, now possessing the ability to destroy all life by the most advanced methods of science. And, more, man's science has developed to the point at which it can dramatically change the environment by pollution, overpopulation, and atomic fallout.

The history of human conflict of the last few years suggests that man has not evolved much beyond his primitive ancestors. Everywhere we look we see conflict—tribal, religious, ideological—escalating to the destruction of human beings. Unless we find new ways to reduce conflict we may not be able to survive as a species and may destroy the ecology of all living things in the process.

Human aggression is clearly a product of both biological and cultural influences. While biologists are working on possible changes in human genetic structures, which may provide the needed breakthrough to the reduction of human aggression, other behavioral scientists must work on the cultural influences. Furthermore, it seems more realistic to hope that the solution will be found in the modification of the environment rather than in the restructuring of human genes, since there will be tremendous ethical, political, and social problems to be solved if we seek a biological solution to man's aggression.

One of the keys to this aggression can be found in ethnocentric concepts, ideological differences, and culturally determined ways of perceiving the social environment. We define *subjective culture* as a cultural group's characteristic way of perceiving its social environment. Differences in subjective culture are responsible for a good deal of intergroup conflict. In this book we hope to provide some concepts and new methodologies for its analysis and some insight into its relation to human conflict.

This work was undertaken in the spirit of cooperation by behavioral scientists concerned with the reduction of human conflict. Several behavioral scientists, from different disciplines, living in four different parts of the world, were concerned with the human condition and hoped to discover new ways to reduce conflict. When right conditions for cooperation were made available, they were ready to join in a common effort.

The opportunity to do large-scale studies which would be freely published and available to all those who read the professional literature, no matter what their tribe, religion, or political persuasion, was most appealing. It is exactly this freedom to do whatever studies we wished to do, to cooperate across highly diverse cultures, and to send our reprints east, west, north, and south that convinced us that we could proceed with these projects.

The strange dialectics of life which dominated social-science support in the 1960's made it possible for the very source of the "by-force-solutions" to open the way to studies aiming to facilitate communication, mutual understanding, and solution by negotiation. In any case, in the early 1960's the "defense establishment" was the only source of research funds available for large-scale studies as controversial as those we planned to do. At that time studies of stereotyping, social distance, and the like were considered by funding agencies as a means of increasing conflict, by detecting it, measuring it, and pointing to it. It was only in the last part of the 1960's that it was realized that conflict cannot be reduced by ignoring it, suppressing it, and pretending that it does not exist; on the contrary, it must be studied, analyzed, and understood.

It was high time to face the problem of cultural differences squarely. Centuries ago Herodotus described such differences in detail. Later the astonished Montaigne observed that what held true on one side of the Pyrenees did not hold on the other. Since then many psychologists have attempted to propose general laws that transcend culture. Yet the application of these laws in different cultural settings has often led to disappointment. Very abstract concepts, such as the strengthening of the bond between stimuli and responses via reinforcement, may be universal, but they are of limited use to those who need to know which stimuli are perceived, how they are categorized, what responses are reinforced, and under what conditions. As soon as we reduce the level of abstraction of our psychological laws, we need to know something about cultural influences. At this greater level of specificity we discover that variables change their relationships from one culture to another. Hence we must rediscover these relationships or find a way to translate them from one system to another. The concepts that we propose in this book may help. Once such translations are made available it may be possible to show the generality of several psychological laws, and we may discover that we are quarreling about something that we actually agree on.

The world of the 1970's is tantalizing because science can provide many of the solutions to its problems. Yet unless we undertand how man's subjective culture is involved in conflict we may find that, as one of us put it, "Anthropos may not avoid the fate of Tantalus." We hope that this book will make a small contribution by providing some concepts and new methodologies for the analysis of subjective culture.

Many people contributed to the studies that finally led to this book. Projects such as this require an extensive network of collaborators, intellectual stimulation, constructive criticism, and encouragement. Most credit in these categories goes to Charles Osgood. We are also grateful to Uriel Foa and Lawrene Stolurow for their stimulating ideas during the early phases of the project. A major share of the credit goes to Fred E. Fiedler, who as codirector with Triandis of the contract which supported the major part of the work, made invaluable contributions.

Earl Davis, in 1963-1966, and David Summers, in 1966-1968, as research associates, made important contributions to this project. Kuo-Shu Yang collected data in Taiwan, Tulsi Saral, in India, Wallace Loh, in Peru, and Keith Kilty and Howard McGuire, in the United States. Most of the analyses were done by McGuire.

This does not complete the list of those who helped make this book a reality. It is only by an accident of timing that some names do not appear in the front of this book. In Illinois Ellie Hall and Robert B. Ewen, Robert Potts and Erich Thomanek, and Gerald Oncken and Tom Stewart represent three "generations" of assistants who collected American data and analyzed cross-cultural data. In Greece Maria Nassiakou and Voula

Argyropoulou, in India, Vijayakumari Shanmugam, and in Japan, Yoko Iwamatsu and Tomoe Abe made important contributions to both data collection and preparation for analysis.

The early work on this project was supported in 1956, 1960, and 1962 by grants to Triandis from the U.S. Public Health Service. The University of Illinois Research Board made a crucial grant in 1961-1962. The Advanced Research Projects Agency, through the office of Naval Research NR 177-472, Nonr 1836 [36]; ARPA Order No. 454) supported this research from 1963 to 1969. The Ford Foundation gave Triandis a senior faculty fellowship which made it possible for him to work full time on this project in 1964-1965 and to spend part of the time in Japan, India, and Greece. The Department of Health, Education and Welfare through its Social Rehabilitation Service (Grant No. RD 2841-G) has been supporting Triandis since 1968. The writing of this book was greatly facilitated by an invitation from the Center for International Studies of Cornell University for Triandis to spend the academic year 1968-1969 in Ithaca. One of the fellows at the Center was Henry Teune, whose considerable experience with cross-cultural research contributed importantly to the writing of the first two chapters. Douglas Ashford, Director of the Center at that time, and his staff made numerous facilities and services available which were greatly appreciated.

Since all the principal authors of this book use English as a second or third language, it was necessary to have editors for our prose. Several chapters were improved by Earl Davis, Keith Kilty, and David Summers; the major editorial work for the entire book as done by Pola Triandis.

W. W. Lambert and Robert T. Holt made valuable suggestions which improved the manuscript.

Special thanks are due to Mrs. Alfreda Mitchell, Triandis' secretary at Illinois, who has helped in many ways and typed most of the manuscript.

We are grateful to all and thank them for their help.

HARRY C. TRIANDIS
GEORGE AND VASSO VASSILIOU
YASUMASA TANAKA
A. V. SHANMUGAM

August 1971

CONTENTS

The Analysis of Subjective Culture

PART ONE

Introduction

CHAPTER ONE

Preliminary Considerations

It is a common observation, even among casual travelers, that groups in different cultures differ in their behavior. No special training is required to note that there are major differences in dress, food, language, or customs of social behavior across cultures. It is almost certain that these differences are reflected in the way individuals experience their social environment. The problem in this book is to explore how reliable, cross-culturally equivalent methods can be developed for the study of such differences in "subjective culture." By subjective culture we mean a cultural group's characteristic way of perceiving its social environment.

Subjective culture refers to variables that are attributes of the cognitive structures of groups of people. The *analysis* of subjective culture refers to variables extracted from consistencies in their responses and results in a kind of "map" drawn by a scientist which outlines the subjective culture of a particular group. In short, when we observe consistent responses to classes of stimuli that have some quality in common, we assume that some "mediators" (attitudes, norms, values, etc.) are responsible for these consistencies. It is the cognitive structures which mediate between stimuli and responses in different cultural settings that we wish to study. The elements of subjective culture are hypothetical constructs that help us simplify our observations of human behavior. They do not "exist" except in the mind of the scientist. There are no physical entities that constitute subjective culture, yet the variables that will be included under this construct do help us to understand, predict, and possibly even control human behavior.

Subjective culture can be analyzed by referring to already well-established concepts such as attitudes, roles, and values. In this book these concepts are defined in ways that will allow cross-culturally equivalent measurement. Our attempt is to reveal the nonequivalence of measurement when equivalence cannot be attained.

Our approach utilizes a large number of cognitive tasks and obtains a

3

large number of responses from each subject. Elaborate statistical analyses of such data permit us to make explicit what is implicit in the responses of the subjects. In short, we produce a "map" of the subjects' subjective culture which makes explicit or visible what is implicit or subjective. In this book we have attempted to illustrate with data collected in Greece, India, Japan, and the United States how various aspects of a group's subjective culture may be studied and how we may establish the validity of these measures.

We do not see this work as a finished product. On the contrary, this is the first step in a research program that may require several centuries for its completion. To develop appropriate ways of describing the subjective culture of most of the significant cultural groups of the world is a task that can be completed only if many people work on it for a long time. To utilize further the elements of subjective culture to modify the generality of some psychological laws and to uncover the principles that interrelate social structural and ecological variables and psychological laws will require extensive work. We have made only a beginning. The reader will have to decide for himself whether the beginning is sufficiently promising to justify his participation in the next steps.

Some Definitions

Culture has been defined as the man-made part of the human environment (Herskovits, 1955, p. 305). *Subjective culture* is a cultural group's characteristic way of perceiving the man-made part of its environment. The perception of rules and the group's norms, roles, and values are aspects of subjective culture.

People who live next to one another, speak the same dialect, and engage in similar activities (e.g., have similar occupations) are likely to share the same subjective culture. Several theoretical systems which have been supported by empirical findings, such as those proposed by Homans (1950, 1961), Whyte (1959), and Newcomb (1961), include propositions that suggest that many of the elements of subjective culture are determined by the propinquity of members of a group. This is true because propinquity, a common language, and similar activities tend to lead to high rates of interaction among members of human groups. Frequent interaction usually leads to similar norms, attitudes, and roles, hence to similar subjective cultures. Similarity in race (physical type), sex, and age also lead to higher rates of interaction, hence to similarities in subjective culture. The causal chains are circular because similarities in subjective culture lead to greater satisfaction in interpersonal interaction, hence to its increased frequency. If we think of interaction as providing rewards or punishments and its

private failure condition. Clear

self-promoting than those of fem

(1982) conclusion that "women's b

expectations of 'feminine modest

attributions" (p. 484) is entirely

theory.

While "feminine Modesty" may

desired impressions in some so

counterproductive in professional

high performing co-workers (Staw

1974), and superiors (Bachman, 19

their lower performing counterpart

of which are non-work related. In

Adams (1974) found that it was the

frequency as a measurement of the degree of enjoyment in an interpersonal relationship, we can see frequent interaction both as a cause and an effect of similarity in subjective culture.

If we are to specify the subjective culture of a human group, we should attempt to control or measure most of the variables mentioned above. In short, we should determine how language, sex, age, race, religion, place of residence, and occupation affect subjective culture and also how subjective culture influences interpersonal behavior.

The Broad Aims

The purpose of analyzing subjective cultures is not limited to understanding the experience and behavior of various specific human groups. This is more an applied than a scientific goal. Of greater scientific importance than such analyses is the improvement in our understanding of how the elements of subjective culture develop and how they are implicated in interpersonal behavior; for example, if we are to study interpersonal attitudes, we must first learn much that is general about attitudes, regardless of culture, and how these attitudes are related to interpersonal interactions. We must develop general or culture-free laws, such as, "the greater the rewards experienced in an interpersonal relationship, the more positive the affect experienced in the presence of the other person."

Other laws may be true only for cultures with certain broad characteristics, such as those that emphasize hierarchical relationships. Thus we may have more specific laws such as, "in cultures that emphasize hierarchical relationships the higher the status of a person, the more rewarding is potentially the interaction with him." (Note that the converse is not true, since interactions with children may be very rewarding.) As we specify more and more conditional variables not only do the laws become more and more specific and limited but also probably more predictive of the limited behaviors described by them; for instance, there might be a law that stated, "in cultures emphasizing hierarchical relationships, a male will avoid interaction with females that are more than 10 years his junior, except for behavior areas X, Y, and Z." This is a complex conditional law, but it probably predicts rates of interaction better than the more general laws. Our aim, however, is to develop the most general laws that predict best, but the complexity of human behavior may put some limits to the success of our attempts. We may need to develop laws that are valid at different levels of abstraction or specificity.

1. At the most general level we would have laws that are valid across cultural groups. These laws would probably concern broad phenomena such as values and rates of interaction.

2. At the next level we would have laws that apply only within particular types of culture and would involve general attitudes such as nationalism or religiosity.

3. At the next level we would have laws that depend on the cultural and demographic characteristics of the actors and would involve rather specific attitudes, for example, toward "old people in hierarchical cultures."

4. At the most specific level we would have empirical generalizations that apply to specific subgroups such as "Portuguese-speaking, Negro, female Brazilian physicians approve of medical insurance plans." They would be extremely specific and would involve attitudes toward limited issues and specific behaviors.

From a scientific point of view laws of types (1) and (2) would be the most interesting; for an applied social science, however, laws of types (3) and (4) may also be required.

Some Specific Aims

We wish to develop concepts that will allow us to analyze subjective culture and to measure its elements equivalently across culture. If we learn how to analyze and measure accurately the way people look at their environments, we may be able to do two kinds of study of great social significance: we may study what causes the particular perceptions of the environment and also learn about the precise consequences of these perceptions; for example, we may explore the way child-training practices, the reading of history, the amount of schooling, the kinds of schools, or the political system of a particular country or cultural group influence such perceptions. In addition, we can see what happens if children are brought up differently, when the school systems are changed, when the political institutions are modified, and so on.

If we learn about the consequences of these perceptions to mental health or economic development, we may be able to design organizations, societies, and other social systems so that cultural influences will help rather than hinder the members of these social systems to reach their goals. In any case, precise analysis and measurement of such perceptions would lead to considerable progress toward an understanding of how the environment influences the beliefs, attitudes, hopes, and values of different people and how these factors, in turn, influence behavior in different environments.

Another important aim is the improvement of intercultural understanding, communication, and adjustment. Studies in which differences in subjective culture constitute the independent variables and interpersonal perception, communication, and adjustment, the dependent variables, can provide critical information for social psychology and also useful information for the solution of many practical problems of interpersonal and intergroup conflict.

About This Book

What is new in this book? *Subjective culture,* as a concept, is not new. It has been used extensively by Osgood (1964, 1965, 1970) and is similar to *mazeway* (Wallace, 1962a), *behavioral environment* (Hallowell, 1955), *world view* (Redfield, 1953), *cognitive map* (Tolman, 1948) and *life space* (Lewin, 1951). We could have used one of these concepts, but we avoided doing so because we do not completely subscribe to the details of the theoretical analyses of any of these theorists. If there is something new about our approach, it is the attempt to define *several* concepts in a way that permits equivalent cross-cultural measurement. What is meant by equivalent is discussed extensively later.

This book is an attempt to describe what has been done by a small research group at the University of Illinois in collaboration with colleagues in three other countries to meet the goal of such equivalent measurement. The heart of the book is the presentation of original research reports covering our particular techniques in detail, describing our findings, and giving interpretations of these findings. In order, however, to help the reader to see this work in perspective, we have devised a theoretical framework that is broader than the focus of this book, and we have referred to the work of others with sufficient frequency to tie our work to the mainstream of the social psychological literature.

The next chapter defines the concepts that constitute the theoretical framework. It presents not only the elements of subjective culture but also some speculations concerning the antecedents and consequents of differences in subjective culture. The third chapter explores methodological problems of cross-cultural research in general and research on subjective culture in particular. The last chapter of the introductory section of the book is an overview of the remaining chapters.

Part II of the book consists of examples of our approach to the analysis of cognitive structures, values, behavioral intentions, and roles. In Part III we present an integration of data obtained with all these approaches in one culture as an example of how such kinds of data are interrelated. The last chapter explores the relationship between subjective culture and behavior and speculates about the relevance of subjective culture analyses in a number of practical situations. We believe our approach will prove

relevant in studies of training persons to interact effectively in another culture and giving advice and technical assistance to governments when a cultural gap exists between adviser and advisee. The implications of analyses
of subjective culture for economic development and for the adoption of
innovations and population control are still unclear, but some suggestions
are included on how these analyses can be helpful in understanding such
phenomena.

CHAPTER TWO

Theoretical Framework

Social scientists can observe two major kinds of regularity: in situations and in behavior. If they detect a common element across situations or across patterns of behavior and discern a consistency in the associations between such common elements, they make inferences about psychological constructs such as attitudes, values, subjective culture, or what have you.

One kind of regularity concerns the presence in situations of respondents that belong to the same cultural or biological group. We arbitrarily define a *cultural group* as one whose members speak the same dialect, share major activities (e.g., have a common occupation), or have a common ideology (e.g., belong to the same religious persuasion). We define a *biological group* as one with some biological characteristic in common which has social significance in that group so that it influences its patterns of social interaction. In many societies, for instance, social interactions are patterned by age, sex, or physical typing (race), and when this happens we have biological groups, according to our definition.

The strategy we employ in analyses of subjective culture places persons who belong to specifiable cultural or biological groups in similar situations, presents them with many kinds of stimuli, and observes their responses. When these responses constitute similar patterns, we infer similarities in subjective culture. Conversely, when the similar patterns obtained in one culture differ from the similar patterns obtained in another, we infer the existence of some differences in subjective culture.

Campbell (1963b) has correctly pointed out that a large number of psychological concepts are inferred from consistencies in situations and responses; specifically, when there is an observation that experience has modified the person's behavior tendencies, we infer that something mediating between situation and response is no longer the same. This something can have many names. He lists about 80 concepts, ranging from *acquired drive* to *value*.

9

In studying subjective culture we selected concepts that are "pancultural" and "show variation across cultures"; for example, customs, roles, or values are useful in the analysis of behavior in all cultures and show variations across cultures. Many concepts from Campbell's list meet these criteria. We note, however, that some of Campbell's concepts are at higher levels of abstraction than others; *cognitive map, cognitive structure,* and *life space* are at the same level of abstraction as subjective culture. Furthermore, many of Campbell's concepts overlap one another. *Anticipations, expectancies,* and *expectations* are difficult to distinguish. For these reasons we include in our definition of subjective culture only the following elements from Campbell's list:

associations	memories
attitudes	opinions
beliefs	percepts
concepts (categorizations)	role perceptions
evaluations	stereotypes
expectations	values

In this chapter we provide operational definitions for some of these concepts and suggest specific methods of measurement. We assume also that it would be helpful to place the concepts in a conceptual scheme, since each concept's definition can be made clearer when its relation to other concepts is shown.

Categorization

Humans often give the same response to discriminably different stimuli. When this happens, we say that they categorize experience. The *category* is probably the most important element in the analysis of subjective culture.

We must distinguish different levels of analysis in studying subjective culture. At the most primitive level we have *discriminable stimuli* and at the higher level, *elementary categories.* The eye is capable of discriminating about 7,500,000 colors (Brown and Lenneberg, 1954) but there are only about 400 color words in English and most English-speaking persons employ only about a dozen of these words with reasonable frequency.

All cultural groups employ categories (Kluckhohn, 1954). They "cut the pie of experience" differently, however. To see this in a clear example we note that Lenneberg and Roberts (1956) found cultural differences in the way color categories are formed; for example, what one group calls green another may call by four different names. Landar et al. (1960) have shown that the Navaho use four different terms which might correspond to the English terms "brown-green," "blue-green," "green-yellow," and "purple-green," whereas English speakers react to "greenness" with little subtlety and differentiation.

There is evidence, reviewed by Triandis (1964a), that there are many cultural differences in categorization which are reflected in the well-known examples of many words for certain domains in certain cultures (e.g., several thousand camel-related words in Arabic, several hundred car-related words in American English—Ford, VW, 1950 Dodge, truck, auto, vehicle, etc.) as well as in the use of different content and different *criterial attributes* for categorization.

Elementary categories can be found not only for visual stimuli but also for auditory, tactical, olfactory, and gustatory. Gibson (1966) has considered each of these sensory inputs as providing a perceptual system that evolved through increased differentiation. The organism learns to pay attention to more and more subtle aspects of stimulation. As a child grows it is capable of larger spans of attention and learns what is important to attend. He learns *by* association the learning *of* associations. He observes much and does so even when he has no linguistic labels. He sees more than he can describe.

As Vygotsky (1962) has clearly shown, thought and word are not connected by primary bonds, although thought is assisted by the availability of labels. In short, thought may utilize *elementary categories* which have no corresponding *meaning category*.

Social psychologists are particularly interested in elementary categories involving social behavior. That elementary categories involving behavior must exist appears to be self-evident from the observation that we may notice aspects of a person's behavior we are unable to describe. Time is also experienced in bundles or categories.

An important kind of elementary unit of sound is the ordinary phoneme. One characteristic of elementary categories, such as ordinary phonemes, is that when they first develop they have no affect. A color *as such* does not elicit affective responses in a child until it is associated with pleasant or unpleasant events. Cross-cultural studies of color meaning suggest that this meaning is not the same in different cultures. This is most probably due, however, to differential associations. In Turkey green is "good," but in other countries that were occupied by the Ottoman empire it is "bad." At the next level of analysis we have *meaning categories*. Here affect is present. A morpheme is an example of a meaning category.

In summary, at the lowest level of abstraction we have discriminable stimuli from which elemental categories are formed; at the next level the elemental categories are combined to form meaning categories. At higher levels we have concepts, sentences, and paragraphs.

Anthropologists have done extensive work in determining the way tribal groups categorize experience; for example, Voegelin and Voegelin (1957) have published a book on Hopi domains, which essentially examines the way the Hopi categorize the physical and biological world, man, intellect, emotions, values, and interpersonal relations. Levi-Strauss (1966) has summarized a vast body of literature on this topic.

Four classes of categories (self, people, objects, behaviors) consist of *domains* that include numerous subclasses; for example, "people" includes a vast number of domains such as American politicians, Javanese dancers, Greek foustanelades, Temple dancers in India, and Geisha girls in Japan.

In order to define a domain it is necessary to have some criteria. To define the domain American politicians some people may use the criteria (a) American citizen who aspires (b) to be or has been elected to political office. We call them *between-domains criterial attributes,* since they help us to discriminate one domain from another. In addition, there are *within-domain criterial attributes*. The latter attributes discriminate members of a domain from one another. In our example the within-domain criterial attributes used by a group may be (a) left-right and (b) Democrat-Republican which immediately define four categories: left Democrat, left Republican, right Democrat and right Republican. If we were to study a subgroup of people and discovered that it gave responses which fall into these four categories, we should be justified in claiming that this sample of people utilizes the two within-domain attributes mentioned above. Thus our definition of categorization still applies: to repeat, if people give the same response to discriminably different stimuli, we infer that they categorize experience.

By discovering what attributes define these domains we can study the way people categorize experience. The advantage of discovering the attributes is that it reduces the work of analysis; for example, there are thousands of American politicians, but we might be able to describe significant aspects of the way people react to them by knowing only where they belong on *two* criterial attributes.

In Chapter 3 we shall study how multidimensional scaling, facet, feature, factor, and componential analysis can provide the methodology for the determination of criterial attributes.

It should be obvious that language is intimately involved in the categorization process. This implies that different language-culture communities will provide different opportunities for the categorization of experience. One of our problems is to determine exactly how this is done. Another problem is to determine the consequences of such differences in language. Triandis (1964a) reviewed this problem in connection with a discussion of the Whorfian hypothesis. He concluded that languages differ not so much in what can be said in them but rather in the ease with which one can say things (Hockett, 1954).

On the other hand, there are demonstrations of effects consistent with the Whorfian hypothesis, although they are often quite subtle. Niyekawa (1968) observed that the Japanese language has an "adversative passive" grammatical form, which implies "am not responsible for it." It is generally used when referring to some unpleasant event. Niyekawa studied the Japanese-to-English and English-to-Japanese translations of several short stories and found that when the translator went from Japanese to English he disregarded this particular implication but when he went from English to Japanese he employed the adversative passive form to describe an unpleasant event. She also employed a perceptual task which utilized stick-figure cartoons that depicted interpersonal conflict situations with negative outcomes. The Japanese subjects were found to have a greater tendency than Americans to attribute responsibility for these unpleasant incidents to others. A sample of English-speaking monolingual Hawaiians of Japanese ancestry was intermediate in this response tendency. The cultural influence (Japanese versus American ancestry) was a more powerful factor in attributing responsibility to others than was the linguistic influence. It was concluded that the Japanese culture provides experiences that are likely to lead to attribution of responsibility to others, but these tendencies are *enhanced* by linguistic factors, thus providing a partial support for the Whorfian hypothesis. We could also argue that Japanese culture is so sensitive to the attribution of responsibility for unpleasant events it has developed particular linguistic forms which make it easier to avoid blame.

A different kind of support for the Whorfian hypothesis may be found in Gay and Cole's (1967) demonstration that the Kpelle of Liberia, whose language makes distinctions between the various forms of disjunction, learn disjunctive concepts (such as *A* or *B* but not both) more easily than do Americans.

Evaluations

Once a category has been formed and becomes "functional" in a particular culture, it can become "conditioned." Staats (1967) argues that the operant laws of conditioning, such as the high frequency of contiguous occurrence of a category with positive or negative "events" leads to the attachment of positive or negative affect to the category, apply to "attitude formation." The amount of affect attached to a category depends on the frequency of this contiguity.

Associations and Elementary Cognitive Structures

Categories become associated with other categories. When this happens they form *elementary cognitive structures*. There are many of these relationships. Given two categories *A* and *B*, we can distinguish negation (*A* is not *B*), inclusion (*A* is part of *B*), equivalence (*A* is approximately the same as *B*), inequality (*A* is larger [smaller] than *B*), proportion (*A* is to *B* as *C* is to *D*), conjunction (that which is common to *A* and *B*), inclusive disjunction (*A* or *B* or both), exclusive disjunction (*A* or *B* but not both), implication (if *A*, then *B*), and transformation (*B* is a modified form of *A*).

Beliefs

Certain kinds of cognitive structure are particularly important. They include *beliefs,* which are implicative relationships between two categories (e.g., Negroes have black hair) and *antecedent-consequent relations,* which link an antecedent to a concept and the concept to a consequent (e.g., Negroes moving to white neighborhoods create a condition of OPEN OCCUPANCY, which leads to equal opportunities for all).

Attitudes

Attitudes are beliefs associated with affective states, predisposing action, so that a person's attitudes include (a) an affective component (how he feels about an attitude object), (b) a behavioral component (what he intends to do with or to the attitude object), and (c) a cognitive component (what beliefs he has about the attitude object). Categorization of the other—for example, it is Joe; it is a Democrat—is necessary before other aspects of interpersonal attitudes become activated. Since categorizations may differ, the analysis of interpersonal attitudes requires the determination of (a) the *criterial attributes* employed by a person to classify other persons in a particular category and his *beliefs* about this category, (b) his *feelings* about the category, and (c) his *behavioral intentions* about the category. Moreover, these elements have different antecedents and different consequents.

Stereotypes

Stereotypes are a special category of beliefs that linking ethnic groups with personal attributes. They too are considered central elements in the analysis of subjective culture.

Expectations

Reinforcement expectations are a subset of general expectations. They are cognitive structures that take the form: "If I do X, such and such will happen, and I will feel 'good' (bad)." When X is expected to be followed by the attainment of a goal, the reinforcement expectations of behavior X are said to be positive. Such expectations are particularly relevant as predictors of behavior (Dulany, 1967).

Norms

Norms involve relationships between a person category and a behavioral category and they usually specify whether the behavior is appropriate. Most of them are proscriptive rather than prescriptive; for example, in Northern India there is the norm "widows must not eat onions." (Human Relations Area Files.)

Justification for norms involves a network of beliefs connecting the norm with values or ideals. Thus there is the belief that "eating onions makes one passionate" and the ideal that "widows should not even imagine being passionate," which in conjunction justify and rationalize the norm.

Ideals

Particular levels of a criterial attribute are sometimes adopted by members of a cultural group as appropriate for defining "good" members of a category; for example, ideal widows are not passionate.

Roles

When certain behaviors are considered appropriate for persons holding a particular position in a social system, we say that there is a role. Thus roles involve links between a category of persons in a social position and behaviors. We believe that the best unit of analysis is the role pair. We might investigate father→son and son→father as separate role pairs, the actor being mentioned first and the person acted on second. The connections between such persons and behavior are both prescriptive (e.g., a father should "advise," "love," and "protect" his son), and proscriptive (e.g., a father should "not hit" his son).

Tasks

Tasks involve a sequence of behavioral categories which refers to a transformation of object categories. Abstract tasks involve transformations of concepts; for example, the presidential decision to support a particular legislative proposal may lead to a transformation of an abstract category (Draft Law X passed by the Congress) to another (Law X signed by the President).

Values

Relationships among abstract categories with strong affective components and implying a preference for certain types of action are called values; for example, when a person "feels good" about the proposition "man should be the master of the universe," this reflects one of his values. Such a value would be consistent with his installing an air conditioner rather than training himself to withstand the heat, supporting a bond issue designed to harness the waters of a river, and thousands of other behaviors. We reserve the term *price* for the value of concrete categories. Three systems of classification of values have been reviewed by Kluckhohn (1959). In addition to his own, there are the systems proposed by Albert (1956) and by Kluckhohn and Strodtbeck (1961).

Kluckhohn (1956, 1959) assumes the existence of binary oppositions which define the different systems of values in different cultures. First, there is the relationship between man and nature. This can be determinate or indeterminate (e.g., fatalism), unitary or pluralistic (e.g., the distinction of body and mind), and evil or good. Second, there is the relationship of man to man. The culture might specify that in this relationship the individual is more important than the group or vice versa, that the individual is the center of things (egoism), or that the other person must be the center (altruism); that he should be autonomous or dependent, active or acceptant, etc. Finally, both the man and the nature categories can be examined in terms of emphasis on their quantity or quality and their generality or uniqueness.

Kluckhohn's system is obviously at a very high level of abstraction. Albert (1956) proposed a system that has explicitly different levels of abstraction. At the lowest level she has what she calls entities, which correspond to what we call meaning categories. At a higher level she has man's virtues (what we call ideals) and vices. The virtues and vices together form man's character. At the same level of abstraction as the virtues and vices are prohibitions and prescriptions of behavior, which correspond to what we called norms. The prohibitions and prescriptions together form what she calls directives. At an even higher level of abstraction the character and the directives form what she calls focal values, centering around the family, possessions, enjoyment, health, individualism, and personal success. At the highest level of abstraction are "value premises," that is, desirable modes, means, and ends; for example, mechanical determinism is a value premise, as is the orientation that sensory experience is the necessary and sufficient test of knowledge.

Kluckhohn and Strodtbeck (1961) consider five basic value orientations: (a) innate human nature—which can be evil, neutral, a mixture of good and evil, or good, mutable or immutable; (b) man-nature—which can be a relationship involving subjugation, harmony, or mastery; (c) time focus—which may be on the past, present, or future; (c) The modality of human activities—which may emphasize the being orientation (a kind of psychedelic ecstasy), the being-in-becoming (self-actualization), or the doing (activity is good for its own sake) orientation; and (d) the modality of man's relationship to other men—which can emphasize the lineal (e.g., submission to the elders), collateral (e.g., agreement with group norms), or individualistic orientations. Each of these orientations provides a system of preferences or rankings of the emphases on different views; for example, one culture may emphasize the time modality by ranking future over present over past, another by ranking present over past over future, and so on. There are six possible ranks on the time modality; in other words, the system could distinguish six kinds of culture. The total system can distinguish 2688 patterns of rankings which is large enough to distinguish the world's known cultures from one another.

Organization of the Concepts by Level of Abstraction

The bottom of Figure 1 includes the most concrete concepts and the top, the most abstract. Discriminable stimuli are grouped to form elementary categories which, in turn, are grouped to form meaning categories which become concepts.

Concepts are organized according to level of abstraction. Different types of concept are related to one another in specified ways to make elemental cognitive structures. Similar concepts constitute domains and domains constitute categories, such as human, object, and behavior. Values deal with relationships between such classes of category—man to man, man to nature, man's activities (behaviors), and man's relation to time.

We defined earlier between- and within-domain criterial attributes. We can now point out that the nature of these attributes depends on the level of abstraction and the heterogeneity of the particular domain. The more homogeneous the domain, the more the within-domain criterial attributes are specific to it; for example, if we consider what within-domain attributes discriminate one job from another (Triandis, 1960), we find that

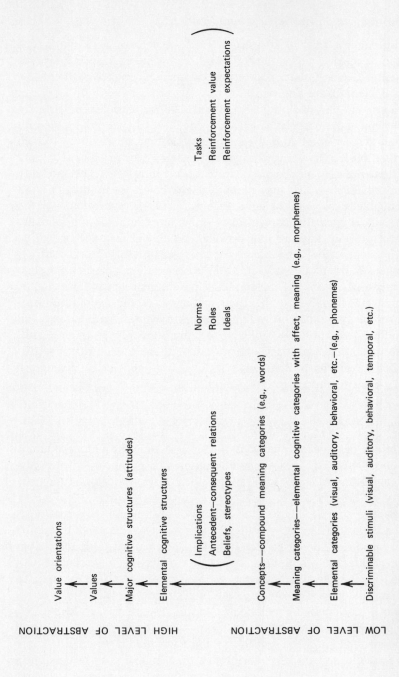

Figure 1. The basic concepts of the theoretical framework.

blue collar is an appropriate attribute. At a higher level of abstraction, however, such as "human activities," this would no longer be an appropriate attribute. For a heterogeneous set of concepts such as those typically used by Osgood, Suci, and Tennenbaum (1957) and in the subsequent studies by Osgood (1965) there appear to be three attributes: *evaluation* (good, fair, honest), *potency* (strong, heavy), and *activity* (active, hot, fast). As we move from such heterogeneous sets of concepts to more and more homogeneous domains of concepts, we discover more and more attributes. Finally, when we consider a specific concept, the number of attributes can be extremely large; for example, the concept "Jawaharlal Nehru" can be characterized by literally thousands of attributes, such as Hindu, dead, dynamic, and intelligent. The domain "Indian political men" obviously cannot involve so many, because not all of them are Hindu, dead, and so on. In fact, the total set of attributes for this domain may be rather limited; it will undoubtedly include the attributes liberal-conservative, member of congress party opposition, but few others. As we move to "people in general" some attributes of the more restrictive domain again have to be discarded. It is, meaningless to consider, for instance, whether a bhavataratyam dancer is a Republican, because that term has a special meaning in the context of American politics. On the other hand, there may be several attributes that are widely useful for "people in general"; for example, the attributes *active* or *powerful*. These would apply to Nehru as well as to people in general. Finally, at the highest level of abstraction we have the evaluation, activity, and potency attributes which appear to apply to *any* concept. Note that since they apply to any concept they apply to Nehru, "Indian political men," "people in general," as well as STONES, DIVORCE, BOOKS, JUSTICE, and FIRE. In short, evaluation, potency, and activity are pancultural and panconceptual attributes. As we consider more specific homogeneous domains of concepts, we find additional specific attributes. In all cases the attributes applicable to a wider domain are also applicable to a restricted domain within it.

Warr and Haycock (1970) make the interesting point that in studies of social perception with the semantic differential we find pancultural evaluation, potency, and activity factors, plus corresponding culture-specific factors. They suggest that Kuusinen's (1969) Finnish person perception factor 6, which includes *young, blond,* and *wholesome,* is a Finnish variant of the pancultural evaluation factor. In short, Warr and Haycock think that one has pancultural evaluation, potency, and activity factors plus some others. This is a viewpoint that agrees, in part, with our own, but we are not sure that the culture-specific factors will typically be variants of evaluation, potency, and activity; for example, in judging *jobs* respondents employ a white-blue-collar dimension, and someone might argue that since white-collar jobs are generally more prestigious this is a variant of the evaluative factor. We note, however, that almost all dimensions of job perception (Triandis, 1960) may be conceived as having something to do with evaluation. Furthermore, the factors or dimensions that emerge will always be a function of the sampling of concepts; for example, if we studied only undesirable jobs and made sure that they matched on undesirability, the evaluative factor would be suppressed and would not emerge. In short, although we are sure that evaluation, potency, and activity are the attributes of heterogeneous samples of concepts, we cannot predict the attributes of other samples. Such attributes will have to be discovered empirically.

Perhaps another way to approach this issue is to consider that evaluation, potency, and activity are *potentially* always relevant attributes of any concept, but when a specific sample of concepts is studied one or more of these dimensions may not be salient. This is typical in human affairs; for example, if someone offers you a job, you do not usually consider factors such as the pollution of the air in the town in which the job is situated but rather talk about salary, supervision, and opportunities. If someone *then* mentioned that accepting the job would reduce your life-span by 10 years, suddenly the pollution dimension would "swamp" the others. What was suppressed and unimportant suddenly becomes the only important dimension. What we have here is a case in which situations are contrasted on a dimension that was not involved in earlier judgments. We can think of this dimension as *potentially* there in the ordinary judgments. We suggest that evaluation, potency, and activity are potentially present in considerations of any concept, whereas other attributes may be potentially present only in the case of particular sets of concepts.

The implication of this analysis is that if we select a specific domain in several cultures, sample a variety of concepts within that domain, and *discover* the attributes that are appropriate to it we can state how people categorize experience with respect to that domain in different cultures. This is because a category is an intersection of attributes. The methodological problem is to do these operations in equivalent ways so that if the obtained attributes have the same character we can say something about equivalence of cognitive functioning in these cultures; if the obtained attributes are different, we may be able to specify in what way they differ.

In this book we have tried to present some studies in which this type of comparison was actually made. In particular, we look at role perceptions and examine the major attributes of social behaviors and roles in several cultures. These are offered as an example of the approach. Similar studies can be done with other concepts of our theoretical framework (e.g., ideals and tasks), but they have not yet been attempted.

Organization of the Concepts by Antecedent and Consequent Relations

The analysis of subjective culture can be helped by an examination of the antecedents and consequents of its elements, since it is from common antecedents and consequents that we infer their existence.

In order to examine these antecedents and consequents it is important to consider a broader "map" of subjective culture[1] than the one provided by Figure 1.

First we define the term *cognitive structures* to include beliefs, associations, and stereotypes, thus eliminating these additional concepts from Figure 2 and making more room for new concepts. Then, in Figure 2*a,* we present the distal antecedents of subjective culture and in Figure 2*b,* the proximal antecedents and the consequents.

Each of the concepts in Figure 2*b* is capable of further analysis in terms of dimensions or variables; for example, the patterns of action may involve a variable such as the "percentage of a cultural group voting for candidate X" or behavioral intentions may be indexed by the "percentage of a cultural group who say they intend to vote for candidate X." The structure in Figure 2*b* has implications concerning the size of the correlations between variables. Those concepts that are directly connected by an arrow will be highly related; it is probable that the direction of causality is as indicated by the arrow. When two concepts are connected by a third and two arrows are required to get from one to the other, the correlation between them will be lower than when only one arrow is required; for example, if we count the frequencies of pairing of particular cognitive structures with affectively pleasant or unpleasant events, we will observe a strong correlation with the affect elicited by these cognitive structures but a much weaker correlation with behavioral intentions and an even weaker correlation with patterns of action.

As an example, a person *P* may have met a person *O* frequently and in pleasant circumstances. The prediction is that *P* will experience positive affect toward *O*. We predict, however, a mild correlation between the appearance of *O* and the behavioral intention "to lend him $100." Just liking somebody does not automatically lead to lending him money. We predict a high correlation between the behavioral intention and the behavior but

[1] Subjective culture is an aspect of *cognition*. Cognition includes recognition, judgment, affect, evaluation, problem solving, and many other aspects. Extensive reviews of the psychology of cognition are available (e.g., Neisser, 1967; Guilford, 1967) but they generally deal in very limited ways with the concepts subsumed under subjective culture. In short, cognition includes subjective culture and many other concepts.

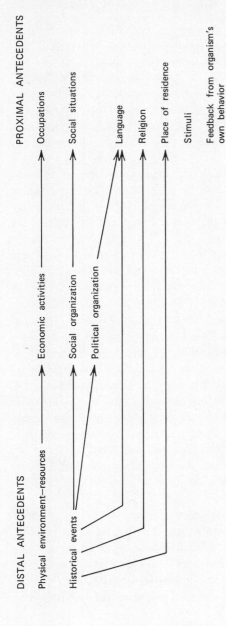

Figure 2a. The antecedents of subjective culture.

22

PROXIMAL ANTECEDENTS   BASIC PSYCHOLOGICAL PROCESSES   SUBJECTIVE CULTURE   CONSEQUENTS

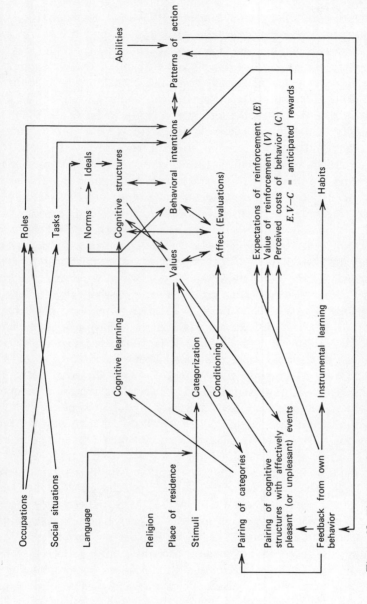

Figure 2b. The antecedents and consequents of subjective culture.

essentially no correlation between affect and action. Our analysis specifies that the action depends on the habits, roles, tasks, and behavioral intentions in the particular situation. More specifically, if O is a well-established merchant and P is a banker who is in the habit of lending money and O appears in P's office and asks for it, the probability is high that the behavioral intention will be to make the loan and in fact it will be made. Relevant here also is the question of P's *ability* to make the loan.

The utility of this framework is limited. It only states the concepts we wish to study and hypothesizes the probable relationships between them. A more useful framework will go further and specify how particular variables subsumed under each of these concepts are related to variables subsumed under adjacent concepts. Such middle-range theories are only now beginning to develop and will have to be tested quite thoroughly before they can be incorporated into the present framework as established relationships rather than mere hypotheses. An example is provided in Triandis, Vassiliou, and Nassiakou's (1968) conception of the relationship between roles and behavior. According to this theory, which we discuss in greater detail in Chapter 8, a role is defined by a set of attributes and a behavior is also defined by a set of attributes. If we wish to predict what behaviors will occur in a given role, we must search for behaviors that match the role on identical attributes; for instance, the role pair father-son is coded as high on the attribute *superordination*. The behavior *to give advice* is also coded high on *superordination;* hence it "fits" the role. Each of the arrows in Figure 2*b* suggests the need for the development of a middle-range theory, but obviously the immensity of this task places it beyond our reach. Different people will have to work on different parts of Figure 2 for several years before we can develop an adequate set of middle-range theories.

We begin to read Figure 2*b* by examining the hypothesized determinants of ACTION. Two influences are shown ₋y behavioral intentions and habits. The empirical evidence that supports these connections will not be reviewed here, since it would require an extensive presentation and can be found elsewhere (Triandis, 1971). It is clear that action can be due to an automatic response, not made consciously, but based on established habit. Roles and tasks operate through modifications in the behavioral intentions. Action provides feedback which eventually influences cognition, which in turn influences both behavioral intentions and affect; affect interacts with behavioral intentions and values; values influence ideals. Cognitive structures are influenced by values, ideals, affect toward the relevant objects of attitudes, and the already existing behavioral intentions. Expectations of reinforcement are multiplied by the value of the expected reinforcement to influence behavioral intentions. The perceived cost of the behavior is subtracted from the product of expectations times values, as suggested by Steiner (1971).

To go back to *P* and *O* and the situation in which *O* asked *P* to lend him $100, *P*'s behavioral intention will depend on his expectation of reinforcement (if I lend him the money, I am *sure* to get $7 interest, approval, or moral support in my election to city hall), the value of this reinforcement (how good does he feel about getting $7, approval, or support), and the cost of the behavior (what do I give up by lending him the money, and what are the chances he will not return it).

Under values in this diagram we also include "personality variables." This conceptualization would suggest that motivational concepts such as needs [as McClelland's (1961) *n*-Ach] belong under values in the diagram. They influence aspects of cognition (e.g., "I must not fail") and affect (e.g., "success feels 'good' ") and via cognition and affect the person's behavioral intentions. Heise (1966) has shown that projective measures of *n*-Ach are correlated with the frequency of occurrence of such cognitions.

Values could have been represented more analytically in the diagram by showing their affect, cognition, and preference for action aspects. This was done for *attitudes,* but we did not repeat this information for values, since it would have complicated Figure 2*b*.

A particular convention used in constructing this diagram should be clarified. When an arrow stops on a line, as in the case in which language and values influence the connection between stimuli and categorization, it is meant to suggest that the particular concept will be implicated in the way this relationship occurs in specific instances; for example, the kind of categories that a particular person is likely to develop and employ will reflect the linguistic conventions of his language-culture community. The kinds of values he has adopted may make it more or less likely that he will attend to some of the stimuli and categorize them.

At the risk of being repetitious we wish to clarify the functions of this diagram. It is simply a guide to facilitate our thinking about the antecedents and consequents of subjective culture. It helps us make sure that we will not eliminate some of the complexities of real life when we consider particular relationships among variables. It functions as a broad map. Each of the arrows could involve a diagram of its own or suggest a particular mathematical relationship. The details will have to be stated after further research. Some of the major theories of social psychology, for instance, are concerned with small aspects of this diagram. More specifically, the theory of cognitive dissonance is concerned with consistencies in cognitive structures, affects and feedbacks from one's own behavior and would be able to account for certain phenomena, but the conditioning of affect or the effects of habits on behavior require additional mechanisms. We suggest that several psychological mechanisms jointly determine the phenomena of interest to social scientists; hence it is desirable to employ several multiple regression equations to describe how the major variables of the theoretical framework are interrelated. Path analysis (Werts & Linn, 1970) is likely to prove helpful in such work.

An important implication of the figure which has already been mentioned should be stated once again now that the reader has gained some understanding of our approach. The figure predicts the size of the correlations among *classes of variables*. Each of the elements of subjective culture can be indexed by several variables; for example, ACTION might be indexed by the probability of occurrence of particular behaviors, such as "to hit." The behavioral intentions are indexed by a set of orthogonal dimensions, such as respect for the other, marital acceptance, or aggression. Aggression would be relevant to the particular behavior "to hit," and we would predict a high correlation between this one behavioral intention variable and the index of behavior.

Among a person's values there is also a large set of independent dimensions, one of which might be "feeling good about one person hitting another." This dimension, we predict, would be correlated with the corresponding behavioral intention more than with the index of behavior. In short, the framework predicts the *rank-order of the correlations* between the index of behavior and the corresponding variables which are relevant to that behavior and which might be used to index each of the elements of subjective culture.

Although the connections among variables that are next to each other are likely to be higher than among variables which belong to sets that are far from each other, there will be substantial and significant relations among remote variables; for instance, "values" may be too far from "behavior" to be strongly associated, yet they may show some relationship because they influence many of the intervening constructs. The correlations between variables that are more than "two steps" away from one another are not likely to be high, but they might be significant and would be theoretically important.

The evidence reviewed by Triandis (1971) is consistent with this theoretical framework, but it is clearly much too soon to determine how useful this framework will prove to be. It is in many ways too complex and summarizes too many potential relationships to permit easy testing. Nevertheless, the vast literature on attitudes, values, roles, and behavior seems consistent with it, and this is the best way we know, now, to show how subjective culture is related to behavior.

The analysis of Figure 2b seems to present most of the arguments of more sophisticated theorists, such as Parsons, in relatively simple language.

Devereux's (1961) explication of Parsonian theory, for instance, argues that the basic elements of this theory are action, which is under the voluntary control of the individual, the situation, other actors, and internal processes such as goals and norms. We have, as can readily be seen, the same elements in that figure. The situation is whatever is meaningful to the actor. This includes not only present stimuli but also experiences (habits) and anticipations (expectations of reinforcement). The actor, according to Parsons, constructs a cognitive map of the situation and evaluates it in terms of its relevance to various goals, values, and norms.

The famous Parsonian "pattern variables" of "affectivity" (we call it affect), "specificity-diffuseness" (we call it level of abstraction), "universalism-particularism" (we have included this variable in the cognitive component of attitudes, since it refers to the use of a universal or a particularistic frame of reference for judging situations), "quality-performance" (also a cognitive variable concerned with ascription versus achievement and the question whether the subject pays more attention to one or the other) and "self- versus collectivity-orientation" (another cognitive variable which reflects the extent of the actor's self-interest or concern for the group) can easily be incorporated in Figure 2*b*.

We feel that Parsonian theory is unnecessarily complicated. In fact, we find Max Black's (1961) paraphrasing of Parsonian theory quite to the point:

1. Whenever you do anything you're trying to get something done. (Behavior is a function of behavioral intentions.)

2. What you do depends on what you want (behavior is a function of affect), how you look at things (cognition), and the position you find yourself in (your role, task, etc.).

3. You cannot do anything without thinking and having feelings at the same time. (Behavior is closely related to cognition and affect.)

4. Human life is one long set of choices. (One kind of behavior is chosen over another.)

5. Choosing means taking what seems best for you or what others say is the right thing. (Choosing one behavior rather than another depends on the total impact of the relevant behavioral intentions, habits, and norms associated with that behavior rather than the other.)

6. When you deal with other people, you always have to take account of what they expect you to do. (Behavior is a function of norms and roles).

7. There is a lasting pattern to the way people behave. (Behavior is a function of habits.)

8. Families, business firms, and other groups of persons often behave

surprisingly like persons. (This proposition is not in Figure 2*b* because the figure refers to the psychological rather than the sociological levels.)

On the other hand, the level of abstraction of the antecedents and consequents in Figure 2*b* is too high for a useful theory; for example, the notion of pairing categories to form cognitive structures does not tell us what categories will be paired in what social settings. For this reason we need to discover antecedents that are more specific. Ideally we need good typologies of cultures which we can employ to make predictions of the kinds of characteristics of subjective culture that will be found in different types of culture.

Unfortunately, the existing typologies of cultures are based on social, political, or economic indicators and the psychological implications seem remote. Starting with Cattell's (1949) interesting factor analysis of social, political, and economic indices of nations and culminating in the most elaborate study by Rummel, Sawyer, Guetzkow, and Tanter (in preparation), we are told that the important variables are the *size* of the population, the *wealth* of the nation (e.g., gross national product per capita), and *political* orientation (communist, neutral, western). The three dimensions are independent of one another because there are, of course, both large and small wealthy nations, both large and small communist nations, and both rich and poor communist nations. We wonder if such dimensions are the major determinants of differences in subjective culture.[2]

Once in a while such analyses do provide clues of relevance to subjective culture: both marriage and divorce rates are positively related to population and wealth and are higher in communist than noncommunist countries; population growth, which presumably reflects a subjective culture in which large families are valued, is negatively correlated with the size

[2] Such analyses provide interesting information; for example, Sawyer's study found that the size of the population of a country is related to "the average length of years during which the last two governments held power"; "wealth" is related to the "number of foreign visitors," "to death rates from heart disease and cancer," and to the "percentages of the population who are Caucasians" or "Protestants," whereas it is negatively correlated with the "mean annual temperature," "death rates from tuberculosis" and "typhoid," "per cent Mohammedans" or "Buddhists," and the "number of language groups which include more than one per cent of the population of the nation." A "Western political orientation" is related to the number of "English translations/number of all translations," "U.S. economic aid," "number of emigrants and immigrants," "number of religious holidays," and "freedom of the opposition to argue its case." A "communist orientation" is related to the "number of Russian translations/number of total translations," "the percentage of females in the labor force," and "protein consumption/calorie content." But are we likely ever to understand why these relationships hold without a better theory of subjective culture?

and wealth of the nation and slightly greater in noncommunist countries. It would appear, then, that communist regimes may be viewed as antecedents of more liberal attitudes toward marriage and divorce and less willingness to have large families, which in turn are reflected in particular behaviors.

A perhaps somewhat more promising approach involved a factor analysis of data from the World Ethnographic Sample of the Human Relations Area File, completed by Sawyer and LeVine (1966), in which the extracted dimensions included both varieties of economic organization (agriculture, animal husbandry, fishing, shelling and marine hunting, and hunting and gathering) and social organization (nuclear family households, patrilineality, matrilineality, cross-cousin marriages, and the degree of sociopolitical stratification). These nine dimensions appear to be of greater relevance to our problem. Further research is needed to determine whether they are sufficiently close to subjective culture variables to permit useful discussions of the determinants of differences in subjective culture. The inclusion of economic and social organization in Figure 2a is intended to suggest the need for such studies.

Many antecedents of subjective culture are suggested in the literature, but it is still premature to state with any degree of certainty that they are important. Lenneberg's (1967) analysis of categorization in different species, including man, and Dawson's (1966) demonstration that protein deficiency, resulting in kwashiorkor and gynaecomastia, is also an antecedent of a "feminine perceptual style" described by Witkin (1954) suggest that definite links may be established between genetic and physiological antecedents and differences in subjective culture. These were not included in Figure 2a to avoid complicating it.

There is no doubt that environmental factors can affect perceptual skills, as demonstrated by Berry's (1966) comparison of Temne and Eskimo ability to perceive. The degree to which the environment is "carpentered" (i.e., has many right angles) is related to the degree of perception of those geometric illusions that depend on previous experience with right angles (Segall, Campbell, & Herskovits, 1966). These authors also found that Western subjects are more susceptible to some illusions than others, and subjects raised in a noncarpentered environment showed exactly the reverse susceptibilities to geometric illusions.

Berry argues that in agrarian societies closely knit and well-organized social institutions create more field dependence, in Witkin's (1954) sense, whereas in hunting environments the more functional perceptual skills would lead to field independence. Witkin (personal communication) has found that parents of field-dependent children in several cultures tend to prefer a child that is obedient to one that is responsible, but the opposite is true of parents of field-independent children. It seems reasonable that cultures in which smooth social functioning is extremely important will emphasize obedience, whereas cultures in which personal skills and successful independent functioning are most important will emphasize responsibility. These comments suggest some functional bases of observed cultural differences in subjective culture.

This point of view is supported by Barry, Child, and Bacon (1959), who studied 104 societies. They predicted, and found, that in hunting and fishing economies, which have low food accumulation, the adults are individualistic, assertive, and venturesome. In agricultural and pastoral societies, which have high food accumulation, the adults are conscientious, compliant, and conservative. Socialization in the two types of society is quite different and reflects the needs of each.

To summarize the argument so far, there is strong evidence that the nature of the physical environment determines the kind of economic basis that is most likely to lead to survival, which in turn determines the kind of personality that can function most effectively in that environment. Parents adjust their child-training practices to the development of children who are most likely to be effective in that kind of social environment. They justify these practices by adopting corresponding attitudes, values, etc., and developing institutions that will support their children's and their own effective functioning in their particular economic structure. Such a model differs but slightly from Whiting's (1961) notion that the maintenance systems (economic structures) influence the child-training practices, which influence the personality variables, which in turn influence the projective systems (e.g., measures of need achievement). Aronoff (1967) has challenged this formulation and has presented data consistent with the notion that three classes of independent variable (historical sociocultural, environmental, and psychological needs) influence the "reciprocal interchange between sociocultural and psychological organizations"; the latter acts on the dependent variables (personality and sociocultural institutions). Aronoff argues that since he found a variety of institutional arrangements within the same economic structures (fishermen, plantation workers) it cannot be true that Whiting's analysis is adequate. He maintains that motivational factors act independently of economic factors in influencing the formation of particular institutions. Such arguments, interesting though they may be, appear to be rather premature. In order to establish cause and effect relationships it is necessary, first, to be able to measure particular variables reliably and, second, to examine these variables over a period of time, analyzing the data within the framework of one of the designs discussed by Campbell (reviewed in Chapter 3). On the other hand, although the arguments about causation are premature, it is clear that they are extremely important to an understanding of the relationship between culture and personality.

It is likely that the chain of events connecting the physical environment and subjective culture will involve several links. Whiting (1964) suggested that (a) in tropical environments (b) it is difficult to raise cattle; hence (c) children do not get milk from sources other than the mother, and (d) it is likely to be functional to have a long post-partum sex taboo (e) so that the mother will not become pregnant and her milk will continue for several years; therefore (f) polygynous families are more likely to develop, and (g) the male child is likely to sleep with its mother; hence (h) when the time comes for the child to adopt its adult male role it is necessary to have a severe initiation ceremony. We can now imagine the host of subjective culture phenomena that are likely to accompany such a chain of events. Norms, roles, and values consistent with polygyny and the particular sleeping arrangements and initiation ceremonies are likely to develop to "explain" to members of such a society why they must behave in particular ways. The perception of interpersonal relationships, sex typing, and many other variables will undoubtedly be affected by the adoption of the polygynous marital patterns. These comments only suggest how environmental factors are likely to determine social structures and how subjective culture is likely to reflect, justify, and determine behavior within such social structures.

An important determinant of cultural differences in subjective culture is familiarity. Hudson's (1960) demonstration that schooled children are more likely than unschooled children, to perceive pictures and photographs three-dimensionally suggests that familiarity with pictures and photographs is a critical factor in their perception. The findings of Segall et al. (1966) point to the same thing. Jahoda (1966) has correctly suggested that Segall's findings are due to both the rectangularity of the environment and the ability of the subjects to interpret two-dimensional representations. Further work is needed to determine how various aspects of differential familiarity with the particular configurations of stimulation involved in geometric illusions influence their perception.

Tajfel (1969) points out that functional salience and familiarity are critical determinants of perception and then states the most obvious and important factor: systems of communication. It is probable that the most important antecedent of differences in subjective culture is the fact that different cultures employ different languages. As already mentioned, Triandis (1964a) has reviewed several studies which suggest that linguistic factors influence the number of categories, the content of the categories, and the consistency with which a particular label is assigned to a particular stimulus.

A variety of subtle differences in subjective culture may also be found in the literature. Little (1968), for instance, has reviewed studies which suggest that different social groups employ different social schemata; for example, Mediterranean subjects prefer shorter distances for social interaction than northern European subjects.

On the consequent side subjective culture probably is neither a necessary nor a sufficient cause of behavior, but it can be considered as a "contributing cause." Behavior is often under the influence of particular tasks, situations, and schedules of reinforcement, so that what the person sees as appropriate, or desirable, is not *necessarily* translated into behavior. Nevertheless, other things being equal, subjective culture has a decisive influence on behavior.

Instead of looking at particular antecedents of subjective culture and their effects, another approach, which may be more fruitful, is to select cultures that differ in their subjective culture and examine their antecedents. This approach may prove more economical, since it guarantees that we will be working with cultural groups that differ in subjective culture. An example can be given from the work of ethnolinguists who classify cultures according to the kinds of relationship among categories typically employed by their members. Lévi-Bruhl (1910) argued that "primitive people" use mostly associationistic thinking; developed people use more abstract thought processes and a larger variety of the higher order relationships, such as implication and cause and effect.

Glenn (1968) has reviewed the ensuing controversy, which pitted some French- against some English-speaking anthropologists. Radin (1953) proposed that both types of thought pattern could be found in both undeveloped and developed societies. Glenn appears to accept Radin's position and elaborates by arguing that societies develop through four stages: associative, abstractive, deductive, and inductive.

The associative level is characteristic of less developed societies, although many members of developed societies employ this pattern as well. It is characterized by mysticism, undifferentiated thought, little use of the canons of logic, and suspicion of the unknown. The prejudiced individual in developed societies employs this thought pattern, at least with respect to the targets of his prejudice. People operating at this level relate to other people intuitively and feel that ingroup members are good but unknown and outgroups are probably bad.

The abstractive level of development involves greater differentiation of both the categories and types of connection between the categories. The categories become more "universalistic" rather than "particularistic" and the connections more differentiated.

At a still higher level the deductive person utilizes his universalistic system to make deductions about what to expect.

At the highest level of abstraction, the inductive, there is a return to particularism, but of a much more sophisticated nature, involving inductive rather than deductive thought patterns.[3]

Although Glenn's theorizing is highly speculative, it fits enough observations and intuitions to be worth serious consideration and empirical testing. It is an example of the development of laws of considerable generality which refer to elements of subjective culture. It classifies cultures into four groups according to level of development and specifies the kinds of differentiation among categories, relationships among concepts, and inferences that should be observed at each level of development. If we had a suitable procedure for the measurement of the aspects of subjective culture referred to by Glenn, we would subject his theorizing to a suitable empirical test. In this book we are describing some procedures that might allow such tests.

So far we have examined a variety of strategies that might be used in studies of subjective culture. They include selecting cultures with different characteristics and examining the subjective cultures found in them or selecting cultures with different subjective cultures and determining whether they differ in their antecedents. One final approach is mentioned, which is to select, and examine the consequences, of cultures differing in the subjective culture of their members. Studies concerning the Whorfian hypothe-

---

[3] Glenn gives an example that illustrates his points: consider the reaction of humans to a crocodile. At the associative level it is connected with magical figures, such as water gods, danger, and witchcraft. At the abstractive level the animal is grouped with other wild and dangerous animals. At the deductive level there is a good deal of knowledge about crocodiles—their major characteristics can be enumerated. The human faced with a crocodile says to himself: "Here is a crocodile; it follows that such and such dangers are facing me." At the inductive, or the highest, level there is a return to particularism in which crocodiles are dangerous only when they are awake, in the water, and the wind blows so that they can smell you. Now the judgment of "dangerous" is reduced to a *case*. The reaction to crocodiles depends on the specific conditions and there are many under which there is no danger. Glenn suggests that cultures go through such cycles, from the undeveloped, which use mostly associative thought patterns, to the highly evolved, in which many of the thought patterns are specified, particularistic, experimentally determined, and empirically derived and in which individual reactions depend on the particular case. Corresponding to such prevailing patterns of thought are systems of law (the deductive French versus the inductive Anglo-Saxon), political systems (the centralized system which corresponds to the deductive versus the decentralized, locally autonomous, diverse system which corresponds to the inductive). Finally, role systems are undifferentiated in the less developed and more differentiated in the more developed cultures; a point which is in agreement with the observations of Foa and Chemers (1967).

sis employ this approach, in which, for example, differences in language are assumed to have behavioral consequences.

To conclude we note that subjective culture has environmental, biological, and social factors as antecedents; for example, protein deficiency, different kinds of social organization, and differential familiarity with certain objects, shapes, or conditions can be antecedents of subjective culture. On the consequent side there are patterns of behavior. This kind of broad conceptualization has been called by Dawson (1969) the "biosocial basis of psychology." Actually we think of the study of subjective culture as only a small segment of social psychology. The task we set for ourselves in this book is to describe the major concepts of subjective culture and their measurement and then to illustrate them with our findings. In this chapter we have described the major concepts; we now turn to problems and issues concerned with their measurement.

CHAPTER THREE

Methodological Problems in Cross-Cultural Research

Purposes of Cross-Cultural Research

One of the important purposes of cross-cultural research is to obtain situations in which the culture functions as the "experimental treatment" (Strodtbeck, 1964). It is often difficult to manipulate certain variables in the laboratory and frequently there are problems of morality associated with the manipulations. When naturally occurring variations provide such extreme conditions, however, observations can result in the improved understanding of their effects.

Another purpose listed by Strodtbeck is to obtain information about the incidence of a particular phenomenon in different ecological environments. An example of such a study is Cantril's (1965) survey. Although it has severe methodological limitations because of the use of a self-anchoring scale whose anchors vary with each individual so that the scores obtained from person to person are not equivalent, the survey helps to show the frequency with which certain hopes and fears occur in different cultures.[1]

A third purpose is to study how cultures differ in their ways of "cutting the pie of experience." By studying key concepts that are typical of particular cultural groups, such as the Greek concept of *philotimo* (Triandis & Vassiliou, 1967a), it is possible to obtain insights into key mechanisms of social behavior employed by different cultural groups. Most of the

---

[1] The methodology used eliminates many of the cultural differences which could have been obtained with another approach, since it eliminates differences in the level of adaptation, thus understating the observed cultural difference. Although the percentages of concerns of different kinds are comparable across samples, the computational use of the scale values is methodologically indefensible, since both the zero point and the intervals on the scale vary from person to person and averaging these numbers produces meaningless information *across* samples.

studies of subjective culture generally fall in this category of cross-cultural studies. Studies of ethnoscience (e.g., Romney & D'Andrade, 1964) are also in this category.

The fourth purpose is the testing of general laws of behavioral science, with data from several cultures. Whiting (1954) has described and justified this important approach to cross-cultural research. The method here involves comparative content analysis of ethnographies, which treat each cultural group as one observation. Potentially any social-science hypothesis can be tested with such data. However, as Naroll (1962) has well documented, it is important to subject the data to quality control. A number of biases are likely to enter the research process and must be controlled by the utilization of control factors, such as the length of stay of the ethnographer in the field and his familiarity with the native language.

Naroll (1968) has also examined the problem of the proper units of analysis and has proposed the term *cultunits*. Cultunits are defined as "people who are domestic speakers of a common district dialect language and who belong either to the same state or the same contact group" (p. 248). Naroll and Cohen (1970) make a further advance in the methodology of this type of research.

Types of Methodologically Indefensible Research

There are many kinds of cross-cultural study, only some of which are methodologically defensible. The central problem in each case is how to develop cross culturally equivalent variables. Certain of them can be criticized for showing little sophistication with respect to this problem. The main offenders are those who have attempted to measure *abilities* cross culturally without equating their cultural groups on such obvious variables as familiarity with the test instrument or format, similarity of interpretation of the social situation of the experiment by the two populations of subjects, response styles, and levels of anxiety generated by testing situations. The claim that some test situations, such as the Porteus (1961) maze, are culture-fair is without foundation: obviously some environments (e.g., Venice or the Chandinichonk area in Old Delhi) give children more opportunities to run mazelike paths than other environments (e.g., a desert). Hudson (1960) has shown that untrained African children are unable to perceive depth in three-dimensional pictures; yet some tests employ such pictures, and some testers claim that because their tests contain pictorial materials they are "culturally fair." Tests that have been developed on the basis of extreme criterion groups in one culture (e.g., the Strong Vocational Information Blank) are inappropriate for cross-cultural research. Of course, an investigator can do all the work done by Strong in each culture, but that leads to instruments appropriate for within-culture studies and not for cross-cultural comparisons unless he can demonstrate some invariance in the patterns of scores across cultures. Good discussions of cross-cultural comparisons can be found in Segall, Campbell, & Herskovits (1966), Przeworski & Teune (1967, 1969), Berry (1966), Frijda & Johoda (1966), Gordon & Kikuchi (1966), Holtzman (1968), and Berrien (1968).

The present authors agree with Gordon and Kikuchi's emphasis on constructing instruments with items that are relevant to culture common constructs rather than to some criterion.

Gordon and Kikuchi also point out that checks of the relevance, acceptability of test items, meaningfulness of the test format and directions, and differential susceptibility to response sets should be performed on the items to be scaled in each culture before undertaking the major task of scale standardization. They emphasize the need for examinations of the factorial structure of the items in each culture, but they do not emphasize the need for "decentering" (having a mixture of items from both cultures) of the items, for which they are criticized by Campbell. Werner and Campbell (1970) correctly point out that the item pool should be developed in both directions so that items developed in each culture are also used by both. This approach is consistent with the one advocated by Berrien (1968) in his reply to Gordon and Kikuchi's admonitions. Gordon's (1968) reply to Berrien, though generally sound, seems unduly concerned about the presence of items that are culture-specific. If such items do not correlate with pancultural (culture-common) factors they will give indications of other dimensions on which the two cultural groups differ and on which the groups cannot be compared; if the items do correlate with the pancultural factors, they will increase the reliability of these factors.

Many cross-cultural personality tests employ a forced choice format which restricts the number of items that can be used and produces other problems identified by Gordon. Gordon's and Kikuchi's (1970) demonstration of a comparability of the forced-choice and Q-sort measurement approaches in personality research should open the field to the use of larger pools of items.

Another methodological issue concerns the equivalence of any experimental manipulations. Interesting studies, such as those of Strodtbeck (1951) and Straus (1966) in which families in different cultures were placed in experimentally produced conflict situations and the modes of resolution of the conflict were the subject of the investigation, need careful qualification, since we are unable to know whether the experimental manipulation is equivalent in strength.

In fact most cross-cultural experiments are difficult to interpret because there are too many competing hypotheses involving interactions of the experimental and cultural variables. The problem here is that it is almost impossible to "control" all of the variables that might make two experimental settings quite different and which might account for the differences in the level of performance across the various cultures. First, consider that the meaning of the stimuli or tasks presented to the respondents may not be the same; second, consider differences in the definition of the experimental situation, with people in various cultures differentially prone to respect, cooperate with, be antagonistic to, be friendly to, or show subordination to the experimenter. Third, consider the extent to which the response alternatives set up by the experimenter might be more or less natural for the respondents and might have high or low probabilities of occurrence in the ecology of the particular cultures.

It should be clear that any of these factors can interact with culture and be responsible for differences in the level of some variables, which appear as cross-cultural differences when in fact they are just differences in reaction to the task, the experimental setting, or the response alternatives. Although the differences are interesting in themselves and some work should be done on the social psychology of the cross-cultural experiment, most of the scientists in this field have an interest in substantive hypotheses. To the extent that the factors outlined contaminate the data, it will be difficult to test the hypotheses.

In planning cross-cultural research we must constantly be on guard against the possibility that some variable may be assumed to be pancultural when in fact it is culture-specific.

An example from the work of Triandis and Vassiliou (1967a) will illustrate what is meant. Greeks used the word *philotimos* to characterize people. Some people have much of this quality and others have little; hence it is a variable. A person is philotimos to the extent to which he conforms to the norms and values of his ingroup. These include a variety of sacrifices that are appropriate for members of one's family, friends, and others who are "concerned with one's welfare"; for example, for a man to delay marriage until his sisters have married and have been provided with a proper dowry is part of the normative expectations of traditional rural Greeks as well as rural Indians (and many of the people in between). A person who does so is praised and, in Greece, said to be more philotimos than one who does not. Now, this variable obviously can be expressed in English by some kind of circumlocution, such as "a person who conforms to the norms and values of his ingroup." Nevertheless the problem is complicated by the fact that ingroups are defined differently in the two cultures (America and Greece). Furthermore it may not be meaningful to employ this variable in the United States, since most Americans give less weight to this dimension in thinking about others than most Greeks. To the extent that the salience of a dimension is different in two cultures it may not be appropriate to make cross-cultural comparisons unless they are made at a higher level of abstraction on which a common dimension can be found.

The Emic-Etic Contrast

Most anthropologists take the position that cultures must be understood in their own terms. Psychologists, on the other hand, search for universal (pancultural) laws of human behavior. The first view emphasizes the best possible description of social phenomena and utilizes concepts developed from the examination of only one culture. It studies behavior from within the culture to discover whatever structure it might have; both the antecedents and consequents of this behavior are found in that culture. The second view emphasizes the most general description of social phenomena, with concepts that are culture-free, pancultural, or universal. It uses a universal perspective. The structure of the observations is created by the scientist. According to this view, the antecedents and consequents of behavior are variables that represent universal aspects of the world. Borrowing Pike's (1966) well-known contrast between *emic* and *etic* approaches, the first approach is emic and the second is etic.

The scientist who adopts the emic approach cannot, by definition, do cross-cultural work. The one who adopts the etic can easily miss the most important aspects of the phenomena he wishes to study. Either of these approaches, however, is preferable to the *pseudoetic* approach used by many psychologists doing cross-cultural research. The pseudoetic approach is in fact an emic approach developed in a Western culture (usually the United States) which is assumed to work as an etic approach. Thus instruments based on American theories, with items reflecting American conditions, are simply translated and used in other cultures. Only rarely does this approach yield useful results.

A particularly serious problem is found in the cross-cultural use of tests and scales. These instruments are typically developed in western cultures (particularly the United States), following a procedure that requires (a) the specification of a content domain, (b) some sampling of an appropriate set of items representing that domain, (c) demonstrations of item homogeneity for groups of items, (d) reliability, and (e) validity studies. Translations of such instruments, omitting most of the abovementioned steps, are often used in other cultures and lead to essentially useless studies.

When scales are applied outside the population in which they were developed, mean differences between cultural groups are essentially uninterpretable in the absence of demonstrations of similarity (Campbell, 1964) against which differences can be interpreted. Such similarity can be demonstrated by (a) following exactly the same procedures in the new culture that were followed in the development of the test or scale in the original culture *and* (b) showing similar patterns of correlation between scores obtained with the instrument and other variables in the two cultures. Partial demonstrations of similarity would include similar construct validity or similar patterns of correlation, as in (a). The explication and rejection of rival hypotheses for the observed differences, which are usually done empirically, is the weakest and most vulnerable strategy; for example, if a variable correlates with five other variables in similar patterns in two cultures but with a sixth variable in entirely different patterns, we can claim that we have observed a genuine cultural difference involving variable 6. If, however, all correlations are different, we can discard the data as uninterpretable; or, if all six variables show similar intercorrelations, differences in the level of some of these variables may be interpretable.

Wober (1969) distinguished centricultural (how well can *they* do *our* tricks) from cross-cultural (how well do *they* do *their* tricks) tests of ability. He suggests that only the test by Cappon, Banks, and Ramsey (1968), which requires the identification of objects in different contexts, presented in the visual, auditory, or haptic (touch) modes, and the Witkin Rod and Frame Test are cross-cultural. In an earlier paper Wober (1966) had argued that different groups have more or less developed abilities in the various sensory modes. Such *sensotypes,* he claimed, are ignored by test constructors.

Irvine (1969) reviewed factor analytic results from several African cultures and shows that the structure of mental abilities is similar, having several apparently etic factors and some emic factors. He suggests, however, that the appearance of etic factors might be due to the common Western schooling to which the respondents were subjected. He questions that the notion of intelligence, even as a construct, may be applied cross-culturally and emphasizes that different ecologies will require the development of different values (interests) and that values determine which skills will be developed; hence intelligence reflects the ecology and may differ from one environment to another.

The emic-etic dilemma has been the focus of considerable interest, and a number of solutions have been proposed. One approach is to start with a construct that appears to have universal status and to develop emic ways to measure it; for example, interviews with local informants suggested that students in Germany, Greece, Japan, and the United States understand the construct "social distance." Triandis and Triandis (1962) and Triandis, Davis, and Takezawa (1965) asked samples of students to generate social distance items; they were then scaled according to Thurstone's successive intervals procedure, which results in an equal interval scale. Stimulus persons that ranged widely and varied simultaneously on the characteristics race, religion, occupation, and nationality were presented to the students, who indicated the amount of social distance they experienced toward each of them. Analyses determined how much of the variance in social distance scores is controlled by each of the characteristics of the stimulus persons. Here then is an etic construct, which allows cross-cultural comparisons, but the students responded to emically developed scales.

A similar approach has been employed by Osgood (1965) in the development of multinational semantic differentials, by Triandis, Vassiliou, and Nassiakou (1968) in developing a method for the measurement of role perceptions, and by others. These studies consist of "independent experiments" done in two or more cultures, the only connecting thread being an etic construct and an identical methodology for generating data. In several of these studies factor analysis has been used to generate etic constructs (factors) consisting of emic elements; for example, Osgood's semantic differential scales *good, fair,* and *clean* correlated very highly in one culture; *beautiful, honest,* and *nectarlike* correlated highly in another culture. Inspection will suggest *evaluation* is the common underlying construct for these correlations. Hence the etic construct (evaluation), which is emically defined in each culture, can be used to make cross-cultural comparisons.

One problem with such essentially emic studies is that judgment has to be used to determine the presence of the etic construct in the emic data. There is no formal mathematical way of comparing factors if the persons studied in each culture respond to different stimuli. On the other hand, there are many good ways to compare (Gulliksen, 1968) if the subjects respond to the same stimuli. One solution, then, is to take the emic items from culture *A* and translate them into culture *B*, and vice versa, and present the same translation-equivalent stimuli to all respondents. This procedure was followed by Triandis, Feldman, and Harvey (1970, 1971a,b,c) and allows the placement of all respondents in the same mathematical space. Of course, the hazards of translation are many, and we will return to them shortly, but this approach allows the researcher to study differences in the meaning of the items while at the same time examining differences in the meaning of the concepts under study.

Problems of Sampling

Several problems of sampling must be considered: the subject, the question, and how, when, and where to ask it.

The sampling of cultures should be guided ideally by extreme positions on either the independent or dependent variables of the study, although focusing on the dependent variables is best, since it guarantees results. Furthermore, a sufficiently large sample of cultures should be studied to allow for randomization of most of the variables that are not of interest in the particular study. Samples of 20 or more cultures seem perfectly appropriate, although few studies so far have utilized such a large number. One problem, of course, is the limitation of funds. Social scientists must educate those who control funds to understand the need for studies that require large samples of cultures.

In the meantime, most of the studies that utilize two or three cultures should be considered as "pilot" studies and used for the development of research instruments, but not for the testing of substantive cultural hypotheses. Many of the studies reported in the present volume are of this nature.

Sampling of subjects sometimes requires consideration of equivalence in subject demographic characteristics. A representative sample of the population of a cultunit (Naroll, 1968) is the ideal, but it may not be economical. Such a sample would permit examination of the demographic correlates of the responses of the subjects and thus permit specification of the limits of generalization. In Chapter 8 we present a study that utilized an approximation to this type of sample in Greece. If variations in subjective culture are not found for different demographic characteristics, it is obviously unnecessary to consider the matter further. However, if there are variations that are correlated with demographic characteristics, it will be necessary to obtain samples that properly reflect the proportions of these characteristics in each cultunit.

This should not mean that in all studies of subjective culture we must try to match our samples. It is obvious that there are conditions under which this is quite unnecessary; as, for example, when the within-culture variance is very small in relation to the between-cultures variance or in studies employing variables on which nonrepresentative samples, such as students, are likely to be quite similar to the majority of the members of the culture. To take a trite example, if we study "preference for speaking English rather than French" in England and in France, the within-culture variance is so small, the between-cultures variance is so large, and the cultures are so homogeneous on this variable that only extreme stupidity could result in inappropriate sampling. This is not to say that extreme stupidity is completely out of the question, since it is possible to select a peculiar sample of French-speaking Englishmen or English-speaking Frenchmen if we really try!

Sampling in some developing countries is likely to present special problems and difficulties. Area ampling, for instance, by blocks and dwelling units, is widely used in the developed countries, but in some developing countries people live in caravans, sampans, houseboats, and streets and set up quarters in vacant lots or government property for short periods until they are evicted. It is still unclear how such mobile groups should be sampled if they are to be compared with "equivalent" groups in developed countries.

The sampling of stimuli and response continua concerns the problem of the equivalence of measurement. Because this is a crucial issue in cross-cultural research it is covered in the next section.

The equivalence in the stimuli is extremely difficult to achieve, since the frequency of their occurrence in each culture, their difficulty, relevance for the samples of subjects, and meaning must be equated or systematically manipulated. For this reason we propose the use of procedures that bypass the problem of stimulus equivalence.

Special checks needed when stimulus equivalence is assumed include the systematic variation of the stimuli by using factorial designs (e.g., Triandis & Triandis, 1960; 1962), administering the test under different conditions, so that some of the influencing factors are randomized across different conditions of administration in each of the cultures, and using tests developed in culture A in culture B and tests developed in culture B in culture A. Thus, if we designate by A_B a test developed and validated in culture A which is administered in culture B, we need to have four experimental groups: (a) $A_B B_B$; (b) $B_B A_B$; (c) $A_A B_A$; and (d) $B_A A_A$, with conditions (a) and (b) administered in culture B and conditions (c) and (d) administered in culture A and the order of administration counterbalanced.

Longitudinal measurement, with appropriate controls [e.g., the Solomon (1949) design] may be highly desirable for certain studies. If cause and effect relationships are to be studied, the use of some variation of cross-lagged panel correlation technique (Campbell, 1963a; Campbell & Stanley, 1963) can be recommended. The argument in this analysis is that $r_{C_1 E_2}$ should be higher than $r_{E_1 C_2}$, if r stands for correlation coefficient, C stands for cause, E for effect, and 1 and 2 stand for successive time periods. Since causal analyses of this type have not been attempted in this book, we will not review the more recent developments of this approach (Rozelle & Campbell, 1969) or the alternative methods of "frequency-of-shift-across median" and "frequency-of-change-in product-moment" developed by Yee and Gage (1968) or path analysis (Werts & Linn, 1970). It is sufficient to say here that techniques are available for the determination of cause and effect relationships in studies of subjective culture.

Equivalent Measurement

The focal problem of the present analysis is the development of procedures that provide equivalent cross-cultural measurement of the central concepts of subjective culture.

Any concept in the framework of Figure 2.b can be described by means of certain within-domain criterial attributes. It is reasonable to expect, however, that different cultures will utilize different attributes. On the other hand, some of these attributes may be pancultural (culture-common) in view of the fact that humans share a common biology and have to solve similar problems of survival wherever they are. If this happens, we have a way to compare concepts across cultures.

An example from the physical world may help. If we are to compare apples and oranges, we can do it only on those dimensions they have in common, such as size, thickness of skin, and acidity, and not on unique dimensions such as apple flavor. We can formulate "laws" that describe the relation between size and price, or thickness of skin and price, that are applicable to all "fruit," but we also need laws that hold for apples, and when modified apply to oranges, and finally laws that are unique to apples or oranges. Similarly, if we describe interpersonal attitudes cross-culturally, we might be able to state some general laws, some laws that have to be modified by variables that discriminate different kinds of cultures, and laws that are appropriate for only certain cultures.

What does equivalence mean? There have already been extended discussions in the literature on this point, most particularly those of Osgood (1965) and Przeworski and Teune (1967, 1969). Equivalent measurement means that a set of indicators i_1, i_2, i_3, . . . , i_k has been found in culture A, which intercorrelates according to a pattern suggesting the presence of a particular criterial attribute, and a different set of indicators i_{k+1}, i_{k+2}, . . . , i_{k+1} has been found in culture B, which correlates according to a *similar pattern,* and *suggests* the *same* criterial attribute. It is possible to employ the first set of indicators to measure the particular criterial attribute in one culture and the second set of indicators to measure the particular attribute in another culture.

We also take the position that the criterial attributes should be validated by further research; for example, if people in culture A drink more water rated high in "evaluation" than water rated low and people in culture B drink more wine rated high in "evaluation" than wine rated low, this suggests that the evaluation scales have a certain validity within each system, *in spite of the need for a different criterion.* A certain flexibility in such validity studies must be allowed, and it is perfectly appropriate to utilize naturalistic observations in the formulation of hypotheses. It is unreasonable to validate the evaluative scales with the same drinking criterion in a water-drinking culture such as Greece and in a wine-drinking culture such as France. On the other hand, one should be able to find subpopulations of wine drinkers in both cultures and then utilize the same criterion, which would be a more elegant study.

The critical point of the discussion offered above is that each culture should be allowed to employ different indicators and different criteria and that the researchers should use a good deal of judgment in making their analyses. Basically what is advocated is the development of "equivalent theories of social behavior" across cultures, theories that will have more or less similar *structures*. As long as they have similar structures (e.g. they resemble Figure 2.b), the fact that different special behaviors (e.g., water versus wine drinking) enter certain categories does not constitute any embarrassment for the theories.

The approach advocated here bypasses the problem of translation. This is not to say that all translations have been eliminated; for example, in giving instructions to subjects we will want to have approximately the same meaning in each language.

Translation. An excellent paper on translation by Werner and Campbell (1970) should prove helpful in improving translation procedures. Of particular value is their discussion of the fact that back-translation, which is so widely used in cross-cultural research, is not foolproof. The strategy of developing several versions of the same instrument is strongly recommended, together with the use of multistage iterative translations, in which one starts from the original language O_1, employs bilinguals to translate to T_1, a new set of bilinguals to go to O_2, and monolingual judges who judge the similarity of O_1 and O_2; one now modifies (usually simplifies) O and makes it similar to a T that might have been developed in the other culture. The new O, let's say O_3, leads to T_2 and the process continues until $T_{n-1} = T_n$ or $O_{n-1} = O_n$. The authors recommend the translation of paragraphs rather than single words. Another recommendation is to avoid repetition of the same term in question after question, since poor translation will carry to all the questions. Rather by systematically sampling the synonyms of a particular concept and employing a set of questions with different synonyms we are most likely to convey the meaning of the concept. Analysis should be done by item, noting the intercorrelations among the items.

Brislin (1970) discusses the major advantages and problems of the method of back translation in cross-cultural research. He presents five criteria for the evaluation of the adequacy of translations and a seven-step procedure for the development of adequate translations, including such ideas as the notion of decentering.

Studies which utilized items that have not been translated by the method of back translation, have not been decentered, and show the country of origin in the best light are highly suspect.

Translation is extremely difficult, not only because the stimuli categorized in supposedly equivalent categories are by no means the same across cultures but also because bilinguals have conceptual structures that are unlike those of monolinguals (Lambert, Havelka, & Crosby, 1958). Furthermore, even if perfect translation could be obtained, it would be most unlikely that the words obtained in two languages would have the same frequencies of occurrence. It is known that work frequencies are important in determining the difficulty of perception and comprehension of words. Thus, at least for some samples of people, among whom comprehension is a problem, translation equivalent items would not be *truly* equivalent. This is particularly critical in intelligence testing, when the fairness of a test depends on the difficulty of the items and when understanding the instructions can be the crucial factor in test performance. We are therefore taking the position that translation should be used as little as possible, and no *assumptions* about the equivalence of translated concepts should be made, if at all possible.

On the other hand, translation is appropriate when the researcher is looking *only* for cross-cultural generalities. Hyman (1967) studied experts on modernization in 13 countries and examined only the *uniformities* in their answers. Such uniformities, obtained in spite of translation, can be extremely interesting.

Summary of Arguments Up to This Point

Our position concerning cross-cultural studies aimed at discovering cultural differences emphasizes the need for scale construction and independent validation in each culture.

The approach advocated here bypasses some of the difficulties in establishing equivalent stimuli for experimental manipulations in cross-cultural research (Schachter et al., 1954; Rommetveit & Israel, 1954). We take the position that such attempts at equivalence are *undesirable* because they give the researcher false, illusory feelings that he is manipulating his variables in equivalent ways. It is much more desirable to do "parallel experiments," which attempt to obtain several measures of some theoretically important constructs in each of the cultures and by a multitrait/multimethod analysis (Campbell & Fiske, 1959) determine the relationship between the constructs, separately in each culture. By obtaining a number of these relationships one can build a nomological network, consisting of a number of theoretically important relationships, some of which may have the same structure, thus providing a cross-culturally general set of laws; others may require the use of cultural moderator variables, and still others may occur only in one culture. The latter two kinds of finding indicate the presence of cultural differences.

Ideally we should establish equivalence of our etic constructs across cultures by showing similar etic antecedents and consequents for each construct.

The approach we advocate also finds little value in cross-cultural studies that involve translations of an instrument developed in one culture for use in another (studies with a "Western bias").

Although it is extremely difficult to present items of equivalent difficulty or equal fairness, when an instrument is translated, we can translate some of the anchors of a given instrument and explicitly *assume* equivalence of *only* these anchors. This approach was used by Triandis and Triandis (1962) and Triandis, Davis, and Takezawa (1965) in studies of social distance. These studies began with the assumption that social distance is a concept that is cross-culturally equivalent and that the anchors "to marry" and "to kill" can be used equivalently in Germany, Greece, Japan and the United States.[2] Once these assumptions were accepted, a set of social behaviors was generated in each culture and scaled by monolingual subjects in each culture, using the Thurstone successive intervals procedure. Thus each cultural group *had its own set of items and its own equal-interval scale*. Complex stimulus persons appropriate to each cultural group were then constructed in order to study the extent to which race, religion, occupation, and nationality determine social distance responses. Not only was the American social distance scale not translated into German or Japanese but the particular German and Japanese hypothetical stimulus persons were employed with American subjects and the American scale items, thus controlling for the fact that each of the samples had responded to a different set of stimulus persons. In this fashion it was possible to examine the stability of the obtained results when the stimuli were changed. It was found, in this instance, that the emphasis of Americans on race as a factor determining their social distance responses was obtained when the Japanese and the German stimuli were employed as well as when the American stimuli were used, thus providing some confidence in the stability of the finding.

The point of this argument is that if we construct separate instruments in each culture, translate them, and administer them in all the cultures we can examine the stability of findings when the data from an *X*-culture generated instrument are compared with those from a *Y*-culture generated instrument. With appropriate "analyses" it is possible, then, to separate the variance that is due to the form of the questionnaire, the cultural origin of the instrument, and the subjects giving the responses.

[2] Although in some hunting cultures killing can be "an act of kidness" when it involves a relative who is sick or in a state of exhaustion, mercy killing is not likely to have been salient in the context of the items employed in that study.

If we *must* translate items, there are some approaches that can reduce nonequivalence and ethnocentric bias. They can include (a) the use of extremely common (easy) words in each language, thus facilitating the tasks for all subjects, regardless of culture, (b) employing a variety of scaling methods, and correlating the items that supposedly measure concept X with items that supposedly measure concept Y (if concept Y behaves equivalently cross-culturally and has been separately validated, we can *estimate* the equivalence of the X measurements from such correlations), and (c) probing with samples of subjects to determine the meaning of the particular questions for them. We can ask questions such as "What do you mean?" (Schuman, 1966a), "What am I trying to learn from this question?" and "What do you understand about this question?"

The use of scales and a variety of psychophysical tasks can lead to internal checks and controls of the items. Since these matters are discussed in the next chapter, we simply mention here the general approach.

How Is Cross-Cultural Research To Be Organized?

A number of contributions in recent years have addressed themselves to this question. Perhaps most notable is Campbell and LeVine's (1970) chapter on field-manual anthropology. As standards of ethnographic reportage are rising, it becomes more and more difficult for a single ethnographer to cover the full range of topics on all aspects of culture. Furthermore, comparisons of two or three cultures typically leave much to be desired. If similarities are uncovered between two highly dissimilar cultures, it is possible to draw conclusions such as, "this construct is etic." If differences are obtained, however, it is almost impossible to interpret them. Field-manual anthropology has the advantage that it allows ethnographers working in a large number of different cultures to collect equivalent data. Its major disadvantage is that it is much more fatiguing for both the ethnographer and the informant. Campbell (1968) also proposed a cooperative multinational opinion sample exchange that would involve a group of social psychologists from several cultures. Segall (1970) proposed to tie "relevant" research with important scientific problems and describes a longitudinal analysis of the physical and psychological development of Tanzanian children known to have suffered protein malnutrition during early childhood.

Berrien (1970) proposed a superego for cross-cultural research and stated the following:

"The best cross-cultural research is that which (1) engages the collaborative efforts of two or more investigators of different countries, each of whom is (2) strongly supported by institutions in their respected countries, to (3) address researchable problems of a common concern not only to the science of psychology but (4) relevant to the social problems of our time. Such collaborative enterprises would begin with (5) the joint definition of the problems, (6) employ comparable methods, (7) pool data that would be "owned" by the collaborators jointly who are free to (8) report their own interpretations to the own constituents but (9) are obligated to strive for interpretations acceptable to a world community of scholars" (pp. 33–34).

In studies in which within-culture individual differences in point of view are likely to be important it is desirable to employ Tucker's (1964, 1966) three-mode factor analysis. An example of such a study which uses subjective culture data was presented by Triandis, Tucker, Koo, and Stewart (1967). The original data were those of Triandis, Tanaka, and Shanmugam (1966) in which the design called for 50 male and 50 female subjects in each of three cultures (Tokyo, Mysore, and Illinois) to respond to semantic and behavioral differentials. The interpersonal attitudes of the subject were assessed with respect to stimulus persons varying in sex, age, occupation, and religion.

Three-mode factor analysis results in three *sets* of factors; one for the stimulus persons, one for the behaviors that the subjects indicate they are willing to engage in with such stimulus persons, and one for the various points of view of the subjects. In addition, a "core matrix" shows the interrelation among the three sets of factors.

In the Triandis, Tucker, Koo, and Stewart study Mode I (the behaviors) resulted in four factors: *respect* (would admire the character of, would not exclude from the neighborhood), *institutionalized marital acceptance* (would marry, would accept as kin by marriage), *friendship acceptance* (would accept as intimate friend, would be partners in athletic game), and *affect with submission* (would love, would be commanded by). Mode II (stimulus persons) resulted in four factors, which were rotated so that they corresponded to the sex, age, occupation, and religion characteristics of the stimulus persons presented to the subjects. Mode III (the subjects) resulted in six points of view, summarized in Table 1.

Subjects with point of view 1 include the Americans and the Japanese males but *not* the Indians. These subjects tend to have equalitarian feelings toward highly respected figures such as physicians.

Subjects with point of view 2 are generally the Japanese. This view is rarely found among Americans, particularly American females. It is characterized by extreme marital acceptance of young physicians and by a deemphasis of differences in religion as determinants of social acceptance.

Table 1   Summary of Points of View Obtained in the
Triandis, Tucker, Koo, and Stewart (1967) Study

	Mode III Points of View					
	1	2	3	4	5	6
American females	H	L	H	L		H
males	H			L		
Japanese females		H	L		L	H
males	H	H			L	
Indian males[a]	L			H	H	

[a] Only male subjects were tested by Shanmugam.

The Japanese are known to emphasize status in interpersonal relations and to de-emphasize religion (Triandis, Davis, and Takezawa, 1965).

The next point of view contrasts American with Japanese females. It involves extreme admiration for female high-status stimuli and was interpreted as a "feminist" point of view.

Factors 4 and 5 represented Indian males, but the first contrasted them with the Americans and the second with the Japanese. Point of view 4 is suggestive of admiration for powerful individuals and religious tolerance; point of view 5 is characterized by great emphasis on the importance of religion in the determination of intimate interpersonal relations, together with a strong marital acceptance of a young female physician of the same religion as the subjects.

The sixth factor was again a female point of view which suggests rejection of powerful males of the same religion, another version of a feminist viewpoint, but this one was acceptable to both Japanese and American females.

The interesting result of this study is that only three of the six points of view can be considered cultural (views, 2, 4, and 5); two (views 3 and 6) are sex-related; one (view 1) is a personality variable.

Although factor analysis has many strengths, it does require prior determination of the variables to be included in the factor analysis. Multidimensional scaling (Torgerson, 1958) does not require any sort of assumptions about the variables that are relevant. It is the most emic of the approaches, since it requires respondents to make judgments only of similarity among concepts; here the criterial attributes that underlie these judgments emerge from the analysis. This procedure, however, has some limitations because it gets rather impractical and difficult to do when there are too many concepts. The procedures developed by Shepard (1962), Kruskal (1964), Lingoes (1965) are also emic and appropriate when the researcher does not know the probable criterial attributes.

Although the use of factor analysis, or multidmensional scaling, is a hypothesis-generating step which requires no theory, there are also hypothesis-testing approaches. Facet analysis (Guttman, 1959; Foa, 1965) and feature analysis (Osgood, 1970) are such hypotheses-testing approaches. In them the investigator hypothesizes the criterial attributes that will be observed in a particular set of constructs and tests his hypotheses by making particular predictions.

A specific example of such an approach concerns the structure of interpersonal behaviors. Let us assume that behaviors are determined by one criterial attribute: positive versus negative affect. This is obviously a much too simple theory, but it is good as our first illustration. Assume that we selected four behaviors that vary on this criterial attribute, from very positive, to positive, to negative, to very negative. The prediction is that the correlations among the responses of the subjects to these four behaviors, when ordered in this fashion, will form a *simplex* order. In a simplex order the highest correlations are observed near the diagonal and there is a reduction in the size of the correlations as we move away from the diagonal; for example,

	to love	to invite	to criticize	to hit
to love	1.00	.50	.00	—.30
to invite		1.00	.70	—.20
to criticize			1.00	.30
to hit				1.00

Now let us complicate our theory a little and assume the existence of *two* criterial attributes: positive versus negative and subordinate versus superordinate. This is a two-dimensional system, with two *facets,* and predicts a circular order and a pattern of correlations called a *circumplex.* The behaviors are now analyzed into positive subordinate (e.g., to obey), positive superordinate (e.g., to invite), negative superordinate (e.g., to criticize), and negative subordinate (e.g., to plead with). The circumplex pattern has high values near the diagonal, but the correlations fall and *then* rise again; for example,

	to obey	to invite	to criticize	to plead with
to obey	1.00	.60	—.60	.45
to invite		1.00	.70	.10
to criticize			1.00	.00
to plead with				1.00

If a circumplex is obtained, as hypothesized, this supports the implication that the postulated facets do, in fact, operate as expected. Thus the particular two-dimensional theory of perception of social behavior is supported. In short, we get empirical evidence that the hypothesized criterial attributes operate as expected.

Guttman's approach is useful also in generating attitude items, as in the following example:

(all states)
(   )
(suggest)   (some states)
(   )   (to)(   )
The government should (impose) regulations on (some cities)
(air pollution)
(   )
with respect to (civil rights).

Subjects may be asked to agree or disagree with such a statement. The statement can be generated from a "degree of coercion" facet (suggest versus impose), a degree of "geographic generality" facet (all states, some states, some cities), and a content facet (air pollution versus civil rights). By systematically manipulating each facet $2 \times 3 \times 2 = 12$ questions can be generated with this design. Correlation of the degree of agreement with each question can be computed to determine the structure of the underlying facets. If similar structures are obtained in two cultures, there is some justification for thinking that the 12 questions are equivalent and can be used in correlational analyses involving other concepts. Note that we do not assume that they can be used in direct comparisons of the *levels* of agreement, since response sets operating in one culture, but not in another, can make the level scores noncomparable. For the purposes of correlation with other variables, however, the particular questions can be quite helpful. If the intercorrelations among the 12 questions are not the same (and our guess is that in this example, which is highly ethnocentric, they would not be), a new set of questions must be constructed.

Osgood's (1970) feature analysis is the last of the methods that we discuss here. It occupies an intermediate position between the dustball empiricism of factor analysis and multidimensional scaling and the facet analytic situation in which the criterial attributes are supposed to be known and the empirical investigation tests the theory. Osgood postulates that certain features (criterial attributes) are culture-common. He then tests to see if this is true.

The test employs the reactions of subjects to word mixtures. The basic insight is that certain words do not go together (i.e., their coexistence is judged by subjects to be anomalous); for example, the sentence "to plead haugtily" is judged as anomalous because "to plead" is coded as subordinate and "haugtily" is coded as superordinate. By presenting mixtures of verbs and adverbs and by asking the subjects to judge whether these word mixtures are "apposite," "permissible," or "anomalous" Osgood is able to extract semantic features such as subordination-superordination and also to test his theory of the features that are culture-common. In short, he assumes the existence of certain criterial attributes and checks empirically if these attributes operate as expected.

Needed Controls

Most of the problems encountered in within culture research are also present in cross-cultural research. The size of the cross-cultural problems makes them more serious, and therefore we must pay special attention to them.

Familiarity with the Instruments. It is clear that in many cultures the approaches we employ may appear to be completely novel or even threatening. Asking questions, interviewing, and the like are probably sufficiently common occurrences in most cultures that they produce less tension, but many questionnaires are likely to be quite strange. As long as we equate the extent to which the respondents from the various cultures are familiar with our various approaches or as long as differential familiarity cannot account for the conclusions of our cross-cultural investigations, we are on relatively solid ground. If familiarity is relevant, it is desirable to manipulate it in pretests or to provide ample opportunity for practice in the particular way of responding before actual testing begins.

Motivational Equivalence. It is difficult to equate the motivations of the respondents in the various cultures. In some cultures the concept of timing a performance simply does not exist. The idea of working at maximum speed does not make sense. In some cultures the subjects are more inclined to boast, to compete with one another, or to differ in their self-esteem from respondents in other cultures. It appears that when such variables are likely to be relevant for the particular research problem the best strategy is to measure them explicitly. We can, for instance, obtain measures of time perception, self-esteem, or competitiveness and use them as statistical controls in covariance analyses.

Response style. Two response styles are particularly critical in cross-cultural studies, since it is known that cultures differ in the extent to which respondents adopt these styles: (a) acquiescence and (b) extreme checking style. Some respondents show acquiescence by agreeing with almost *any* question. Others utilize the most extreme positions on a scale (1 or

9 on a 9-point) much more frequently than usual. Triandis and Triandis (1962), for instance, found that on nearly every Likert-type item used in their study their Greek subjects showed more acquiescence and a more extreme checking style than their American subjects. One suggested method for controlling acquiescence is to reverse the items, but this method appears to be unsound because different items have different neutral points; for example, the item, "An insult to our honor should always be punished," is a pretty aggressive statement; the reverse item, "An insult to our honor should never be punished," is not necessarily so far from the neutral point as the first statement in the direction of being nonaggressive. One can play with words (e.g., "it is generally best to ignore insults to our honor"), but it is extremely hard, if not impossible, to reverse the item and get the exact same degree of deviation from the neutral point. Kerlinger's (1967) theory of attitude structure, which appears to have considerable merit, holds that all items should be considered unipolar; hence the very concept of reversing is nonsensical. Probably, a *Q*-sort methodology, with a forced distribution of responses, such as is obtained when asking subjects to sort about one-third of a set of statements in an "agree" bin, one-third in a "disagree" bin, and the rest in an "I am indifferent" bin, seems best to avoid the problems associated with response style. Other approaches include the use of a forced-choice format or of correlations rather than levels. Correlations would eliminate the extreme checking style effects, since these effects will appear equally in all variables measured in a given culture. The use of standard scores is also possible, but it must be done with care; otherwise it will eliminate all cultural differences!

Test Conditions and Experimenters. It is desirable to equate these conditions as much as possible by using experimenters from the host culture and similar conditions of test administrations. If these controls are not possible, it is wise to follow Campbell's suggestion and vary widely and systematically both the conditions of administration and the type of experimenter. With such variations it is possible to determine the effects of these shifts in conditions on the observed results. Explicit measurement of the attitudes of the respondents toward experimenters, psychologists, and the like is also desirable. The behavioral differential (Triandis, 1964b) can measure tendencies to respect, cooperate with, or be antagonistic or subordinate to the experimenter.

Social Desirability. Obtaining data on the social desirability of items is in itself a most interesting cross-cultural study. It is probably best to use the obtained data in covariance analyses rather than in a forced choice format (Gordon, 1968). The cross-cultural study of social desirability is interesting in its own right.

Anonymity. Different cultures have different views about anonymity. In some cultures, such as in Greece and Japan, subjects tend to feel complimented when asked to give their opinions and wish to have their names placed on questionnaires. In other cultures, such as in Scandinavia, subjects feel that questioning involves invasion of their privacy but may be induced to cooperate in studies under conditions of anonymity. Pretests and careful interviewing of subjects are required to determine the conditions under which the instruments are most acceptable.

Experimenter Bias. The vast literature on experimenter bias suggests the need for controls. Lewis (1953) states that the use of field teams, rather than individual ethnographers, might control some of the theoretical biases of particular anthropologists. A similar approach seems desirable in studies of subjective culture.

Problems of Interpretation. Both the coding of the data, if any, and their interpretation can introduce ethnocentric biases. The most desirable way to control such biases is to show the data to persons from different cultures who have different kinds of biases. Blind interpretations may also be helpful.

Appendix   How to Develop Cross-Cultural Tools: a Cook Book

1. Get in touch with competent social scientists in the cultures in which you plan to work. Select your cultures to be interesting on theoretical grounds and to have enough available social scientists to make this enterprise practical.

2. Develop the design jointly with these social scientists so that data will have both theoretical significance for psychology and practical implications in the various countries. In designing the project, consider the theoretical variables (constructs) that are likely to be etic and develop emic methods for their measurement; for example, if you determine that the "social distance" construct makes sense in all the cultures you wish to study, develop items appropriate for each culture to index this construct.

3. Sample people, stimuli, and responses in ways that are maximally representative within your budget. This means that you will want a range of different kinds of people, a good sample of the stimuli (e.g., social distance questions), and a good sample of responses (e.g., would you do that,

would a friend of yours do that, would your relatives do that, rank the order in which you are most likely to do, agree/disagree, rate, substitute words in blanks).

4. The preceding step is done emically so that each culture does its own development of concepts. Some of these concepts or response continua may happen to be pancultural or easily adapted to a format acceptable in all cultures.

5. Translate a substantial portion of the potentially etic items by the method of decentering (Werner and Campbell, 1970) from one language to another until you have a set of items that is not particularly appropriate to any one culture but is acceptable to all.

6. Obtain a new sample of persons and this time give them the etic judgments, plus those emic judgments that appear to be most appropriate to their culture. Before responding to this task these persons should respond to a set of items with obvious answers (e.g., *Paris* is in France, Italy, Greece, or Germany) (*carpenters* use mostly wood, iron, plastic, or air). The format of the "comprehension check items" should be identical to the format of the questionnaire or test. Persons who give bizarre answers to the comprehension check items should be questioned and excused if they prove incapable of learning the task.

7. Analyze the data by looking for invariances. These invariances may be revealed in pancultural factors, facets, features, components, or patterns of correlations among various indices of the relevant variables. It is only when similarities which constitute the background are obtained that one can see the figure (differences) the way one sees a figure against a background.

8. Once equivalence of measurement is obtained, consult with your associates in the different cultures to examine the possibility that the obtained cultural differences might be explained by competing hypotheses. Here are some of the hypotheses you should check:

Differences in the definition of the experimental situation.

Differences in the respect, antagonism, cooperation, friendliness, or subordination toward the experimenter.

Differences in the extent to which the members of each culture are likely to make particular responses, their response biases, familiarity with the tasks, and motivation.

Could experimenter bias account for the observations?

Could differences in anonymity account for the observations?

It should be noted that good experimental design allows an experimenter to answer these questions by pointing to empirical evidence. This means that data from control groups, and other kinds of additional data, may have to be gathered to render interpretation unambiguous. Systematic variation of the conditions of administration is one way to obtain additional data.

9. Each scientist should report his own conclusions to his own fellow social scientists in his own country. In addition, a joint report should be presented for the international scientific community. The data are owned by the collaborators, jointly, so that no one should publish without giving full credit to the others.

10. When conflicts over timing of the publication occur, the one who wishes to publish first should be allowed to do so, as long as he gives proper credit, and the other members of the team should be allowed to add comments in which they suggest why, in their opinion, it is premature to publish the study and what further work has to be done before it is published. If all understand that a particular report is simply preliminary to a more complete and careful report, there should be little conflict. Because cross-cultural studies require unusually long periods of time to be brought to completion, it is necessary to employ a double standard in their publication in which some reports are considered preliminary and others final.

CHAPTER FOUR

Relation of the Theoretical Framework
to the Other Chapters of This Book

In this chapter we review a number of specific approaches that have been or could be employed with profit in cross-cultural studies. We present this review in exactly the same order as the one used in Chapter 2 to define our concepts.

Categorization

How are experiences categorized in different cultures? Our previous discussion suggested that in order to answer this question we must employ procedures that study the criterial attributes that define categories in each culture. A variety of procedures has been or can be employed.

We can distinguish two basic approaches: one inductive, the other deductive. In the inductive the researcher has no theory but presents stimuli to subjects and asks them to make various judgments. He infers how they categorize from the consistencies in such judgments. In the deductive he has a theory concerning the attributes that define a particular set of categories. Of course, in many investigations one begins with an inductive approach and develops a theory which he tests with a deductive approach.

There are two types of inductive approach; one is employed when the characteristics of the stimuli have a physical correlate and the other when they have no correlate.

The Inductive Approaches. A good example of an inductive study with stimuli which have physical correlates can be found in the work of Lenneberg & Roberts (1956) on color categorization. These investigators presented color charts to their subjects and asked them to draw the boundaries of particular color names. They found only a rough correspondence between certain Navaho and supposedly equivalent English color names. A similar approach can be employed when the investigator has physical objects, such as botanical or animal specimens or tools, and can ask his informants to name them, categorize them, or judge their similarity.

This approach can provide useful information about the determinants of categorization, as was done by Landar et al. (1960) in their demonstration that bilinguals categorize stimuli in ways that constitute compromises between the categorizations employed in their two linguistic communities.

Another inductive approach requires the presentation of objects that the researcher cannot characterize beyond the fact that they belong to the same cognitive domain, such as names of tools and names of diseases. Ethnolinguists have developed a series of "frames" for asking questions which permit explorations of domains of concepts. "What is that?" "What kind of a . . . is it?" "Are there other kinds of . . . ?" "What is a good . . . ?" "What is a bad . . . ?" are the sorts of questions that they employ (Metzger & Williams, 1966).

A variety of cognitive domains, explored by means of such procedures, include names of diseases (e.g., Frake, 1961), botanical terms (Conklin, 1954), kinship names, and even "firewood" (Metzger & Williams, 1966). The result of such work is typically a taxonomy, that is, structured along two dimensions; a horizontal one of discrimination (poodle, collie, terrier) and a vertical one of generalization (poodle, dog, animal).

The critical purpose of such attempts is to discover the contrasts inherent in the data obtained in each culture and not according to any a priori notions of what the categories should be. The methodology usually reveals the criterial attributes employed for making the various contrasts by the people who speak the particular language. Elaborate procedures, such as those described by Frake (1962a,b) and Metzger and Williams (1966), have been published. It is not yet certain that this is the most economical way to extract information, and there are also several ambiguities concerning the relationships between these empirical studies and the formal analyses proposed by the supporters of componential analysis and other such formal techniques (Hammer, 1966).

Wallace (1962b) has presented a good introduction to componential analysis. Consider, as an example, the analysis of kinship data. First, collect a large sample of kinship terms. Second, translate these terms to a common notation which utilizes a minimum number of simple elements, such as Fa (Father), Mo (Mother), and Br (Brother). Now each term can be described in terms of these basic components. Next the total domain can be examined and its structure, determined. For American English an adequate analysis of kinship terms requires only three elements: A, the sex of the relative, with (a_1) being male and (a_2) female; B, the generation of the relative, with (b_1) two generations above ego, (b_2) one generation above ego, (b_3) same generation as ego, etc.; C, the lineality of the relationship, with (c_1) lineal [a direct line], (c_2) colineal, as in uncle, niece, and (c_3) ablineal, as in cousin. The final stage of this analysis involves defining each member of the original domain by using the above-mentioned components; for example, grandfather is $a_1b_1c_1$; mother is $a_2b_2c_1$; aunt is $a_2b_1c_2$ and $a_2b_2c_2$. Each term is defined so that no term overlaps or includes another; each term is discriminated by at least one elemental component; and all terms can be displayed on the same paradigm.

The most general inductive approach is to ask for judgments of similarity in a sample of concepts from a particular domain of meaning. Given the stimuli "your mother, your oldest sister, and your current girl-friend," all selected from a student's list of "important women," the student can be asked "Which one is more different from the other two?" Such a judgment of similarity implies that the two that have not been chosen are more similar than the one that has been chosen; the two unchosen may be grouped in the same category. From a large number of such judgments, and by means of multidimensional scaling (see Torgerson, 1958, for a review) it is possible to determine the attributes that were used by the subjects in making these judgments.

We have already indicated that the determination of such attributes is the most efficient way to study categorization. In general, m trichotomized attributes, distinguishing between the positioning of the stimulus on the "high," "middle," or "low" side of an attribute (a relatively crude judgment), give 3^m categories. Even this crude system of categorization can generate enough categories with a small number of attributes. Considerations derived from studies of the human attention span suggest that about seven attributes may be attended to at any given time (Miller, 1956). Since $3^7 = 177,147$ and most cultures have vocabularies that do not exceed this number, it is easy to see that if we could discover the seven critical attributes that distinguish the meaning of the words used in any linguistic community we would have a highly efficient system based on only seven items of information to describe a most complex array of stimuli. Unfortunately, this can only be approximated but the direction of research is relatively clear.

Another way to attack this problem is to ask subjects to judge the sample of concepts on dimensions generated by members of their culture, as appropriate for the particular domain. An example may be taken from the work of Osgood (1965) and his associates; 100 culture-common nouns were used to elicit qualifiers, and the most frequent and general qualifiers were used in a new task in which subjects judged the extent to which each noun is associated with each qualifier. Factor analysis of the correlations among these judgments resulted in the same three criterial attributes (factors) in each culture.

Still another approach, used by Kelly (1955), presents triads of concepts and asks not only for judgments of similarity/difference but also for the bases of these judgments. In the example used earlier a subject might indicate that his mother is different from his sister and girl-friend in that she is *older.* Age, then, is the basis for that judgment. An analysis of such judgments can lead to the extraction of the most frequently used criterial attributes. A slight variation of this procedure combines it with Osgood's semantic differential (Osgood, Suci, & Tannenbaum, 1957) in that the most frequently mentioned bases for these judgments are used as semantic differential scales (Triandis, 1959a,b).

An important aspect of this work is the incorporation in the list of semantic differential scales employed in each culture of the scales derived from the other culture; for example, one may derive 20 scales from culture *A* and 20 scales from culture *B* and employ a 40-scale semantic differential in both cultures. Factor analyses of the 40×40 matrices of correlations (or covariances) in each culture lead to two factor structures that can be compared. If the scales derived from culture *A* are more meaningful to subjects from the culture, it is probable that these scales will have higher loadings than the scales derived from culture *B* in the factor analysis of culture *A* data and conversely for culture *B*. Nevertheless, if the common meaning of factors obtained from two cultures is similar, it is possible to compare concepts across cultures, since such comparisons are made on attributes that have common meaning. As Osgood (1965) has pointed out, if data from one culture result in a factor with high loadings on *clean, beautiful,* and *good,* whereas data from the other culture result in factors with high loadings on *valuable, delightful,* and *nectarlike,* the common meaning of the first three words and the second three words is sufficiently similar to permit comparisons. Thus a concept is defined by attributes that are extracted from the factor analysis in equivalent ways. This is the strength of the Osgood approach that makes it most attractive in studies of categorization across cultures.

The last approach to be mentioned here is the most direct and requires subjects to categorize stimuli into groups "which seem to you to belong together." The early work of Gardner (1953) has led to a number of investigations dealing with such variables as personality organization (Gardner, Jackson, & Messick, 1960) or cultural background (Mercado, Diaz-Guerrero, & Gardner, 1963). The extensive program by Scott (1962, 1963, 1966) which deals with cognitive complexity has often employed this method. The determinants of categorization behavior include not only cultural variables but also the nature of the domain (e.g., personally relevant stimuli are grouped in fewer categories, whereas objects are grouped in a larger number of categories: Glixman, 1965; Glixman & Wolfe, 1967).

Although this direct approach is appropriate for the determination of the categories utilized by members of a particular group, the fact that a study has to be done for each domain of meaning, and the results have to be presented in a relatively complex form, suggests that the less direct approach (e.g., Osgood's) is more promising. Furthermore, the problems of cross-cultural equivalence are so overwhelming when the direct categorization approach is employed that we cannot recommend it for cross-cultural work.

The Deductive Approaches. The two major deductive approaches, facet analysis and feature analysis, have already been discussed in Chapter 3. Presentation of these approaches is therefore unnecessary here, but a few points of clarification and discussion appear desirable.

Note the similarity between componential and facet analysis. It should be clear that the "components" extracted in componential analysis are "facets" in facet analysis. This means that we could begin by doing a componential analysis and then hypothesize how people will respond to stimuli containing different combinations of components. According to the facet analytic "principle of contiguity" (see e.g., Foa, 1965), variables that are more similar in their facet structure will be more related to one another in empirical studies than other variables. This could be tested, for instance, by using a behavioral differential (Triandis, 1964b) and concepts such as grandfather and father, to be judged on behavior scales such as "admire the ideas of" or "invite to dinner." The prediction is that the responses of subjects to such stimuli will be correlated in such a way that the greater the similarity in the facet structure, the greater the correlation. If this prediction is not supported, it would indicate that the hypothesized facets (components) are not operating as expected and a new componential analysis is needed.

One could also take components from one culture and predict the correlations among the stimuli that are defined by these components in another culture. If the predicted correlations are observed, it would suggest that a new analysis is not required and the same components predict the responses of subjects in the second culture.

In addition to the contiguity principle, facet analysis utilizes the so-called principal component principle (see Foa, 1965). This is most easily explained by examining a set of eight stimuli, defined by three dichotomous facets:

$$a_1 b_1 c_1$$
$$a_1 b_1 c_2$$
$$a_1 b_2 c_2$$
$$a_1 b_2 c_1$$
$$a_2 b_2 c_1$$
$$a_2 b_2 c_2$$
$$a_2 b_1 c_2$$
$$a_2 b_1 c_1$$

These stimuli are ordered in such a way that each changes as little as possible from the one above it. If this order turns out to be correct, facet A is the first principal component because it changes its value from a_1 to a_2 only once. Facet B is the second principal component because it changes value twice; facet C is the fourth principal component because it changes four times. Such an order indicates that facet A is the most important, facet B the next most important, etc. Foa (1965) has shown that in order to predict a unique order for eight stimuli defined by three facets it is necessary and sufficient to identify (a) the principal component and (b) the first stimulus of the order. Once this has been done everything else falls into place.

Osgood's (1970) feature-analytic model is one in which criterial attributes are assumed and predictions are made about the structure of the responses of subjects to word mixtures containing congruent or incongruent features. The model assumes that these subjects respond in an all-or-nothing manner, so that when two words have the opposite sign on a given feature their word mixture will produce a feeling of "anomaly." There is evidence, however, reviewed by Osgood, that a continuous model rather than an all-or-none model predicts somewhat better.

To the extent that feature analysis utilizes a dichotomous system of features it makes predictions that are similar, though not identical, to those made by facet analysis. On the other hand, when a continuous model is adopted, feature analysis approximates the rationale of factor analysis.

The basic difference between *feature* and *factor* analysis, both of which have been used in Osgood's (1970) study as strategies for the discovery of criterial attributes, determines whether one approaches the problem deductively or inductively. It is possible to examine word mixtures without a theory and subject the data to factor analysis, in which case this approach becomes inductive as do those we described in the preceding section.

Evaluations

The association of a category with affect leads to evaluative responses. The greater the frequency and recency of such associations, the stronger the evaluation. Staats (1967) has presented an elaborate statement relevant to these points.

The affective dimensions of subjective culture have been the focus of an intensive investigation by the University of Illinois Center for Comparative Psycholinguistics. The semantic differential, which was developed by Osgood in the early 1950's, is one of the most widely used instruments in the social sciences. Snider and Osgood (1969) published a book of readings which selected some of these studies and a bibliography which in 1968 consisted of more than 1000 titles. Most of this work was done in the United States, but since 1963 a major cross-cultural project, involving more than 25 cultural groups and representing the major languages of the world, has been in progress.

In the present section we give only a brief account of this work, since summaries of it are already available elsewhere (Osgood, 1964; 1965; 1967; Jakobovits, 1966; Tanaka, 1967a). It is inappropriate for us to summarize the work that has not yet been published, in spite of the fact that most of us have been involved in some parts of it. The major publications of this work will be in the form of several books by Osgood, Miron, Jakobovits, and Archer, the probable titles of which are *The Generality of Affective Meaning Systems* (which reports that in most cultures the evaluation, potency and activity dimensions of the semantic differential appear to be the most important criterial attributes of concepts); *The Atlas of Affective Meaning* (which will present the basic data on the loadings of 550 concepts on the three dimensions of affective meaning, various transformations of these scores, as well as information concerning the polarization and familiarity of the concepts in each of the cultures); and *The Affective Dimension of Subjective Culture* (which will report comparative analyses across communities of the meanings of the 550 concepts).

In order to present a brief account of this monumental work, we list its major phases:

1. One hundred young male monolinguals in each culture were asked to give qualifiers of 100 "culture fair" and "universal" substantives, such as HOUSE, TRUTH, and POISON, by completing sentences of the type "The house is . . ." or "the . . . truth."

2. The 10,000 responses obtained in each culture were analyzed in terms of frequency and diversity (number of times the qualifiers was given as an associate to different substantive stimuli). The qualifiers were then

ranked according to a measure that considers both their frequency and diversity. Those that were most frequent and most diverse and relatively independent in their use were employed in the next phase.

3. New samples of 200 males judged 100 concepts on 50 bipolar scales. The 5000 judgments required were randomly divided among 10 groups of 20 subjects.

4. The ratings given by the 20 subjects when responding to a substantive on a particular scale were summed so that a matrix of 100×50 numbers was obtained.

5. The 50×50 matrix of intercorrelations among the scales, based on 100 observations, was subjected to a principal axis factor analysis with varimax rotation.

6. Shorter (12-scale) forms of the semantic differential were constructed to represent each of the three (evaluation, potency, activity) factors obtained in each culture. A sample of 550 concepts, some of which were obtained from a reverse elicitation task in five communities and the rest contributed by the cooperating social scientists in different parts of the world, was judged by a new sample of subjects on 12 scales. These data were then summarized in the *Atlas*.

In addition to this basic sequence of phases, a large number of studies was undertaken by the group of cooperating social scientists and is reported in the books mentioned above. Among the most interesting are the following:

1. Pancultural factor analyses of the data in which the scales obtained from each culture were correlated, using an $N = 100$ (the culture-equivalent substantives). The general result is that the three classic factors appear, although there are a few "dissonant" findings. Among the dissonant findings are a dynamism factor (mixture of potency and activity) in the Arabic language and a difficult to interpret factor (fickle-serious, soft-hard, thin, slim-thick, difficult-easy) in the Hindi sample. The broad structure is clear, however, for there seems to be little doubt that the three classic factors appear both in within-culture analyses and in pancultural factor analyses.

2. Jakobovits (1966) lists a number of specialized studies, such as the analysis of the concepts that appear to have similar semantic differential profiles in most cultures; for example, in 14 out of 15 cultures MAN, GAME, FRIEND, and FREEDOM are *good, strong,* and *active.* In 12 out of 15 cultures NOISE and BATTLE are *bad, strong,* and *active.* In 13 out of 15 cultures BIRD is *good, weak,* and *active.*

3. Tanaka (1967a) reports a number of exceptions to the general findings described above among Japanese subjects; for example, he reports

two evaluative factors in Japan: one is "moral" (right-wrong; superior-inferior; good-bad) and the other is "sensory" (pleasurable-painful; beautiful-ugly). Some evaluative criteria change as concept classes and cultures are changed; some change as subjects are changed.

4. Many of the findings are difficult to interpret without a detailed knowledge of the cultures; for example, PEACE is the most positive of concepts in most cultures, but in Kannada (Mysore, India) WORK, LUCK, and POLICEMAN get slightly more positive ratings on evaluation. What does this mean? THIEF is very bad in Japan, but not as bad in India. Does this mean anything?

5. Jakobovits (1967) presents an interesting analysis of the meaning of certain' concepts in six "economically advantaged" countries, such as France, Italy, Japan, and the Netherlands, and six "economically disadvantaged," such as India, Lebanon, and Thailand. Table 1 lists some of his findings:

Table 1

Concept	In the Advantaged Countries	In the Disadvantaged Countries
WORLD	Very active	Very passive
BODY	Very active	Slightly active
I (MYSELF)	Very active	Slightly active
BORROW MONEY	Bad	Very bad
COMPETITION	Very strong, active	Slightly strong, active
PRAYER	Very passive	Slightly passive
FUTURE	Active	Passive
TRADITION	Very passive	Active
PAST	Very passive	Slightly active
DEATH	Very passive	Passive
SUNDAY	Very good, weak, passive	Good, slightly weak, active

6. The SELF seen cross-culturally provides some fascinating data. Some groups appear to see it as very good, strong, and active, whereas others see it as relatively weak and passive. Osgood has hypothesized that when two groups in conflict see themselves as good, strong, and active they may become engaged in conflict such as war as a natural consequence of such perceptions. Obviously, this is an important prediction, for if it can be supported by empirical evidence it would give social scientists a method for the prediction of certain kinds of international behaviors.

To summarize, the studies by Osgood and his associates, around the world, suggest that evaluation, potency, and activity are the basic criterial attributes for the perception of heterogeneous concepts in all cultures. The procedure they used established the common framework for studies of affective meaning, and evaluation in particular, in any culture. Many studies so far completed are extremely promising, but validation of the findings by behavioral and other kinds of measures has not yet been done.

In Chapter 9 we present a descriptive summary of subjective culture results obtained from American and Greek samples in which semantic differential data are integrated with other kinds of evidence, thus giving some suggestions of validity.

One final clarification is needed: the qualification that Osgood's results concerning the generality of evaluation, potency, and activity is restricted to studies of heterogeneous concepts should be made clear.

As we move to more homogeneous sets of concepts, we discover attributes that are appropriate to them. Thus, when we study jobs (Triandis, 1960), we find the attribute "blue-white collar"; when we study social issues (Davis, 1966), we find the attribute "important" (interesting, profound, important), the attribute "familiar" (near, familiar, believable), as well as the more general attribute "evaluation" (fair, good, valuable).

In person perception the attributes are, as expected from such arguments, more specific than the three classic Osgood attributes. In one study Davis (1966) found two kinds of evaluation (*esthetic,* such as sensitive and good, and *moral,* such as wholesome, clean, and moral), a *potency* factor (tough, masculine), a special kind of activity factor (*excitability,* such as excitable, emotional, impulsive) and an additional factor which he called *sociability* (sociable, typical, extroverted). It is clear that in the more homogeneous domains we obtain nonevaluative attributes with greater frequency than in the most heterogeneous domains.

Associations and Elementary Cognitive Structures

An analysis of cognitive functioning by Guilford (1967, 1968) considers three modes: the *content* of categories (figural, symbolic, semantic, and behavioral), the *activities of the organism* (recognition, discovery, comprehension, evaluation, memory, convergence, and divergence), and the *products* of such activities.

One relationship of long standing in psychological research is *association.* There is a large number of techniques, ranging from free association to restricted associations, such as filling blanks of sentences. The structure of word associations has been studied cross-culturally in both free (e.g., Rosenzweig, 1957, 1961) and restricted formats (e.g., Miron & Wolfe, 1962). The data suggest that there is enough similarity in the structure of word associations to justify the comparison of word association norms developed in different linguistic communities. Correlations of the frequencies of such norms across a sample of, say, 100 words give interesting information about the similarity of various cultural groups. Lambert (1968) has shown that English Canadians give associations that correlate .87 with the associations given by Americans and only .33 with those given by French Canadians; bilinguals in Canada, however, give associations that correlate about .60 with both Canadian linguistic groups.

Word associations have been used to determine the dominant themes present in the thinking of some Korean and American students by Szalay and Brent (1967) and Szalay, Windle and Lysne (1970); for example, in response to HUNGRY American students give words like food, eat, thirsty, and starve, and Korean students, words like cooked rice, beggar, food, and poverty. Differences in the "themes" and values of the two groups can be suggested from such observations. Riegel (1968) compared restricted associations among six language groups.

Deese (1962) demonstrated that associations can be employed to determine similarities in the meaning of concepts. Ten different methods for measuring verbal relatedness were reviewed by Marshall and Cofer (1963). In general the rated similarity of concepts agrees quite closely with the similarity obtained from most indices of associative similarity (Forster, Triandis, & Osgood, 1964). When the concepts studied vary in connotative meaning, as determined by the semantic differential, the correlation between rated similarity and semantic differential profile differences is negative; when differences in connotative meaning are controlled, associative meaning becomes the best predictor of rated similarity (Forster et al., 1964).

Although much work has been done on associations, very little has been done with other forms of relation among categories, yet it is probable that studies of other forms of relation would prove equally informative. A variety of such studies is suggested below:

INCLUSION. Is *A* part of *B*? One might ask, for example, "In your culture do all the people who consider themselves *honest (A) pay their taxes (B)*?"

NEGATION. *A* is not *B*. One might ask, for example, "In your culture are there any honest people *(A)* who do not pay their taxes *(B)*?"

EQUIVALENCE. *A* is just like *B*. "In your culture is paying taxes a good indication of honesty?"

INEQUALITY. *A* is smaller (bigger) than *B*. "In your culture is crime *A* more or less serious than crime *B*?"

PROPORTION. *A* is to *B* as *C* is to *D*; for example, "Is crime *A* to crime *B* as crime *C* is to crime *D*?"

CONJUNCTION. *A* and *B*. "In your culture what kinds of people (*A*) are considered lucky (*B*)?"

INCLUSIVE DISJUNCTION. *A* or *B* or both. "In your culture are males considered desirable (*A*), powerful (*B*), or both?"

EXCLUSIVE DISJUNCTION. *A* or *B* but not both. "In your culture are males considered reliable (*A*) or unreliable (*B*)?"

IMPLICATION. If you have *A*, then you have *B*. "If you have OPEN HOUSING, then you have JUSTICE."

TRANSFORMATION. *A* is a transformed version of *B*. "In your culture does owning 100 cows confer the same status as having three wives?"

It is obvious from the above discussion that a variety of questions, taking many forms, might be asked. The crucial question is "How much information can one derive from such questions about the subjective culture of subjects?" The answer appears empirical. For this reason we have undertaken some studies that utilize this approach. In particular we studied implications (Davis & Triandis, 1965; Kilty, 1967; Thomanek, 1968) and the perception of antecedent-consequent relationships (Chapter 7). Stereotypes are a special form of association involving a group of people and their various characteristics. Chapter 5 and 6 present two studies of stereotypes which exemplify our approach.

Beliefs

Two kinds of belief, which are essentially restricted associations, have been studied in our research program. The first are implicative relationships such as "If you have INTEGRATED HOUSING, then you have. . . ." The format used required the subjects to make their judgments on probability scales (probable-improbable) which referred to six implicates, such as "slums," "justice," "equal rights for all," and "more crime." The other kind included both antecedents and consequents of the concept under study.

Attitudes

We conceptualize attitudes as having cognitive, affective, and behavioral components. The cognitive can be studied by examining the associations, beliefs, and categorizations described above. The affective can be investigated as described in the Section on evaluation. The behavioral has not yet been described and it is to this aspect that we now turn.

The behavioral differential (Triandis, 1964b) was developed to measure behavioral intentions. A typical item of this instrument might take the following form:

A Japanese female physician, 53 years old
would___:___:___:___:___:___:___:___:___would not
admire the ideas of this person

Our theoretical framework suggests that behavioral intentions are central to our understanding and prediction of interpersonal behavior. For this reason it is important that we learn how people perceive behaviors and the kinds of behavioral intentions they have toward various categories of people.

The earliest conceptualization of behavioral intentions was unidimensional; Bogardus (1928) labeled this dimension social distance. Cross-cultural studies of social distance (Triandis & Triandis, 1962; Triandis, Davis, & Takezawa, 1965; Brewer, 1968) have employed the unidimensional model, but the empirical evidence pointed increasingly to the need for a more complex model. Although the dimension of approach-avoidance, which is implicit in the notion of social distance, is certainly the most powerful of all the dimensions of interpersonal behavior, later work showed that superordination, intimacy, and overt hostility are important dimensions that are often orthogonal to one another. In short, the Bogardus conceptualization corresponds to the turn of the century view of intelligence as a unitary trait, whereas the current view of the multidimensional nature of interpersonal behavioral intentions corresponds to the post-Thurstonian view of intelligence as consisting of several specific, though interrelated, aspects.

The first multidimensional study of interpersonal behavior resulted in five factors: *respect* (admire the ideas of, admire the character of); *marital acceptance* (date, marry); *friendship acceptance* (gossip with, accept as intimate friend); *social distance* (exclude from the neighborhood); and *superordination* (command, criticize) (Triandis, 1964b). The first cross-cultural study was done by simply translating the most highly loaded scales from this study and using them in three cultures (Triandis, Tanaka, & Shanmugam, 1966). Subsequent studies (Triandis, Vassiliou, & Nassiakou, 1968) generated lists of social behaviors in each of the cultures by using appropriate pretest samples of subject before proceeding with the main study. Naturally, as the samples of behavior scales became more diverse, the comparability of the factors obtained when the intercorrelations among these scales were subjected to factor analysis became less clear. Nevertheless, these studies revealed enough communality in the meaning of the factors across cultures to permit cross-cultural comparison of interpersonal behaviors.

Let us turn to a more specific examination of these results. Triandis,

Tanaka, and Shanmugam (1966) tested American, Japanese, and south Indian students on behavioral differential scales. They found three culture-common factors: *respect, friendship,* and *marital acceptance.* The factors were clearly similar across the three cultural groups, although various subgroups in certain cultures had relatively idiosyncratic ways of perceiving social behaviors; for example, the Japanese *respect* factor (would admire the character of and would obey) had a very strong element of subordination which was not found in the other two cultures; the Japanese *friendship* factor was also much more loaded with respect elements than was the case for the corresponding factors in the other two cultures. The Japanese *marital acceptance* factor, although similar to the *marital* factors of the other cultures, contained some behaviors that did not load in the other cultures. Specifically, in the case of the Japanese males there was a strong loading of the scale *would treat as a subordinate,* and in the case of the Japanese females a strong loading of the scale *would be commanded by.* In short, although there was considerable generality in the factor structures across the three cultures, there was also a certain amount of cultural specificity that changed somewhat the meaning of the factors obtained in each culture.

Triandis, Vassiliou, and Nassiakou (1968), testing Greek and American subjects, found six American factors which closely replicated the earlier findings of Triandis (1964b). The factors were *respect* (praise, admire, enjoy meeting, depend on); *hostility* (argue with, correct, blame for failure, dislike); *marital acceptance* (love, marry); *friendship* (help, protect wish good luck to); *superordination* (treat as a subordinate, command); and *deep emotional involvement* (confess sins to, cry for). The correspondence with the *respect, social distance, marital acceptance, friendship* and *superordination* factors of the preceding study is good. The Greek factors included *association* (show love, help, reward, thank for goods), *hostility* (hate, fear, feel inferior to), *friendship* (study with, apologize to, cooperate with, have fun with), *superordination* (reprimand, scold), *active avoidance* (have difficulty understanding, show abhorrence of), and *attempts to gain attention* (complain to, boast to, boast of success to).

Obviously the correspondence across cultures is not perfect. It appears that four factors are similar across the American and the Greek samples (*association* has some resemblance to *respect* and *hostility, friendship,* and *superordination* are reasonably similar to factors obtained earlier). The lack of a *marital* factor in Greece is not easy to interpret. Taking the American, Greek, Indian, and Japanese results together, it would appear that *respect, marital acceptance, friendship, hostility,* and *superordination* (which were the factors of the original Triandis (1964b) study) may be cross-culturally general, although we cannot be sure that all of them will appear in any particular study since only the *friendship* factor appeared in every one of the four cultures.

Triandis (1967) has shown that the factors obtained in such studies depend very much on the types of stimulus persons presented. This is obvious, if we consider peculiar factors such as the American *social distance* factor (would not accept in my neighborhood, would prohibit from voting) obtained in the first behavioral differential study. This factor can be obtained only when prejudiced subjects respond to Negro stimuli. If Negro stimuli are not included in the study, the factor will not emerge. In view of this fact we tend to believe that the nonreplication of certain factors in some of the studies is not sufficient evidence for the conclusion that the factors are culture specific. Tentatively, then, we hypothesize that an adequate sampling of stimulus persons and behavior-scales will result in five cross-culturally common factors dealing with *respect, marital acceptance, friendship, hostility,* and *superordination.*

What is the structure of interpersonal behaviors in role perceptions? This has been extensively discussed by Triandis, Vassiliou, and Nassiakou (1968). Suffice it to say here that it appears that the structure of behaviors obtained from the role differential is quite similar to that obtained with the behavioral differential. This conclusion is reinforced from Loh and Triandis' (1968) finding of *respect* (admire the ideas of, help, admire honesty of), *marital acceptance, formal friendship* (accept as business partner, invite to party, accept as game partner), *rejection* (refute word of, not trust word of), and *superordination* (punish, be boss of) among Peruvian subjects, responding to a role differential.

Additional evidence presented by Triandis, Vassiliou, and Nassiakou (1968) from the Thrustone scaling of a sample of social behaviors on four dimensions (association, superordination, intimacy, hostility) suggests that association, superordination, and intimacy may be truly the basic dimensions of interpersonal behavior. It could be argued that social behavior in all cultures occurs among persons who are (a) in primary groups (e.g., family, friends) or in secondary groups, (b) similar or different in status, and (c) in a social relationship involving cooperation or competition. *Intimacy* is appropriate in primary groups, whereas *formality* is appropriate in secondary groups, *superordination* is appropriate when the status of the actor is high, *friendship* when it is equal, and *subordination* when it is low relative to the status of the other person, *cooperation* occurs when people have similar goals and agree about the means of reaching them. When they have similar goals but disagree about the means, there is some tension; when they have different goals, there is competition and a great deal of tension. If this analysis is correct, certain types of social behavior should be particularly common under the circumstances just described. Table 2 shows what these behaviors might be. The fact that we have not obtained all of these types of behavior factors in either role or behavioral differential studies so far may simply reflect inadequate sampling of the appropriate domains of stimulus person and behaviors. Table 2

Table 2   The Conditions for the Occurrence of Different Types of Social Behavior

Type of Group	Agreements	Relationship Between Status of Actor and Other		
		Higher	Equal	Lower
Primary	On means, goals	Protection *Nurturance*	*Marital acceptance*	*Respect*
	On goals, not on means	*Scolding, control*	Controlled hostility	Rebellion
Secondary	On means, goals	*Superordination*	*Friendship*	*Subordination*
	On goals, not on means, or on neither	*Social distance*	Overt *hostility*	Revolution

italicizes the factors we have found in our current studies. Further work needs to include a sufficient number of stimulus persons and scales to obtain factors such as *rebellion* and *revolution,* which have not yet appeared in any studies.

Although this table is essentially speculative, we are encouraged to think that the distinctions among the various factors found so far are real by two kinds of evidence. First we note that some of these distinctions correspond to the work of other investigators; for example, Foa (1964, 1966) and Lorr and McNair (1965) have worked with factors that correspond to our *association* and *superordination* factors. The distinction between *respect* and *liking* (friendship) seems fruitful in the social psychological laboratory (Kiesler & Goldberg, 1968) and predicts behavior as it is expected to do (Goldberg, 1968). The analysis of social behavior as determined by solidarity (intimacy) and status found in both Brown's (1965) and Lambert's (Lambert & Tucker, 1969; Tucker, Lambert & Viera, 1969) analyses of the determinants of interpersonal modes of address supports this viewpoint. Second, there are different antecedents to *respect* and *friendship* (Triandis, Vassiliou, & Thomanek, 1966), and it is probable that similar differences in antecedents will be obtained for the other factors. Specifically, *respect* increases as the status of the other increases and decreases as the status of the subject giving the responses increases. On the other hand, *friendship* increases as the similarity in the status of the other and the subject increases.

We believe that the factors in Table 2 are largely normatively determined, since personality appears to be unrelated to responses to the behavioral differential (Posavac & Triandis, 1968). The table summarizes a theory of normative social behavior which is complex but not much more complex than other analyses of social norms such as that of Gibbs (1965). The table predicts specific relationships between different kinds of behavioral intention, since it is organized by facets such as the primary-secondary group, and so on. Specifically it predicts high correlations among behaviors that are adjacent in the table and low correlations among behaviors that are distant. Further work is needed to test these speculations.

Stereotypes

In our research program we have been particularly interested in the effects of contact on stereotyping. This problem has a long history which has recently been reviewed by Amir (1969). Our studies test specific hypotheses concerning the changes of stereotypes that can be attributed to contact. Chapter 5 presents the details; we therefore will not review the literature in this chapter.

Expectations

In our program we have not yet studied this important aspect of subjective culture. Current work by Malpass on black-white expectations of the instrumentalities of certain means for certain ends will fill this gap.

Norms

Norms are closely related to behavioral intentions and can be studied with only slight modifications of procedure. The behavioral differential requires subjects to indicate how they *would* behave; the norm differential requires subjects to indicate how they *should* behave. In one study reported by Triandis, Vassiliou, and Nassiakou (1968) there were similar factorial structures in the judgments of the subjects to these two types of instruction, although the "should" instructions tended to be less sensitive and more gross than the "would" instructions.

Ideals

Our research program has not yet studied this aspect of subjective culture.

Roles

An extensive study of role perceptions was published by Triandis, Vassiliou, and Nassiakou (1968). The study is reviewed in detail in Chapter 8 in which we report an extension of this work to several additional cultures.

Tasks

The cross-cultural perception of tasks has not yet been studied. This, too, is an aspect of subjective culture that requires study in the near future.

Values

A central theme in cross-cultural analyses of subjective culture has been the analysis of values.

Values have been defined in a large number of ways. Albert and Kluckhohn (1959) have compiled a bibliography of 2006 references which portrays an amazing variety of definitions. Their own work (Albert, 1956; Kluckhohn, 1956, 1959) has already been discussed in Chapter 2, and examines the concept at a high level of abstraction. We feel that their conceptualization is the most defensible; hence our definition of values as "relationships among abstract categories having a strong affective component and implying a preference for certain types of action." This definition implies a rank order of preferences for certain events or outcomes; for example, the relationship between man and nature can be conceived in abstract terms, such as man is a master over nature, man is subjugated to nature or in harmony with nature (Kluckhohn & Strodtbeck, 1961); at an even higher level of abstraction it can be seen as determinate (mastery) or indeterminate (fatalism), unitary (a oneness merging man and nature) or pluralistic (Decartian dualism, etc.), and evil or good (Kluckhohn, 1959). Each of these views implies preferences for certain outcomes.

Although we are sympathetic to this conception, we note also a variety of definitions that appear equally defensible. Fallding (1965) defined values as "satisfactions that are self-sufficient." He distinguished them from instrumental satisfactions, pleasures, interests, compulsions, and benefits. He conceived of five types of value; for example, one of these is membership—one may experience satisfactions for their own sake with respect to membership in a group.

Others have defined values in terms of sensitivity to some aspects of the environment. Such a conception would include the Spranger values, which were reflected in Allport's work and which has generated much research [see Dukes (1955) for a review], McClelland's (1961) work on various needs, Cantril's (1965) analysis of human concerns, and Diaz-Guerrero's (1967a) active-passive syndrome which implies sensitivity to and preference for either active (change environment) or passive (change yourself) adjustment to stress.

Some analyses of values suggest that certain cultural groups utilize central themes (Opler, 1945) in looking at the world. Examples of studies utilizing such central themes include Foster's (1965) argument that most peasant societies have an image of a limited good, an analysis by Ziller et al. (1968) of Indian and American self-orientations, Triandis and Vassiliou's (1967a) analysis of Greek culture, Iacono's (1968) analysis of southern Italian culture, and Banfield's (1958) description of familism.

Still another approach utilizes values from the perspective of human adjustment, as seen by the clinical psychologist. Buhler's (1962a,b) argument that values are need-satisfying (comfort, love), adaptive (fitting-in), creative-expansive (self-realization), and aim at upholding an internal order (seek internal harmony) is an example of this approach.

Anthropologists have often thought of values as conceptions of the *proper* relationships between categories. Hall's (1959, 1966) work on proper behavior with respect to time, interpersonal distances, etc., fits this notion. Psychologists, such as Little (1968), have generalized this conception. Related to this is the definition of values as an ideal type, as, for example, in Pearlin and Kohn's (1966) analysis of American and Italian conceptions of what is an "ideal child." Vogt and Albert (1966) have provided an excellent study of values in five cultures which utilize similar perspectives.

Riecken and Homans (1954) and particularly Scott (1965) have presented still another point of view which argues that values are those characteristics of people that we like to see in others in unlimited amounts; for example, honesty is a value, but wealth is not, because we like our friends to be as honest as possible, but not necessarily as wealthy as possible.

The final approach to be mentioned is that of Morris (1956) who conceived of values as "ways of life."

Morris developed 13 "ways of life" representative of the most important known philosophical positions found anywhere in the world. He asked respondents in several cultures to rank them according to their preference. In a pioneer study which employed multivariate analyses in the area of values Morris and Jones (1955) studied the values of American and Indian students, using Morris' ways of life.

The diversity of these approaches is apparent. Is there any way to choose among them? We propose four criteria for preference of one approach over another. Other things being equal, we prefer approaches that provide (a) more reliable measurements, (b) more complete coverage of the value systems of both individuals and cultures, (c) lawful relationships with other intrapsychic events, such as cognitions, behavioral intentions, norms and roles, and (d) lawful relationships with behaviors.

The Kluckhohn approach has provided a satisfactory measurement procedure (Kluckhohn & Strodtbeck, 1961) and the best coverage of the value systems in terms of completeness. There is little information, however, about lawful relationships with other intrapsychiac events or behaviors.

Fallding (1965), who does not favor specific measurement procedures but advocates the observation of groups, argues that different groups are formed in order to express different values. We find this approach unsatisfactory because it will probably lead to unreliable measurements; also, it is doubtful that a complete coverage of values can be obtained from such observations.

Those who examined the sensitivity of man to certain aspects of his environment have been reasonably successful in measuring it. Certainly the Allport-Vernon-Lindzey Scale is widely used, reliable, and appears related to both cognitive and behavioral events. On the other hand, it seems to cover a small aspect of the total value structure and is probably culture-bound.

McClelland's (1961) approach has utilized content analyses of TAT's, which have had a disappointing reliability. Heise (1966), however, has measured need achievement with the semantic differential and Kahl (1965) has been successful in measuring achievement orientations with Liket-type attitude items. Rogers and Neill (1966) have used sentence completions in studies of farmers in several cultures. McClelland's research program which is utilizing this approach is impressive because it has provided interesting mappings of both the antecedents and behavioral consequents of need achievement.

Those who focus on a particular theme have utilized a variety of approaches to extract the theme from observations. Triandis and Vassiliou, in Chapter 9, for instance, utilized semantic, behavioral and role differentials, the antecedent-consequent meaning method, and informal observations. The same themes seem present in all the data. Some of these procedures are presented in later chapters.

Buhler used value statements, such as "to have the necessities of life" and asked her subjects to rate them on a scale ranging from *essential,* through *important, desirable, not my concern,* to *I reject this.* The measurement is probably satisfactory but of limited coverage. There is little evidence of how it is related to behavior.

Most of the work of Hall is based on observations. The reliability of each observation may be small, but a large number of observations may result in reliable knowledge. Again the coverage is narrow. On the other hand, the relationship to behavior is clearly specified. Little (1968) has employed specially devised figures which the subject places on a sheet of paper. He arrives at his generalizations about social schemata by measuring the distance of placement of the figures. This is reliable measurement, but narrow coverage, and although closely related to certain behaviors the behaviors themselves are rather specific.

Scott (1965) employed a questionnaire which explored the traits considered particularly admirable by college students. He developed four- or five-item scales for 12 traits, such as kindness, loyalty, status, physical development, honesty, religiousness, self-control, and independence. The stability of the scales was around .70 and they correlated with reported behaviors around .25. There is some discussion in his book about the correlates of such values, particularly with respect to their consequences for organizational life in fraternities and sororities. Thus Scott's work meets three of our four criteria reasonably well, but he does not demonstrate that the 12 traits he investigated are important values outside his population of American college students. There is a great need for replication of this study in other cultures.

Morris (1956) did some of the pioneer work on values. He presented his "ways of life" to subjects and asked them to indicate the degree to which they liked them. This type of measurement is reliable and the 13 "ways of life" may provide wide coverage.

The evaluation provided above suggests that in general those approaches that have been best on measurement have been least good on coverage and those that have been good on coverage have been least good on measurement or the relationships with other intrapsychic events or behaviors. The work of Kluckhohn and of Morris provides compromises with good coverage and measurement, but there is still little empirical work which relates such values to other intrapsychic events or behaviors.

In sum, none of the approaches seems to have met completely our four criteria. The reason for this situation is readily apparent: the amount of work required to meet all four criteria is extremely large.

It may be a useful exercise now to examine some of the major approaches to the measurement of values in terms of the same criteria.

First, there is content analysis. This was used by Gillespie and Allport (1955) in their important study of the outlook of young people in 10 countries, by Goodman (1957) in her study of American and Japanese children, and by others. LeShan (1952) asked lower class and middle-class children to tell a story and content-analyzed the stories to determine the period covered in the story; lower class children told stories that covered short periods of time, such as one hour, whereas middle-class children told stories that covered longer periods of time. If we assume that the lower class subjects value the present and the middle-class subjects, the future, this would be evidence of a cognitive correlate of this value. A related approach is Ayal's (1963) content analysis of Japanese and Thai philosophic and religious points of view.

Content analysis seems to have the same problem that we detected in the general study of values: the richer the coverage, the less satisfactory the measurement. If one wishes to measure some specific aspect of the value system, this method can provide reliable measurement; however, if one wishes to measure the value structure exhaustively, either analysis time will be very high or the reliability of measurement will be lower. Finally, most of the studies do not assess the relationships of values to other intrapsychic events or behavior. Ayal's attempt to relate values to economic development is well done, but it is difficult to exclude alternative interpretations of the data.

Projective approaches, such as the analysis of drawings (Dennis, 1966) or TAT's (McClelland, 1961), generally lead to lower reliability of measurement. Dennis has published a fascinating volume because of the interesting pictures of children's drawings but the validity of the approach remains to be tested.

Morris' (1956) approach is somewhat more focused, since the paragraphs that describe the ways of life do cover the structure of values, yet it is done in sufficiently specific terms to permit rating or ranking. Beg (1966) presented a recent study that utilized this approach. One of its methodological problems concerns the probability that the ways of life do not mean the same thing in different cultures because of the problems of adequate translation discussed in Chapter 3. Translation of paragraphs, however, is more defensible than the translation of single words. The Morris approach is certainly promising enough to deserve further work, particularly on validity.

The use of attitude items to measure specific values has a long history. Wickert (1940) used such items to measure personal goal values. He measured nine values: personal freedom, helpfulness, new experience, power, recognition, response (enjoying intimacy, friendship), security, submission, and workmanship. He found the reliability of the items too small, however, for individual prediction, although conceivably high enough for group comparisons. A large number of studies have utilized such items with satisfactory reliabilities; for example, in the area of personality measurement Kikuchi & Gordon (1966) and Berrien (1965); in the area of organizational values Shartle et al. (1964), England (1967), and Whitehead & Takezawa (1968); in the area of modernization Inkeles (1969), Smith & Inkeles (1966), Dawson (1967), and Kahl (1968); on political values Almond & Verba (1963) and Jacob, Teune & Watts (1968).

Although the ordinary use of items, without matching for social desirability, response style, etc., can produce problems of interpretation discussed in Chapter 3, the use of various kinds of structured cognitive tasks is likely to control for such effects and to produce reliable measurement. Peck (1967) asked Americans and Mexicans to rank-order 15 concepts; he found that his Mexican college students gave much higher ranks to career success, honor, and economic security than his American men, whereas the latter gave higher rankings to love, freedom, and character. The Mexican sample responded in ways that do not fit the stereotypes of Mexicans, but this may be because of the unusual nature of the sample, which was highly select and elite. Rokeach (1968) used the ranking technique with 18 value concepts with considerable success.

One problem with the ranking technique is that only a limited number of concepts can be studied. The forced-choice technique used by Gordon (1968) and by Gorlow and Noll (1967a,b) appears to be quite promising and can sample a much larger domain of items.

In general the forced-choice technique appears to be most promising in achieving both reliability and coverage in a limited amount of time. Direct observation suffers from the difficulty of estimating reliability and coverage is uncertain. On the other hand, it has direct implications for behavior.

In sum, we tend to think that the Q-sort methodology is most likely to meet most of the criteria, although some of the other approaches are quite promising and need to be explored further.

One consideration that is generally not faced in most of these studies of values is that generally most values are desirable; hence we can measure the potency of values best when we pit one against another. In a pilot study Triandis employed 90 values, selected from all those utilized in the research just reviewed. The subjects were instructed to respond in two different ways: (a) according to the Bühler instructions, to indicate whether the values were essential, important, and so on, and (b) by distributing 100 points among the 90 values. The results of this pilot study showed that subjects give rather different responses under these two kinds of instruction. The Bühler instructions result in most values being rated as "desirable"; very few are rejected. The distribution of 100 points among 90 values results in the rejection of most of the values, since most of them receive no points. The values that were rated as "essential," however, received several points, and some of those rated "important" received some. Further work is needed to validate these scoring systems, but our guess is that the 100-point system will provide more valid results. On the other hand, subjects have difficulty understanding the instructions, and they feel unhappy about having to sum the points they give to each value, several times, in order to ensure that the total does add to exactly 100.

Critical Comments About Current Research on Values. One of the characteristics of much current research on values is that it consists of the simple administration of a questionnaire to two or three culturally diverse groups; the description of cultural differences in values is done in terms of differences in such responses. Such research gives the investigator a quick and easy publication, but it makes a small contribution to the advancement of social psychology. A slightly more sophisticated version of this approach consists in administering several questionnaires. Typical of this approach is a paper by Singh, Huang, and Thompson (1962) who administered the Allport-Vernon-Lindzey Scale, the Morris, the Sanford and Opler, and the Edwards Personal Preferences Survey to American, Chinese, and Indian students.

Another shortcoming in the literature is the use of minute and detailed observations of a small segment of behavior, with little reference to anything else. An instance of such an approach is Adler's (1967) observation that the majority of children around the world draw apple trees when picturing fruit trees. Almost 3000 pictures, from 13 countries on five continents, were analyzed and the data supported this notion, but the author had no satisfactory explanation of the reasons why this is happening. Adler (1968) extended this study to more than 4000 children in 24 countries, but with no insights concerning the basis of this phenomenon. Certainly it is important to establish the generality of certain observations, but a single observation of this kind, even though very general, cannot advance our understanding unless it is related to antecedents and consequents.

Our Own Approach. We have employed cognitive tasks on the grounds that this is the most likely procedure to lead to high reliability of measurement and good coverage of the value structures in a limited amount of time. We have assumed that the frequency with which a theme appears in the judgments made by subjects reflects its importance in part. If the same theme appears in different tasks, under different instructions, or in response to different stimuli, it is more important than if it does not. We also looked at the structure of the responses and the interrelationships among the responses, assuming that important attributes of the objects that are being judged will reveal something about the underlying themes and that values will be attached to these themes.

In addition, it appears to us that the antecedent-consequent procedure, which is described in Chapter 7, provides information relevant to the analysis of values. It is a highly reliable procedure with a test-retest reliability of .94 (Haried, 1969). It allows for extensive coverage of the values of individuals or cultural groups. There is some evidence that it is related to behavior as well as interpersonal attitudes. Certainly the data discussed in Chapter 10 suggest that measures such as the antecedent-consequent measure will predict some of the variance of behavior. Further work is needed to test this expectation.

Summary. In this chapter we have reviewed work by others and our own group relevant to the analysis of various aspects of subjective culture. We have referred to the relation between this work and the chapters that follow. Each of the following chapters can be read without reference to this chapter or related chapters of the book, although the present chapter, hopefully, points out how each of the aspects of subjective culture is related to other aspects.

A Final Comment. The chapters of this part of the book have examined the analysis of subjective culture at the broadest and most inclusive level of analysis. The reader will find a considerable difference between this level and the levels used in the next several parts of the book in which we are dealing with actual data. An analogy is appropriate: The theoretical framework of Chapter 2 and the review of this chapter correspond to maps of the globe; the chapters that follow correspond to detailed maps of particular countries. Our optimistic expectation is that after many years of research with maps of countries we will be able to put them together into maps of continents and later into a map of the globe resembling the one provided in Chapter 2. With this warning to the reader about the impending major change in the level of abstraction, we turn now to the data.

PART TWO

Examples of Approaches
to the Study of
Subjective Culture

In this part of the book we get much more specific, closer to the data, and much less inclusive than in Part I.

We present four empirical studies concerned with stereotypes, values, and roles. In our research program we have not yet worked at an empirical level with all the concepts developed in Part I. The empirical work represented in Part II is offered as a sample of what can be done with studies utilizing the concepts developed in Part I.

The first two chapters concern stereotyping, the next is an approach to the analysis of values, and the final chapter of this part reports our latest unpublished cross-cultural study of behavioral intentions and role perceptions. Each of these studies has published antecedent studies. The published studies will not be reproduced, since they are readily available in the journals, and the critical arguments are summarized in the introductions to each of the chapters that follow.

In the preceding chapters we outlined our broad approach. In the chapters that follow we are going to get very specific. What follows might have been published in one of the social psychology journals. It is hoped that by getting close to the data the reader will obtain some of "the feel" of how one proceeds and the kinds of hypotheses one needs to work with.

The first paper in this part of the book is concerned with interpersonal contact and stereotyping. We examined the extent to which data about stereotyping obtained from Americans and Greeks conform to hypotheses tested and supported in our previous research (Triandis and Vassiliou,

1967b). In this new study the autostereotypes and heterostereotypes of 435 Americans living in Greece, concerning Greeks, and the autostereotypes and heterostereotypes of 668 Greeks representative of the population of the two largest cities of Greece, concerning Americans, were studied in a modified semantic differential interview. The data replicated all five hypotheses from our previous work; closer consideration, however, suggested some revisions to the theory of stereotyping which we formulated in 1966. This paper, then, proposes a new theory of stereotyping which integrates previous theories, such as Campbell's (1967) and Triandis and Vassiliou (1967b) and also accounts for all the data in this latest study of stereotyping.

Chapter 6 examines several kinds of stereotype, national and political among Japanese and American respondents. This chapter is offered as an example of the flexibility of the semantic differential in the analysis of subjective culture.

Chapter 7 introduces a new method of analyzing subjective culture. Here we explore "implicative relationships" such as "if you have X then you Y." We believe this method is an important way to consider how concepts are subjectively interrelated and we suggest how it can be used in the analysis of values. Furthermore, some forms of this method can be used to measure the extent to which a person feels potent, since a potent person feels that what he does (X) leads to definite outcomes (Y) with great reliability, whereas people who feel weak and at a loss see little connection between what they do and what happens to them. We suspect that this is similar to Rotter's (1966) internality-externality dimension of personality orientation, but we still have no empirical support for this speculation. The data for this chapter were obtained from 1500 male students from Illinois, Athens, southern India, and Tokyo. *Very* briefly, we found reliable differences in the values of these samples; the Americans and the Japanese were similar in their values, the Indians most different from the Americans, and the Greeks somewhere in between. The major values of the Americans in these samples were achievement, self-development, and peace of mind; of the Japanese, achievement, self-development, and aesthetic satisfaction; of the Greeks affiliation; and the Indians, status.

Finally, in Chapter 8 we present a large study of role perceptions. The data were obtained from 1620 people from the United States, Greece, India, Peru, and Taiwan. We were interested in the extent to which a few pancultural role attributes might account for most of the variance in role perceptions. We found only three pancultural attributes, whereas in most cultures five or six attributes were employed in role perceptions. However, the three pancultural factors account for about half of the variance of role perceptions and can be used in the cross-cultural comparison of roles. We show how different kinds of role (ingroup, outgroup, and conflict roles) vary on the dimension of "giving versus denying affect" and how roles that differ in status do show the expected variation on the status attribute. Superimposed on this pattern of similarities is a set of findings about cultural differences in role perception that is meaningful in terms of known influences on social behavior in the specific cultures.

CHAPTER FIVE

Interpersonal Contact and Stereotyping

VASSO VASSILIOU, HARRY C. TRIANDIS,
GEORGE VASSILIOU, AND HOWARD MCGUIRE

Our theoretical framework included the concept of categorization as a fundamental element in the analysis of subjective culture. When humans categorize other humans, they tend to use stereotypes; that is, they give the same response to several different individuals (categorization) and associate specific attributes to each category. The categories may refer to Negroes, Americans, Greeks, Indians, Japanese, physicians, street cleaners, Christians, women, children, or what have you. The attributes deal with the characteristics that people in a particular category are supposed to have—intelligent, moody, pious, rednosed, or what have you. Stereotypes involve bonds of association between the category and the attribute.

Campbell (1967) pointed out that "the greater the real differences between groups on any particular custom, detail of physical appearance, or item of material culture, the more likely it is that that feature will appear in the stereotyped image each group has of the other" (p. 821). Whether or not a group will be stereotyped depends on many factors, some of which are discussed below. Stereotypes have a kernel of truth, but often they reveal more about the person doing the stereotyping than about the group being stereotyped.

An example may clarify this last point. Suppose that there is a universal trait, such as "washing one's hands X times a day," and the distribution of frequencies around the world has an average of three times a day, further, suppose that in culture A people wash 10 times a day but in culture B they wash seven times a day. The prediction from Campbell's theory would be that people in culture A will see those in culture B as *filthy,* particularly if they are parochial enough not to know how deviant they are in relation to the rest of the world.

One of the major predictions from Campbell's theory is that stereotypes will change with contact by becoming clearer and more reliable. However, the effects of contact on stereotyping are quite complex.

There is considerable theoretical and practical interest concerning the effects of contact on ethnic relations. Amir (1969) has reviewed a large number of studies relevant to this problem and has concluded that the relationship is complex. Contact influences not only the direction of attitudes but also their intensity; for example, initially positive attitudes tend to become more positive and initially negative attitudes tend to become more negative as a result of contact. Attitude change is specific and does not generalize to all attitudes held by members of ethnic groups about each other. Improved interpersonal attitudes are observed when there is equal status contact between the members of the ethnic groups, when the contact is between members of a majority group and higher status members of a minority group, when authorities are in favor of good intergroup relations, when the contact is intimate rather than casual, when the contact is rewarding and pleasant, and when the members of both ethnic groups reach some important goals as a result of such contact. The latter point, of course, is consistent with Sherif's well-known theory of intergroup conflict and its reduction by the development of superordinate goals.

Unfavorable conditions for contact include situations that are competitive, when the contact is unpleasant, when the prestige of the group is lowered as a result of contact, when members of one group are frustrated, when the groups have moral or ethical standards that are objectionable to one another, and when the members of the minority group are of lower status than members of the majority group.

Stereotypes vary on a number of dimensions.

1. *Complexity*. The number of traits assigned to the other group.

2. *Clarity*. (a) *Polarization* of the judgments on each trait dimension; that is, the extent to which people from one group assign non-neutral values of the trait to people from another group. (b) *Consensus,* that is, agreement among people in assigning the trait to another group.

3. *Specificity-Vagueness*. The extent to which the traits are specific or vague (abstract).

4. *Validity*. The extent to which the stereotypes correspond to substantially realistic assignments of traits.

5. *Value*. The favorability of the assigned traits.

6. *Comparability*. The extent to which the framework of the perceiver

is involved in the stereotyping so that a comparison is made between auto-stereotype (group looking at itself) and heterostereotype (one group looking at another). When such a comparison is made and the mean difference on any characteristic between groups A and B, $(\bar{X}_A - \bar{X}_B)$, is large, there may occur a contrast phenomenon; that is, group A may see itself as more different from group B than it really is. If $\bar{X}_A - \bar{X}_B$ is small, group A will see no difference between itself and group B.

If we select two groups of people, A and B, in whom some characteristic X is normally distributed, with $\bar{X}_A$ being a rather different value than $\bar{X}_B$, the greater the actual difference between $\bar{X}_A$ and $\bar{X}_B$, the more likely it is that X will appear in the stereotypes of these two groups. Contact has the effect of making the difference between $\bar{X}_A$ and $\bar{X}_B$ more salient. Thus the greater the contact, the greater the clarity of the heterostereotype. In addition, contact will lead to greater complexity, specificity, validity, and comparability. Favorability is affected by contact in a complex manner, as can be seen from the following example of American-Greek contact.

When Greeks and Americans meet, one of the most salient differences between them is their work habits. The Greeks find Americans as systematic as "well-oiled machines." The Americans find the Greeks unsystematic.

Both cultures value work. Middle-class Americans, however, have learned to approach work methodically, planning and estimating time schedules on the basis of previous experiences. Such an approach allows them to keep deadlines reasonably accurately. In short, living in a more predictable environment, they are systematic. The Greeks tend on the average to be unaware of the value of planning and systematic procedures. Throughout the centuries they have learned to rely on spontaneous total mobilization of their resources in moments of crisis. They feel that work can be accomplished primarily by means of enthusiasm and devotion rather than by planning.

When Greeks "explain" cognitively such differences in work behavior, they justify (rationalize) their unsystematic approach by thinking of the American work habits as "unworthy for human beings." Greeks value the "spontaneous." On the other hand, Americans are unaware of such differences in point of view. As a result they see the Greek work behavior as indicative of disinterest in work. Nevertheless they do perceive the Greeks as "warm," because they see them as strongly intending to complete the work enthusiastically. Our previous data (Triandis & Vassiliou, 1967b) showed that the greater the degree of contact, the more accentuated the tendency of the Greeks to see the Americans as "systematic but cold" and themselves as "unsystematic but warm." Similarly, the greater the contact, the more the Americans saw the Greeks as "unsystematic but warm" and themselves as "systematic."

The favorability of stereotyping is a function of the extent to which a group sees itself or another group as able to reach valuable goals. When a group is unable to reach such goals with respect to another group, it may develop a stereotype of "inferiority" versus that group. Conversely, success may lead to "superiority" which cognitively explains such success as well as the lack of success of the other group. From such considerations it may be predicted that when Americans and Greeks meet the American view of the Greeks will become unfavorable and the Greek view of Americans will become favorable.

Triandis and Vassiliou tested hypotheses derived from this framework. The data obtained from six samples of Americans and Greeks with different amounts of heterocultural contact supported most hypotheses. In that study, however, the samples were selected so that they had different amounts of contact. It is possible that "high-contact" Greeks (in that study Greek students in American universities) became members of a high-contact group because they had favorable attitudes; "high-contact" Americans (doing a job in Athens, Greece) may have only appeared to have unfavorable stereotypes of Greeks because they were compared with "no-contact" Americans (college students in Illinois) who had a norm of giving "liberal" answers to questions involving foreign peoples. The present study was designed to test the relationship between contact and stereotyping by examining only the responses of Greeks and Americans living in Greece.

More specifically, Triandis and Vassiliou tested the hypothesis that the greater the degree of contact the more "favorable" the Greek stereotype of Americans; their data supported ($p < .001$) this hypothesis. They also tested the hypothesis that the greater the contact the more "unfavorable" the stereotype of Greeks held by Americans. This hypothesis was also supported ($p < .0001$).

Triandis and Vassiliou further hypothesized that the greater the contact the greater the clarity of the stereotypes, as measured by the amount of polarization as well as agreement among the Ss from a particular culture when they assign characteristics to members of their own or another culture. This hypothesis was supported by the American auto- and heterostereotypes but not by the Greek. It is conceivable that in a small country autostereotypes are influenced by a variety of contacts with foreigners which are not specific to contact with Americans, and the Greek stereotypes of Americans were formed by the mass media and other determinants and therefore they did not depend on the amount of contact.

Finally Triandis and Vassiliou hypothesized that the autostereotypes of

Americans will become more "favorable" with contact and those of Greeks, less "favorable." The hypothesis was confirmed for Americans but was completely disconfirmed for Greeks, whose autostereotype also improved with contact.

The disconfirmation of that hypothesis may not invalidate the theoretical arguments behind it. The maximum-contact Greeks were college students in American universities, whereas the no-contact Greeks were college students at the University of Athens. By several kinds of criteria the former are "privileged" and the latter "underprivileged." Such differences may influence their self-esteem, hence their autostereotypes. Thus we propose in the present study to retest the hypotheses in the Triandis and Vassiliou study.

1. The greater the degree of contact, the clearer the autostereotypes and the heterostereotypes.

2. The greater the degree of contact, the more "favorable" the Greek stereotype of Americans.

3. The greater the degree of contact, the more "unfavorable" the stereotype of Greeks held by Americans.

4. The greater the degree of contact, the more "favorable" the American autostereotype.

5. The greater the degree of contact, the less "favorable" the Greek autostereotype (Triandis & Vassiliou, 1967b, p. 317).

Since in the present study we used better sampling and slightly better controls, we may obtain more insight in the relationships of contact and stereotyping.

The major differences between the present and the previous study are methodological. In the present study we employed "reported amount of contact" as a measure of contact. In the previous study we selected our samples to have different degrees of contact, but as is clear from the points made earlier such a selection leads to many ambiguities in interpretation. If the results of the present study are consistent with those of the previous study, the theoretical premises on which both are based will be supported. Discrepancies between the two studies will have to be explained by differences in the methodology.

Method

Samples. The American sample consisted of 435 males and females. Thirty-two American interviewers were asked to collect responses from 10 couples each. This procedure allowed for sampling by household, thus making it equivalent to the sampling of the Greek respondents. However, because some of the interviewers were unable to obtain their quotas of 10 pairs, they were allowed to interview single individuals. Some were unable to meet their quotas because all the people they approached had already been interviewed. Two samples of Greeks were interviewed: (a) a representative sample of the adult population of Metropolitan Athens (one adult in 500 of the existing Athenian households) and (b) a representative sample of the adult population of the city of Thessaloniki (one adult in 250 households). The population of Metropolitan Athens is more than 2 million and represents about 25% of the population of Greece. The population of Thessaloniki is about 350,000 and therefore represents close to 5%. Thus our sample consisted of most of the urban population of Greece.

Mortality of the Sample. A high mortality of the sample was obtained among low-education female respondents. Since there was none of this type among the American subjects, the mortality of the American sample was insignificant. The mortality of the Athens sample was high; of the 400 interviewed only 324 were both willing and able to respond. The mortality of the Thessaloniki sample was even larger; of the 600 persons interviewed only 444 were both able and willing to respond. Our analysis of the location of mortality within the samples suggests that the majority of the nonrespondents were unable rather than unwilling to respond.

Interview. Triandis and Vassiliou (1967b) performed a factor analysis of 41 characteristics given by Americans and Greeks in unstructured interviews in which they described their coworkers from the other culture (Triandis, 1967). Fifteen of the 41 characteristics, having high loadings on the obtained factors, were retained in the present study. These 15 characteristics were presented together with sentences of the form "In general Americans (Greeks) tend to be. . . ." Since a total of four target groups was used, there was a total of four[1] times 15, or 60, judgments to be made by each *S*. The judgments were made by pointing the finger at a cardboard containing a seven-point scale. The 15 characteristics were used by the interviewer as labels for this scale. Thus an interview equivalent of the semantic differential judgments made by the subjects in the Triandis and Vassiliou (1967b) study was used in the interview; for example, one item was the following:

In general Greeks tend to be
systematic:__:__:__:__:__:__:__:unsystematic

---

[1] In addition to Greeks and Americans we used two other groups as "filler" items to distract the subjects from our focus of concern.

Half the items had the favorable characteristic to the right and the other half on the left of the cardboard.

The interviewer recorded the subject's sex and asked a number of questions. The American interviewers asked the American respondents "How many Greeks do you know as intimate friends?", "How many Greeks are your relatives?", "How many Greeks do you know as close acquaintances?", and "How many Greeks do you know as remote acquaintances?" For control purposes the same questions were also asked for two other national groups.

The Greek interviewers asked the Greek respondents corresponding questions about Americans. In addition, the Greeks answered five questions concerning their education, three questions concerning date and place of birth and the date of their moving to the metropolitan area in which they were interviewed, and other questions about their occupations, their father's occupation, the household income, and the number of employed persons living in the household. Finally the interviewer provided a rating of the "kind of house" (luxurious to substandard) in which he found the interviewee. From all this information the social status of the subject was estimated by two raters[2] on a nine-point scale.

Analyses

Contact. Examination of the reported contact showed that few subjects had relatives in the other culture. These subjects were separated from the main samples and analyzed separately. It was hoped that the intimate friend, close, remote, and no acquaintance items would result in a Guttman scale, but the data did not support this expectation. In fact, those who reported having intimate friends did not necessarily report having remote acquaintances. As a result we established four categories and judgmentally placed each interviewee in one of them. The categories were (a) maximum contact, several intimate friends; (b) much contact, some intimate friends, many close acquaintances; (c) some contact, no intimate friends, few close acquaintances, many remote acquaintances; (d) no contact, no intimate, no close, no remote acquaintances. Table 1 shows the number of subjects who completed interviews classified in each of these categories.

Characteristics. The response obtained from the Americans and the Greeks (separating the Athens and Thessaloniki samples) to the items ". . . Americans tend to be," "Greeks tend to be," were factor-analyzed.

[2] The interrater reliability was high and the average rating of the two raters was employed in the analyses.

Table 1   Number of Americans and Greeks with
Different Amounts of Contact

Contact Category	Americans	Greeks
Maximum[a]	112	43
Much	148	63
Some	149	83
No	26	580
Total	435	769

[a] When interpreting these results, it should be kept in mind that the concept "intimate friend" has a different meaning for Americans and most Europeans. Europeans tend to have a *few* intimate friends with whom they are *really* intimate, whereas Americans tend to have many friends, but not really intimate ones. It is our guess that the 112 Americans who report having several Greek intimate friends are talking about friends whom they see once a week socially and perhaps three times a week in work-related social settings. By contrast the Greeks are likely to see their intimate friends daily and to discuss many personal (intimate) topics with them.

Since there were 15 characteristics, the maximum possible number of factors was 15, but actually five or six factors were obtained from each sample.

Plots. The means and standard deviations of the responses of each sample to each item were recorded. The responses of the subjects homogeneous in the amount of reported contact, sex, and social class were plotted in separate graphs.

Results

Stereotypes of the Total Samples. Tables 2, 3, and 4 summarize the stereotypes obtained from the three samples. Before examining these results it is necessary to describe the differences between Athens and Thessaloniki.

Athens includes groups from all of Greece. About 75% of its present inhabitants come from the provinces. Thus the Athens sample is the "best" urban Greek sample possible. Thessaloniki is in the North where the climate is more rigorous, whereas Athens has a mild climate. Corresponding to these climatic differences are a number of widely held regional stereotypes which, according to each subgroup, differentiate the one from the

Table 2   American Stereotypes

Stereotype	Interpretive Label for Factor	Scales Loading High on Factor
Americans see Americans as	pragmatic	drive carefully, accept change readily
	innocent	naïve, trusting
	nice	modest, obliging
	flexible	flexible
	effective	systematic, witty, decisive
Americans see Greeks as	impulsive	unsystematic, emotionally uncontrolled, drive competitively
	distrusting outsiders	egotistic, sly, suspicious
	ineffective	follow procedures approximately, indecisive
	charming people	witty, obliging, honest
	rigid	rigid

Table 3   The Stereotypes of Athens Greeks

Stereotype	Interpretive Label for Factor	Scales with High Loadings
The Athens Greeks see Greeks as	spontaneous	witty, emotionally uncontrolled
	distrusting outsiders	egotistic, sly, suspicious
	reliable	modest, honest, systematic
	maneuvering antagonists	flexible, competitive, suspicious
	cooperating inexactly	obliging, follow procedures approximately
The Athens Greeks see Americans as	effective	systematic, follow procedures exactly, decisive
	naïvely competitive	naïve, competitive, rigid
	arrogantly witty	arrogant, witty
	rationally competitive	competitive, emotionally controlled
	straightforward (*philotimous*)[a]	obliging, honest

[a] Uniquely Greek, untranslatable concept (see Chapter 9).

Table 4   The Stereotypes of the Thessaloniki Greeks

Stereotypes	Interpretative Label of Factor	Scales with High Loadings
The Thessaloniki Greeks see Greeks as	distrusting outsiders	egotistic, suspicious, sly
	competitively progressive	competitive, follow procedures approximately, accept change readily
	philotimous[a]	obliging, honest
	controlled	systematic, emotionally controlled, drive carefully
	socially enjoyable	witty, modest
The Thessaloniki Greeks see Americans as	arrogant	arrogant, haughty
	distrusting outsiders	suspicious, sly
	effective	systematic, witty, decisive
	self-righteous	rigid, honest, emotionally controlled
	flexible	follow procedures approximately, accept change readily

[a] Uniquely Greek, untranslatable concept (see Chapter 9 for discussion of this concept.)

other. Thus Thessaloniki is supposed to be "full of" hardworking, vigorous, realistic, honest, effective, but also rigid people, but Athens is more mixed.

Athens had about 100,000 Americans at the time of this study; Thessaloniki had probably fewer than 5000. Some of these differences are properly reflected in our samples: the Athens Greeks reported "no contact" with Americans in 56.5% of the cases; the Thessaloniki Greeks reported "no contact" in 89.5% of the cases.

Turning now to Tables 2 to 4, we note that the Americans have an autostereotype (pragmatic, innocent, nice, flexible, effective) consisting of entirely positive attributes, but they view the Greeks negatively on four out of five of the factors. The "charming-people" factor is exceptionally interesting because it was quite salient in interviews conducted by Triandis (1967), and the factor analysis confirmed the interviewer's intuitive feeling that this was an important dimension of American-Greek relations in Athens.

In a comparison of the two Greek samples we note first that the Thessaloniki Greeks have a somewhat more positive autostereotype than the Athens Greeks. They both see Greeks as distrusting outsiders, but the Athens sample emphasizes that Greeks are spontaneous, reliable, and cooperating inexactly; the Thessaloniki sample emphasizes that they are competitively progressive and controlled.

This difference in the autostereotype can also be seen in the mean differences in the ratings on the various traits obtained from the two samples. Some of the widely held regional stereotypes referred to above appear to be reflected in the autostereotypes of the two cities.[3]

Both Greek samples see Americans as effective. But although the Athens sample saw Americans as arrogantly witty, naïvely competitive, and straightforward (*philotimos*), the Thessaloniki sample saw them as flexible, yet arrogant, distrusting outsiders and self-righteous. This difference is stereotyping may be due to the amount of contact with Americans, since 43.5% of the Athens but only 10.5% of the Thessaloniki samples report at least *some* contact with Americans. In general, it would seem that the Athens sample is more positive toward Americans. The differences that could be established by *t*-tests were not numerous, however; the Athens sample saw Americans as more *naïve,* not so extreme in *emotional control* (i.e., more "human"), and more *willing to adopt changes* (i.e., more progressive) than did the Thessaloniki Greeks. Differences in these scales do not appear to be convincing proof of a more positive stereotype. On the other hand, the strong correlation of *suspicious* and *sly* in Thessaloniki and the fact that Americans are seen as having these characteristics by that sample suggests that this sample is less favorable toward Americans than the Athens sample.

The Effect of Reported Contact on Stereotyping. First we shall examine our five hypotheses. The *first hypothesis* was that the higher the degree of contact the clearer the autostereotypes and heterostereotypes. In the previous study this was supported with data obtained from the American subjects and was not supported with data obtained from the Greeks. In the present study we investigated this problem by counting the number of traits (out of the possible 15) on which the judgments made by a sample of subjects differed significantly (tested by *t*-test, $p < .01$) from neutrality (scale-value 4). This test requires that the samples respond to the trait in non-neutral terms and that the standard deviation of the judgments be sufficiently small so that the mean of the judgments can be significantly different from the midpoint of the scale. Using this test, the American

---

[3] Significant differences (by *t*-test beyond $p < .01$) were obtained as follows: the Athens Greeks saw Greeks as more unsystematic, less modest, more emotionally uncontrolled, more flexible, less decisive planners, more competitive drivers, and less willing to adopt changes than did the Thessaloniki Greeks.

"no-contact" group showed "significant autostereotypes" on only four scales, whereas the other three American groups that did report contact averaged 10 out of 15 "significant stereotypes." Thus the trend is definitely in favor of the hypothesis. There was no such trend for the Greek sample. The American stereotypes of Greeks showed a similar pattern of results, with the "no-contact" group having only three "significant stereotypes" and the groups with contact, 9, 10, and 11, respectively. Again there was no such trend in the Greek data. Thus the present data replicate *exactly* the Triandis and Vassiliou (1967b) conclusion: the hypothesis is supported for Americans and rejected for Greeks.

The *second hypothesis* was that the greater the contact the more "favorable" the Greek stereotype of Americans. The *third hypothesis* was that the greater the contact the more "unfavorable" the stereotype of Greeks held by Americans. To test these hypotheses we examined the graphs that related the amount of contact and stereotyping for each of the samples and for each of the traits. Figure 1 shows a sample of these graphs. Table 5 is a summary of this inspection. A graph that had a definite, uninterrupted slope was considered as implying "improvement" in the stereotype

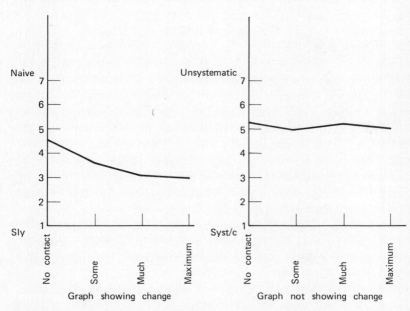

Figure 1. Examples of graphs used to construct Table 5 and other similar tables. The mean rating given by four groups of Americans (no contact, some, much, maximum contact) when responding to Greeks. Graph to the left shows change; the one to the right does not.

Table 5   Changes in Heterostereotypes as a Result of Contact

Characteristic	Americans See Greeks See Americans					
	Improve	Same	Deteriorate	Improve	Same	Deteriorate
Systematic		1		1		
Witty	1				1	
Naïve			1	1		
Unselfish			1		1	
Modest		1		1		
Trusting			1	1		
Cooperative		1			1	
Obliging	1			1		
Emotionally controlled			1		1	
Flexible		1			1	
Honest	1			1		
Follow procedures exactly			1			1
Decisive			1		1	
Drive carefully			1		1	
Accept work change			1		1	
Total	3	4	8	6	8	1

to the extent to which it increased with contact, with respect to the pole of the characteristics listed in Table 5, or decreased with respect to the opposite characteristic. It was assumed to imply "deterioration" of the stereotype if it decreased with respect to the pole listed in Table 5 or increased with respect to the opposite of the listed pole. This procedure forced all 15 characteristics to be evaluative. The decision regarding what was considered favorable was in part based on the results of the factor analysis by Triandis and Vassiliou (1967b) and the correlations observed in each culture between the particular scale and the scale "good-bad"; for example, "naïve" people were judged as "good." Hence naïve is listed in Table 5 as being a "good" trait.

Table 5 shows that on six of seven occasions in which there was a detectable relationship between the amount of contact and stereotyping hypothesis II is supported; on 8 of 11 occasions in which there was a detectable relationship hypothesis III is supported.

The control stimuli employed in this study showed no such relationships. Fischer exact tests show our observations as deviating significantly from chance ($p < .05$; one-tailed) for hypothesis II and as tending toward significance for hypothesis III. Another way to test these hypotheses is to assume that if chance were operating when there is a relationship between contact and stereotyping it would result in an improvement half the time and a deterioration of the stereotype half the time, in which case the binominal test may be used. When this is done, hypothesis II is supported at $p < .06$ and hypothesis III, at $p < .11$ (both one-tailed). In view of the fact that these results constitute replications of previously obtained results, with a different methodology, we accept the hypotheses.

The *fourth hypothesis* stated that the greater the contact the more favorable the American autostereotype, and the *fifth hypothesis* stated that the greater the contact, the less favorable the Greek autostereotype. Table 6,

Table 6   Changes in Autostereotypes as a Result of Reported Contact

Characteristics	Americans			Greeks		
	Better	Same	Worse	Better	Same	Worse
Systematic		1				1
Witty	1				1	
Naïve		1			1	
Unselfish	1					1
Modest	1				1	
Trusting	1				1	
Cooperative		1			1	
Obliging		1			1	
Emotionally controlled		1				1
Flexible		1				1
Honest	1			1		
Follow procedures exactly	1					1
Decisive	1					1
Drive carefully		1				1
Accept work change		1			1	
Total	6	9	0	1	7	7

which was constructed the same way as Table 5, shows the relevant data. The fourth hypothesis is supported for six out of six and the fifth hypothesis is supported for seven out of eight of the observations. These results are significant at $p < .016$ and $p < .035$, respectively (both one-tailed), by the binominal test. We therefore accept the fourth and fifth hypotheses.

Exploratory Studies. The characteristics of the stereotypes presented above prompt some further exploratory studies.

COMPLEXITY. There is obviously a trend (Table 5) to assign more traits when there is reported contact for the American subjects (11 out of 15 traits) but not for the Greeks (7 out of 15). The Greeks have a stereotype of Americans regardless of contact, and apparently contact does not influence its complexity.

SPECIFICITY. The range of specific and nonspecific traits was insufficient to explore this variable.

VALIDITY. Underlying our theoretical scheme is the notion that the greater the actual differences on a trait the greater the probability they will be perceived, that is, the greater the validity of the stereotype. The problem of establishing the existence of real differences is overwhelming. Schuman (1966b) has demonstrated that it can be done and that stereotypes can be shown under certain conditions to have validity. Given the kind of data we have, can we obtain any evidence in support of this notion?

We will argue that there are several ways of testing this basic notion and, though none of them is satisfactory in itself, if several unsatisfactory but adequate methods give convergent results, we can feel reasonably secure that our underlying assumptions are valid. We turn, then, to a number of ways to test these notions.

First, we might examine the degree of agreement of the autostereotype of Group A and the heterostereotype of other groups with respect to Group A. When such stereotypes are in agreement, this *may* be due to the fact that they reflect real differences.

Second, we can determine whether reported contact brings a heterostereotype "in line" (into greater agreement) with the target group's autostereotype. In our case we can provide a good test of the hypothesis by this approach, since the Triandis (1967) study has already reported the degree of agreement of the Greek autostereotypes and the American stereotypes of Greeks and the agreement of American autostereotypes with Greek stereotypes of Americans.

Third, we can examine the similarities or differences in the trends of the relationships between our measures of contact and the judgments of a particular group concerning the characteristics of another group. Thus we can see whether the American stereotypes of Greeks change the *same way* as a function of (a) reported contact (present study) and (b) actual contact (Triandis & Vassiliou, 1967b).

Examination of the Greek autostereotypes and the American stereotypes of Greeks showed that there was agreement on the characteristics listed in Table 7.

As can be seen in Table 7, for 9 of 11 characteristics on which the two cultural groups are in agreement concerning what the characteristics of Greeks are, the greater the amount of reported contact, the more extreme the rating of Greeks by Americans on that characteristic. This constitutes extremely strong confirmation of our theoretical notion ($p < .033$ by binomial, $p < .025$ by Fischer test), particularly since it incorporates *two* criteria of stereotype validity: (a) agreement of hetero- with autostereotypes and (b) change of the heterostereotype in the *direction* indicated by such agreement, as a function of the amount of contact.

Table 7 American Heterostereotypes of Greeks Showing Functional Relationships with the Amount of Contact

Characteristics	Relationship to Contact
Unsystematic	None
Witty	Yes
Suspicious	Yes
Competitive	Yes
Emotionally uncontrolled	None
Rigid	Yes
Obliging	Yes
Honest	Yes
Follow procedures approximately	Yes
Drive competitively	Yes
Resist changes in working conditions stiffly	Yes

Note 1. This table contains only characteristics on which the Greeks' autostereotype is in agreement with the American heterostereotype, as determined in the Triandis and Vassiliou (1967b) study.
Note 2. This table indicates that on those traits on which the Greeks see themselves the same way as the Americans see them, the greater the contact, the more likely the Americans will see the Greeks as witty, suspicious, competitive, emotionally uncontrolled, obliging, etc.

The theoretical notion, however, can also be tested by inspection of the relationships between contact and stereotyping for the remaining four characteristics. On these four characteristics the Americans and the Greeks disagreed. But do the results of the present study agree with those of Triandis and Vassiliou (1967b)? Specifically, if there is a relationship between contact and stereotyping in the present data, does it also appear in the previous data? Replication would suggest a "real" relationship. Table 8 presents the relevant summary. In two out of four of these characteristics (sly and egotistic) the greater the contact (by whatever estimate) the more the Americans see the Greeks as having these characteristics. For the other two characteristics (arrogant and indecisive) it appears that even the no-contact Americans (who, after all, live in Greece) agree with

Table 8   Greek Characteristics[a] Showing Functional Relationships
with the Amount of Contact

Characteristic[a]	Reported Contact (present study)	Actual Contact in (Triandis and Vassiliou 1967b)
Sly	Yes	Yes
Egotistic	Yes	Yes
Arrogant	Flat curve (but with definite elevation)	Yes
Indecisive	Flat curve (but with definite elevation)	Yes

[a] Characteristics on which there is disagreement between Americans and Greeks in the Triandis and Vassiliou (1967b) study.

the maximum-contact Americans, so that there is no relation between the amount of reported contact and the responses of the subjects. (Even the no-contact Americans drive their cars and make inferences about Greek traits from driving habits.) On both traits the previous study had shown a relationship with contact. Thus these results must also be considered as supporting the basic theoretical notion. There are reasons to believe (see Chapter 9) that the Greeks have the characteristics listed in Tables 7 and 8, and the greater the contact, by whatever measure, the greater the likelihood that the Americans will give an extreme rating to the Greeks on those characteristics. A fuller explanation of the way these characteristics are integrated in Greek self-perceptions can be found in Chapter 9.

Table 9   Greek Heterostereotypes of Americans, Showing Functional Relationships with the Amount of Contact

Characteristics[a]	Relationship to Contact
Systematic	Yes
Naïve	Yes
Egotistic	U-shaped relation
Trusting	Yes
Emotionally controlled	None
Honest	Yes
Follow procedures exactly	Flat in Athens, reverse in Salonika
Decisive about making plans	None
Accept changes in working conditions	Yes

[a] Characteristics that agree with American autostereotype (Triandis & Vassiliou, 1967b).

Table 10 American Characteristics Showing Functional
Relationships with the Amount of Contact

Characteristics[a]	Reported Contact (present study)	Actual Contact [Triandis & Vassiliou (1967b)]
Dull	None	Yes
Arrogant	Reverse	Yes
Competitive	Reverse	Reverse
Haughty	Reverse	Yes
Inflexible	None	None
Drive competitively	None	None

[a] Characteristics on which there is disagreement between Greek, and Americans (Triandis & Vassiliou, 1967b).

Tables 9 and 10 list the characteristics that the majority of Greeks assign to Americans. Table 9 includes those characteristics on which the Americans and the Greeks agree and Table 10, those on which they disagree. First, we note that on five out of nine characteristics on which the American autostereotype agrees with the Greek stereotype of Americans we have the expected relationship between amount of contact and stereotyping. On two items (emotional control and decisiveness) there is no relationship. On both characteristics the Greeks without contact consider the Americans quite extreme and apparently contact does nothing to change this perception. A similar result can be seen in Athens with the item "follows procedures exactly." In Thessaloniki, however, the "no-contact" Greeks appear to imagine that Americans act like robots (i.e., are superexact), but the contact groups see the Americans are more "human"; hence a reverse relationship is obtained.

The results of Tables 9 and 10 are also impressive in another sense. It appears that Greeks without contact have negative stereotypes of Americans and those with contact have much more positive stereotypes. The simplest way to summarize the total set of obtained results is this: Americans with no contact have vague and undefined stereotypes of Greeks. The greater the contact with the Greeks, the more the American stereotypes of Greeks approach "reality." On the other hand, the "no-contact" Greeks have a definite set of stereotypes concerning Americans. They see Americans as most effective (systematic, following procedures exactly), though slightly on the dull side and a bit arrogant. This view is challenged by contact. The greater the contact, the more the Americans become "normal" on effectiveness and less arrogant.

We summarize these results by stating that the evidence obtained in the present study is strongly in favor of the general theoretical notion underlying the Triandis and Vassiliou (1967b) study and the present study and the specific hypotheses tested in both studies.

Demographic Characteristics and Stereotyping. There is an impression that American women in Greece are more dissatisfied with their husbands' assignment than their husbands are. To test this we employed matched *t*-tests on the American couples who were in our sample. If the argument is correct, the stereotype of Greeks held by American females should be more negative than the stereotype held by their husbands. None of the tests proved to be significant, although there was a tendency for the American females to be higher than their husbands on the extent to which they saw the Greeks as *arrogant* and *sly*. The data obtained from the two cultural groups, when broken down by sex, are conspicuously consistent across same-culture, sex groups and very different across different culture groups.

The samples of 202 American females and 241 American males showed strong agreement in their judgments. However, there are some consistent differences in the way they stereotyped Greeks: regardless of degree of contact, the males tended to see the Greeks as *duller* and more *rigid* than did the females.

Turning now to differences between Greek males and females, there was a tendency for the Athens females to see Americans as less *systematic, naïve,* and *trusting,* more *competitive,* less *emotionally controlled, honest, exact,* and *decisive in making plans* than did the Athens males. These sex differences tended to be exaggerated with the amount of reported contact.

We also asked the Americans how long they had been in Greece. We split the sample into those who had lived there for more than 18 months ($N = 198$) and those who had lived there for less than 18 months ($N = 227$). We examined the graphs relating contact and stereotyping for those two groups of Americans. Over-all, the 15 graphs obtained from the "short stays" did not differ from the 15 graphs obtained from the "long stays." However, on a few characteristics there were statistically significant differences. Thus the long-stay-no-contact group tended to see the Greeks as more *egotistical* and as *following procedures approximately* to a greater extent than did the remaining groups. Such people are obviously "resistant to contact" and probably unhappy with their overseas assignments; hence their deviation from the judgments of the other American groups. Nevertheless, their judgments are veridical (see Chapter 9). The "long stays," regardless of amount of contact, tended to see the Greeks as more competitive than the "short stays." This perception is also veridical (Triandis & Vassiliou, 1967a). We conclude that the comparison of the responses of the "long stays" with those of the "short stays" leads to the discovery of

"real" characteristics, that is, "valid" stereotypes as far as can be determined from other kinds of analyses, such as those of Chapter 9.

What is the effect of age and social status on stereotyping? Table 11
supplies some answers. First, we note that the older the Greek subject,
the more positively he sees "Greeks." On 7 of the 15 characteristics there
was such a tendency, whereas on only two there was the oppositive tendency (this is almost significant). Second, age appears unrelated to hetero-
stereotyping. Third, the higher the social status, the more favorable the
stereotyping of Americans and the less favorable the stereotyping of
Greeks. This is very clear in the Athens sample ($p < .01$) but not detectable in the Thessaloniki sample. Similarly, in Athens there were six

Table 11   The Relationship Between Demographic Characteristics
and Stereotyping

(age and social status as determinants of stereotyping)

			Sample			
			Athens		Saloniki	
	Age		Social Status		Social Status	
Characteristic	A	H	A	H	A	H
Systematic	+	−	−	+	0	−
Witty	0	0	0	−	−	−
Naïve	+	−	0	+	+	+
Unselfish	+	0	0	0	+	+
Modest	0	0	−	−	−	−
Trusting	+	0	0	+	0	0
Cooperative	0	0	0	+	−	0
Obliging	0	0	0	+	−	0
Emotionally controlled	−	0	−	0	0	−
Flexible	0	+	0	0	0	+
Honest	0	0	0	+	−	0
Follows procedures exactly	+	+	−	+	0	−
Decisive	+	0	−	+	+	0
Drive carefully	−	−	−	+	−	−
Accepts work change	+	0	0	+	0	+

Notes. A means autostereotypes.
   H means heterostereotype.
   + means that age (or social status) is related to the listed characteristic.
      (favorable stereotype).
   0 means that age (or social status) is unrelated to the characteristic.
   − means that age (or social status) is related to the opposite pole of the listed
      characteristic.

occasions on which the autostereotype of Greeks was worse among upper than among lower status people and none in the opposite direction ($p < .01$ by Fischer exact test, two-tailed).

Changes in Factor Scores as a Function of Contact. We have already examined the major stereotypes of the various groups in terms of the grouping of characteristics that was obtained from the factor analyses. Do the factor scores of a particular group, as judged on all scales with high loadings on a given factor, shift systematically with the amount of contact? For example, the Americans see the Greeks as impulsive (Table 2) and this factor is defined by three scales. Do the shifts in the judgments of the Americans as a result of contact on one of these scales follow the same patterns as the shifts on the other two scales? Surprisingly, the answer is that generally this is *not* the case. Nevertheless, we examined some of these shifts systematically, and we also looked at the possible influences of demographic characteristics. Below we note those cases in which there is a strong trend for the judgments of the several interrelated scales to shift in the same way as a result of contact.

AMERICANS SEE GREEKS. There is a tendency for the factor scores to shift with contact, so that the greater the contact, the more the Americans see the Greeks as *distrusting outsiders* (see Table 2). This trend is strong among the long-stay Americans. The factor *ineffective* (see Table 2) seems to follow the same pattern; that is, the greater the contact, the more the Greeks seem to the Americans to be ineffective, and this phenomenon is exceptionally strong for the "long stays." Similarly, the *charming-people* factor follows this trend.

AMERICANS SEE AMERICANS. No trends.

GREEKS SEE AMERICANS. On the *effectiveness* factor the scores shift with contact, males see Americans higher than do females, upper-class subjects give higher responses than lower-class subjects, and the young higher effectiveness responses than the old.

GREEKS SEE GREEKS. The greater the contact with Americans the more the Greeks see themselves as *philotimos* (obliging and honest). This trend is less pronounced for the upper social classes.

Summary

Contact has definite effects on stereotyping. This chapter illustrates these effects. Specifically, the five hypotheses of the Triandis and Vassiliou

(1967b) study were supported. The first of these, that the amount of contact will be related to clearer autostereotypes and heterostereotypes, was supported for the American data but not the Greek. This result is consistent with our previous findings. It might be that Americans know little about Greeks and they learn a good deal about them as a result of contact. On the other hand, Greeks respond as if they knew a good deal about Americans and do not change so much in their stereotypes as a result of contact.

Another explanation of the obtained results can be derived from the great importance in Greece of the ingroup-outgroup distinction, which has already been reported (Triandis & Vassiliou, 1967a,b) and is discussed in detail in Chapter 9. The Greek ingroup consists of "family, friends, friends of friends, and people who are concerned with my welfare"; the outgroup consists of all other Greeks. Greeks tend to place people in one or the other of these groups as fast as possible, and once placed the other person acquires some characteristics appropriate to this placement. Simple contact between an American and a Greek will not necessarily make the American a member of the ingroup. Therefore simple contact will not produce a measurable effect on the Greek stereotype.

The second and third hypotheses stated that the greater the contact, the more the Greek stereotype of Americans will "improve" and the American stereotype of Greeks will "deteriorate." These hypotheses were supported, as in the previous study. The fourth and fifth hypotheses dealt with the effects of contact on autostereotypes: they postulated that the American autostereotype will "improve" and the Greek will "deteriorate." Both hypotheses were supported in the present study.

The Greeks have a definite stereotype about Americans, which at low levels of contact is particularly exaggerated. Thus the Americans appear like robots, in complete control and totally efficient. Contact humanizes this image of the Americans held by the Greeks.

It is now necessary to discuss in greater detail what is meant by "favorable," "unfavorable," "improvement" and "deterioration" of the stereotypes. Returning to Tables 7, 8, 9, and 10, we note that although Greeks, in agreement with Americans, assign to themselves certain "unfavorable" traits (e.g., unsystematic, suspicious, competitive, emotionally uncontrolled) these traits do not necessarily hold an unfavorable connotation for them. Each of these traits taken singly correlates somewhat with the "bad" pole of the "good-bad" semantic differential scale (Triandis & Vassiliou, 1967b). In the context of Greek culture, however, the importance of these traits is small and their existence justifiable; for example, since Greeks are surrounded by outgroup members (see above for definition), they find it functional to be suspicious and competitive. Since they value spontaneity, they find no obvious advantage in being systematic and emotionally controlled.

On four traits (Table 8) the Americans and Greeks disagree about Greek attributes. First, the Americans see the Greeks as *sly;* the Greeks do not see themselves as sly but as *suspicious.* They probably have this characteristic, but this is tactical behavior that is required for the placement of the other person in the ingroup or the outgroup. This behavior might be "interpreted" by Americans as *slyness.* Second, the Americans see the Greeks as *egotistic* and *arrogant* because the Greeks are unyielding in their opinions and hold their positions obstinately. The Greeks behave this way because they hold their opinions as "representatives" of the ingroup; that is, they defend positions shared by their ingroup and perceive such behaviors as leading to support for the ingroup. Therefore, these behaviors are not seen as egotistic. Such behaviors function to increase the Greek's self-esteem because they increase his acceptance by the ingroup and his perceived prestige in the outgroups. Finally, the Americans see the Greeks as *indecisive,* but the Greeks see themselves as *decisive.* It should be remembered that in the early phase of contact, which is, of course, more characteristic of American-Greek interactions, the Greeks are indeed suspicious and indecisive because they are deciding whether the American will become a member of their ingroup or their outgroup. Once this decision has been made they behave decisively. The latter phase is the one that is important to the Greeks; hence they see themselves as *decisive.*

It should be clear, from the above discussion, that changes previously described as "unfavorable," or as a "deterioration" of the stereotype *do not necessarily imply changes in self-esteem.* The above interpretation is probably an important insight into the functioning of autostereotypes, which was lacking in our previous study. It also adds understanding concerning the relationship between stereotyping and intercultural interaction.

The present replication of our previous study illustrates the value of replication of studies employing different methodology. We changed our independent variable's measurement (degree of contact), but in this process we also changed the *meaning* of contact in our two studies. The meaning of contact for a Greek who has frequent contact with an American in Greece, is comparable only to the meaning of contact of an American who has frequent contact with Greeks in the United States rather than in Greece.

In spite of such changes in methodology and meaning of the variables, the present results agree well enough with the previous study to support the theoretical conception behind both studies. Our present findings do not only support our theory but also suggest modifications. Specifically, the model proposed by Triandis and Vassiliou to account for contact and stereotyping is too simple. It does not allow for the level of stereotypes that exists *before* contact or for the modification in the meaning of traits. The model appears to be applicable when a population has no strong pre-conceptions about a group of people (e.g., American views of the Greeks), but it does not apply to populations with strong preconceptions about other groups (in our study: the Greek view of Americans). These preconceptions, formed in response to historical events, tradition, the mass media, and the "educational systems" of various countries, create a *normative stereotype*—that is, a stereotype that is a cognitive norm for thinking about a group of people. Contact modifies the normative stereotype so that it approaches what Bogardus called a "sociotype," that is, a substantially realistic assignment of traits to a group of people.

We therefore restate our theory of stereotyping as follows: when members of Group *A* are exposed to the cognitive norms of Group *A* about Group *B*, they develop a "normative stereotype" about Group *B*. When Group *A* lacks a normative stereotype about Group *B* with whom they have friendly relations, members of Group *A* will begin by thinking about Group *B* as being "like me."

In Figure 2 we present the theoretical paths of the stereotypes relevant to trait *X*. When members of Group *A* are exposed to information or norms of thinking about Group *B*, they will have a stereotype represented by point *E*. Contact brings this stereotype to a more realistic level, such as point *F*. The sociotype of *B*, for characteristic *X*, is well below point *F*. On the other hand, when members of Group *A* have not been exposed to cognitive norms about *B*, they begin at point *C* and contact changes their stereotype so that it is represented by point *D*. We hypothesize a certain amount of contrast and point *D* is again higher than the actual sociotype would indicate. With respect to autostereotyping, Group *A* begins at point *G* and as a result of contact sees itself as being at point *H,* which is somewhat lower than the sociotype for Group *A*.

Figure 2 fits most of the observations of our study. We assume that Tables 7 and 8 represent the sociotypes of Greeks. Contact has the effect of making the American stereotype approach these sociotypes. Similarly, Table 9 presents mostly sociotypes of Americans and the Greek stereotypes change in the direction of these sociotypes. Table 10 presents normative stereotypes that Greeks have about Americans and contact produces the reverse relationship (or no relationship) (i.e., the stereotypes follow the *EF* line of Figure 2).

The theoretical model does not imply anything about favorability, since characteristics *X* can be positive, negative, or neutral.

The argument that contact leads to stereotypes that are closer to socio-

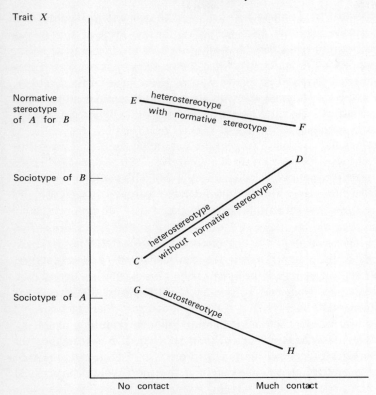

Figure 2. Theoretical changes in stereotypes as a result of contact.

types is also supported by the observation that the Americans who have stayed in Greece for a longer time make judgments that are more consistent with our analysis of Greek national character (presented in Chapter 9) than do the Americans who have been in Greece for less than 18 months.

Our findings concerning the clarity of the stereotypes are also consistent with the analysis of Figure 2. Most of the American stereotypes of Greeks change along the *CD* line, that is, Americans do not have normative stereotypes about Greeks. Hence the greater the amount of contact that Americans have with Greeks, the clearer their stereotypes. This is exactly what we observed. On the other hand, Greeks have definite normative stereotypes of Americans. Hence clarity, in the sense of within-group agreement, is already present without contact and is not changed by it.

The major qualification of this theory must be emphasized. The theory applies in the case of non-normative stereotypes only when the "other group" is friendly. It is assumed that when the other group is not friendly the ingroup will develop appropriate normative stereotypes, so that the *EF* rather than the *CD* line will be appropriate.

Our theory of stereotyping can now be stated:

1. The larger the difference between the sociotypes of Groups *A* and *B*, on characteristic *X*, the more likely it is that *X* will appear in the stereotypes of the two groups.

2. Contact has the effect of changing the stereotypes to match the sociotypes; that is, it increases the validity of stereotypes.

3. Non-normative stereotypes change very much with contact.

4. Normative stereotypes change very little with contact.

5. The greater the contact, the greater the clarity of non-normative stereotypes.

6. Contact has no effect on the clarity of normative stereotypes.

7. The greater the contact, the more contrastive the autostereotypes.

8. The greater the contact, the greater the complexity of stereotypes.

9. The greater the contact, the greater the specificity of stereotypes.

10. When $\bar{X}_A - \bar{X}_B$ is large, there will be a contrast phenomenon; that is, the two groups will see each other as more different than they really are.

11. When there is neither contact nor a normative stereotype, the nature of heterostereotypes will be purely projective. The greater the contact, the less projective the stereotype [and the more valid, as per (2) above].

12. When $\bar{X}_A - \bar{X}_B$ is small and contact is large, there will be no differences perceived between auto- and heterostereotypes.

13. Autostereotypes are coordinated with other self-percepts to maximize self-esteem.

Implications for International Understanding. Social scientists have known for some time that simple contact is not sufficient for improving intercultural understanding. In fact, more contact has a negative effect in interpersonal perception among cultural groups who are "superior" on some dimension. However, social scientists have not been clear about the parameters of this phenomenon. The present study sheds some light on the effects of contact in person perception.

One of our previous studies (Triandis & Vassiliou, 1967a) showed the complexity of the analysis of the subjective culture of national groups. We now see that intercultural contact can lead to negative stereotypes. It seems probable that understanding the subjective culture of a national group will improve effective intercultural relations, but this must be tested in future research. Since *mere* contact is not likely to lead to such an analysis or understanding of subjective culture, it is now easy to see that some more powerful forms of intervention are necessary to improve international understanding.

Intervention can occur at least at two points. First, the educational systems of various countries might provide information that will lead to more accurate normative stereotypes. Second, extensive training may be provided to prepare a person for interaction in another culture. The degree of training required to avoid cross-cultural misunderstanding may be greater than required to master a foreign language. Very few people in any culture ever get that much training. It is not suggested that such intensive programs of intercultural training should lead to the elimination of cultural differences. What is needed is enough knowledge of the basic value premises of each culture to allow increased predictability of the "other person" in a cross-cultural encounter. Otherwise, intercultural contact may result in a number of defensive patterns, intensive negative stereotyping, confusion, hostility, scape-goating, and similar undesirable interpersonal phenomena.

CHAPTER SIX

A Study of National Stereotypes

YASUMASA TANAKA

Image and Reality in the Conduct of Human Affairs: an Introduction to the Chapter

We cannot know what we call reality in a direct fashion. We certainly know the evidence of our senses, but we also have the evidence that these senses are easily deceived. We make inferences about others from what they say and what they do, but they are often wrong, partly because of the perceived image we have of people, their words and behavior, which depend largely on the signs that only fragmentally describe the object persons. Thus most Japanese will never know what the Americans o' the Indians are *really* like and vice versa.

Reality consists of numerous cognitive events, both physical and human. From these cognitive events we have images, and these images in turn tend to be susceptible to distortion by a number of causes, such as misconception, prejudice, lack of accurate information, or the noises made when information is transmitted through a communication channel.

In the arena of government and politics the real dilemma for decision makers in any nation arises from this: that there is a scarcity of objective facts and that images are most often all that they have regarding crucial events about which they must make critical decisions.

Some of the studies reported here were supported, in part, by grants from the National Institute of Mental Health (MH 07705) and the National Science Foundation (NSF GS 160) to Charles E. Osgood and the Center for Comparative Psycholinguistics, University of Illinois. I am indebted to Charles E. Osgood for his invaluable insights into the psychological dimensions of international relations, to William May for his assistance in computing, and to Yoko Iwamatsu for her help as a research assistant.

Note, for instance, how the image plays a dominant role in the conduct of foreign affairs. The dynamics of the nuclear arms race may be the case in question. The development of a new nuclear weapon (e.g., a MIRV), which may be intended by the developer as a totally *defensive* weapon, can easily be viewed by his opponent as totally *offensive*. The original developer's intentions may be never to strike first to create hell on earth. He might believe that such a formidable new weapon would only deter his opponent from striking first because of his fear of retaliation. His opponent's reaction to the new challenge, however, is that his enemy is now attempting to take advantage of him and he in turn builds his own nuclear weapon. Thus the nuclear arms race escalates indefinitely in a spiral of terror. The reciprocated image one has toward his opponent, or the *mirror image* as the psychologist calls it, results in nuclear arms escalation.

To the extent that humans make crucial decisions political scientists and psychologists share some common research interests as well as goals. During the last decade, therefore, there has been a growing number of theoretical and empirical investigations of the dynamics of human behavior in the conduct of international relations and politics.[1] It has been noted that these investigations are increasingly cross-cultural or cross-national, which makes possible a preliminary analysis of crucial similarities and dissimilarities in national perceptions and judgments. Relatively new research techniques have also been devised.

In the following sections problems of national stereotypes are discussed and empirical evidence is presented: The findings reported here are based in part on larger cross-cultural projects carried out at the University of Illinois between 1963 and 1968. Their major purposes were (a) to evaluate cross-culturally the usefulness of an application of *multilingual semanitc differentials* to the study of national stereotypes and (b) to find cross-cultural consistency in what may be called a *psycho-logic* which might be operating in the perception of nations.

The Measurement of National Stereotypes

An important problem in scientific research is the extent to which the methodology and conclusions of one discipline can be applied to the data

[1] Psychological aspects of international relations were studied both by political scientists (Farell & Smith, 1967; Finley, Holsti, & Fagen, 1967; North, Holsti, Zaninovich, & Zinnes, 1963; Shelling, 1966; Singer, 1968) and by psychologists (Kelman, 1965; Klineberg, 1964; Osgood, 1960, 1962, 1966, 1967; Stagner, 1967; Tanaka, 1962, 1965a, 1965b, 1967a, 1967b, 1969, 1970). An increasing number of psychologists are interested in the study of international relations and many political scientists have become concerned with psychological theories of political behavior.

of another. This chapter is essentially an attempt to take a measurement instrument developed by experimental psychologists and apply it to data that have been primarily the concern of sociologists, cultural anthropologists, and pollsters interested in the cross-cultural investigation of national stereotypes.

Since Walter Lippman (1922) invented the word *stereotype* and defined it as a mental image, there have been a number of studies of national stereotypes.

Katz and Braly (1933) established one method of studying such stereotypes. Buchanan and Cantril (1953) and others repeated this method in cross-cultural studies. Some difficulties have been indicated. Brown (1958) and others have pointed out that the *adjectives* used in these studies are commonly evaluative and it is difficult to separate their evaluative aspect from their specific implications.

It would be extremely helpful, therefore, if we could discover the common ingredients that constitute the judgments people make of one another. A double value may be derived from such an approach. Psychological instruments have been developed and validated mostly in the context of Western civilization. To what extent can conclusions based on these instruments be universally extended to other human groups? This can be investigated only by studying peoples with a non-Western cultural and linguistic heritage.

In studies reported here only a limited number of problems of national stereotypes were examined. First, the judgment of an object, material, or human is considered to involve what may be called "evaluative" elements. Evaluative judgment may most often reflect certain built-in criteria of preference and morals in the specific cultural context. That many such evaluative judgments are based on previous learning leads to the second problem.

As many studies have shown, stereotypes are not simple abstractions from direct personal experience; rather they have been "learned" verbally and nonverbally in a given linguistic or cultural community over a period of time. The process of stereotyping most often is a process of what Osgood (1953) terms "assign learning." The meaning of assigns is literally "assigned" to them by association with other signs rather than by direct association with the object signified. Most often stereotypes are learned via the mass media and other secondhand sources. Such learning, then, may be bound to cultural criteria. It should be recalled that many studies to date have shown evidence that those individuals who are in a position to know best about an ethnic group often are least susceptible to culture-bound ethnic stereotypes (Kramer, 1951; Deutsch & Collins, 1951).

Finally, there are in national stereotypes some important elements of "national consciousness." National consciousness can be defined as "attachment of secondary symbols of nationality to primary items of information" (Deutsch, 1953). The symbols of nationality such as "Japanese" or "American" are labels added to objects or actions to elicit appropriate corresponding reactions in the individuals. Their lexical meaning is clear, but their connotative or affective meaning is implicit and may vary according to the semantic environment in which they are presented. Examples of a tendency of "extension of Ego" have been given by Buchanan and Cantril (1953) in this connection. These authors reported that each sample population tended to rate itself *best* in relation to other nationalities by selecting a greater number of "positive" adjectives for the description of its own nationality.

This chapter summarizes several cross-cultural studies which validate and suggest the utility of *multilingual semantic differentials.*

The instrument will be regarded as having cross-cultural validity if it reflects previously found (a) cross-cultural general elements or (b) cross-cultural differences discovered in other studies. It will be considered as useful if it can be applied with ease and will help to formulate or test the hypotheses developed from a variety of theoretical perspectives.

Multilingual Semantic Differentials and the "Semantic Space" Hypothesis

Values essentially reflect what is "good" and what is "bad." Thus we can assume that there are a number of subjective, evaluative criteria by which values are conceptually represented. The average Japanese may value "diligence" most highly, whereas the average American may hold "cleanliness" to be most desirable. Similarly, the typical lawyer may believe in "law abiding" and the typical professor may emphasize intellectual competence. These are only a few typical examples of evaluative criteria used daily in our subjective cultures.

One may also note that values are either positive or negative, that the positive values are "good" and the negative values, "bad." Each value can be classified according to its unique quality and direction, and two "opposite" values can be verbally transposed into a linear, bipolar scale which is defined by the two "opposite" value-qualities, such as "diligent-lazy," "clean-dirty," and "law-abiding-law-breaking." If we assume that values can be transformed thus into bipolar scales, the semantic differential method developed by Osgood et al. (1957) for the measurement of affective meanings provides a useful theoretical approach to the systematic analysis of the evaluative process.

A typical semantic-differential form is displayed in Figure 1. When a

Ugly	___:___:___:___:___:___:___	Beautiful
Thick	___:___:___:___:___:___:___	Thin
Active	___:___:___:___:___:___:___	Passive
Unpleasant	___:___:___:___:___:___:___	Pleasant
Light	___:___:___:___:___:___:___	Heavy
Slow	___:___:___:___:___:___:___	Fast
Undemocratic	___:___:___:___:___:___:___	Democratic
Powerful	___:___:___:___:___:___:___	Powerless
Industrious	___:___:___:___:___:___:___	Lazy
Foolish	___:___:___:___:___:___:___	Wise
Large	___:___:___:___:___:___:___	Small
Quiet	___:___:___:___:___:___:___	Noisy

Figure 1. A 12-scale semantic differential form.

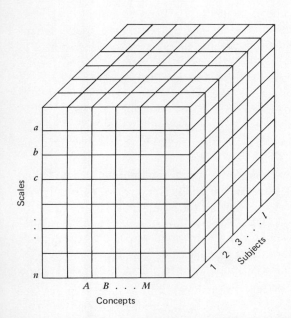

Figure 2. The cube of data generated when l subjects judge m concepts against n scales.

group of people rates a set of concepts, such as JAPANESE, against a set of appropriate semantic-differential scales such as "ugly-beautiful" and "thick-thin," a cube of data is generated (Figure 2). The rows are defined by scales, the columns by concepts being judged, and the "slices" from front to back by the people doing the judging. Each cell includes a number from 1 to 7 which represents a particular individual's judgment of a particular concept on a given scale. A suitable statistical method for dealing with such a cube of data is factor analysis. Usually, but not always, the interest is in the correlations among the scales. These correlations may be obtained across subjects, across concepts, or across both simultaneously. Separate analyses may be done for single subjects (to examine the cross-subject generality) or for single concepts (to examine the cross-concept generality, or we collapse either the subject dimension (when we are interested in cultural meanings) or the concept dimension (when we are interested in concept-class characteristics). Indeed there are many alternative ways in which this data cube can be sliced and each is appropriate for answering a different kind of question.

During the last decade Osgood et al. (1963) have constructed standard multilingual semantic differentials and analyzed such data cubes in more than 20 language/culture communities. In this continuing extensive cross-cultural work each language/culture community provides an independent replication of the original studies done in the United States. They have found that despite variations in the kinds of subjects used, three salient, orthogonal factors keep appearing: an *evaluative* factor (represented by scales like "good-bad" or "honest-dishonest"), a *potency* factor (represented by scales like "strong-weak" or "hard-soft"), and an *activity* factor (represented by scales like "active-passive" or "fast-slow"). Thus they have empirically demonstrated that this basic, *evaluation-potency-activity* framework, or the structure of *semantic spaces* in our terminology, is a cultural universal that is present despite obvious differences in language and culture.

There is general consensus about the psychological nature of the evaluative process: (a) that it is learned and implicit, (b) that it is a predisposition to respond evaluatively to certain attitude objects, and (c) that the evaluative predispositions may fall anywhere along a scale from "extremely good" through "neutral" to "extremely bad." In most of the factor analyses done by Osgood et al. (1963) the first, most salient factor has nearly always been clearly identifiable as *evaluation*. Being a bipolar factor which is graded in intensity and in both directions from a neutral point, the *evaluative* factor meets the criterion of reflecting predispositions from "extremely good" through "neutral" to "extremely bad." In the general mediation theory of meanings, of which the semantic differential measuring operations are part, meanings of concepts are implicit reactions to given signs which are learned. Multilingual semantic differentials may tap the general but implicit evaluative framework in which people experience, perceive, and judge various kinds of cognitive event in different subjective cultures.

Very broadly, there seem to be two different kinds of problem involved in the analysis of national stereotypes via multilingual semantic differentials: one is related to the scale composition of an *evaluative* and other semantic factors and another concerns the intensity with which each valued concept is associated to the "positive" or "negative" polarity. The numerous semantic-differential studies carried out to date, especially in Japan and America, provide a useful pool of information on these problems.

Evidence for Concept/Scale Interaction

Many semantic differential studies to date have indicated that the semantic factor structure is sensitive to variations in concept populations. This conclusion was foreshadowed in Suci's early finding, reported in *The Measurement of Meaning* (Osgood, Suci, & Tannenbaum, 1957), that the usual three-factor semantic space coalesced into two (benevolence and dynamism) for political concepts. It became clear when Triandis (1960) examined judgments towards jobs. Tanaka, Oyama, and Osgood (1963), Tanaka and Osgood (1965), and Tanaka (1969) showed how the semantic space is modified, depending on the objects of judgment.

We have also noted that the following three alternative modifications may occur in concept/scale interaction:

1. A coalescence of two or more factors into one (e.g., potency and activity into a dynamism factor, as in Triandis & Osgood, 1958).

2. A *differentiation* of the factor structure which appears as a reduction in the total amount of variance explained by evaluation, potency, and activity, along with the emergence of additional meaningful factors (e.g., the emergence of a white-collar versus blue-collar factor in judgments of jobs).

3. A *coloring* of the extracted factors in terms of specialized scales applicable to the restricted concept domain.

The development of a personality differential (or PD) and its subsequent applications in another concept domain can illustrate these points further.

The original development of personality differential was carried out by Ware and Osgood (reported in Osgood, 1962). Ware's unpublished data on the factor composition of ratings of 40 diverse personality concepts (e g., MYSELF, MY FATHER, or MY FRIENDS) showed a highly differentiated structure made up of eight interpretable dimensions shown in Table 1. The eight factors were *morality* (variant of evaluation), *rationality, uniqueness, excitability* (variant of activity), *sociability, toughness* (variant of potency), *urbanity,* and *tangibility.* Note the clear indication of *differentiation* and *coloring* as judgmental scales interact with concepts in

Table 1   Varimax Rotation of Eight Personality
Differential Factors

Factor I	*Morality (7.9% TV)*	
	Moral-immoral	.78
	Reputable-disreputable	.78
	Wholesome-unwholesome	.73
Factor II	*Rationality (7.1% TV)*	
	Logical-intuitive	.66
	Objective-subjective	.66
	Rational-irrational	.60
Factor III	*Uniqueness (6.7% TV)*	
	Unique-typical	.77
	Unusual-usual	.74
	Individualistic-regular	.70
Factor IV	*Excitability (6.6% TV)*	
	Excitable-calm	.81
	Tense-relaxed	.77
	Emotional-unemotional	.52
Factor V	*Sociability (6.5% TV)*	
	Gregarious-self-contained	.76
	Sociable-solitary	.72
	Extroverted-introverted	.66
Factor VI	*Toughness (6.0% TV)*	
	Tough-tender	.78
	Insensitive-sensitive	.71
	Rugged-delicate	.63
Factor VII	*Urbanity (5.2% TV)*	
	Proud-humble	.65
	Sophisticated-naïve	.58
	Deliberate-casual	.53
Factor VIII	*Tangibility (4% TV)*	
	Formed-amorphous	.72
	Predictable-unpredictable	.56
	Tangible-intangible	.42

this uniquely restricted concept domain. In this space defined by eight factors each factor accounts for no more than 8% of the total variance; evaluation, potency, and activity in this space emerge as morality, toughness, and excitability.

Japanese Only, POLDI-I Study

Tanaka (1965a) used a variation of the personality differential in order to study the images of 32 nations held by three Japanese samples. Based on American results reported by Osgood (1962), the 20 highest loading personality differential (PD) scales and seven standard semantic differential (SD) scales representing the ordinary evaluation, potency, and activity (E-P-A) domains were used in the ratings of 32 *nationality* concepts such as JAPAN, UNITED STATES, COMMUNIST CHINA, and SOVIET UNION. It was assumed that this particular modification of the PD, which we shall term *POLDI* or a *political differential,* would "tap" unique semantic qualities within this specific concept domain.

Scale-by-Scale Factorization. Three groups of Japanese (52 male and 54 female college students and 70 "experts" attending a special foreign-service training school in Tokyo) participated in the experiment. The data obtained were tabulated separately for male and for female students and for the experts, and an averaged 27 (scales) × 32 (concepts) matrix was generated for each group. For the student groups the two matrices were then combined to make up a new 54 × 32 matrix, on the basis of which scale-by-scale correlations were computed. The intercorrelation matrix was then subjected to a principal component analysis and, finally, the extracted factors were rotated by the varimax method. For the expert group a 27 × 27 scale-intercorrelation matrix was obtained and subjected to a principal component analysis. The extracted factors were rotated by varimax.

Table 2 summarizes the results of this first Japanese-only POLDI study. First, five semantic factors are defined similarly by the three groups and are clearly identifiable as *evaluation, dynamism, volatility, uniqueness,* and *familiarity,* in each group. Second, there are apparent deviations from the earlier Ware-Osgood study. *Excitability* and *rationality,* previously found to be orthogonal factors independent of each other, now appear to coalesce completely into one large *volatility* factor. Third, in terms of the amount of variance removed by each factor, there is a marked deviation from the previous study. The first two factors, *evaluation* and *dynamism,* account for more than 60% of the combined variance in each group and appear to be most important in the judging of nationality concepts. To put it another way, the Japanese use two major criterial attributes when they judge the images of these nations: *evaluation* and *dynamism.*

It should also be noted that the results of factorization clearly show unique metaphorical qualifications of the evaluative processes of the Japanese. Common to all the three groups are not only general *evaluative* scales

Table 2 Highest Loading POLDI-I Scales (Varimax-Rotated Factors)

Male students (N = 52)

Factor I (32% TV) Evaluation		Factor II (30% TV) Dynamism (P + A)		Factor III (17% TV) Volatility	
Loved-hated	0.95	Sensitive-insensitive	0.92	Excitable-calm	0.88
Tangible-intangible	0.93	Active-passive	0.90	Emotional-unemotional	0.81
Reputable-disreputable	0.91	Fast-slow	0.85	Intuitive-logical	0.80
Predictable-unpredictable	0.91	Proud-humble	0.85	Immoral-moral	0.71
Tender-tough	0.89	Sophisticated-naive	0.84	Irrational-rational	0.66
Democratic-undemocratic	0.83	Strong-weak	0.74	Subjective-objective	0.57
Relaxed-tense	0.80	Extroverted-introverted	0.66		
Sociable-solitary	0.78	Large-small			
Wholesome-unwholesome	0.75				

Female students (N = 54)

Factor I (41% TV)		Factor II (27% TV)		Factor III (12% TV)	
Loved-hated	0.96	Proud-humble	0.93	Excitable-calm	0.91
Reputable-disreputable	0.96	Active-passive	0.93	Intuitive-logical	0.88
Tangible-intangible	0.94	Fast-slow	0.93	Immoral-moral	0.79
Predictable-unpredictable	0.93	Sensitive-insensitive	0.90	Emotional-unemotional	0.64
Tender-tough	0.87	Strong-weak	0.90	Subjective-objective	0.56
Democratic-undemocratic	0.85	Sophisticated-naive	0.87	Irrational-rational	0.53
Sociable-solitary	0.82	Large-small	0.70		
Relaxed-tense	0.80	Subjective-objective	0.69		
Wholesome-unwholesome	0.78	Extroverted-introverted	0.67		

Experts (N = 70)

Factor I (41% TV)		Factor II (27% TV)		Factor III (12% TV)	
Loved-hated	0.95	Sensitive-insensitive	0.95	Excitable-calm	0.90
Tangible-intangible	0.95	Fast-slow	0.95	Emotional-unemotional	0.88
Reputable-disreputable	0.93	Active-passive	0.93	Intuitive-logical	0.83
Tender-tough	0.89	Strong-weak	0.89	Immoral-moral	0.77
Predictable-unpredictable	0.86	Familiar-unfamiliar	0.86	Subjective-objective	0.72
Democratic-undemocratic	0.85	Proud-humble	0.85	Sophisticated-naive	0.65
Sociable-solitary	0.83	Extroverted-introverted	0.83	Irrational-rational	0.63
Tense-relaxed	0.77				
Wholesome-unwholesome	0.70				

	Factor IV (7% TV) Uniqueness		Factor V (3% TV) Familiarity	
Male students (N = 52)	Unique-typical	0.73	Familiar-unfamiliar	0.75
	Individualistic-regular	0.68		
	Unusual-usual	0.62		
Female students (N = 54)	Individualistic-regular	0.72	Familiar-unfamiliar	0.68
	Unique-typical	0.71		
	Unusual-usual	0.62		
	Factor IV (7% TV)		Factor V (3% TV)	
Experts (N = 70)	Individualistic-regular	0.85	Familiar-unfamiliar	0.48
	Unique-typical	0.82		
	Large-small	0.69		

like "loved-hated" and "democratic-undemocratic" but also the *morality, tangability, toughness,* and *sociability* scales. This particular factor configuration appears to indicate that, for the Japanese generally, a nation is highly valued (i.e., viewed as *loved, reputable,* and *wholesome*) if it is seen simultaneously as *democratic* (in terms of political system), *tender* and *sociable* (with respect to international relationships), *predictable* and *tangible* (in whatever it says and does), and *relaxed* (just as any mentally sound person should be). The *volatility* factor also shows an interesting configuration, presumably because of concept/scale interaction. Contrary to our original expectation, three *rationality* scales and a *morality* scale rotated similarly toward this factor in the three groups. Thus an *excitable* nation was seen as being both *irrational* and *immoral.*

In summary, the use of the scales by the Japanese as a whole appears reasonably constant across subjects, despite differences in sex, age, and professional backgrounds. That several scales are shown to interact uniquely with concepts but similarly across the three subject groups may be taken as evidence of concept/scale interaction and the reasonably high sensitivity of the measuring system which "tapped" it.

Composite Scores and the Octant Analysis. A composite score is defined as the average of several scale means along the same factor dimension and serves to simplify interpretation of data. In order to index the affective meanings of nationality concepts a total of five composite scores, each representing one of the factors, was computed for each concept in the "student" and "expert" groups. In computing the factor scores the male and the female student groups were combined into one "student" group. The indices were computed from stable scales that had the highest factor loadings on a given factor for all the three subject groups. Specifically, six scales were employed for each of the *evaluation, dynamism,* and *volatility* factors, three for *uniqueness,* and one for *familiarity.*

Intracultural Consistency in Perceiving National Images. "Experts" in the foreign service and "students" belong to the same culture but their roles differ; we expect the former to know more about the world and its people. Hence the question, do the "experts" perceive the nations in the same way as the students do? If they do, we shall have evidence of intracultural consistency concerning the way educated Japanese see other nations.

Two separate analyses were made, both based on the composite scores. First, we correlated the composite scores between the expert and student groups over 32 nationality concepts, separately for each of the five semantic factor dimensions. Five correlation coefficients were thus obtained.

If they are near unity, one group sees the 32 nations exactly as the other sees them. If they are near zero, there is no consistent way of seeing the 32 nations by the two groups. The correlations for *evaluation, dynamism, volatility, uniqueness,* and *familiarity* were .97, .91, .86, .62 and .94, respectively. Except for *uniqueness,* both groups are in near-perfect agreement (accounting for more than 80% variance in four out of five cases) in the judging of the 32 nations: for example, a nation that is both "loved" and "reputable" as seen by one group is also viewed as such by the other and *vice versa.*

Second, to the extent that the image of a nation is in the present case characterized by five composite scores, each representing one factor, it is possible to examine the correspondence that might hold among these five characteristics. A statistically significant correlation will then indicate a more-than-chance correspondence between any two "traits" of the nations; that is, if *dynamism* correlates highly with *familiarity,* it implies that the Japanese tend to perceive more *dynamic* nations as more *familiar* or more *static* nations as more *unfamiliar.* This proved to be the case. Table 3 sum-

Table 3   Correlations Among the Five Composite Scores
(N = 32 nations)

	E	D	V	U	F
E	.97	.03	− .52	− .03	.38
D	− .17	.91	− .21	.45	.60
V	− .53	.08	.86	− .06	− .24
U	− .02	.65	− .11	.62	.29
F	.32	.56	.06	.40	.94

Notes. 1. Figures above the diagonal represent the student group; figures below the diagonal represent the expert group.

2. Bold italic figures indicate correlations significant beyond the .01 level.

3. *E, D, V, U,* and *F* represent *evaluation, dynamism, volatility, uniqueness,* and *familiarity,* respectively.

marizes the correlations that result. It is clearly seen in both groups that significant correlations were obtained exclusively in the following pairs of "traits": *evaluation/volatility, dynamism/uniqueness,* and *dynamism/familiarity.* Note that *evaluation* correlates inversely with *volatility.* In other words, the Japanese tend to perceive as more *loved* those nations that are viewed as less *excitable* or less *emotional* and *vice versa.* Similarly, the likelihood is that the nations are considered more *dynamic* if they appear to be *unique* and more *familiar*. To the extent that the 32-nation-concept sample is fairly representative of the total nation-concept population, such significant correspondence among traits may be taken to be both general among the Japanese and unique to nation perception.

In summary, we have a clear indication that within-culture consistencies do in fact appear in nation perception. Although no immediate diachronic explanation is possible at this point, these findings will provide useful information for future research in cultural communications and cultural concept formation and will suggest as well the usefulness of such an approach to the study of implicit cultural norms.

The Octant Analysis. In order to summarize the meanings of nation concepts, the 32 concepts can be allocated in a five-dimensional semantic space, each dimension being defined by a semantic factor. To make our understanding easier at this point, let us consider a three-dimensional rather than a five-dimensional semantic space, defined by the first three salient factors; that is, *evaluation, dynamism,* and *volatility.*

The three-dimensional space can be divided into eight regions or octants, each of which is defined by the end point of the three dimensions taken in all possible combinations. Thus, for example, a nation concept would be assigned to Octant I if that concept has composite scores toward the positive end of the *evaluative* factor (*E⁺—loved*), *dynamism* factor (*D⁺—active*) and *volatility* factor (*V⁺—excitable*). The octant allocation of a concept in the three-dimensional meaning space is a shorthand statement of its affective meanings.

Table 4 displays the 32-nation concepts assigned to each octant. These allocations reflect the basic "nuance" each nation concept has for the Japanese subjects. Generally, there seems to be a reasonably high stability of the nuances of each concept across both subject groups. All the major Western nations are allocated in the positive region along the *evaluation,* whereas many Communist nations and developing nations are assigned to the negative region along the same dimension. Thus many smaller Western nations are allocated to Octant III (seen as being *loved* but *static* and *calm*) for experts as well as students, whereas many developing nations are assigned to Octant VIII (viewed as being *hated, static,* and *excitable*) for both. It is interesting to note that the Japanese see differences between the Soviet Union and Communist China in that Russia is viewed as being *hated, active,* and *calm* and China is *hated, active,* but *excitable.*

In some cases within-culture differences also appear. The experts view Japan as *loved, dynamic,* and *excitable,* whereas the students perceive the same as *loved, static,* and *excitable.* The experts assigned France and the

Table 4 Octant Allocations of the POLDI-I Nationality Concepts

Octant	Students	Experts
Octant I $E^+D^+V^+$	Italy	Italy, Japan, France, America
Octant II $E^+D^+V^-$	West Germany	West Germany, Yugoslavia
Octant III $E^+D^-V^-$	New Zealand, Holland, Sweden, Finland, Poland, Greece	New Zealand, Holland, Sweden, Finland, Poland
Octant IV $E^+D^-V^+$	Ethiopia, Thailand, Mexico, Japan, India	Ethiopia, Thailand, Mexico, Greece
Octant V $E^-D^+V^+$	Comm. China, N. Vietnam, Cuba	Comm. China, N. Vietnam, Cuba, N. Korea, S. Korea, Formosa, Algeria
Octant VI $E^-D^+V^-$	Soviet Union	Soviet Union, E. Germany
Octant VII $E^-D^-V^-$	…	…
Octant VIII $E^-D^-V^+$	S. Vietnam, Afghanistan, Iran, Turkey, Nigeria, Lebanon, Venezuela, N. Korea, S. Korea, Formosa	S. Vietnam, Afghanistan, Iran, Turkey, Nigeria, Lebanon, Venezuela, India

Exceptions

Code	Students	Experts
$E^+D^+V^0$	France, America	…
$E^-D^0V^+$	Algeria	…
$E^-D^0V^-$	E. Germany	…
$E^-D^-V^0$	Yugoslavia	…

United States to Octant I along with Japan. The students see them some-what differently; they rate them as being *loved* and *dynamic* but *neutral* along the *volatility* dimension. What about the perception of Japan? The students place Japan with favorably developing nations like Thailand and Ethiopia, but the experts place her with advanced Western nations such as France and the United States. Figure 3 is a graphic representation of the three-dimensional model of semantic spaces for experts and students in which 16 typical nation concepts are allocated. By inspection the loca-tion of one nation concept in the semantic space in relation to all the others can be examined within each group and further compared across both. Generally, the students appear to see Japan somewhat isolated from other nations, even from those that Japan in fact must deal with closely, such as the United States and the Soviet Union. For the experts, however, Japan appears to be close to France and Italy and fairly close to the United States but remote from Communist China or the Soviet Union. The experts place Japan close to countries that have achieved levels of economic develop-ment similar to its own.

These findings appear to show that differences between the students and the experts in the cognitive mapping of the world are relatively small and subtle but real. We have already seen that a powerful within-culture con-sistency operates in nation perception. We now have evidence of minor intracultural differences which have implications concerning the achieve-ment of national concensus in foreign-policy decision making.

Japanese-German, POLDI-II Study

Subsequent to the POLDI-I study, a modification referred to as POLDI-II was constructed for a cross-cultural study of Japanese and Ger-mans. Four subject groups, each consisting of 30 individuals, were used in Japan to check the possible sex differences and interference by concept order. Thirty-six persons were studied in Germany. A total of 32 national-ity concepts were rated on a 27-scale form of a translation-equivalent POLDI-II in Japan and Germany.[2]

Scale-by-Scale Factorizations. A combined factorization was done for the four groups of Japanese. Specifically, a total of 108 scales (i.e., 27 scales $\times$ 4 groups) was considered. A 108 (scales) $\times$ 32 (concepts) scale-mean matrix was first computed and a 108 $\times$ 108 scale-intercorrela-tion matrix was generated. For the Germans a 27 (scales) $\times$ 32 (con-

[2] I am grateful to Mr. Georg Blome, then at the Institute of Communications Research, University of Illlinois, for collecting data in Germany.

A. Students

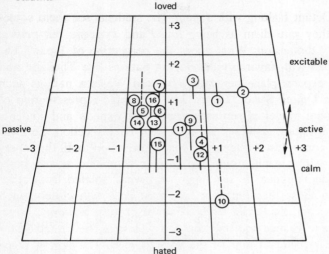

B. "Experts"

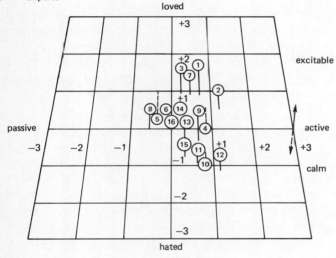

[Key]

1. France	5. Holland	9. Cuba	13. Formosa
2. United States	6. Sweden	10. Soviet Union	14. South Korea
3. Italy	7. Japan	11. North Vietnam	15. North Korea
4. West Germany	8. India	12. Communist China	16. South Vietnam

Figure 3. Three-dimensional models of the semantic spaces for Japanese students and "experts." Each of 16 concepts is numbered according to key. The base of projection from concept gives the ratings on composite scales *love-hated* and *active-passive*. The length of projection from concept to base gives the ratings on composite scale, *excitable-calm,* a solid projection indicating a rating toward the excitable end, and a broken projection indicating a rating toward calm end of the composite scale. Key: 1. France; 2. United States, America; 3. Italy; 4. W. Germany; 5. Holland; 6. Sweden; 7. Japan; 8. India; 9. Cuba; 10. Soviet Union; 11. North Vietnam; 12. Comm China; 13 Formosa; 14. South Korea; 15. North Korea; 16. S. Vietnam.

cepts) scale-mean matrix was obtained to generate a 27×27 scale-intercorrelation matrix. These scale-intercorrelation matrices were then submitted to factorization, separately for each nationality group. The factor analytic results are shown in Table 5.

POLDI-II factors, derived by a principal component analysis and rotated by varimax, seem quite consistent across the subject groups. Common to all, the first four salient factors are clearly identifiable as *pleasantness* (variant of evaluation), *development* (variant of dynamism), stability (opposite of volatility), and *strength* (pure potency). Again, the factors are similar for the five subject groups differing in culture, sex, and the order of stimulus presentation; no major interaction is found either with sex, with culture, or with the order of the concepts. Despite somewhat different scale composition of POLDI-II, deviations of the POLDI-II factor configuration from that of POLDI-I appear relatively small.

Both the Japanese and Germans use four major criterial attributes when they perceive the 32 nations: whether they are *pleasant* and *happy* or *unpleasant* and *sad;* whether they are *active* and *sophisticated* or *passive* and *naïve;* whether they are *constant* and *calm* or *changeable* and *excitable;* and whether they are *big* and *strong* or *small* and *weak.* This can be taken as evidence of cross-cultural generality of the affective meaning systems that operate in nation perception.

In addition to evidence of cross-cultural generality, however, some interesting cultural differences also appear in this study. First, the Japanese associate *excitable-calm* with *immoral-moral* in both POLDI studies. Furthermore, in this study both scales are highly associated with *tough-tender* and *changeable-constant.* In other words, those nations that the Japanese view simultaneously as *excitable, tough,* and *changeable* connote *immoral* to them. The opposite is also true; what the Japanese would perceive as *moral* should be *calm, tender,* and *constant.* It should be recalled at this point that the Japanese are said to be tradition-oriented and in this sense more conservative. This unique configuration of the *stability* factors seems quite consistent with their traditional values of calmness and constancy and their persistent attachment to them. The measuring instrument seems to tap this implicit trait underlying typical Japanese thinking. No such culturally unique pattern holds for the corresponding German factor.

Second, Germans are found to show their own cultural uniqueness. In Table 5 it is clearly seen that *immoral-moral* alone loads very highly, and the loadings of *tender-tough* and *happy-sad* are only secondary on the *morality* factor. Unlike the Japanese, Germans appear to use a unique, independent criterion of morality when they perceive nations. From these factor loadings it looks as though Germans would perceive *immoral* nations as being simultaneously somewhat *tender* and *happy;* one might even get

Table 5 POLDI-II Scale Factorizations: Japanese and German

Factor I (Pleasantness)	Factor II (Development)	Factor III (Stability)	Factor IV (Strength)	Factor V (Morality)
JM-N (N = 30)				
Sad-happy .87	Naïve-sophisticated .87	Excitable-calm .84	Little-big .90	
Ugly-pretty .84	Slow-quick .85	Immoral-moral .73	Light-heavy .70	
Unpleasant-pleasant .84	Passive-active .82	Tough-tender .68	Weak-strong .61	
Solitary-sociable .83	Humble-proud .79	Changeable-constant .66	Shallow-deep .57	
Disagreeable-agreeable .81	Insensitive-sensitive .78	Impetuous-quiet .66		
Tense-calm .78	Weak-strong .69	Shallow-deep .56		
JM-R (N = 30)				
Sad-happy .89	Humble-proud .90	Immoral-moral .78	Little-big .85	
Solitary-sociable .88	Naïve-sophisticated .88	Excitable-calm .78	Weak-strong .62	
Tense-calm .84	Slow-quick .86	Changeable-constant .69	Light-heavy .59	
Unpleasant-pleasant .84	Passive-active .85	Tough-tender .68	Shallow-deep .46	
Ugly-pretty .82	Insensitive-sensitive .78	Impetuous-quiet .64		
Disagreeable-agreeable .80	Weak-strong .69	Shallow-deep .62		
JF-N (N = 30)				
Sad-happy .96	Naïve-sophisticated .90	Excitable-calm .88	Little-big .92	
Unpleasant-pleasant .93	Humble-proud .83	Immoral-moral .81	Weak-strong .65	
Disagreeable-agreeable .88	Passive-active .83	Changeable-constant .75		
Tense-calm .85	Insensitive-sensitive .82	Shallow-deep .74		
Solitary-sociable .81	Slow-quick .81	Tough-tender .70		
Ugly-pretty .85	Weak-strong .66	Impetuous-quiet .69		
Per cent TV 30	Per cent TV 25	Per cent TV 20	Per cent TV 10	
JF-R (N = 30)				
Unpleasant-pleasant .96	Humble-proud .89	Excitable-calm .81	Little-big .87	
Sad-happy .95	Naïve-sophisticated .87	Immoral-moral .74	Weak-strong .66	
Disagreeable-agreeable .91	Slow-quick .86	Changeable-constant .73		
Solitary-sociable .86	Passive-active .85	Impetuous-quiet .69		
Ugly-pretty .86	Insensitive-sensitive .81	Tough-tender .68		
Tense-calm .85	Weak-strong .66	Shallow-deep .68		
Per cent TV 25	Per cent TV 22	Per cent TV 20	Per cent TV 9	
GM (N = 36)				
Insensitive-sensitive .85	Passive-active .93	Impetuous-quiet .98	Little-big .89	Immoral-moral .90
Unpleasant-pleasant .84	Slow-quick .90	Excitable-calm .94	Light-heavy .69	Tender-tough .47
Disagreeable-agreeable .81	Unfamiliar-familiar .87	Changeable-constant .88	Weak-strong .56	Happy-sad .40
Solitary-sociable .71	Weak-strong .75	Tense-calm .84	Shallow-deep .43	
Sad-happy .69	Naïve-sophisticated .72	Unpredictable-predictable .82		
Ugly-pretty .68	Shallow-deep .46	Proud-humble .61		
Per cent TV 21	Per cent TV 22	Per cent TV 26	Per cent TV 7	Per cent TV 7

135

the impression that Germans would look at the nations with strongly stoic feelings. Although there is no way of determining in this study whether this unique associative pattern is in fact consistent to implicit *Weltanschauungen* Germans might have toward other nations, the finding certainly seems to call for further research on this intriguing point.

In summary, scale factorizations of both the Japanese and the German POLDI-II data clearly indicate that a high degree of cross-cultural generality operates in the semantic spaces of the Japanese and Germans. It is also shown, however, that some cultural uniqueness is present in the semantic spaces; for the Japanese *moral-immoral* is inversely related to *stability,* whereas, for the Germans, it has a unique position in nation perception.

The Generalized Distance Analysis. There are several alternative ways of analyzing the meanings of concepts. As we have seen in the preceding section on POLDI-I, both the correlations among the composite scores and the octant analysis provide a useful method for such an analysis. In analyzing POLDI-II data, however, still another method, the *generalized distance analysis,* is used, since it is a more stringent method of semantic analysis and provides more useful information.

Although simple and useful as an over-all index of similarity between two semantic profiles, the correlation coefficient does not give a fully valid or stringent representation of semantic relations. In Figure 4 we reproduce

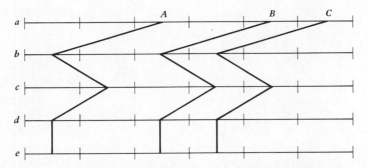

Figure 4. Profiles for three subject groups *(A,B,C)* judging five concepts *(a,b,c,d,e)* in one factor dimension.

a hypothetical system of three groups *(A, B, C)* rating five concepts *(a, b, c, d, e)* along the same factor dimension (in terms of the composite score). The groups are shown to co-vary perfectly in the judging of the five concepts; hence, despite the gross absolute discrepancies, intercorrelations among them would be 1.00. Thus it can be stated that the product-moment correlation is useful only when our interest lies in finding evidence of consistent co-variation among the groups under investigation. When we are interested in the discovery of semantic similarities or differences among different groups of people beyond obtaining evidence of over-all consistency, the correlation not only distorts the information but may be inapplicable. As described above, a perfect correlation between the two groups only indicates such over-all consistency; no information whatsoever can be derived from the correlation about the actual intensity and direction of judging.

What is required to express semantic similarity or difference across groups is some measure of relation that takes into account both the profile co-variation between groups and the discrepancies between the meanings of the same concepts judged by both groups. Such a measure is provided by the *generalized distance formula* of solid geometry (cf. Osgood et al., 1957, p. 91 f.):

$$D_{xy} = \left(\sum_j d_{xy}^2 \right)^{\frac{1}{2}},$$

where D_{xy} is the linear distance between the points in the semantic space representing concepts X and Y (i.e., in the present case the same concept as judged by two groups) and d_{xy} is the algebraic difference between the coordinates of X and Y on the same factor dimension j. Summation is over k dimensions. This D is computed by taking the difference between the composite scores of the same concept rated by two groups, squaring the difference, summing the squares, and taking the square root of the sum. If any two concepts are in a perfect *homonymous* relation, the two concepts should have the identical location in the given semantic space; each d_{xy} is zero and D is therefore zero. If any two concepts are in a perfect *semantically opposite* relation, that is, if the coordinates of X are $+3$, -3, and $+3$ when those of Y are -3, $+3$ and -3, $[+3 - (-3)]^2 + [-3 - (+3)]^2 + [+3 - (-3)]^2$ equals 108, the desired D^2. The square root of this value, 10.39, is the desired distance, or D, which is most often used to index the distance between, or similarity among, concepts judged by an individual or a group. It can also be applied in the comparison of two or more groups of subjects judging the same set of concepts.

Instead of obtaining D for separate pairs of concepts, all $n(n-1)/2$ pairs can be studied simultaneously. By using the D formula the distance between each concept and every other concept can be computed and entered into an $n \times n$ matrix. This matrix represents the semantic structure of the set of n concepts, giving the distances or similarity relations among all concepts.

D-Computation from POLDI-II Data. For the generalized distance analysis on POLDI-II data the following procedures were utilized. Based on the factor analytic results reported in the preceding section, three composite scores were computed for each concept, but separately in the four Japanese and one German groups. For the Japanese five *evaluative* scales (*sociable-solitary, pleasant-unpleasant, pretty-ugly, happy-sad,* and *agreeable-disagreeable*), five *development* scales (*proud-humble, sensitive-insensitive, sophisticted-naïve, quick-slow,* and *active-passive*), and five *stability* scales (*moral-immoral, calm-excitable, tender-tough, constant-changeable,* and *quiet-impetuous*) were used to compute the composite score. Because of somewhat different factor composition, the composite score for the Germans was computed over *sociable-solitary, sensitive-insensitive, pleasant-unpleasant, happy-sad,* and *agreeable-disagreeable* for evaluation, over *familiar-unfamiliar, sophisticated-naïve, strong-weak, quick-slow,* and *active-passive* for development, and over *calm-excitable, predictable-unpredictable, calm-tense, constant-changeable,* and *quiet-impetuous* for stability. A total of 480 (5 groups $\times$ 3 factors $\times$ 32 concepts) composite scores were thus computed in all groups.

Subsequently, *D*'s were computed by using these composite scores. In computing *D*'s for the Japanese each concept location in every group is paired with every other concept location in every group in the entire "cultural" semantic space. This is considered legitimate because of near-perfect consistency which appears to operate in the semantic space across the four Japanese groups. Thus a 128 (32 concepts $\times$ 4 groups) $\times$ 128 *D*-matrix was generated to represent the over-all semantic structure of the 32 nation concepts, giving the differences or similarities among all concepts in all groups. For the Germans a separate, 32 $\times$ 32 *D*-matrix was computed, following the same procedure.

"Conceptual Congruence" Among the Four Japanese Groups. The "conceptual congruence," or the degree of agreement in the allocation of any two concepts put into comparison in the common semantic space, would be maximum if the distance *D* between the concepts is minimum or zero. Distances were compared among the same concepts (e.g., JAPAN) judged by four Japanese groups. No Japanese-German comparison was made at this point because of the somewhat incompatible factor structures of the Japanese and Germans. If there is a high degree of conceptual congruence held by the four Japanese groups toward the same concept, each *D* should be relatively small, near zero.

Table 6 displays a part of the 128 $\times$ 128 *D*-matrix in which each row and column represents the corresponding concepts; that is, the first row and the first column represent JAPAN, the second POLAND, and the

Table 6 Distance Measures Relating Concepts: A Partial Reproduction of the 128 × 128 D-Matrix for the Japanese

	1	2	3	4	5	6	7	8	9	10	11	12	13	14	15	16	17	18	19	20
1	.00																			
2	1.19	.00																		
3	1.08	.57	.00																	
4	2.25	2.01	.86	.00																
5	1.23	.62	.64	.73	.00															
6	1.25	.49	.96	2.30	1.11	.00														
7	1.20	1.34	1.83	3.17	1.64	1.21	.00													
8	1.85	1.20	.87	3.14	.81	1.63	2.43	.00												
9	.72	.75	1.29	2.47	1.04	.73	.70	.79	.00											
10	1.12	.93	1.42	2.84	1.27	.82	.43	2.06	.44	.00										
11	.62	1.19	1.67	2.68	1.31	1.25	.70	2.04	.52	.73	.00									
12	.88	1.91	2.44	2.77	2.08	1.77	1.59	2.62	1.37	1.66	1.26	.00								
13	1.31	.96	1.02	2.16	.53	1.39	1.52	1.21	1.09	1.27	1.14	2.19	.00							
14	2.48	2.03	1.72	2.62	1.66	2.40	3.25	.90	2.58	2.90	2.80	3.14	2.04	.00						
15	.92	.54	.82	1.83	.33	.83	1.40	1.06	.21	1.09	.39	1.76	.62	2.77	.00					
16	2.35	.95	1.48	2.65	1.22	2.48	.52	.98	.76	.40	2.74	2.95	1.20	.45	.94	.00				
17	1.15	2.13	.92	.42	1.74	1.17	3.26	1.10	1.02	2.95	1.20	2.01	2.09	2.07	.88	2.76	.00			
18	.95	.70	.77	1.73	.13	1.25	.13	.86	.84	1.31	.86	1.83	.49	1.68	.28	1.19	1.73	.00		
19	2.01	.87	1.10	2.08	.53	1.94	1.35	1.28	2.03	1.12	2.23	2.78	.36	1.93	.41	.95	2.06	.43	.00	
20	.98	1.50	1.72	1.01	1.04	.61	2.67	.34	.69	2.33	2.08	2.72	1.37	.68	1.28	2.22	.86	1.06	1.44	.00
21	1.27	.27	.67	1.73	.95	.45	1.25	1.14	1.14	.99	.44	2.07	.92	1.42	.71	.90	1.98	.58	.75	.42
22	1.25	.70	1.45	.77	.30	.95	1.35	1.36	.61	1.49	1.06	1.90	.81	1.86	.36	1.38	1.48	.34	.75	.86
23	1.30	.44	.88	1.45	.26	1.37	.99	1.84	.59	.57	1.38	2.15	1.08	2.46	.45	.74	2.56	1.00	1.00	.91
24	1.43	.47	.92	1.05	.70	1.60	1.69	.75	1.48	1.32	1.73	1.37	.77	1.61	.82	1.26	1.71	.37	1.00	1.04
25	1.60	1.00	1.72	1.66	1.13	2.44	2.17	.50	1.06	1.83	.73	2.71	1.17	1.10	.42	1.68	1.13	.71	.75	.68
26	2.10	1.37	1.49	1.60	1.60	1.20	1.43	1.75	2.40	1.37	2.48	1.22	1.87	2.36	.80	1.02	.49	1.01	1.09	.84
27	.79	2.07	2.59	.76	1.19	2.52	3.06	1.49	2.14	2.79	1.33	1.62	2.10	.83	.90	2.56	1.81	1.55	.70	.89
28	1.42	1.13	2.10	2.23	2.03	1.73	2.44	2.25	1.24	1.55	1.89	.77	1.67	1.95	1.71	1.27	2.08	1.91	1.24	1.64
29	.52	2.32	1.33	2.08	1.60	1.29	2.56	2.11	1.09	2.51	1.03	1.44	1.16	2.43	1.86	2.13	2.38	1.50	1.82	.89
30	1.66	1.66	.64	2.28	.87	1.19	1.64	1.22	1.55	1.62	1.19	2.38	1.36	2.59	1.32	1.23	1.62	.79	1.31	2.20
31	.74	1.05		1.52	1.10		1.75	.59		1.52	1.92			1.75	.67	1.23	1.42	.93	.87	2.34
32	1.70	.88		1.27	1.31		2.20			1.80				1.24	.98	1.76			1.15	.89
1	.23	1.10	1.59	2.15	1.22	1.10	1.25	1.79	.71	1.12	.77	.87	1.38	2.41	.90	.76	2.29	1.15	1.03	1.97
2	1.05	.27	.71	1.84	.66	.53	1.42	1.17	.76	1.04	1.19	1.73	1.06	1.93	.51	.97	1.99	.71	.90	1.45
3	1.43	.35	.28	1.78	.56	.76	1.68	1.34	2.62	1.28	1.49	1.01	1.01	1.73	.65	1.29	1.88	.68	1.00	1.23
4	2.33	2.21	2.09	.28	1.90	2.50	3.31	.88	.87	3.01	2.79	2.81	2.29	.77	1.98	2.79	.41	1.88	2.20	1.17
5	1.22	.38	.48	1.77	.27	.86	1.56	1.09	1.43	1.19	1.27	2.02	.73	1.73	.35	1.14	1.95	.37	.68	1.16
6	1.18	.25	.61	1.80	.65	.55	1.51	2.48	.18	1.12	1.30	1.86	1.09	1.86	.57	1.08	1.39	.72	.96	1.39
7	1.18	1.35	1.87	3.16	1.72	1.13	.26	.36	.43	1.47	.80	1.46	1.67	3.24	1.46	.55	3.28	1.71	1.47	2.73
8	1.57	.85	.59	1.39	.46	1.63	2.06	1.81		1.70	1.70	2.37	.92	2.57	.72	1.63	1.39	.54	.97	.66
9	.58	.82	1.37	2.42	1.10	.77	.78	2.05		.58	.53	1.21	1.19	2.89	.79	.27	2.54	1.07	.90	2.05
10	1.12	.90	1.40	2.82	1.31	.76	.47		.43	.07	.77	1.64	1.30		1.09	.41	2.93	1.32	1.15	2.33

139

third AFGHANISTAN. The order of the 32-nation concepts can be found in Appendix 2 of this chapter. The value in each cell indicates the distance: the first column in the table shows distances from Japan to every other concept in the same group and to 10 concepts in the next group. Along the same column the values are seen to vary from the lowest of .23 (between the two JAPAN's as rated by two groups) to the highest of 2.48 (between JAPAN and UNION OF SOUTH AFRICA in the first group). It will also be noted that all *italicized* critical values, which show the diagonal of the same concepts across the two groups, seem small indeed

Table 7   Highest, Lowest, and Median *D*'s for Each Nation Concept

Nation Concepts	Median *D*	Highest *D*	Lowest *D*
Greece	0.20	0.27	0.12
Finland	0.25	0.38	0.07
Holland	0.27	0.30	0.16
Australia	0.27	0.38	0.12
Communist China	0.29	0.45	0.15
Turkey	0.30	0.42	0.22
Mexico	0.31	0.42	0.14
Venezuela	0.32	0.60	0.15
Iran	0.32	0.37	0.17
Lebanon	0.34	0.47	0.15
Thailand	0.36	0.48	0.24
England	0.38	0.49	0.15
Egypt	0.38	0.43	0.28
Afghanistan	0.40	0.71	0.17
Nigeria	0.40	0.48	0.17
West Germany	0.40	0.63	0.27
Japan	0.41	0.61	0.21
Sweden	0.41	0.53	0.34
Cuba	0.43	0.71	0.18
Indonesia	0.44	0.61	0.29
Italy	0.45	0.58	0.22
Yugoslavia	0.47	0.61	0.16
Poland	0.49	0.90	0.25
U.S.S.R.	0.50	0.84	0.27
Ghana	0.54	0.88	0.29
Brazil	0.58	0.73	0.11
France	0.58	1.04	0.51
United States	0.59	1.03	0.22
Formosa	0.60	0.84	0.36
India	0.63	1.20	0.22
East Germany	0.83	0.98	0.33
Union of South Africa	0.86	1.21	0.40

compared with other values in the same row and column. How consistently does this "congruence" tendency hold in the total data?

Table 7 summarizes D's between the same concepts computed in a total of six subject-group pairs, giving only the highest, lowest, and median D's related to each concept. On the basis of these D's we can examine the interrelation among the four subject groups with respect to the relative locations in the common semantic space of the same concepts. The highest "conceptual congruence" would be obtained between any two groups if D is zero or near zero. Although no direct statistical test of significance of D is available, the D's we obtained for each concept between the two groups are certainly small by any standard. On the average, the subject groups would differ by a tenth of a scale unit along each semantic dimension when judging GREECE and by less than half a scale unit when rating UNION OF SOUTH AFRICA. It must be recalled at this point that Osgood et al. (1957) and Tanaka (1962) have reported that composite score differences greater than half a scale unit are statistically significant beyond the .05 level. Using this criterion, most D's in the table would be taken as statistically nonsignificant. It would be safe to state, therefore, that a reasonably high degree of "conceptual congruence" has been achieved among the four Japanese groups. This would reflect the within-culture stability of the cultural meanings associated with the 32 nation concepts.

The Relative Distances Among 32 Nation Concepts: A Cross-Cultural Comparison

In perceiving 32 nations we find that some may be similar in their meanings when compared with others. The distance measure D would then serve as a useful index of the distances or similarity relations among the nation concepts. Such relations basically concern the relative locations of the concepts in the semantic space and can easily be examined by inspecting a 32×32 D-matrix which represents the over-all semantic structuring of the set of 32 concepts.

Before we proceed, however, it must be stated in advance that our conceptual task is confounded by two "noise" factors in the measuring system. First, as pointed out earlier, there is no direct statistical test of significance of D-data. In other words, there is no way of knowing with confidence whether a D of 4.00 is significantly greater than a D of 3.50. Thus mere inspection of the values in a 32×32 D-matrix (there is a total of 496 elements in the matrix) not only does not immediately create a clear picture of the conceptual structure but mere comparison of two or more values in the matrix does not lead to a statistically sound conclusion. Second, we have already seen in the preceding section, on the scale-by-scale factorization, that the semantic space structures for the Japanese and the Germans were similar but not exactly identical; for example, both cultural groups used *stability* as a salient factor in their semantic systems. Nonetheless the scale compositions of Japanese *stability* and German *stability* were somewhat different. In other words, a D of 3.00 derived from the composite scores of the Japanese may be incompatible with the same value derived from those of the Germans if we use the most stringent criterion.

With these limitations in mind, it is considered appropriate to take inter-D relationships into account rather than the single values of D. We can examine a pattern of variations among D's from each concept to every other concept within a group. We can also investigate a profile of co-variations among two or more sets of D's, each set representing a group of subjects judging the same concept pairs. To simplify the analysis in the present study the two Japanese male and the two Japanese female groups were collapsed into one male and one female group to be compared with the Germans. Table 8 shows this analysis.

It can be seen clearly in Table 8, I, that for both Japanese males and females the five most perceptually similar nations to JAPAN are SWEDEN, GREECE, ITALY, AUSTRALIA, and WEST GERMANY, whereas the UNION OF SOUTH AFRICA, COMMUNIST CHINA, INDONESIA, CUBA, and NIGERIA are the most distant. For the Germans, on the other hand, the UNITED STATES and WEST GERMANY are the most similar to JAPAN; and CUBA, COMMUNIST CHINA, and INDONESIA differ the most. It is interesting to note that the Germans tend to view the UNITED STATES and JAPAN as alike, whereas for Japanese males and females the UNITED STATES is rather different from JAPAN. The co-variation profile between groups can be examined by an ordinary product-moment correlation coefficient computed in each pair of subject groups over the 31 concepts. All three correlations are found to be significant beyond the .01 level; an indication that D's for the concept JAPAN co-vary with reasonable consistency across the three groups of subjects. To determine whether these three r's are significantly different from one another, they were subsequently z-transformed and submitted to the appropriate tests. The results indicate that an r of .88 differs significantly from either an r of .61 or an r of .53 beyond the .05 level. These results lead to the conclusion that the over-all similarity in the semantic structure with respect to Japan is reasonably high across all three samples but still higher within than across the culturally different groups.

Similar comparisons were made for WEST GERMANY, the UNITED STATES, the U.S.S.R., and COMMUNIST CHINA. In summary, the three groups were found to be semantically "distant" in relation to WEST GERMANY and the U.S.S.R., all the correlations being very low. Their

Table 8 I. Relative Distances Between Japan and
Other Nations as Perceived by Japanese Male and
Female and German Subjects

Nation Concepts	D/JM	D/JF	D/G
Sweden	0.57	0.84	1.29
Greece	0.63	0.93	2.29
Italy	0.75	1.03	1.93
Australia	0.76	1.06	1.37
West Germany	0.76	0.93	0.97
France	0.82	1.13	1.66
U.S.S.R.	0.82	1.31	1.90
Egypt	0.86	1.02	2.62
Yugoslavia	0.96	1.31	1.64
England	1.00	1.31	1.31
Mexico	1.00	1.01	2.02
Poland	1.06	1.27	1.46
Brazil	1.10	1.09	2.13
Finland	1.11	1.33	1.64
Thailand	1.14	1.25	1.95
India	1.15	1.24	1.78
Venezuela	1.16	1.25	2.33
Holland	1.20	1.65	1.75
Turkey	1.20	1.11	1.73
Iran	1.31	1.40	2.53
Ghana	1.45	1.71	2.61
Afghanistan	1.51	1.64	2.83
Formosa	1.56	1.27	2.17
United States	1.65	1.63	0.49
Lebanon	1.68	1.51	2.71
East Germany	1.78	1.71	2.36
Nigeria	1.86	1.92	2.54
Cuba	2.18	1.93	3.55
Indonesia	2.20	1.65	3.12
Communist China	2.25	1.83	3.17
Union of South Africa	2.32	1.79	2.31

	r: JM/JF	.88*
	JM/G	.61*
	JF/G	.53*

Notes. 1. D indicates distance; JM, JF, and G represent
Japanese male, Japanese female, and German groups,
respectively.

2. Correlations marked by * are significant beyond the
.01 level.

Table 8   II. Relative Distances Between West Germany and Other Nations as Perceived by Japanese Male and Female and German Subjects

Nation Concepts	D/JM	D/JF	D/G
U.S.S.R.	0.50	0.70	1.99
Japan	0.76	0.93	0.97
Egypt	0.83	0.97	3.12
Yugoslavia	0.85	1.13	1.98
Italy	0.85	1.69	2.72
Ghana	0.96	1.33	2.95
Mexico	0.97	1.36	2.66
Formosa	0.97	0.80	2.57
France	0.99	1.79	2.47
Turkey	1.00	1.07	2.17
Venezuela	1.00	1.16	2.84
Poland	1.04	1.37	1.55
Iran	1.08	1.11	2.88
Greece	1.14	1.41	3.02
East Germany	1.18	0.91	2.62
India	1.20	0.75	2.13
Brazil	1.20	1.38	2.78
Lebanon	1.21	1.02	3.02
Sweden	1.23	1.32	0.45
Thailand	1.28	1.26	2.11
United States	1.28	1.90	0.93
Nigeria	1.31	1.37	2.77
Afghanistan	1.32	1.37	2.91
Australia	1.35	1.40	0.64
Cuba	1.47	1.40	4.12
Indonesia	1.47	1.05	3.70
England	1.49	1.86	0.47
Communist China	1.50	1.12	3.55
Finland	1.62	1.68	1.02
Union of South Africa	1.66	1.37	2.63
Holland	1.84	2.18	0.93

r: JM/JF   .52*
JM/G   −.10
JF/G   −.37

Notes. 1. D indicates distance; JM, JF, and G represent Japanese male, Japanese female, and German groups, respectively.

2. Correlations marked by * are significant beyond the .01 level.

Table 8   III. Relative Distances Between the United
States and Other Nations as Perceived by Japanese Male
and Female and German Subjects

Nation Concepts	D/JM	D/JF	D/G
France	1.12	1.61	1.82
West Germany	1.28	1.90	0.93
Italy	1.40	1.49	2.30
U.S.S.R.	1.54	2.03	1.78
Cuba	1.60	2.27	3.79
Japan	1.65	1.63	0.49
Communist China	1.73	2.20	3.27
Indonesia	1.75	2.12	3.37
Formosa	1.89	2.53	2.53
Mexico	1.90	2.03	2.44
Ghana	1.93	2.65	3.00
England	1.94	2.15	2.16
East Germany	2.03	2.62	2.47
Egypt	2.04	2.43	2.89
Yugoslavia	2.08	2.74	1.93
Venezuela	2.10	2.56	2.75
Sweden	2.11	2.35	1.33
Nigeria	2.12	2.66	2.97
Turkey	2.14	2.50	2.17
Lebanon	2.17	2.63	3.12
Greece	2.23	2.43	2.68
Brazil	2.23	2.37	2.54
Iran	2.23	2.69	2.95
Union of South Africa	2.24	2.67	2.55
Poland	2.28	2.77	1.75
Australia	2.37	2.56	1.46
India	2.41	2.47	2.17
Thailand	2.48	2.72	2.38
Afghanistan	2.51	2.93	3.24
Finland	2.71	2.86	1.83
Holland	2.81	3.04	1.81

r: JM/JF	.87*
JM/G	.09
JF/G	.29

Notes. 1. D indicates Distance; JM, JF, and G represent Japanese male, Japanese female, and German groups, respectively.
   2. Correlations marked by * are significant beyond the .01
level.

Table 8   IV. Relative Distances Between the U.S.S.R. and Other Nations as Perceived by Japanese Male and Female and German Subjects

Nation Concepts	D/JM	D/JF	D/G
West Germany	0.50	0.70	1.99
Japan	0.82	1.31	1.90
Yugoslavia	0.82	1.64	1.56
Egypt	0.92	1.55	2.10
Poland	0.99	1.84	1.62
India	1.05	1.33	2.09
Formosa	1.06	1.31	2.16
Turkey	1.14	1.66	2.32
Greece	1.15	1.84	2.67
Ghana	1.17	1.85	2.67
Venezuela	1.19	1.75	2.65
East Germany	1.19	1.12	1.17
Iran	1.20	1.61	2.78
France	1.22	2.05	1.77
Thailand	1.23	1.80	2.69
Italy	1.23	2.18	2.44
Mexico	1.29	1.93	2.52
Afghanistan	1.31	1.81	3.16
Sweden	1.33	1.78	2.38
Lebanon	1.35	1.48	2.89
England	1.35	1.92	1.78
Australia	1.35	1.82	2.03
Brazil	1.43	1.93	2.55
Nigeria	1.50	1.76	2.78
United States	1.54	2.03	1.78
Communist China	1.58	1.03	1.86
Finland	1.59	2.07	2.71
Cuba	1.72	1.70	2.84
Indonesia	1.65	1.31	2.55
Union of South Africa	1.75	1.84	1.67
Holland	1.83	2.57	2.79

r: JM/JF	.49*	
JM/G	.32	
JF/G	.32	

Notes. 1. D indicates Distance; JM, JF, and G represent Japanese male, Japanese female, and German groups, respectively.

2. Correlations marked by * are significant beyond the .01 level.

Table 8   V. Relative Distances Between Communist
China and Other Nations as Perceived by Japanese Male
and Female and German Subjects

Nation Concepts	D/JM	D/JF	D/G
Indonesia	0.50	0.66	1.24
Cuba	0.77	0.96	1.27
Union of South Africa	0.80	1.47	1.33
East Germany	0.99	0.90	0.97
Formosa	1.09	1.45	1.97
Nigeria	1.23	1.23	2.69
Lebanon	1.36	1.37	2.59
Ghana	1.43	1.55	2.31
West Germany	1.50	1.12	3.55
U.S.S.R.	1.58	1.03	1.86
United States	1.73	2.20	3.27
Iran	1.83	1.69	2.54
Turkey	1.85	1.91	2.56
Yugoslavia	1.86	1.92	1.93
Venezuela	1.91	1.91	2.37
Afghanistan	1.93	1.82	3.16
Egypt	1.97	1.84	1.22
Poland	2.02	2.36	2.38
Mexico	2.10	2.05	2.40
India	2.15	1.46	2.32
Italy	2.16	2.50	2.35
Japan	2.25	1.83	3.17
France	2.27	2.72	2.04
Brazil	2.30	2.12	2.33
Thailand	2.33	2.15	3.10
Greece	2.51	2.47	2.32
Sweden	2.70	2.39	3.88
Australia	2.74	2.47	3.43
England	2.81	2.80	3.44
Finland	2.91	2.72	3.99
Holland	3.24	3.24	4.25

	r: JM/JF	.89*
	JM/G	.73*
	JF/G	.62*

Notes. 1. *D* indicates Distance; JM, JF, and G represent Japanese male, Japanese female, and German groups, respectively.

2. Correlations marked by * are significant beyond the .01 level.

conceptual structures seem markedly different, especially between the Japanese and the Germans as a whole. This probably reflects differences in the subjects' learning experiences, which might have been affected by differences in cultures and to some extent by differences in sex. In connection with the UNITED STATES, however, the Japanese male and female groups seem to have similar conceptual structures, which, however, are apparently different from those of the Germans. Finally, in regard to COMMUNIST CHINA all three groups are "close" to one another, yet there continues to be greater similarity within than across cultures. (Z-test results indicate than an r of .89 is significantly different from both an r of .73 and an r of .62 at the .01 level.)

The uses of the D-measure exemplified above may not only illustrate the usefulness of that measure in the analysis of some aspects of subjective culture but may also demonstrate that conceptual structures, or the complex process of cognitive mapping, are, in fact, highly culture-bound. The relative placements of the 32 nation concepts in the semantic space vary more within than between the cultural boundaries. This may be an indication of the uniqueness of national stereotypes within a culture, which in turn may be due to persistent and homogeneous "assign-learning" experiences with the nation concepts via various channels of communication available in that culture.

Evidence for Interactions Among Concepts

Using the semantic differential measuring system, Osgood and Tannenbaum (1955) formulated the general theoretical approach, which they termed the congruity model, to the problems of semantic interaction between two or more cognitive events. More recently this approach has been used in several cross-cultural studies and has provided good predictions of *person concepts* (Triandis & Fishbein, 1963; Triandis, Tanaka, & Shanmugam, 1966), *perceptual signs* (Tanaka, 1964) and *national stereotypic concepts* (Tanaka, 1965b) across different language-culture communities.

The Congruity Model. The congruity model developed from the work of Osgood, Suci, and Tannenbaum (1957) on the measurement of affective meaning. Cognitive interaction was approached in the following way: cognitive elements in the congruity model are equated with the affective meanings of signs (i.e., words, colors, figures, or sound—any stimuli that elicit symbolic processes). In the measurement system provided by the semantic differential technique the factorial meaning of a concept is given by its location along factor dimensions. It follows that "if two (or more) signs associated with different meanings occur near-simultaneously, only one cognitive reaction can occur in the system, and this must be a compromise." (Osgood, 1960, p. 347.) Such a compromise, which Osgood calls "congruity resolution," between the interacting concepts reflects itself both in the change in the meaning of input concepts (i.e., the meaning of the cognitive elements originally put into interaction) and in the locus of resolution between the interacting conceps (i.e., the meaning of the compound concept). This theoretical approach, which Osgood, Suci, and Tannenbaum (1957) called the *congruity hypothesis,* is given in the following general statement:

"Whenever the two concepts are related in an assertion, the affective meaning reaction characteristic of each concept shifts toward congruence with that characteristic of the other, the magnitude of the shift being inversely proportional to the intensities of the interacting reactions."

The present work is an extension of the work of Osgood and Ferguson (cf., Osgood, Suci, & Tannenbaum, 1957, pp. 275–284), in which combinations of qualifiers and nouns, or word mixtures, were used as interacting concepts for English-speaking American subjects. Osgood and Ferguson, using eight qualifiers and eight nouns, predicted the meanings of the 64 possible word mixtures (i.e., compound concepts, e.g., SINCERE PROSTITUTE) from the meanings of the component qualifiers and nouns (i.e., component concepts, e.g., SINCERE and PROSTITUTE). The predicted meaning of each compound concept (symbolically, P_R), which is estimated from the polarization (p) of the concept, that is, its location close or far from the point of neutrality (i.e., ranging from -3 through 0 to $+3$), was computed by using the following congruity formula (Osgood & Tannenbaum, 1955):

$$p_R = \frac{|p_1|(p_1)}{|p_1| + |p_2|} + \frac{|p_2|(p_2)}{|p_1| + |p_2|},$$

where $|p_1|$ and $|p_2|$ are the *absolute* values of polarization of the components (i.e., the qualifiers and nouns), and (p_1) (p_2) are the *signed* algebraic values corresponding to the polarization of the components.

Using this formula, several studies obtained satisfactory predictions. In the first study the correlations between *predicted* and *obtained* meanings, reflecting accuracy of predictions, were .86 for the *evaluative* factor, .86 for *potency,* and .90 for *activity.* By examining the case of unsuccessful predictions, Osgood and Ferguson found evidence of what was called "pessimistic evaluative stickiness." The direction of errors was consistently found in the evaluative dimension and toward the socially more derogatory components in the word mixtures.

In the present study somewhat more restricted classes of qualifiers and nouns were used—that is, nationality concepts such as JAPANESE or AMERICAN as qualifiers and political concepts such as NUCLEAR TESTINGS or FOREIGN POLICY as nouns. The congruity hypothesis was tested across two groups of subjects differing in both language and culture—that is, Japanese and Finns. Some additional diachronic comparisons were also made with the Japanese data.

Japanese-Finnish, Political Stereotype Study

To test the congruity hypothesis cross-culturally three semantic differential experiments were administered, two in Japan in 1961 and 1966 and one in Finland in 1961. Totals of 40 (15 male and 25 female) and 47 (19 male and 28 female) college students majoring in Arts and Design served as subjects in the 1961 and 1966 Japanese experiments. Except that the experiments were administered during a five-year period, subjects in both groups were assumed to be relatively homogeneous in age and education. It must be noted, moreover, that most subjects in the first group were born in 1943 and consequently had only a little experience with World War II and its aftermath and that most subjects in the second group were born in 1948 and therefore had no experience whatsoever with war. In other words, subjects in both groups were a sample of what may be called "postwar children" who have had little or no experience with war. The second experiment was carried out in November of 1966 shortly after Communist China's successful test of a nuclear missile.[3] In Finland a total of 50 (25 male and 25 female) college students majoring in psychology served as subjects.[4]

The concepts used as stimuli in the present work consisted of five *nationality* components (i.e., the UNITED STATES, COMMUNIST CHINA, FINLAND, JAPAN, and the SOVIET UNION), five nouns denoting political phenomena (i.e., GOVERNMENT, PEOPLE, NUCLEAR TESTINGS, FOREIGN POLICY, and MILITARY STRENGTH), and their 25 compounds (e.g., AMERICAN GOVERNMENT or COMMUNIST CHINESE PEOPLE) for the 1961 Japanese and Finnish experiments and four *nationality* components (less FINLAND in the 1966 nationality concepts) and the same five noun components used in 1961 and their 20 compounds for the 1966 Japanese experiment. In the latter a compound concept, COMMUNIST CHINESE NUCLEAR TESTINGS,

---

[3] Part of the Japanese portion of this analysis has been published elsewhere. (Cf. Tanaka & Iwamatsu, 1968a; Tanaka, 1970.)

[4] I am indebted to President Marti Takala of the University of Jyväskylä, Jyväskylä, for arranging data collection in Finland.

was repeated as a reliability check. Thus totals of 35 and 30 concepts were used in the 1961 Japanese and Finnish and the 1966 Japanese studies, respectively. The reduction of the number of concepts in the 1966 Japanese study was dictated by limited time.

To index the affective meaning of concepts a 26-scale semantic differential was constructed in Japanese and Finnish. The scales, which represented each of the three most salient affective factors—*evaluation, policy,* and *activity*—were included on the basis of the preceding studies (Tanaka, 1962; Tanaka, Oyama, & Osgood, 1963), along with scales that loaded highly on *personality* factors isolated in the Osgood-Ware study (Osgood, 1962). These *personality* scales were translated from English, since no scale had been constructed for the Japanese or the Finns, nor were they immediately available in Japanese or Finnish at the time of the first testing in 1961. The same set of 26 scales was used throughout after they had been randomized in order and direction. Appendix 3 shows the 35 concepts and the 26 scales used in this study.

Scale Intercorrelations and Factor Analysis. Scale-by-scale factor analysis in the present work was carried out to determine the structure of the affective dimensions of attitudes and to obtain evidence that the same attitudinal criteria had been used across the Japanese and the Finnish groups and over time by the Japanese. Principal axes solutions and varimax rotations were used throughout.

In connection with the Japanese data each of the 1961 and 1966 subject groups was divided into two subgroups consisting of nearly equal numbers of subjects in order to test the over-all generality of the affective meaning system both through time and across subjects. The data thus obtained was tabulated separately for each subgroup. Consequently an averaged 26 (scales) × 35 (concepts) matrix was obtained for each of the two 1961 subgroups and an averaged 26 (scales) × (30 concepts) matrix was obtained for each of the two 1966 subgroups. For the 1961 data the two matrices were then combined to make up a new 52 (scales) × 35 (concepts) matrix on the basis of which a 52 × 52 matrix of intercorrelations was computed. This was factored and the extracted factors were rotated by the procedures mentioned above. For the 1966 data exactly the same procedure was repeated; a new 52 (scales) × 30 (concepts) matrix was generated and a 52 × 52 matrix of intercorrelations was computed, factored, and the factors rotated. The purpose of these factor analyses was clearly that of finding not only the *within-culture* but also the *diachronic* consistencies in the affective system of the Japanese subjects in their judgment of international political concepts. The same factor analytic procedure was repeated for the Finnish data as a whole; an averaged 26 (scales) $\times$ 25 (concepts) matrix was obtained, a 26 $\times$ 26 scale intercorrelation matrix was computed; this matrix was factored and the obtained factors were rotated. The results are shown in Table 9.

The three most salient factors extracted in all groups are clearly identifiable as *evaluation, dynamism,* and *familiarity.* The first factor in every case accounts for more variance and is defined by scales such as *bad-good, unpleasant-pleasant,* and *ugly-beautiful;* the second factor is defined by scales such as *strong-weak, large-small, sturdy-fragile;* and the third, which accounts for less variance than the other two, is defined by scales such as *near-far, familiar-unfamiliar,* and *common-rare.* It was also found that several *personality* scales, such as *moral-immoral, rational-irrational,* and *tangible-intangible,* have high loadings on the *evaluative* factor.

It is evident in the table that the coefficients of these factors overlap in magnitudes to such an extent that both the subgroups in the 1961 and 1966 Japanese studies and the 1961 Finnish group contribute similarly to each of the factors; for example, the first factor is composed of the scales of the two subgroups in the 1961 Japanese data, of the scales of the two subgroups in the 1966 Japanese data, and of the scales of the 1961 Finnish data. Identical meanings and nearly identical factor loadings can be noted despite their different origins. The dimensions, in other words, are culture-common and almost equally defined by all samples; no separate factors for the three separate experiments or for four Japanese subgroups are found, as might have been expected if there had been great cultural differences and diachronic inconsistencies in the affective use of scales. We thus have clear over-all evidence of the cross-cultural generality of the affective system across the Japanese and Finns and for its within-culture, diachronic stability among the Japanese.

The Cognitive Interaction Analysis. The prediction of subject judgments of complex concepts from a knowledge of subject judgments of components concepts was attempted in the present work with the *congruity* formula (Osgood, Suci, & Tannenbaum, 1957) and the *simple-average* formula (Anderson, 1965; Tanaka, 1965b). The purpose of this analysis was to determine the extent to which cognitive interaction is consistent in judging complex international political events and to discover under what conditions such consistency in cognitive interaction fails to be found in culturally heterogeneous groups.

As stated earlier, the congruity formula basically weighs the cognitive elements (or attitude objects) that enter into interaction by their relative polarization. The simple-average formula, on the other hand, does not weigh the cognitive elements but simply provides the arithmetic means. At least in one cross-cultural study (Tanaka, 1965b) the two approaches

Table 9 Varimax-Rotated Factors and High-Loading Scales in the 1961 and 1966 Groups

Factors	Factor I (E)					Factor II (D)					Factor III (F)				
	1961-F	1961-J		1966-J		1961-F	1961-J		1966-J		1961-F	1961-J		1966-J	
Years and Groups		A	B	A	B		A	B	A	B		A	B	A	B
Bad-good	.90	.95	.94	.96	.96										
Unpleasant-pleasant	.98	.97	.97	.95	.95										
Ugly-beautiful	.94	.93	.94	.95	.95										
Dark-light	.80	.97	.97	.86	.90						(.39)			(−.40)	(−.37)
Unwholesome-wholesome	.88	.96	.96	.89	.95										
Undemocratic-democratic	.89	.95	.93	.76	.80						(.35)			(−.51)	(−.42)
Strong-weak						.85	.94	.94	.97	.98					
Large-small						.72	.92	.94	.95	.94	(.36)				
Sturdy-fragile						.91	.92	.88	.89	.92					
Thick-thin						.91	.82	.82	.85	.89					
Fast-slow						.74	.80	.85	.78	.77		(.37)		(.46)	(.53)
Near-far											.90	.92	.91	.92	.91
Familiar-unfamiliar	(.61)	(−.49)		(−.42)	(−.44)						.75	.81	.90	.84	.85
Common-rare											(.50)	.81	.84	.61	.70
% TV	41.5	37.2		34.2		21.3	26.4		28.7		12.8	19.8		17.1	

Notes. 1. 1961-F, 1961-J, and 1966-J represent 1961-Finnish group, 1961-Japanese group, and 1966-Japanese group, respectively; A and B subgroups.

2. *E*, *D*, and *F* represent *evaluation*, *dynamism*, and *familiarity*, respectively.

3. Parenthesized figures indicate secondary factor loadings greater than .33.

153

provided equally good predictions for judging national stereotypic concepts of Japanese and American subjects.

Congruity and Simple-Average Predictions. Both congruity and simple-average predictions in the present work were based on group means. By applying the congruity formula an appropriate predicted value was computed from the composite-polarity score of a nationality component (e.g., AMERICA) and the composite-polarity score of a noun component (e.g., NUCLEAR TESTINGS). It will be recalled at this point that the composite score is an average of several scale values representative of each of the major semantic dimensions. The polarity score is obtained from the composite score by transforming the latter from —3 to +3. A total of 60 (20 compounds × 3 factors) predictions was therefore made in the 1961 and 1966 Japanese groups, separately, to make between-group, diachronic comparisons possible. These predicted meanings were then compared with the corresponding obtained meanings of the compound (e.g., AMERICAN NUCLEAR TESTINGS) within each subject group. Basically the same procedure was followed for the simple-average predictions; an arithmetic mean was computed from the composite-polarity scores of a nationality and a noun component, which enter into interaction, and then compared with the corresponding obtained value of the compound concept. In both approaches in the Japanese groups the compounds containing FINLAND as a component were excluded, since they were not used in the 1966 experiment. For the Finns, on the other hand, a total of 150 (25 compounds × 3 factors × 2 models) predictions was made. Except for the deviation in the size of concept sample (25 compounds, instead of 20, were subjected to the present analysis), exactly the same procedure was employed for the analysis of Finnish data.

The Accuracy of Predictions: Correlation and Absolute Deviation Between Predicted and Obtained Meanings. Comparisons of the results of predictions from different models such as were attempted in the present case permit a number of alternative ways of evaluating the accuracy of prediction. There are at least three possible measurements by means of which the accuracy of prediction can be compared and evaluated. First, a *correlation* indicates the degree of correspondence between the locations of the predicted and obtained scores on the scales of measurement. Second, signed *constant deviations* between the predicted and obtained meanings can be used and tested for statistical significance by matched *t*-test. When such *t*-tests are nonsignificant, this indicates that the theories are predicting correctly. One difficulty of this method, however, is that cancellation of errors is possible by errors occurring in alternate directions. Third, the most stringent measure of accuracy of predictions is *absolute deviation* between the predicted and obtained meanings, since no such cancellation of errors is possible. Although no direct test of statistical significance is possible for this measure, the average absolute deviation can be checked against the general reliability of the measurement system. In the present study *correlation* and *absolute deviation* between the predicted and obtained meanings were used to compare the accuracy of prediction from the congruity and the simple-average models.

To generalize the predictability of both the congruity and the simple-average methods correlations between corresponding predicted and obtained values were computed for 20 meanings separately in each semantic dimension for the two Japanese groups and for 25 meanings in each semantic dimension for the Finnish group. They will indicate the degree of correspondence between the locations of the predicted and obtained meanings on the scale of measurement. The results are summarized in Table 10. It can be seen that all correlations are significant ($p < .05$) both for

Table 10 Correlation Analysis of Congruity and Simple-Average Predictions

	Congruity Prediction			Simple-Average Prediction		
	E	D	F	E	D	F
1961-F ($N = 25$)	.87†	.51†	.66†	.93†	.62†	.78†
1961-J ($N = 20$)	.92†	.70†	.49*	.91†	.77†	.54†
1966-J ($N = 20$)	.85†	.63†	.54†	.86†	.78†	.63†

Notes. 1. 1961-F, 1961-J, and 1966-J represent the 1961-Finnish group, the 1961-Japanese group, and the 1966-Japanese group, respectively.

2. *E*, *D*, and *F* represent *evaluation, dynamism,* and *familiarity,* respectively.

3. * is $p < .05$, and † is $p < .01$.

the congruity and the simple-average predictions, although the predictability of both models for *dynamism* and *familiarity* are somewhat poorer than for *evaluation* in all three groups.

Next, a total of 60 (20 concepts × 3 factors) absolute deviations in each Japanese group and a total of 75 (25 concepts × 3 factors) absolute deviations in the Finnish group were computed separately for congruity and simple-average predictions. These absolute deviations were then averaged over 20 concepts for each factor within each Japanese group and over 25 concepts for each factor within the Finnish group. In addition, *t*-tests were computed to determine whether the congruity predictions are significantly different from simple-average predictions with respect to the magnitude of errors in prediction. The results displayed in Table 11 clearly

Table 11   Mean Absolute Deviation Analysis of Congruity and Simple-Average Predictions

Factors	Years and Groups	Predictions	Mean Absolute Deviation (scale unit)	t
Evaluation	1961-F	Congruity	.54	.23
		Simple-Average	.53	
	1961-J	Congruity	.36	2.70*
		Simple-Average	.57	
	1966-J	Congruity	.38	.43
		Simple-Average	.40	
Dynamism	1961-F	Congruity	.50	1.57
		Simple-Average	.42	
	1961-J	Congruity	.48	.05
		Simple-Average	.48	
	1966-J	Congruity	.51	1.32
		Simple-Average	.37	
Familiarity	1961-F	Congruity	1.09	2.72*
		Simple-Average	.82	
	1961-J	Congruity	.72	2.63*
		Simple-Average	.51	
	1966-J	Congruity	.66	5.39*
		Simple-Average	.37	

Notes. 1. 1961-F, 1961-J, and 1966-J represent the 1961-Finnish group, the 1961-Japanese group, and the 1966-Japanese group, respectively.

2. * indicates $p < .05$ by two-tailed test.

indicate that the mean absolute error per concept is of a relatively small magnitude in most cases; on both the *evaluative* and the *dynamism* dimensions the maximum error approximates only 0.6 scale units, which is only slightly larger than the average absolute error found in test-retest checks of reliability (cf., Osgood, Suci, & Tannenbaum, 1957). In the *familiarity* domain, however, the absolute errors are greater both in the congruity and in the simple-average predictions, presumably because of a factor of "incredibility" operating as a noise. It also appears to be clear that the congruity and the simple-average models predict almost equally well; the only exceptions are found in the 1961 Japanese group in which congruity predictions were significantly superior to simple-average predictions for *evaluation* and in *familiarity* in which simple-average predictions were superior to congruity predictions in all three groups. Even so, the mean differences of less than 0.3 scale unit may not be considered as substantial from a practical point of view.

It seems quite reasonable to conclude from these results that both approaches are effective and a law of cognitive consistency holds in judging international political events for both the Japanese and Finnish groups. It must be emphasized at this point that these "conceptualized" events may differ from ordinary laboratory-produced stimuli in that they are considered as far more susceptible to contamination by unknown, uncontrolled factors. The fact that the meaning of a complex compound concept can be lawfully predicted both in the Japanese and the Finnish samples from the knowledge of the meaning of its components suggests that the "meaning" we deal with in perceiving international political events is universally subject to lawful variations.

Some Unique Errors in Prediction. Despite this over-all evidence of the cross-cultural consistency in cognitive interaction, some unique errors found in predictions are also of considerable interest. Before we enter into the problem, however, let us present graphically some patterns of cognitive interaction from our data.

Figure 5 displays somewhat different patterns of interaction found in the two Japanese groups for the four compounds having NUCLEAR TESTINGS in common. In (A) the locations of the obtained meaning of two components (a nationality concept and a noun), which are subject to interaction, are shown in a two-dimensional space for 1961 and 1966. This space is defined by the two most salient factors of *evaluation* and *dynamism*. It can be seen that the location of NUCLEAR TESTINGS is fixed throughout, whereas the location of the interacting component varies. In (B) the relative locations of the obtained meaning (o) of the compound concepts are given against those of the predicted meaning of the corresponding compound. In the diagram the subscript o indicates an obtained meaning, p, a congruity prediction, and m, a simple-average prediction. It should be remembered at this point that both the congruity formula and the simple-average method require that the predicted meaning always fall between those of the interacting components, whereas the position of the obtained meaning of the compound, reflecting either the actual effect of cognitive interaction or a constant error, may fall anywhere on the composite scale. In order to index whether the predicted meaning significantly differs from the obtained meaning, the half-a-composite-scale-unit criterion may be used as rough estimation.

First, in the AMERICAN (*good-strong*) versus NUCLEAR TESTINGS (*bad-strong*) and in the SOVIET (*bad-strong*) versus NUCLEAR TESTINGS (*bad-strong*) interactions predictions appear to be reasonably accurate, each prediction falling between the interacting components. Second, in predicting COMMUNIST CHINESE NUCLEAR

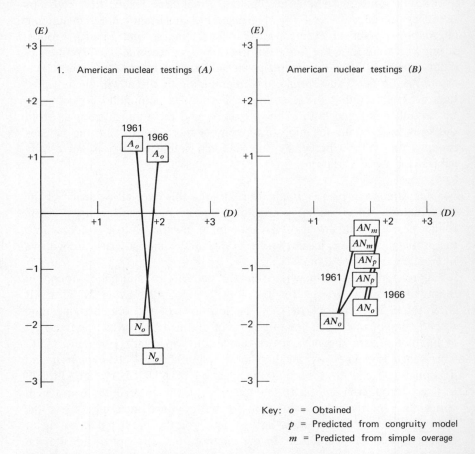

Figure 5. Patterns of cognitive interaction for the NUCLEAR-TESTING-related compound concepts in the Japanese.

TESTINGS from COMMUNIST CHINA (*bad-strong*) and NUCLEAR TESTINGS (*bad-strong*), however, a unique type of error appears in our 1961 Japanese data; that is, predictions along the *dynamism* dimension do not fall between the interacting components but "pulled" toward the less dynamic end of the composite scale by more than a full scale unit for both models (congruity or simple-average). This suggests that, with regard to dynamism, COMMUNIST CHINESE NUCLEAR TESTINGS may have been an incongruent complex concept for the Japanese in 1961; hence a factor of "incredulity" interfered with actual interaction. It should be recalled that Communist China did not have a nuclear weapon in 1961.

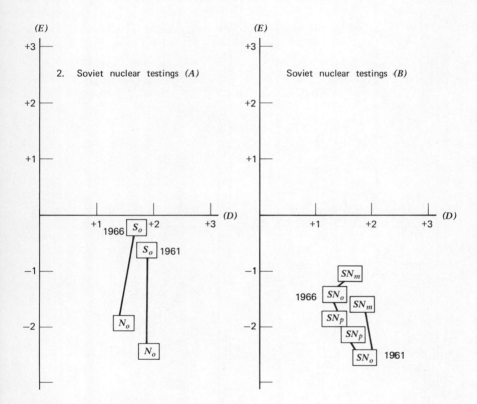

Figure 5 *(continued)*.

Near-perfect congruity is achieved in 1966 both on evaluation and on dynamism after Communist China had, in fact, completed its own nuclear experiments and incredulity was removed. Finally, the interaction between JAPANESE (*good-weak*) and NUCLEAR TESTINGS (*bad-strong*) presents a unique case of the same type of error. Both in 1961 and in 1966 predictions are a complete failure for both models. Theoretically, it should be *bad* and *strong*, but the "pulling power" of the noise factor is so strong along the *dynamism* factor that not only does the actual resolution occur far outside the interacting components in each case but it is "pulled" from the theoretical point of resolution by as much as one and one-half scale units and enters into the semantically opposite negative *dynamism* domain!

For the Finnish data the same type of error is also found with respect to COMMUNIST CHINESE NUCLEAR TESTINGS, JAPANESE NUCLEAR TESTINGS, and FINNISH NUCLEAR TESTINGS, none of

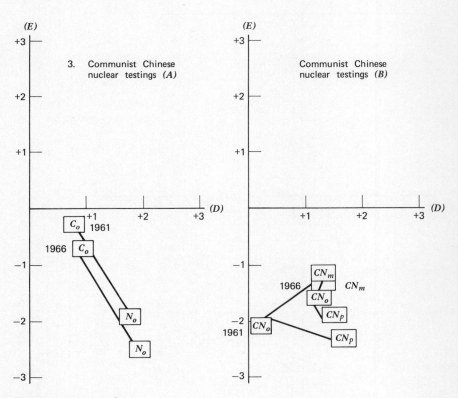

Figure 5 (*continued*).

which appeared "thinkable" in 1961. Figure 6 illustrates the predictions of FINNISH NUCLEAR TESTINGS from FINNISH (*good-strong*) and NUCLEAR TESTINGS (*bad-strong*). In theory it should be *slightly bad* and *quite strong,* but the interference of the noise factor is so strong both along *evaluation* and *dynamism* that the actual point of resolution falls far off the interacting components. Along *evaluation* the actual point of resolution is "pulled" from the theoretical point by more than a full scale unit (*quite bad*), whereas along the *dynamism* factor it is "pulled" toward

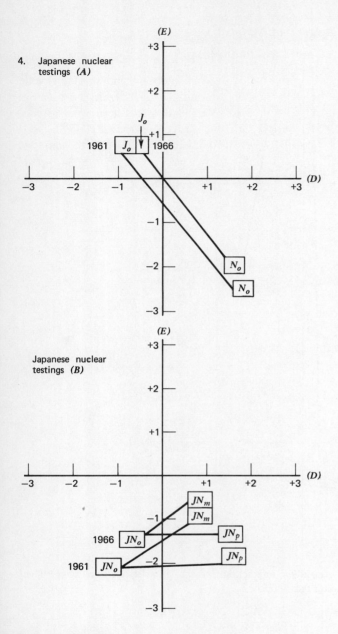

Figure 5 (*continued*).

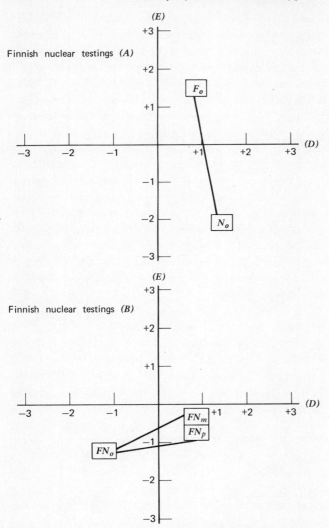

Figure 6. Patterns of congnitive interaction for the NUCLEAR-TESTING-related compound concepts among the Finnish.

the negative end of the composite scale by more than two scale units (*fairly weak*)!

We speculate that the failure in these cases might be attributable to incredibility as a psychological noise that causes disturbance in cognitive interaction. As shown above, COMMUNIST CHINESE NUCLEAR TESTINGS in 1961 for both the Japanese and Finns, JAPANESE NUCLEAR

TESTINGS in 1961 and in 1966 for the Japanese, and FINNISH NU-CLEAR TESTINGS in 1961 for the Finns seem to illustrate an unpredictable abnormal interaction pattern. Such disturbance appears to occur most frequently when there is a small probability that the interacting concepts would co-occur in real life—COMMUNISH CHINESE NUCLEAR TESTINGS in 1961, for example. In the previous study by Osgood and Ferguson, SINCERE PROSTITUTE might have been a similar case. It also appears worth noting that the interfering noise would "oscillate" and completely block normal cognitive interaction, especially when both Japanese and Finnish subjects judge at the same time highly "hypothetical" and very "unthinkable" cognitive events related to their own countries.

In the last analysis, then, we must emphasize that the dynamics of cognitive interaction is complex. Even so, the foregoing analyses and their results would seem to indicate that some theoretical criteria of cognitive interaction, such as the congruity or the simple-average model, might provide a useful analytic instrument to predict the direction of attitude change and detect some sources of noise that might be present in the subjects' cognitive system.

The Multiple Regression Analysis. Multiple regression, a method of using scores on two or more variables to predict scores on another variable called the criterion, can be applied in the analysis of semantic interaction. In an unpublished cross-cultural study Tanaka (1960) used a multiple regression equation to find the degree to which the meanings of qualifier/noun compounds could be linearly predicted from the meanings of their components, taking the qualifier and noun values as the independent variables and the compound as the dependent variable. Four translation-equivalent nationality concepts (qualifiers such as AMERICAN or JAPANESE), five translation-equivalent common nouns (such as WOMEN or ART) and their 20 translation-equivalent combinations were rated on a translation-equivalent 12-scale form semantic differential by culturally heterogeneous subject groups, American and Japanese.

Factor analysis of the data yielded four very similar factors across the two groups—identifiable as *pleasantness, industriousness, potency,* and *activity*—and four composite scores were computed for each concept within each of the subject groups.[5] Out of 80 (20 concepts $\times$ 4 factors) multiple R's computed over the subjects for each of the compound/composite-score combinations within each subject group, roughly 70% for the Americans and 55% for the Japanese, were found to be significant beyond the .05 level. In other words, the qualifier and noun values used as the independent

[5] For the details of this cross-cultural factor analysis see Tanaka (1962).

variables proved to predict the compound values used as the dependent variable better than chance in a majority of cases both within the Japanese and within the American group.

With respect to the regression weights assigned to the qualifiers and nouns, 51 out of 80 comparisons for the American and 52 for the Japanese were found to be greater for the qualifier than for the noun. The relative "adjectival dominance" in semantic interaction, which had been reported by Osgood, Suci, and Tannenbaum (1957), was shown both in the Japanese and in the American groups, although an entirely different method was used. In other words, the meaning of the compound could be better predicted by the meaning of the qualifier than by the meaning of the noun.

Subsequently, using colors and line-forms as the independent variables to predict the dependent variable, judgments of color-form combinations, Tanaka (1963) obtained basically similar results from Japanese and Finnish subjects. It was then demonstrated that the obtained meanings of compounds could be linearly predicted with high accuracy from a weighted composite of the obtained meanings of their color and form components, and this was true both across the compounds and across individual subjects differing in language and culture. Again, evidence of the relative "adjectival dominance" was shown to hold similarly across both groups in the sense that color terms were always "adjectival" and form terms "nominal" when the two are combined in nominal phrases in the languages of the Japanese and Finnish under investigation. The colors were found to be better predictors than the forms in roughly two thirds of the total comparisons in each group.

Multiple Correlations and Regression Weights in the Japanese/Finnish Political Stereotype Study. Data obtained from Japan in 1961 and 1966 and from Finland in 1961, with respect to the cross-cultural study of political stereotypes, were analyzed by the multiple-regression method. The purpose of this analysis was to determine the extent to which the meanings of complex compounds can be linearly predicted from the meaning of the nationality and the political concepts put into interaction and to arrive at the relative weights of the components in that linear prediction.

Four separate analyses were computed within each of the three (1961-Finnish, 1961-Japanese, and 1966-Japanese) subject groups, each based on the group means. *First,* we were interested in learning whether such predictions were possible from our data as a whole. Consequently, multiple correlations and regression weights (standardized) were computed for each factor dimension over 25 (5 nationality concepts × 5 political concepts) combinations for the Finns and over 20 (4 nationality concepts × 5 political concepts) combinations for the Japanese, using the composite scores for the nationality and the political concept as independent variables to predict the dependent variable, the composite score of their compound. In addition, $1 - R^2$ was computed to determine the proportion of variation in compound scores which is independent of variation in component scores and so must be attributed to other sources of variation. This measure indicates the magnitude of "noise" that may accrue from many sources unrelated to the present prediction system, such as "incredulity." The results are summarized in Table 12. In *evaluation* it is clearly seen that all the

Table 12 Multiple Regression Analysis for All Compounds, by Factors and Subject Groups

	Evaluation			Dynamism			Familiarity		
	1961-F	1961-J	1966-J	1961-F	1961-J	1966-J	1961-F	1961-J	1966-J
R	.92†	.91†	.90†	.74†	.96†	.95†	.86†	.51	.63*
$1 - R^2$	.15	.18	.20	.46	.09	.10	.26	.74	.59
B_A	.79	.14	.29	.81	.96	.94	.61	.50	.61
B_N	.70	.81	.85	.11	−.31	.13	.19	.12	.18

Notes. 1. $N = 25$ for the Finnish and $N = 20$ for the Japanese.
2. Figures with * are significant beyond the .05 level and those with † are significant beyond the .01 level by F-test.
3. B_A indicates regression weights for nationality (adjectival) concepts, whereas B_N suggests those for political (nominal) concepts.

multiple correlations are high and only less than 20% of the variance is accounted for by the unrelated "noise" sources similarly in all the three groups. We have evidence that the *evaluative* meanings of the compounds are highly predictable, given the *evaluative* meanings of nationality and political concepts. The high predictability is attributable, however, to the fact that larger weights are assigned to adjectival nationality concepts than to political noun concepts in the Finnish group, whereas larger weights are assigned to nominal concepts than to qualifying concepts in both Japanese groups. In other words, the *evaluative* meanings of the compounds can be better predicted from those of the nationality concepts for the Finns than from those of the political concepts for the Japanese. On *dynamism* multiple correlations were high in the Japanese groups but somewhat lower in the Finnish. In the latter case nearly 50% of the variance was accounted for by unknown sources of noise. It was also shown that the regression weights assigned to nationality concepts were greater than those assigned to political concepts. This was true for all groups. Thus, regardless of whether the compounds are *dynamic* or *static*, they can be predicted from the meanings of their qualifier components better than from those of their nominal components.

In *familiarity* an interesting phenomenon was noted. Despite evidence of the relative "adjectival dominance" in each group in terms of the greater regression weights associated with qualifying components than with nominal components, multiple correlations for the two Japanese groups were low. The correlation was not significant even at the .05 level in the 1961 group, and as much as 75% variance remained unaccounted for by the two independent variables alone in this case. To the extent that people hold a unique "idiosyncratic" image of certain cognitive events the low correlations should be taken for granted; for example, even if two components put into interaction (e.g., COMMUNIST CHINA and NUCLEAR TESTINGS) are *familiar,* their compound (i.e., COMMUNIST CHINESE NUCLEAR TESTINGS) might not necessarily be viewed as *familiar.* In fact, it was an *unfamiliar* or even *"incredible"* cognitive event for most Japanese in 1961. Under such a condition it is quite likely that the independent variables fail to predict the dependent variable with reasonable accuracy. From this point of view the result obtained in the 1961 Finnish group may be considered as a case of "lucky coincidence" in which the selected combinations of both component and compound concepts used in our study happened to permit accurate predications.

Second, we are interested in determining whether the meanings of the compounds could be accurately predicted from their components if we "sort" the compounds by nationality. In other words, if we take the five AMERICA-related compounds, can we expect that the meanings of these compounds would vary as lawfully as those of their components vary? To answer this question multiple correlations and regression weights were computed for each of the five groups of the common nationality-related compounds over 15 (5 nominal concepts $\times$ 3 factors) "observations." This analysis was not made for the Finland-related compounds in the Japanese groups because of lack of data. The results are shown in Table 13. Except for 3 of the 13 comparisons, the multiple correlations are high, leaving the less than 25% variance unexplained. With respect to the low predictability index, however, the magnitude of the "noise" in predictions seems to increase when the Japanese judge the JAPAN-related compounds and the Finns, the FINLAND-related. Although there is no way of generalizing this puzzling trend from our data alone, it seems quite conceivable that somewhat more discrete stereotyped images, unique to each of the interacting components and the compound, would generally prevent accurate linear predictions. It is assumed that both the Japanese and the Finns have sufficient but discrete information about cognitive events associated

Table 13   Multiple Regression Analysis, by Nationality Concepts and by Subject Groups

	America			Soviet Union			Communist China		
	1961-F	1961-J	1966-J	1961-F	1961-J	1966-J	1961-F	1961-J	1966-J
R	.91†	.86†	.92†	.92†	.89†	.93†	.88†	.87†	.95†
$1 - R^2$	.17	.26	.16	.15	.21	.14	.23	.25	.10
B_A	1.18	.95	.41	.97	.61	.73	.74	.43	.69
B_N	.52	.86	.68	.20	.48	.43	.56	.56	.43

	Japan			Finland		
	1961-F	1961-J	1966-J	1961-F	1961-J	1966-J
R	.91†	.76*	.76*	.73*	...	...
$1 - R^2$	.18	.43	.42	.47	...	...
B_A	.93	.58	.56	.68	...	...
B_N	.54	.60	.61	.70	...	...

Notes. 1. $N = 15$ for the Finnish and for the Japanese.

2. Figures with * are significant beyond the .05 level and those with † are significant beyond the .01 level by F-test.

3. B_A indicates regression weights for nationality (adjectival) concepts, whereas B_N suggests those for political (nominal) concepts.

with their own countries, and so it would not be so surprising if they held some unique "incongruent" conception of a specific, complex cognitive event, quite independent of their conception of its components. In connection with the regression weights the previously noted "adjectival dominance" is seen in 8 of 12 comparisons.

Third, our interest also lies in determining whether the meanings of the compounds could be predicted from their components if we "sort" the compounds by nominal concepts. To examine this problem multiple correlations and regression weights were computed for each of the five groups of compounds each containing the same nominal concept as a component, over 15 (5 qualifying concepts $\times$ 3 factors) observations in the Finnish group and over 12 (4 qualifying concepts $\times$ 3 factors) observations in the Japanese. The results shown in Table 14 clearly indicate that all the correlations are significant and thus all predictions are reasonably successful, although those for NUCLEAR TESTINGS- and FOREIGN POLICY-related concepts in the Finnish group and FOREIGN POLICY-related concepts in the 1961 Japanese group are somewhat poorer. By inspection of the regression weights nationality concepts clearly appear to be the better predictors for those concepts related to GOVERNMENT, PEOPLE, and FOREIGN POLICY. It seems that the judgments of these complex

A Study of National Stereotypes

Table 14   Multiple Regression Analysis by Nouns and Subject Groups

	Government			People			Nuclear Testings		
	1961-F	1961-J	1966-J	1961-F	1961-J	1966-J	1961-F	1961-J	1966-J
	.92†	.95†	.86†	.94†	.92†	.97†	.64*	.80†	.85†
$1 - R^2$	.16	.10	.26	.12	.16	.05	.59	.36	.29
B_A	.86	.81	.77	.75	.93	1.01	.38	.16	.19
B_N	−.92	.37	.32	−.41	.12	.16	.41	.76	.77

	Foreign Policy			Military Strength		
	1961-F	1961-J	1966-J	1961-F	1961-J	1966-J
R	.66*	.75*	.91†	.94†	.91†	.94†
$1 - R^2$	.57	.43	.18	.12	.16	.12
B_A	.52	.58	.68	.83	.50	.51
B_N	.29	.34	.41	.51	.65	.65

Notes. 1. $N = 15$ for the Finnish and $N = 12$ for the Japanese.

2. Figures with * are significant beyond the .05 level and those with † are significant beyond the .01 level by F-test.

3. B_A indicates regression weights for nationality (adjectival) concepts, whereas B_N suggests those for political (nominal) concepts.

concepts tend to depend heavily on the judgments of the nations associated with them. On the other hand, the regression weights are obviously higher for the nominal concepts than for the nationality concepts with respect to NUCLEAR TESTINGS and even more so in the two Japanese groups. Presumably because of their first-hand knowledge of nuclear hazards, including Hiroshima and Nagasaki, and their high sensitivity toward any such nuclear disasters, the Japanese discount the meanings of nationality concepts in semantic interaction. The meaning of NUCLEAR TESTINGS thus becomes the major determinant of the related complex concepts. A similar trend can also be noted for MILITARY STRENGTH: the meanings of the complex concepts are to a greater extent determined by the meaning of MILITARY STRENGTH than by the meanings of the nationality concepts. On the other hand, the meanings of the nationality concepts contribute more to the meanings of the related compounds in the Finns. We maintain that these results are quite consistent with the strong anti-nuclear-weapon, antiwar sentiments that are known to have existed in Japan since the end of World War II. They would also seem to reflect the unique culture-bound, semantic "stickiness" which is similar to what Osgood, Suci, and Tannenbaum (1957) termed "evaluative stickiness"— resistance to change of concepts with strong evaluative loadings. In the present analysis the results seem to indicate that the notion can be extended to other factor dimensions, although they support the findings by Osgood, Suci, and Tannenbaum, which emphasized the occurrence of this phenomenon on the evaluation dimension.

Fourth, and last, we speculate that the meanings of nationality concepts should show lawful variations, contingent on the variations in the meanings of the concepts associated with them. In other words, inasmuch as JAPANESE GOVERNMENT, JAPANESE PEOPLE, etc., are representative of certain aspects characteristic of JAPAN as a whole, we have good reason to expect that the meanings of these complex concepts related to Japan might not be entirely independent of the meanings of JAPAN itself and vice versa. This hypothesis can be empirically tested by a statistical design in which, for example, the evaluative meanings of JAPAN can be systematically compared with the evaluative meaning of JAPANESE GOVERNMENT, JAPANESE PEOPLE, JAPANESE NUCLEAR TESTINGS, JAPANESE FOREIGN POLICY, and JAPANESE MILITARY STRENGTH. We thus took the composite scores of the five compounds as independent variables to predict the composite scores of the corresponding nationality concepts and computed multiple correlations and regression weights across the three factor dimensions and over five nationalities in the Finnish group and across the three factors and over four nationalities less Finland in the two Japanese groups. It is clear from the results shown in Table 15 that all the correlations are high, leaving less than 5% variance

Table 15   Multiple Regression Analysis, by Subject Groups

	1961-F	1961-J	1966-J
R	.97†	.98†	.99†
$1 - R^2$	.05	.05	.03
$B_{GOVERNMENT}$	$-.10$	$-.35$	$-.49$
B_{PEOPLE}	.84	.36	.61
$B_{NUCLEAR\ TESTINGS}$	.11	$-.79$	$-.32$
$B_{FOREIGN\ POLICY}$	.11	1.30	.46
$B_{MILITARY\ STRENGTH}$	.28	.28	.22

Notes. 1. $N = 15$ for the Finnish and $N = 12$ for the Japanese.
   2. Figures with † are significant beyond the .01 level by *F*-test.

unexplained in each case. We have evidence here that the meanings of the nationality concepts as a whole can be predicted nearly perfectly from the meanings of the five "related" concepts. The high degree of predictability, however, is attributable to different sources in different groups. In the Finnish group it is almost exclusively attributable to PEOPLE, in the 1961 Japanese group, to FOREIGN POLICY and inversely to NUCLEAR TESTINGS, and in the 1966 Japanese group, to PEOPLE and FOREIGN POLICY and inversely to GOVERNMENT. We speculate that these differences among the three groups in the relative importance assigned to the predictors would reflect at least some important aspects of the subjects' real-life cognitive experience unique to each group. In retrospection, the Japanese subjects used in the 1961 experiment are assumed to have gone through what is known in the current Japanese history as the 1960 Anti-U.S.-Japanese-Security-Treaty Movement in which several hundreds of thousands of Japanese protested against the U.S.-Japanese military alliance, the American military installations in Japan, and American nuclear experiments. The movement led to the cancellation of the late President Eisenhower's trip to Japan. Japan in 1961 was trying politically, diplomatically, and economically to emerge as an independent nation from under the powerful U.S. umbrella. That FOREIGN POLICY and NUCLEAR TESTINGS were the major predictors of the images of nations in the 1961 Japanese group does not seem to be a mere chance occurrence but a rather faithful projection of the general psychological milieu present at that time among the Japanese. To put it in another way, the relative weights of the predictors might suggest a specific cognitive frame of reference according to which the Japanese judged the images of the nations in 1961. The impact of this political excitement faded away as time passed, and so we find the 1966 Japanese and 1961 Finnish groups displaying a fairly compatible pattern with respect to the relative importance of the predictors, despite differences in culture and time of experiment. In summary, it is clearly shown that the images of nations can be predicted from the images of the related political concepts with high accuracy, and yet the relative importance assigned to each predictor varies as the groups vary. We hold that such variations in regression weights would in some way reflect real-life cognitive experience of the subjects, although much is left for future studies.

Evidence for Subject/Scale Interaction

We have reviewed evidence so far for the two major areas of cognitive interaction—the concept/scale and concept/concept interaction in perceiving national stereotypes. In each area we have limited ourselves to those problems uniquely relevant to the affective meaning system. With this limitation, however, many empirical studies are found to offer evidence that various complex cognitive interactions are by no means random but generally consistent through time and across cultures. The consistency of such interactions and their cross-cultural generality were illustrated particularly with regard to the first two areas.

It will be an oversimplification, however, if we totally disregard what may be called the subject/scale interaction, the interaction between subject samples and scale samples. Many examples of this sort are quoted in Tanaka, Oyama, and Osgood (1963), Tanaka and Osgood (1965) and Tanaka (1967a). Table 5 of the present chapter also displays a clear case of subject/scale interaction; for example, a volatility scale, *immoral-moral,* is highly associated with *excitable-calm* and *changeable-constant* in every Japanese group, as if *excitable* and *changeable* nations implied something *immoral* to the Japanese. For the Germans, however, *immoral-moral* appears to constitute an independent criterion of judgment, loading alone on the *morality* factor. The loading of *tender-tough* and *happy-sad* are only secondary on the *morality* factor. *Insensitive-sensitive* also displays a clear interaction with subjects. In each of the four Japanese groups it is a *development* scale that highly correlates to *naïve-sophisticated,* whereas it is a *pleasantness* scale that highly correlates with *unpleasant-pleasant* for the Germans. A sensitive nation, therefore, may mean a *sophisticated, proud, active,* and *quick* nation to the Japanese, whereas it may mean a *pleasant, agreeable,* and *sociable* nation to the Germans. We assume that such scales as *moral-immoral* and *sensitive-insensitive,* interacting with the subject samples, happen to tap the culturally unique temperament, sensitivity, or criterion of values held by subjects.

Further evidence of subject/scale interaction was reported by Tanaka (1965b) in his cross-cultural study of national stereotypes. First, an *N* of 36 Japanese and 32 American college-graduate subjects rated a total of 29 complex national stereotypic concepts such as AMERICAN WOMEN or JAPANESE PRESS on a 12-scale-form semantic differential constructed in the subjects' respective language. The 12 scales and the 29 concepts used in this study are listed in Appendix 4 of this chapter. The data were then subjected to a centroid factor analysis. The semantic structure of the Japanese and Americans as a group was found to be similar across the two groups (cf. Tanaka, 1962). Subsequently, scale intercorrelations were computed over an *N* of 30 concepts for each of the 36 Japanese and the 32 American subjects. Then a total of 68 scale-intercorrelation matrices was correlated across corresponding cells, the resultant 68×68 subject-intercorrelation matrix was subjected to a principal axis analysis, and the extracted factors were varimax-rotated. The first unrotated factor was found to account for 77% of the total variance, all Japanese and American subjects loading high on it. This is a clear indication that all 68 subjects used the 12 scales similarly. It should be noted that

Table 16　First Two Varimax-Rotated Principal-Axis Subject
Factors of Combined Japanese and American Subjects

Japanese Subjects			American Subjects		
Subjects	Factor I	Factor II	Subjects	Factor I	Factor II
F	**.73**	.28	F	.51	**.66**
F	**.78**	.37	F	.43	**.55**
F	.49	**.77**	F	.45	**.77**
F	**.66**	**.57**	F	.48	**.64**
F	**.59**	**.69**	F	.39	.54
F	**.77**	.34	F	.36	**.77**
F	**.79**	.34	F	.48	.40
F	**.67**	.37	F	**.55**	.53
F	**.63**	.31	F	.41	**.65**
F	**.67**	.28	F	.46	**.61**
M	**.62**	.48	F	.50	**.61**
M	**.73**	.44	F	.33	.40
M	**.72**	.49	M	.41	**.79**
M	.48	**.74**	M	.51	.48
M	**.63**	.54	M	.41	**.81**
M	**.61**	**.61**	M	.54	.43
M	**.67**	.36	M	.21	**.86**
M	**.67**	.54	M	**.57**	**.58**
M	**.76**	.33	M	.29	**.82**
M	**.69**	.40	M	.36	**.85**
M	**.80**	.19	M	.47	.36
M	**.68**	.41	M	.40	.36
M	**.79**	.22	M	.40	**.75**
M	**.73**	.53	M	.23	**.86**
M	**.78**	.51	M	.41	**.62**
M	**.65**	.24	M	.52	.50
M	**.58**	.48	M	**.64**	**.59**
M	**.60**	**.61**	M	.41	.75
M	**.74**	.28	M	.32	**.76**
M	**.67**	.43	M	.14	**.89**
M	**.72**	.49	M	.38	**.63**
M	**.65**	**.62**	M	.47	.52
M	**.69**	.39			
M	**.62**	**.55**	Per cent TV	23	21
M	**.67**	.43			
M	**.67**	.28			

Notes. 1. Bold figures indicate factor coefficients greater than /.55/.
　　2. M indicates a male subject, F, a female subject.
　　3. Reprinted from Tanaka & Iwamatsu (1968b).

172

this is true, despite the fact that differences in culture, language, and sex were included. On the other hand, inspection of the rotated data, displayed in Table 16, demonstrated that Factor I (23% total variance) can be termed a Japanese factor, a majority of the Japanese and a few American loading high on it, whereas Factor II (21% total variance) can be called an American factor, on which a majority of the Americans and a few Japanese loaded high. In order to ascertain the extent to which each factor is unique to one of the two cultural groups, Mann-Whitney U tests were employed on the rotated data. The U test results clearly demonstrated that the Japanese subjects on Factor I and the Americans on Factor II do indeed load significantly ($p < .001$) higher than subjects in the other cultural group. These results confirm the assumption that despite the great extent of over-all similarity in semantic structure between the Japanese and Americans as a group (Tanaka, 1962) there are still significant differences cross-culturally in the structures of individual subject spaces.

How consistent is semantic structure across different subjects? The foregoing subject factor analytic results indicate that the consistency of subjects' semantic structure is reasonably high across both the Japanese and the Americans but sill higher within than between the cultural boundaries. To focus further on this question, the semantic structures of each subject were first examined and then compared across subjects. Thus the 12×12 scale intercorrelation matrix for each of the 68 (36 Japanese and 32 Americans) subjects was factored by the principal component method and the extracted factors varimax-rotated. Inspection of the rotated data demonstrated clearly that subjects use certain sets of scales quite consistently; for instance, *pleasant-unpleasant* and *beautiful-ugly, thick-thin, large-small* and *heavy-light,* and *active-passive, fast-slow,* and *powerful-powerless* tend to cling together in spite of subjects' different cultural origins and sex. On the other hand, some scales were found to display clear interaction with subjects: for example, the *quiet-noisy* scale is usually associated with *fast-slow* and *beautiful-ugly* among the majority of the Japanese, whereas it is related to *small-large* and *powerless-powerful* among the majority of the Americans. In fact, there are few Japanese who used *quiet-noisy* in association with *small-large* or *powerless-powerful,* whereas only a few Americans associated it with *beautiful-ugly.* Variations in the subjects' use of this scale appear to be greater across than within the cultural groups.

Table 17 summarizes the results obtained from the 68 separate scale-factor analyses for individual subjects. In summarizing the results the following procedures were taken. For each subject factor coefficients of each scale on different factors were compared in such a way that we can find what may be termed "affectively synonymous" relations among scales; for instance, one Japanese subject used *ugly-beautiful* and *unpleasant-pleasant*

Table 17   Affectively Synonymous Relations among the 12 Semantic
Differential Scales in Japanese and American Subjects

	1	2	3	4	5	6	7	8	9	10	11	12
1. Ugly-beautiful		1	1	27	1	0	5	0	6	4	0	14
2. Thick-thin	7		17	2	32	3	2	24	3	6	25	4
3. Active-passive	1	4		0	14	15	7	20	5	6	20	7
4. Unpleasant-pleasant	30	6	2		2	3	9	0	4	5	0	8
5. Light-heavy	4	23	7	3		3	2	23	4	7	24	5
6. Slow-fast	1	1	20	0	3		20	6	6	11	6	13
7. Undemocratic-democratic	11	1	4	11	3	3		2	4	7	3	11
8. Powerful-powerless	1	6	20	1	8	17	3		5	7	24	1
9. Industrious-lazy	1	2	16	1	1	13	5	13		16	0	8
10. Foolish-wise	10	3	9	12	3	5	9	5	16		5	7
11. Large-small	5	23	8	5	25	4	1	11	3	3		2
12. Quiet-noisy	7	11	8	7	11	11	2	13	7	9	14	

Notes. 1. Figures above diagonal represent Japanese data; figures below diagonal represent American data.

2. Bold figures indicate frequencies greater than 55% of *S*s in each cultural group.

3. Directions of association among scales are not indicated in the table.

4. Frequencies of scale use, independent of any other scales, are not shown in the table.

5. Reprinted from Tanaka & Iwamatsu (1968b).

as "affectively synonymous" scales, since these two scales and these two alone load highly on a factor. Similar "affectively synonymous" scale relations were sought on other factors for the same subject. Finally, these relations were tallied separately for 36 Japanese and 32 American subjects.

Table 17 clearly shows that there are two kinds of scale; those that are definitely less susceptible to interaction with subjects and those that are definitely more susceptible to interaction with subjects. Note, for example, that the *ugly-beautiful* and *unpleasant-pleasant* scales appear together for 27 of the 36 Japanese and in 30 of the 32 Americans tested—clear evidence that the use of these two scales is stable across subjects differing in sex and culture. On the other hand, scales such as *industrious-lazy* or *foolish-wise* show no such clear, consistent synonymous relations with any other scales, reflecting great cross-subject variations. Furthermore, some more exceptional cases of subject/scale interaction were noted, although they are not specified in the table. One is known as "factorial nuance reversal" (cf. Tanaka, Oyama, & Osgood, 1963). In the present case many subjects in both cultural groups tended to associate *industrious-lazy* with *wise-foolish*. A few Japanese and Americans, however, used the *industrious-lazy* scale in association with *foolish-wise,* thus totally reversing the direction of association. For a majority of Japanese and American subjects being *industrious* is seen as being *wise,* but for a minority of subjects, both Japanese and American, it is seen as being *foolish.* Next many subjects in both groups used certain scales entirely independently of any other scales; for example, 6 of 36 Japanese used the *industrious-lazy* scale as an independent criterion of judgments, it and it alone loading highly on a semantic factor. Similarly, 9 of 32 Americans used the *undemocratic-democratic* scale with no association whatsoever with any other scale.

In summary, the foregoing analyses of the semantic spaces of individual subjects clearly confirm that individual differences in semantic structures do indeed exist, although we also have evidence of the over-all consistency of such spaces. The reported variations in these spaces may suggest that somewhat different sets of scales are serving as indicants of semantic factors for different individuals. Such variations seem to be somewhat greater across subjects with different cultural origins than across subjects with culturally homogeneous backgrounds.

Summary and Conclusions

Cross-cultural studies were reported to examine the generality of cognitive mechanisms, which operate in perceiving national stereotypes. Cognitive interaction was discussed with regard to three general areas—that is, concept/scale interaction, interaction among cognitive elements, and subject/scale interaction. First, over-all cross-cultural generality was demonstrated along with cross-concept uniqueness. With respect to the cross-concept uniqueness, it was found that the earlier Osgood-Ware personality factors nearly completely decompose and coalesce into a new set of political differential factors. The political differential factors were found to be similar across two culturally heterogeneous groups. These factors are similar across cultural groups and are almost equally well defined by both, despite differences in language, culture, sex, and concept orders. Second, it was demonstrated that laws of cognitive interaction hold universally for various cognitive elements put into interaction, in spite of differences in the concept class sampled and the language/culture base of subjects doing the judging. On the other hand, it was also shown that somewhat different semantic structures are needed to account for the judgments of different subjects. Variations in the spaces of individual subjects seem to be greater across than within the cultural groups. Here we have evidence, for a culturally universal framework of political judgments, within which there is variation, with more between- than within-cultures variation.

The results of the studies reported, however, indicate that the effect of interaction between the scale sample and the subject sample is relatively small in the determination of semantic structure. Furthermore, Levin's (1963) re-examination of the Ware-Osgood data on the personality differential, employing the three-mode factor analysis developed by Tucker (1966), also suggests that variance accounted for by the subject variables in the semantic space is minimal, compared with variance explained by the scale variables and variance accounted for by the concept variables. Thus we may generally hold that greater generality operates across different cultures than does within-culture uniqueness in our cognitive system.

Appendix 1   POLDI-I Scales and Concepts

Scales

01. Familiar-unfamiliar
02. Active-passive
03. Undemocratic-democratic
04. Weak-strong
05. Moral-immoral
06. Logical-intuitive
07. Unique-typical
08. Calm-excitable
09. Loved-hated
10. Tender-tough
11. Proud-humble
12. Unpredictable-predictable
13. Fast-slow
14. Reputable-disreputable
15. Subjective-objective
16. Unusual-usual
17. Tense-relaxed
18. Sociable-solitaly
19. Sensitive-insensitive
20. Intangible-tangible
21. Unwholesome-wholesome
22. Rational-irrational
23. Individualistic-regular
24. Emotional-unemotional
25. Extroverted-introverted
26. Sophisticated-naive
27. Small-large

Concepts

01. Japan
02. Poland
03. Afghanistan
04. Communist China
05. Turkey
06. France
07. East Germany
08. India
09. Holland
10. North Korea
11. Lebanon
12. Greece
13. Finland
14. South Vietnam
15. New Zealand
16. Sweden
17. Venezuela
18. Ethiopia
19. North Vietnam
20. Mexico
21. Nigeria
22. West Germany
23. Yugoslavia
24. Thailand
25. Algeria
26. South Korea
27. Iran
28. Formosa
29. Italy
30. Cuba
31. U.S.S.R.
32. United States

Appendix 2   POLDI-II Scales and Concepts

Scales

01. Big-little	02. Familiar-unfamiliar
03. Moral-immoral	04. Calm-excitable
05. Tender-tough	06. Proud-humble
07. Predictable-unpredictable	08. Tense-calm
09. Solitary-sociable	10. Sensitive-insensitive
11. Sophisticated-naive	12. Unpleasant-pleasant
13. Pretty-ugly	14. Happy-sad
15. Strong-weak	16. Deep-shallow
17. Quick-slow	18. Active-passive
19. Agreeable-unagreeable	20. Heavy-light
21. Changeable-constant	22. Impetuous-quiet

Concepts

01. Japan	02. Poland
03. Afghanistan	04. Communist China
05. Turkey	06. India
07. Holland	08. Lebanon
09. Greece	10. Finland
11. Sweden	12. England
13. Brazil	14. Union of South Africa
15. Egypt	16. Australia
17. Indonesia	18. Venezuela
19. Mexico	20. Nigeria
21. Yugoslavia	22. Ghana
23. Thailand	24. Iran
25. Formosa	26. Italy
27. Cuba	28. U.S.S.R.
29. United States	30. France
31. West Germany	32. East Germany

Appendix 3   Political Stereotype Scales and Concepts

Scales

01. Beautiful-ugly	02. Dark-light
03. Relaxed-tense	04. Bad-good
05. Rare-common	06. Slow-fast
07. Unpleasant-pleasant	08. Wise-foolish

Appendix 3 (continued)

09. Weak-strong
11. Civil-government
13. Intangible-tangible
15. Thin-thick
17. Simple-complex
19. Sturdy-fragile
21. Wholesome-unwholesome
23. Small-large
25. Unpredictable-predictable

10. Far-near
12. Lazy-industrious
14. Moral-immoral
16. Undemocratic-democratic
18. Irrational-rational
20. Static-dynamic
22. Easy-difficult
24. Peaceful-hostile
26. Familiar-unfamiliar

Concepts

FIVE NATIONALITY CONCEPTS
01. America
03. Communist China
*05. Finland

02. Soviet Union
04. Japan

FIVE POLITICAL CONCEPTS
06. Government
08. Nuclear testings
10. Military strength

07. People
09. Foreign policy

TWENTY-FIVE COMPOUND
CONCEPTS
11. American government
13. Communist Chinese nuclear
    testings
*15. Finnish military strength
17. Communist Chinese people
*19. Finnish foreign policy
21. Communist Chinese
    government
*23. Finnish nuclear testings
25. Soviet military strength
*27. Finnish people
29. Soviet foreign policy

*31. Finnish government
33. Soviet nuclear testings
35. Japanese military strength

12. Soviet people
14. Japanese foreign policy

16. Soviet government
18. Japanese nuclear testings
20. American military strength
22. Japanese people

24. American foreign policy
26. Japanese government
28. American nuclear testings
30. Communist Chinese military
    strength
32. American people
34. Communist Chinese

Notes. 1. Concepts with * were not used in the 1966 experiment. 2. A Latin square design was used in order to obtain the compound concepts.

Appendix 4   National Stereotype Scales and Concepts

Scales

01. Ugly-beautiful
02. Thick-thin
03. Active-passive
04. Unpleasant-pleasant
05. Light-heavy
06. Slow-fast
07. Undemocratic-democratic
08. Powerful-powerless
09. Industrious-lazy
10. Foolish-wise
11. Large-small
12. Quiet-noise

Concepts

01. Women
02. Japanese
03. Science
04. Chinese
05. Products
06. American
07. Arts
08. Russian
09. Press
10. Japanese women
11. Chinese science
12. American products
13. Russian arts
14. Japanese press
15. Chinese women
16. American science
17. Russian products
18. Japanese arts
19. Chinese press
20. American women
21. Russian science
22. Japanese products
23. Chinese arts
24. American press
25. Russian women
26. Japanese science
27. Chinese products
28. American arts
29. Russian press

CHAPTER SEVEN

Cognitive Structures and the Analysis of Values

HARRY C. TRIANDIS, KEITH M. KILTY,
A. V. SHANMUGAM, YASUMASA TANAKA, AND
VASSO VASSILIOU

In Part I of this book we discussed various cognitive forms that appear to be particularly important in the analysis of subjective culture. One form is the implication that ties one concept to another. The idea that if you have X then you have Y is basic to Western thought and may be significant in other settings. We decided, then, to explore the use of this cognitive form in two Western (United States and Greece) and two Eastern (India and Japan) cultures. We assumed that cultural influences are not only important to a determination of the content of categories but also to the subjective probabilities that one category is related to another. Such subjective probabilities are worthy of analysis; for example, when a particular individual sees a definite connection between the category OPEN OCCU-PANCY and the category SLUMS, the affect associated with SLUMS is transferred to OPEN OCCUPANCY (Peak, 1955; Rosenberg, 1956; Fishbein, 1961; Vroom, 1964). Thus analyses of the subjective connections among categories is relevant to (a) any analysis of the phenomenological field (McLeod, 1947), (b) analyses of cognitive structures and their relationship to affective responses (Rosenberg, 1956; Fishbein, 1961), and (c) the relationship between the phenomenal field and behavior (Vroom, 1964). Because such subjective probabilities are influenced by cultural factors (Triandis, 1964a, pp. 23–25), it is important to develop procedures for the study of these influences.

Deese (1966) has argued that the meaning of a word is given by the potential distributions of the responses to it. He takes the associations to a word, obtained by the usual method of one response per subject, as a sample of this distribution. He proposes that this sample defines a subset of the general meaning of the world and calls it the *associative meaning* of the word. Szalay and Brent (1967) have shown that cultural meanings of words may be obtained from analyses of the free verbal associations of subjects from different cultures.

Tanaka, Iwamatsu, and May (1968) have demonstrated a close correspondence between the *associative meaning* and the *affective meaning* of nation concepts. Using an associative index that measures "international discomfort" they found that when a nation is associated with discomfort-increasing events such as war or ideological conflict the affective meaning of that nation tends to be low on semantic differential evaluation and high on instability and *vice versa*.

Although free associations have much to recommend them in the analysis of meaning, naturalistic observations suggest that the full range of these associations is not involved when two people disagree about an issue; for example, if blacks and whites are asked to negotiate a variety of civil-rights issues in the laboratory, as done by Davis and Triandis (1965), they usually disagree only about the consequences of various negotiation agreements. Specifically, the concept OPEN OCCUPANCY was seen as leading to JUSTICE, EQUALITY, etc., by Negroes and to SLUMS, DEPRESSED PROPERTY VALUES, etc., by prejudiced whites. Thus, although OPEN OCCUPANCY may elicit a variety of associations, such as "brick houses" and "debate in the Senate," only a *limited set* of these associations appears in disagreements about this concept. Furthermore, Davis and Triandis (1965) have shown that analyses of the subjective *implications* of OPEN OCCUPANCY predict the behavior of naïve white subjects when they negotiate with Negro confederates on this issue.

Thus, if we are interested in studying cultural differences in the meaning of words so that we may observe the way in which people from different cultures resolve their conflict over issues involving these words, it seems more efficient to study *controlled-word associations,* rather than free-word associations. This chapter presents a method that allows the study of controlled-word associations.

In studying the meaning of words it is often desirable to make a distinction between the connotative meaning of a word and the denotative meaning of the same word. Osgood's semantic differential (Osgood, Suci, & Tannenbaum, 1957) is a widely used instrument for the measurement of connotative meaning. Results obtained with this instrument suggest that certain aspects of meaning escape measurement; for example, GOD and COCA-COLA have rather similar semantic differential profiles for certain kinds of people, that is, both concepts are "good," "powerful," and "active." Nevertheless, it is obvious that the two words mean something very different.

"It is clear on purely intuitive grounds that the concepts HERO and SUCCESS, which have similar semantic differential profiles, do not mean the same thing. It is, therefore, important for studies of the behavior of culturally heterogeneous groups to develop additional procedures for the measurement of similarity of concept meaning" (Forster, Triandis, & Osgood, 1964, p. 1).

Starting from this observation, Osgood and Triandis proceeded in two different directions. Osgood initiated his *semantic features analysis* (Osgood, 1970), which, when fully developed, is likely to be the most powerful technique for the measurement of denotative meaning. Triandis developed the present procedure, which is only a modification of the well-established free association procedures but which appears directly relevant for studies of subjective culture.

As stated above, the implications or consequences of a particular concept appear particularly relevant in an analysis of interpersonal conflict. However, a secondary source of irritation and disagreement among negotiators concerns the antecedents of a concept; for example, both labor and management may value INDUSTRIAL PEACE, but they see different events as leading to this desirable state of affairs. Labor may see "profit sharing" or the "Scanlon plan" as related to INDUSTRIAL PEACE, but management may see no connection between these concepts. Thus it appears worthwhile to examine not only the perceived consequences of a particular event or state of affairs but also the perceived antecedents of the event.

This chapter describes a new technique for the study of implicative relationships, called the "antecedent-consequent method," and data from the United States, Greece, India, and Japan that illustrate the use of this method in a description of differences in the meaning of concepts. To illustrate the method we studied the implicative relationships associated with 20 concepts. It also provides a procedure for the cross-cultural study of values.

Method

Samples. The samples were male students (upper level of high school or lower level of college). When we employ the word Americans, we mean residents of Illinois; the Phase I subjects were high school students in Rockford and the Phase II subjects were students at the University of Illinois. When we employ the word Greeks, we mean residents of Athens.

The Greek sample was taken from a representative sample of the population of Athens by sending interviewers back to interview further those males who gave "student" as their occupation in a previous interview. The sample of Indians consists of male students at the Agricultural University of Bangalore. Their language is Kannada, which is spoken by about 40 million people. When we used the word Indians, then, the reader should translate it into "Kannada-speaking residents of the State of Mysore, in Southern India, attending an urban university." Finally, the Japanese were students attending a number of universities in the Tokyo area. Most of them were from Gakushuin University, which is an upper class private university.

It is clear that the samples are not so equivalent as is desirable; for example, in social class the American and Greek samples are probably reasonably representative of the middle class in those countries, whereas the Indians and Japanese are probably more upper than middle class. It should be remembered, however, that in studying cross-cultural differences it is impossible to employ truly representative samples when a large number of responses per subject is required. Rather it is more economical to select homogeneous samples of known characteristics and to keep in mind, when interpreting the results, that the findings do not apply to the whole country but only to a specific sample. Certainly, to describe a country like India, which has 400 million people, 70 major languages, and all the major religions of the world, is beyond the scope of any research project.

Concepts. Twenty concepts were selected from a list of 100 words utilized by Osgood (1964) and his associates in the development of semantic differentials for different cultures. These words have the property that bilinguals from several cultures are able to translate them from English into their own languages, and different groups of bilinguals usually translate them correctly back into the original English. The selection of concepts from Osgood's list had the further advantage that the semantic differential profiles of these words, obtained from indigenously developed semantic differentials, were available as part of the *World Atlas of Affective Meanings* (Osgood, Jakobovits, & Miron, in preparation).

The 20 selected concepts were chosen because they covered a wide range of significant categories. They were also quite abstract and thus likely to allow for the discovery of cultural differences in values.

The following words were used:

Emotions: anger, courage, fear, and laughter.
Ambiguous political or individual concepts: freedom, peace.
Abstract philosophical: truth.

Social control: punishment.
Social disruption: crime.
Achievement: knowledge, power, progress, success, and wealth.
Nonachievement: death and defeat.
Basic social relations: love, respect, sympathy, and trust.

Instruments

PROCEDURE FOR PLASE I. The 20 concepts were translated into Greek, Kannada (southern India), and Japanese. A different group of bilinguals translated them back into English. Modifications in the translations were made when necessary. This method of double translation has been used throughout this project. They were then placed into sentences that approximated the following English format:

"If you have . . . , then you have ANGER."

The subjects supplied three fill-ins to such sentences for each of the 20 concepts. Thus a list of the antecedents of the 20 concepts was obtained. Similarly, the subjects were asked to fill in sentences in the following form:

"If you have ANGER, then you have . . ."

Again, the subjects supplied three responses for each of the 20 concepts, thus providing a list of "consequents" for the concepts.

A total of 100 males from each of the four cultures supplied a total of 6000 antecedent and 6000 consequent responses in each culture. The tabulation of the 6000 antecedents or consequents was made according to concept. Thus the 300 antecedents or consequents for each concept in each culture were tabulated in descending rank-order of frequency.

All these responses were then double translated and the English equivalents were shipped to Illinois. Inspection of the lists allowed judgments that followed three steps:

1. For each concept and each culture the 10 most frequent antecedents (*A*s) and the consequents (*C*s) were selected.

2. The 10 most frequent *A*s or *C*s for each concept were examined to determine if an *A* or *C* with a high frequency in one culture also had a high frequency in *one* other culture. Those antecedents (or consequents) that appeared in more than one culture were labeled "culture-common."

3. The process of comparison was continued until we had a list of five culture-common antecedent or consequent words for each of the 20 concepts. In addition, we developed lists of five "uniquely American," five "uniquely Greek," five "uniquely Indian," and five "uniquely Japanese" antecedents or consequents. Finally, five "hunch" words were selected be-

cause they represented an unusual point of view. These hunch words needed no specific frequency but appeared to be "interesting." One of the characteristics of the "hunch" *A*s or *C*s is that they were "theoretically interesting"; for example, there are disputes in anthropology concerning whether there are "guilt cultures" and "shame cultures." The implications of such disputes would be that the consequences of CRIME would be different. CRIME should be seen as leading to guilt or to shame with differential frequencies in these two types of culture.

To summarize: from the procedures adopted in Phase I we developed a list of 30 *A*s and 30 *C*s for each concept which consisted of five culture-common concepts, five concepts from each of the four cultures, and five "hunch" *A*s or *C*s.

PROCEDURE FOR PHASE II. The following instructions were used in this phase:

INSTRUCTIONS

We would like to learn what certain CONCEPTS mean to you. On the following pages you will find these words capitalized in a standardized sentence which you are to complete.

There will be two kinds of sentences on each page. The first will be like the following sample:

If there is ————, then there is MURDER.

Beneath each sentence will be six sets of five words each. Here is an example of one such set:

```
_____

1.
revenge         _____
hate               ×
insanity        _____
theft           _____
fear            _____

_____
```

In *each* set of five words you are to check the *one* which, in your opinion, *best* completes the sentence. As you can see in the sample, "hate" has been checked. What we are asking you for in the first sentence is what *goes before, precedes,* or *causes* the concept to come about.

Note that all five anternatives in the set are reasonable. We want you to pick the *best* one which you think *goes before, precedes,* or *causes* the concept to come about.

In the second sentence on each page we will ask you for the *result, consequence,* or *outcome* of the capitalized concept. The following is an example of this second kind of sentence:

If there is MURDER, then there is _____.

Again, beneath the sentence you will find six sets of *five* words each:

1.

imprisonment	
grief	×
execution	
disgust	
police	

Once more you are to check *one* of the five words in *each* set, as in the example above.

Please note again that all five words in the set are reasonable, but we are asking you to pick the *best* one which you think is a *result, consequence,* or *outcome* of the concept.

Please make sure that you check *one* of the words in *each* of the six sets; the one out of the five words you think is best. Work at a fairly high speed and try to give us your *best* "first impressions." But please do not be careless because we want your true impressions.

Thank you very much for your cooperation.

The format of the instrument is exemplified by showing the sheet for the antecedents and consequences of PROGRESS (Table 1).

It is intuitively obvious that the context of judgment will determine whether a particular *A* or *C* is chosen as the best *A* or *C*. Clearly, if a particular *A* is imbedded in a set of *A*s that is most inappropriate, it will be chosen by all subjects. For this reason we controlled the context. Each basic set of five words had the following characteristics: (a) it had one culture common, one American, one Greek, one Indian, and one Japanese *A* or *C*; (b) the frequencies of these *A*s or *C*s (obtained in Phase I) were approximately the same; (c) the order of presentation was varied systematically.

Ideally, the order of presentation of the words and of the six sets of five *A*s or five *C*s should have been randomized. However, the clerical work of mimeographing and assembling the instrument was formidable. We compromised by using only 18 different variations of the questionnaire.

The basic format of the questionnaire followed the arrangement shown in Table 2a.

Table 1

If there is _____, then there is PROGRESS.

	1.			2.			3.	
research	_____	knowledge	_____	study	_____
ambition	_____	ability	_____	education	_____
diligence	_____	willpower	_____	interested learning	_____
courage	_____	strength	_____	unity	_____
endeavor	_____	invention	_____	improvement	_____

	4.			5.			6.	
hard work	_____	money	_____	cooperation	_____
initiative	_____	drive	_____	friends	_____
peace	_____	luck	_____	foresight	_____
enthusiasm	_____	good conduct	_____	honesty	_____
seriousness	_____	thinking	_____	help from others	_____

If there is PROGRESS, then there is _____.

	1.			2.			3.	
success	_____	wealth	_____	glory	_____
achievement	_____	ability	_____	money	_____
well-being	_____	civilization	_____	improvement	_____
respect	_____	courage	_____	good name	_____
expansion	_____	increasing	_____	convenience	_____

	4.			5.			6.	
power	_____	knowledge	_____	scientific development	_____
inventions	_____	automation	_____	moral decline	_____
development	_____	satisfaction	_____	speed	_____
unfolding of intelligence	_____	sorrow	_____	friends	_____
affluence	_____	happiness	_____	thrill of deeds	_____

Table 2a   Arrangement of Antecedents *or* Consequents in the Basic Format of Phase II

Type of Word	Frequency of Word in Phase I					
	10–50	8–15	5–10	4–7	4–7	4–7
Culture-common	C1	C2	C3	C4	C5	H1
American	A1	A2	A3	A4	A5	H2
Greek	G1	G2	G3	G4	G5	H3
Indian	I1	I2	I3	I4	I5	H4
Japanese	J1	J2	J3	J4	J5	H5

Note. C = culture-common; A = American; G = Greek; I = Indian;
J = Japanese; H = hunch word.

The frequencies that head the columns of this table are intentionally overlapping. This allows us to place a word from a particular column into an adjacent column. Thus the 18 variations of the questionnaire could allow for manipulation of the context while keeping the frequencies approximately matched; for example, one of the formats was the one shown in Table 2b.

Table 2b Example of One Arrangement
of Antecedents or Consequents

A5	C4	I3	G2	J1	H3
J4	A4	C2	I1	G1	H5
G4	J5	A3	C3	I2	H1
C5	G5	J2	A1	C1	H4
I4	I5	G3	J3	A2	H2

Note that each column has one C, A, G, I, and J. The hunches always stayed in the same set but they were rotated. The frequencies in a set were about the same. In the form shown in Table 2b Columns 1 and 2 have words with frequencies of 4–7 (of course, there are more words to choose from in this frequency range than in the ranges with larger frequencies). Column 3 has words with frequencies of 5–15; Columns 4 and 5 have words with frequencies of 10 or more.

In addition to the six formats of the questionnaire, we developed three forms that contained a different set of words. Forms A, B, and C had the words shown in Table 3. All forms began with the word PROGRESS and ended with the word TRUTH.

The six formats and the three forms, then, made a total of 18 different questionnaires. Each questionnaire was given to about 20 Ss from each culture. A total of about 360 Ss per culture responded to Phase II, all of whom were male students. The task took about 45 minutes.

ANALYSIS OF PHASE II. The responses of the subjects to the 30 As and 30 Cs for each concept in each culture were summed. As can be seen from the description of the procedure, the concepts [except for the concepts PROGRESS and TRUTH which were present in all three of the forms (A, B, and C)] appeared in two of the three forms. Thus each concept appeared in two forms and six formats or 12 different questionnaires. The questionnaires were distributed to large classes of students and all variations of the questionnaire were handed out at the same time. By chance some of the 18 variations were taken by slightly more or slightly

Table 3   The Words Used in the Study
and the Forms (A, B, or C) in Which
They Were Placed

PROGRESS	A	B	C
LOVE		B	C
FEAR	A	B	
SYMPATHY		B	C
PEACE		B	C
DEFEAT	A	B	
TRUST	A	B	
KNOWLEDGE		B	C
CRIME		B	C
RESPECT		B	C
SUCCESS	A		C
PUNISHMENT	A	B	
FREEDOM	A		C
POWER	A	B	
DEATH	A		C
COURAGE	A	B	
WEALTH	A		C
ANGER	A		C
LAUGHTER	A		C
TRUTH	A	B	C

less than the intended 20 students per variation. If exactly 20 students had taken each of the questionnaires, each concept would have been responded to by 40 students. Since there are six formats of the context of the responses, we would have judgments by 240 students it we disregard the format. Since each of the students made six responses on the antecedent and six on the consequent side, there would be a total of $240 \times 6 = 1440$ responses to each concept. Examination of Tables 10 to 49 shows that the number of responses per culture ranged from 1100 to 1533. For the concepts PROGRESS and TRUTH the numbers ranged between 2086 and 2259 instead of the 2160 that would have been obtained if exactly 20 subjects had responded to the concepts.

Correlations Among the Cultures. To obtain an impression of the overall similarity in the obtained data from Phase II the frequencies recorded in Tables 10 to 48 were correlated across cultures. These correlations are based on a typical N of 30 (the number of As or Cs). Since there are four cultures, there are six possible correlations among them. Since there are 20 concepts there are 120 correlations based on the antecedents and 120 based on the consequents.

Results

Reliability. Since the instrument was designed to study cultural differences, test-retest reliability would provide an overestimate of the *needed* reliability. Data supplied by Haried (1969) show a test-retest reliability of .94. The needed reliability may be called intracultural reliability and is obtained across samples from within the same culture. Accordingly, the responses of the 180 male high school, 120 female high school, 139 male university, and 85 female university American students to five of the 20 concepts, chosen randomly, were employed to compute reliabilities. The correlations between the frequencies of the responses of the high school and college students for the five concepts are shown in Table 4. When

Table 4 Intracultural Reliabilities
(American high school versus American
college students)

Concept	Antecedents	Consequents
DEFEAT	.54	.88
KNOWLEDGE	.71	.62
LAUGHTER	.89	.82
RESPECT	.75	.71
WEALTH	.63	.82

these coefficients are converted to Z-scores, averaged and reconverted, a mean correlation of .76 is obtained. Since this is a lower bound of the intracultural reliability of the instrument, it appears that the instrument has sufficient reliability for cross-cultural comparisons.

Kilty did a number of additional studies with the above samples. He compared the responses of males and females, as well as male high school versus male college students, and examined the results among five forms, using the proportional Z-test (Ferguson, 1966, pp. 176–178). In this study he had five concepts, five sets per concept, and both antecedents and consequents. Thus he computed $5 \times 5 \times 5 \times 2 = 250$ Z-tests for each comparison. He found 93% of the Z-values to be nonsignificant (at $p < .05$). Thus there are no characteristic ways in which American males and females or high school and college students differ in their responses to this instrument.

Consistency Across Cultures. A set is defined here as the five responses from which a subject chooses one. Each concept has six sets of antecedents and six sets of consequents. There are six formats of the instrument. For every format we have a different arrangement of the words in each set. Therefore to keep everything controlled our cross-cultural comparisons must be made for each set and for each format. Since we have six sets and six formats, there are 36 chi-squares to be computed for each concept on the antecedent side and 36 on the consequent side; for example, consider the responses to the concept PROGRESS for a particular set by subjects in the four cultures (Table 5).

Table 5   Number of Subjects Choosing Each Antecedent of PROGRESS

Antecedent	Americans	Greeks	Indians	Japanese
Cooperation	10	10	7	2
Friends	4	6	7	5
Foresight	12	5	8	22
Honesty	6	4	11	11
Help from others	4	12	7	2

The Americans chose cooperation and foresight, the Greeks cooperation and help from others, the Indians honesty, and the Japanese foresight and honesty. We can conclude that there are cultural differences because the chi-square is significant at the .001 level.

Table 6 shows the distribution of the chi-square obtained from these analyses.

Table 6   Number of Significant Chi-squares

Format No.	Number of Chi-squares Significant at					Out of a Total of
	$p > .05$	$p < .05$	$p < .02$	$p < .01$	$p < .001$	
I	15	7	8	33	177	240
II	22	18	10	29	161	240
III	19	13	8	30	170	240
IV	16	12	7	34	170	239[a]
V	16	4	11	24	185	240
VI	12	17	5	37	169	240

[a] Insufficient marginal frequencies prevented the computation of one chi-square.

It is obvious that the overwhelming majority (93%) of the chi-squares is significant. Thus, although the majority of the within-culture chi-squares is nonsignificant, the majority of the across-cultures chi-squares is significant.

Correlations Among the Cultures. The 20 concepts times the six possible comparisons among the four cultures allowed for 120 comparisons based on the antecedents and an equal number based on the consequents. Table 7 shows the number of times the correlations between two cultures reached

Table 7 Number of Correlations Between the Four Cultures
that Reached Beyond the .05 Level of Significance
(antecedents above and consequents below diagonal)

	Americans	Greeks	Indians	Japanese
Americans	...	11	6	17 ⎫
Greeks	16	...	6	12 ⎬ 56
Indians	5	6	...	4 ⎭
Japanese	20	10	3	...
		60		Total: 116

the .05 level of significance. The maximum possible entry in Table 7 is 20 (the number of concepts). It can be seen that the American frequencies agreed with the Japanese frequencies to such an extent that 85% of the antecedent correlations and 100% of the consequent correlations were significant. Since one of the correlations in each cell of Table 7 is likely to be significant by chance, we can state that the Greeks are equally close to the Americans and the Japanese on the antecedent side and closer to the Americans on the consequent side than to any other culture. The Indians are the most remote from the other three cultures and equally far from the Americans and Greeks on both the antecedent and consequent sides.

Table 8 presents the same data, with a more stringent level of significance. The pattern of similarities among the cultures does not change.

It seems notable that 47% of the correlations are significant on the antecedent side and 50%, on the consequent side (Table 7).

A more detailed analysis of the kinds of concepts on which the cultures agreed revealed no major shifts, except that the Greeks and the Indians agreed closely on FREEDOM and PEACE and on these two concepts the Americans and the Japanese were particularly close.

Table 8   Number of Correlations Between the Four Cultures
that Reached Beyond the .01 Level of Significance
(antecedents above and consequents below diagonal)

	Americans	Greeks	Indians	Japanese
Americans	. . .	8	2	14 ⎫
Greeks	8	. . .	2	9 ⎬ 37
Indians	3	3	. . .	2 ⎭
Japanese	19	8	0	. . .
	41			Total: 78

On those concepts on which two cultures are in close agreement we
would expect no serious communication problems. On those concepts on
which the correlation is small or negative we would expect the maximum
difficulty in communication.

Relations Between Phases I and II. Do the subjects in each culture
prefer the *A*s or *C*s that their culture provided in Phase I? The answer
to this question is largely affirmative. We examined the percentages of the
times that members of a culture chose the *A*s and *C*s provided in Phase
I by other members of their own culture. If the choice were random, then
20% of the time they would have chosen the Phase I response that we
considered "culture unique" for their culture. Actually, they chose it 43%
of the time. (The six formats gave 44, 43, 41, 45, 41, and 44%, respectively.) The stability of these results is high; there is no doubt that the
cultures have "preferred antecedents or consequents" which they chose
over the *A*s and *C*s provided by the other cultures. In fact, examination
of the response patterns shows strikingly that the subjects tend to pick
either the culture common or the *A*s or *C*s of their own culture most of
the time. This implies that the *A*s and *C*s obtained in Phase I should be
similar to those obtained in Phase II.

This conclusion, however, is not entirely justified if we examine only
those *A*s or *C*s that were chosen significantly frequently in Phase II. In
Table 9a we traced the origin in Phase I of those *A*s that were significantly
frequently chosen by various samples in Phase II. The table is based on
five of the 20 concepts, chosen randomly. It is clear that only 50% of
the significant (Phase II) American antecedents were also emitted by
Americans in Phase I. For the other samples the percentages were Greeks
50, Indians 72.5, and Japanese 74.4. For the consequents these percentages were somewhat larger: Americans 77, Greeks 75, Indians 83, and
Japanese 71. In other words, the procedure in Phase II introduced "sugges-

tions" to members of each culture which they had not produced spontaneously in Phase I. In the matter of antecedents the Americans and the Greeks are the most "suggestible"; the Japanese the least "suggestible." On the other hand, in the matter of consequents the Americans were the most suggestible and the Indians, the least.

Table 9a   Phase I Origin of As Chosen Significantly Frequently in Phase II

Sample (in Phase II)	Origin in Phase I					
	Culture-Common	American	Greek	Indian	Japanese	Total
Americans	11	7	7	2	9	36
Greeks	5	2	9	4	8	28
Indians	7	5	3	14	0	29
Japanese	14	2	7	1	15	39
Total	37	16	26	21	32	

Table 9b   Phase I Origin of Cs Chosen Significantly Frequently in Phase II

Sample (in Phase II)	Origin in Phase I					
	Culture-Common	American	Greek	Indian	Japanese	Total
Americans	13	7	5	4	7	36
Greeks	8	4	13	3	0	28
Indians	7	1	0	8	2	18
Japanese	9	1	3	3	8	24
Total	37	13	21	18	17	

By looking at Tables 9a and 9b we can also tell which culture supplied the most attractive suggestions. We note that the Americans and Greeks were most susceptible to the Japanese suggested As and that the Americans were also susceptible to Japanese Cs. The Indians and the Japanese apparently are more idiosyncratic in choosing As and Cs, since they are less suggestible than the other cultures.

We conclude that Phase I and Phase II give similar, but not identical, results. The Phase II results, since they allow the subjects to consider a wider range of As and Cs, are probably the most interesting. The difference between Phase I and Phase II results might be conceived as the difference between recall and recognition. In Phase I something stored in the subject's cognitive system is strong enough to be recalled. In Phase II the subject is confronted with several potential responses and he chooses one because he recognizes its importance (or suitability).

The Main Analysis

For the main analysis we collapsed all 18 variations of the questionnaires and simply counted the frequencies of choice of each A and C. Since there are 30 As and 30 Cs for each concept, we simply tabulated the frequencies of choice of each A and C for each culture, as shown in Tables 10 to 49.

As mentioned earlier, the totals of the columns in these tables ranged from 1100 to 1533 for most concepts, except for the two that appeared in all three forms of the questionnaire, which had totals ranging from 2086 to 2259. By dividing those totals by 30 it is possible to obtain the mean frequency for any A or C. If the responses were random, most of the observed frequencies would be similar to these mean frequencies. By chi-square analysis it is possible to determine the limits of frequencies that are either significantly higher or lower than the corresponding mean frequency. We chose the .01 level of significance because with $p < .05$ and with 30 frequencies one or two would be significant by chance. We use boldface type for the frequencies that are significantly higher and italics for those significantly lower than the mean frequencies. These appear in the even numbered Tables 10 to 48. We also listed in Tables 11 to 49, in descending order of frequency, the As and Cs that appeared significantly more frequently than chance. Thus inspection of Tables 10 to 49 will give the reader an over-all glance at the main results.

The 20 concepts employed in the present study were also used by Osgood, Jakobovits, and Miron (in preparation) in the *Atlas of Affective Meaning*. They employed a short form of the semantic differential specially developed for each culture (see Osgood, 1964; Jakobovits, 1966). Since the semantic differential data were available for all the cultures studied in the present project, it was possible to include in Tables 11 to 49 (odd-numbered) a selected set of semantic differential indices.

These indices were obtained from Osgood et al. (in preparation) and consist of the evaluation, potency, and activity of each concept, the same information in standard score form relative to the way the subjects of a particular culture rated the 500 Atlas concepts (indices Z_E, Z_p, Z_A), ratings of the familiarity of each concept obtained from a "familiar-unfamiliar" semantic differential scale and "conflict indices" (Cn) that measure the extent of within-culture disagreement in the semantic differential ratings. High conflict indices imply a variety of points of view about concepts in the particular culture.

A Note on the Interpretation of Cultural Similarities and Differences. In the pages that follow there are discussions of cultural similarities and differences in the responses of subjects to a variety of concepts on both semantic differentials and the antecedent-consequent meaning instruments. First, we should remember that unless there is a substantial *similarity* in the obtained results we will be unable to determine whether the concepts have been properly translated across cultures. It is essential to have enough similarity to feel some assurance that the concepts have been properly translated. Second, in looking for cultural differences we must remember that a single statistical significant result *may* be due to a real difference or a translation difficulty. Thus we emphasize differences mostly when they are seen to occur in *several* logically interrelated antecedents or consequents rather than in a single antecedent or consequent. Single results may be important when a cultural interpretation of the results can be readily supplied. When such explanations are not available they may be used as "hypotheses for further research," but until they are anchored with some other set of empirical data their status must be considered uncertain. On the other hand, when some common theme emerges from the analysis, we can be reasonably certain that it is not random or due to translation difficulties.

Cultural Differences in the Meaning of Emotions

ANGER. The data that Osgood et al. (in preparation) collected on the semantic differential judgments of 500 concepts in 23 cultures shows that all four cultures evaluate ANGER negatively. The Greeks see this concept as low in activity but high in familiarity.

Examination of Table 11 suggests that the main themes of the antecedents of ANGER around the world are injury to self-esteem, frustration, and deviation from "correct" conditions. The Americans and Greeks correlated .41 ($p < .05$) and emphasized the first theme (*hate, injustice, insult, ridicule*) but also mentioned frustration (*jealousy*). The Indians were quite idiosyncratic and emphasized mostly frustration (*scolding, failure, enemies*) but also emphasized injury to self-esteem (*nickname, no patience*). The Japanese agree with the Americans (see Table 11) and emphasize the deviation from appropriate conditions (*betrayal, injustice, dissatisfaction, a lie*), injury to self-esteem (*insult*), and frustration (*jealousy*).

Especially interesting are the *A*s which have significantly high frequen-

Table 10 Frequencies of Antecedents and Consequents of ANGER

Antecedents	American	Greek	Indian	Japanese	Consequents	American	Greek	Indian	Japanese
Bad manners	13	64	26	38	Animosity	76	49	72	46
Bad temper	104	31	67	45	Break in relations	34	47	38	34
Betrayal	76	48	19	130	Brute force	11	31	33	55
Contempt	74	30	22	68	Calamity	16	37	55	19
Defeat	48	56	42	43	Crime	8	49	30	18
Disappointment	49	58	53	30	Deformation	14	24	63	9
Disobedience	57	24	65	21	Destruction	27	51	63	63
Dissatisfaction	52	18	27	106	Discord	80	53	35	89
Enemies	33	26	91	37	Displeasure	103	37	28	135
Failure	28	35	91	37	Dispute	58	49	35	45
Fear	15	21	25	11	Errors	31	59	41	39
Guilt	15	15	31	37	Fear	22	15	30	33
Hate	102	55	60	91	Hate	81	54	65	128
Ignorance	28	24	52	46	Injustice	28	46	35	41
Injustice	87	90	24	123	Jealousy	13	44	69	19
Insult	79	106	35	86	Lack of control	105	81	40	53
Jealousy	72	74	28	67	Madness	64	37	67	35
Lie	17	54	27	83	Murder	9	55	62	21
Love	22	34	24	19	No friends	27	70	44	14
Madness	38	25	34	11	Pain	121	38	40	56
Nickname	1	47	91	2	Quarrel	98	69	70	56
No patience	53	75	70	43	Repentance	13	37	56	44
Quarrel	88	69	73	43	Revenge	60	39	31	40
Revenge	59	47	84	54	Roar of anger	18	37	37	53
Ridicule	38	69	29	50	Self-hatred	36	37	49	116
Uneasiness	14	24	31	44	Sorrow	17	35	59	55
Scolding	15	32	97	14	Suicide	2	28	45	5
Weakness	18	47	40	20	Temper	66	78	41	37
					Violence	93	39	43	65
					War	43	32	62	51

Table 11 The Antecedents and Consequents of ANGER
Presented According to the Rank Order of Their Frequencies

American	Greek	Indian	Japanese

The Top Antecedents

American	Greek	Indian	Japanese
Bad temper	Insult	Scolding	Betrayal
Hate	Injustice	Enemies	Injustice
Quarrel	No patience	Failure	Dissatisfaction
Injustice	Jealousy	Nickname	Hate
Insult	Quarrel	Revenge	Insult
Betrayal	Ridicule	Quarrel	Lie
Contempt		No patience	Contempt
Jealousy		Bad temper	Jealousy

The Top Consequents

American	Greek	Indian	Japanese
Pain	Lack of control	Animosity	Displeasure
Lack of control	Temper	Quarrel	Hate
Displeasure	No friends	Jealousy	Self-hatred
Quarrel	Quarrel	Madness	
Violence			
Hate			
Discord			
Animosity			
Temper			

Correlations Among Cultures
(based on antecedents above and consequents below diagonal)

	A	G	I	J
A	. . .	.41[a]	−.03	.60[c]
G	.37[a]	. . .	−.11	.40[a]
I	−.06	.06	. . .	−.45[b]
J	.55[c]	.04	−.09	. . .

Affective Meaning Indices of ANGER

Z_E	−1.97	−1.84	−2.09	−1.81
Z_P	0.06	−0.51	−0.64	−0.67
Z_A	0.67	−0.39	1.13	0.58
$C\eta$	0.60	0.59	0.87	0.37

[a] $p < .05$
[b] $p < .01$
[c] $p < .001$

cies in some cultures and significantly low frequencies in others. For the word ANGER we note from Table 10 that the antecedents *betrayal, contempt, injustice,* and *jealousy* are chosen significantly more frequently in America and Japan (and tend to be high in Greece) but less frequently than expected by chance in India. In fact the Japanese and Indian frequencies correlate (—.45†). In Japan *betrayal* and *injustice* are considered extremely unethical acts, both in interpersonal relations and in politics. This explains the high frequencies of *A*s. Since injury to self-esteem appears to be the basic theme behind the responses to all but the Indians, we conclude that some of the Hindu teachings have had some influence in "disconnecting" injury to self-esteem from anger. It may also be that the powerful influence of the Bhagavad Gita which explicitly states that frustration leads to anger has influenced the Indians. On the other hand, a minority of the Indians must have adopted the injury to-self-esteem theme, since it is reflected in the connection between nickname and anger.

The latter finding is exceptionally interesting in view of the extreme cultural differences in the frequencies of the connection between nickname and anger (Table 10). Vassiliou and Shanmugam report that nicknames tend to be derogatory, insulting, or derisive in their cultures. Tanaka reports that nicknames are used in Japan mostly in intimate relationships. Certainly, in America nicknames are rarely deliberately insulting. Thus the frequencies reported in Table 10 are explained in terms of the relatively endearing or derogatory qualities of the nicknames employed in the four cultures.

Turning now to the consequents of ANGER, we note that the basic themes in America and Japan ($r = .55$, $p < .001$) suggest a "displeasure with the imperfection of the personality" which has led to ANGER. All cultures see ANGER as leading to *quarrel, lack of control,* and, to some extent, *hate,* but the American emphasis on *pain* and the Japanese emphasis on *self-hatred* suggest that it is a shameful event that would cause a person to feel unhappy. In Japan a display of ANGER is strongly associated with "immaturity." Therefore hate is directed at the ego, rather than the alter, for being unable to control it. The Greeks are mostly worried about losing their friends. On the other hand, the Indians are rather matter-of-fact about ANGER and show significantly low displeasure as a consequence of it.

In sum, the Americans and Japanese see injury to self-esteem or deviation from appropriate conditions as leading to ANGER, but a person should perhaps be above such considerations and getting angry is an indication of an imperfection in the personality. The Greeks are not made unhappy by ANGER, but they do worry about its consequences. The Indians accept it as a natural consequence of frustration and feel no pain or displeasure in connection with it.

COURAGE. Affectively, courage is positively evaluated in all four cultures. It is evaluated particularly high in Japan and not very high in India. It is seen as powerful in Japan and Greece and less powerful in India. It is very active in America.

Bravery, fearlessness, idealism, leadership, power of determination, self-confidence, strength, and *willpower* receive frequent choices as antecedents in most cultures. The responses of all cultures are highly intercorrelated (see Table 13).

Character and *dedication* are American antecedents that are underchosen by other cultures. The Greeks do not show any idiosyncratic meanings. The Indians emphasize *tact, a stable mind,* and *encouragement* as antecedents of COURAGE. It is notable that the Americans consider *encouragement* as a unlikely antecedent (Table 12). Finally, the Japanese emphasize a *sense of justice* and *love* as internal bases for courage. The American emphases appear to suggest an "individual basis of power" resulting in COURAGE, the Indian, a "social basis" (encouragement) and also concern for "subtle power" (tact), whereas the Japanese emphasize the power that comes from the knowledge that one is right and from the awareness that he has good leadership.

The consequents of COURAGE are in all cultures *bravery, progress, strength, success,* and *victory.* All cultures agree that they are *not death, defeat, failure, fear, foolhardiness,* and *insolence.* Thus the respondents around the world are similar and quite idealistic. The Americans emphasize the consequences of social recognition (*respect, faith,* and *honor*) to a larger extent than the other cultures. The Greeks emphasize success (*job success* and the *bypassing of difficulties*). The Indians emphasize *fame, honor,* and *praise* (i.e., social recognition) but also de-emphasize *satisfaction* and *self-confidence.* The Japanese are very low in *faith, honor,* and *power* and very high in *fearlessness.* The consequences of COURAGE for the Japanese seem to be more "personal" than "impersonal."

For both Americans and Japanese we also note a circularity between the antecedents and consequents of COURAGE: both *self-confidence* and *strength* lead to COURAGE, which, in turn, leads to these two concepts. Thus these three concepts appear highly associated in the American and Japanese cultures. The duality of the point of view of the Indian consequents (social recognition but no individual satisfaction) is probably reflected in their ratings on the semantic differential (relatively low evaluation and potency and activity).

Table 12 Frequencies of Antecedents and Consequents of COURAGE

Antecedents	American	Greek	Indian	Japanese	Consequents	American	Greek	Indian	Japanese
Anger	14	28	38	48	Bravery	160	85	48	104
Bravery	115	57	73	71	Bypassing of difficulties	42	67	39	26
Character	79	51	21	9	Death	2	15	23	10
Child rearing	3	28	16	2	Defeat	7	13	18	10
Dedication	75	29	31	16	Determination	151	82	12	105
Encouragement	8	33	75	34	Failure	2	9	12	19
Endeavor	33	52	50	38	Faith	88	43	41	28
Experience	16	45	25	51	Fame	11	51	118	32
Faith	96	62	47	68	Fear	16	12	22	27
Fear	8	11	11	24	Fearlessness	47	45	30	70
Fearlessness	41	70	73	85	Fear of opponent	13	47	39	20
God	35	51	33	17	Foolhardiness	8	16	29	13
Heredity	0	20	17	1	Gain	29	26	49	11
Honesty	24	40	57	58	Honor	66	41	77	31
Idealism	71	81	61	53	Insolence	5	28	19	7
Ignorance	3	31	31	27	Job success	17	77	72	16
Justice	15	45	23	68	Job	13	31	47	65
Knowledge	25	37	35	44	Love	12	28	29	44
Leadership	146	69	105	110	Power	41	64	61	25
Love	55	35	28	73	Praise	24	42	103	34
Power	35	52	67	11	Progress	93	90	83	141
Power of determination	57	80	66	89	Refreshingness	19	40	56	33
Respect	40	23	47	6	Respect	103	41	56	55
Self-confidence	163	93	41	137	Satisfaction	44	43	22	46
Sense of justice	45	43	26	103	Self-confidence	112	66	24	125
Stable mind	31	60	76	41	Sense of superiority	19	48	50	34
Strength	91	53	86	102	Strength	133	69	70	131
Stupidity	6	15	5	6	Success	83	74	40	89
Tact	16	13	103	14	Trust	34	49	51	63
Willpower	97	84	73	92	Victory	97	59	100	84

202

Table 13　The Antecedents and Consequents of COURAGE Presented According to the Rank Order of Their Frequencies

American	Greek	Indian	Japanese
		The Top Antecedents		
Self-confidence	Self-confidence	Leadership	Self-confidence
Leadership	Willpower	Strength	Leadership
Bravery	Idealism	Stable mind	Sense of justice
Willpower	Power of determination	Tact	Strength
Faith	Fearlessness	Encouragement	Willpower
Strength	Leadership	Bravery	Power of determination
Character		Fearlessness	Fearlessness
Dedication		Willpower	Love
Idealism		Power	Bravery
		The Top Consequents		
Bravery	Progress	Fame	Progress
Determination	Bravery	Praise	Strength
Strength	Determination	Victory	Self-confidence
Self-confidence	Job success	Progress	Determination
Respect	Success	Honor	Bravery
Progress	Strength	Job success	Success
Faith	Bypassing of difficulties	Strength	Victory
Success	Self-confidence		Fearlessness
Honor			

Correlations Among Cultures
(based on antecedents above and consequents below diagonal)

	A	G	I	J
A	...	.72^c	.41^a	.68^c
G	.70^c	...	.43^a	.71^c
I	.02	.38^a	...	.38^a
J	.78^c	.70^c	.16	...

Affective Meaning Indices of COURAGE

Z_E	0.97	0.68	0.42	1.31
Z_P	1.40	1.75	0.92	2.23
Z_A	1.03	−0.00	−0.16	0.22
$C\eta$	0.28	0.26	0.88	0.50

[a] $p < .05$
[b] $p < .01$
[c] $p < .001$

FEAR. In all four cultures FEAR is affectively bad and passive. In Greece it is also low in potency, whereas in the other three cultures it is high. It is more familiar in Greece and in India and less familiar in the other two cultures.

All four cultures see FEAR as a consequence of *danger* and *lack of confidence*. America and Japan, but *not* India, see uncertainty (e.g., *ignorance* and the *unknown*) as antecedents of FEAR. It is possible that in industrial societies knowledge is seen as a way to reduce uncertainty and therefore fear, whereas in India this view has not yet become important. It is also possible that in India, with the extended family, one does not experience loneliness or uneasiness in connection with fearful circumstances, but in the industrial societies there are signs of alienation (i.e., *loneliness, uneasiness*).

India is the only culture in which a *demon, excess wealth,* and *lack of manliness* are seen as antecedents of FEAR. *Fantasy* is high in both Greece and India. In India *excess wealth* in the form of gold may cause fear, for if one has gold the government may confiscate it (Gold Control Order of the Government of India). The response to the supernatural is a strong antecedent in India and to some extent in Greece. *Death* is very high in Japan as an important antecedent of FEAR. This is understandable in view of the political situation and Japanese concern with war and peace.

In all four cultures *fear* leads to *flight, panic,* and *uneasiness,* but the Americans, Greeks, and Japanese also mention freezing (*hesitation*) to which the Indians disagree significantly. The American emphasize *weakness* and *nervousness* as a consequent, the Greeks, *failure,* the Indians, a *bad dream,* and the Japanese, *shaking.*

We note that the Greeks and the Indians, on the one hand, and the Americans and the Japanese, on the other hand, are more like one another in their antecedent-consequent meaning of this concept, although the Greeks are also similar to the Americans. This obliquely supports Hebb and Thompson's (1954) argument that culture creates a protective cocoon which reduces the fear that man may experience. Specifically, if knowledge is equated to industrialization, Hebb's argument would be translated into "the greater the knowledge, the smaller the fear." In America and Japan fear is caused by uncertainty (*ignorance* and *the unknown*), whereas in Greece, and to an even larger extent in India, it is caused by supernatural wants such as *demons* and *fantasy*. The consequences are physiological in America and Japan and indirect in Greece and India.

LAUGHTER. *Happiness, joy, humor, funny things, fun, the unexpected* (traces of Freud!), and *love* are antecedents of laughter in all cultures. However, although most cultures also consider *tickling* a good antecedent,

Table 14 Frequencies of Antecedents and Consequents of FEAR

Antecedents	American	Greek	Indian	Japanese
Accidents	20	50	49	58
Blind belief	13	19	39	38
Conscience	27	59	26	16
Cowardice	**88**	**93**	58	45
Crime	14	36	**69**	47
Danger	**135**	**71**	68	**96**
Darkness	55	32	81	56
Death	31	29	37	**121**
Demon	19	12	**90**	39
Disease	17	43	42	33
Enemies	28	37	45	46
Excess wealth	1	33	**103**	22
Fantasy	22	**67**	78	33
Fearfulness	47	**70**	**91**	67
Hate	34	20	13	30
Human nature	28	45	47	34
Ignorance	**105**	57	14	**84**
Lack of confidence	**139**	**81**	65	**103**
Lack of manliness	24	49	**77**	17
Lies	25	27	59	47
Loneliness	**89**	57	65	**108**
Love	9	32	13	24
Mental disease	6	41	21	14
Nerves	13	52	25	11
Pain	66	21	21	14
Past life	6	47	15	10
Shock	**76**	46	37	37
Superstition	**75**	37	37	10
Uneasiness	80	59	27	**122**
Unknown	**166**	64	30	**108**

Consequents	American	Greek	Indian	Japanese
Bad dream	14	23	**74**	31
Black magic	2	16	47	3
Cowardice	39	65	54	45
Crying	22	24	54	33
Death	7	18	39	19
Defeat	31	57	67	36
Enemies	25	24	21	45
Failure	25	**74**	58	28
Flight	**164**	63	**137**	**128**
Fright	**105**	33	42	31
Hatred	35	34	33	25
Hesitation	**146**	**66**	30	**126**
Illusions	34	**66**	66	44
Inferiority complex	25	**80**	**80**	28
Madness	11	40	31	25
Mental worry	**118**	63	44	**88**
Nervousness	**74**	65	50	20
No faith	50	64	43	45
No unity	40	57	**68**	39
Pain	34	35	14	11
Panic	**101**	**104**	**86**	48
Ruin	20	58	53	40
Shake	16	19	19	**151**
Stagnation	12	21	19	39
Suicide	6	35	37	9
Trouble	**89**	31	56	**114**
Turn of mind	34	36	37	84
Uneasiness	**134**	**108**	35	**151**
Weakness	**87**	37	46	23

Table 15   The Antecedents and Consequents of FEAR Presented
According to the Rank Order of Their Frequencies

American	Greek	Indian	Japanese

The Top Antecedents

American	Greek	Indian	Japanese
Unknown	Cowardice	Excess wealth	Uneasiness
Lack of confidence	Lack of confidence	Fearfulness	Death
Danger	Danger	Demon	Loneliness
Ignorance	Fearfulness	Fantasy	Unknown
Loneliness	Fantasy	Lack of manliness	Lack of confidence
Cowardice		Crime	Danger
Uneasiness		Danger	Ignorance
Shock			
Superstition			

The Top Consequents

American	Greek	Indian	Japanese
Hesitation	Uneasiness	Flight	Shake
Uneasiness	Panic	Panic	Uneasiness
Mental worry	Inferiority complex	Inferiority complex	Flight
Fright	Failure	Bad dream	Hesitation
Panic	Hesitation	No unity	Trouble
Trouble	Illusions		Mental worry
Weakness			
Nervousness			

Correlations Among Cultures
(based on antecedents above and consequents below diagonal)

	A	G	I	J
A	...	.56[c]	−.03	.64[c]
G	.53[c]	...	.13	.41[a]
I	.34	.41[a]	...	.15
J	.62[c]	.27	.08	...

Affective Meaning Indices of FEAR

	American	Greek	Indian	Japanese
Z_E	−1.61	−1.90	−1.82	−2.20
Z_P	0.33	−0.91	1.01	0.10
Z_A	−0.06	−0.96	−0.18	−1.32
C_η	0.72	0.59	0.98	0.49

[a] $p < .05$
[b] $p < .01$
[c] $p < .001$

Table 16 Frequencies of Antecedents and Consequents of LAUGHTER

Antecedents	American	Greek	Indian	Japanese	Consequents	American	Greek	Indian	Japanese
A peculiarity	46	53	51	40	Anger	1	20	47	19
Booze	60	47	36	54	Calamity	1	24	36	2
Chain reaction	16	15	71	40	Entertainment	22	60	59	14
Children's play	49	45	70	38	Freedom	52	41	36	45
Comical event	47	42	71	20	Fun	95	79	59	61
Contempt	2	8	36	12	Good time	96	87	36	87
Entertainment	24	70	56	28	Happiness	125	57	52	91
Friends	35	15	38	54	Happy feeling	133	59	58	102
Fun	79	47	58	31	Hate	3	18	38	9
Funny things	94	74	77	44	Health	19	52	36	94
Good mood	46	68	52	41	Humor	129	58	65	110
Good time	61	49	57	63	Jokes	46	46	50	28
Happiness	169	120	53	146	Joy	98	49	41	121
Humor	122	95	64	100	Laugh to death	3	54	47	6
Idiocy	15	33	56	8	Loneliness	9	29	46	65
Insane person	0	7	64	5	Love	24	46	33	72
Irony	16	22	47	15	Mental peace	59	63	49	57
Jokes	52	64	60	40	Misunderstanding	4	47	50	4
Joy	131	114	43	183	Noise	172	65	61	49
Love	50	45	41	70	Peace	58	40	31	100
Nervousness	5	26	27	2	Pleasantness	67	55	60	80
Peace	12	37	25	65	Rest	5	48	41	39
Pleasant things	29	27	30	77	Satisfaction	32	40	49	63
Sadness	3	12	19	6	Shamefulness	3	40	42	48
Sarcasm	27	28	36	43	Sign of sorrow	5	10	46	14
Satisfaction	17	15	24	90	Stimulation to others to laugh	39	41	91	13
Success	15	22	24	27	Stomachache	4	22	39	7
The unexpected	78	81	46	76	Sympathy	8	40	38	9
Tickling	61	60	91	22	Tears	42	71	44	46
					Vacancy	8	17	50	29

Table 17　The Antecedents and Consequents of LAUGHTER Presented According to the Rank Order of Their Frequencies

American	Greek	Indian	Japanese
		The Top Antecedents	
Happiness	Happiness	Tickling	Joy
Joy	Joy	Funny things	Happiness
Humor	Humor	Chain reaction	Humor
Funny things	The unexpected	Comical event	Satisfaction
Fun	Funny things	Children's play	Pleasant things
The unexpected	Entertainment		The unexpected
	Good mood		Love
		The Top Consequents	
Noise	Good time	Stimulation to others	Joy
Happy feeling	Fun	to laugh	Humor
Humor	Tears		Happy feeling
Happiness			Peace
Joy			Health
Good time			Happiness
Fun			Good time
Pleasantness			Pleasantness
			Love

Correlations Among Cultures
(based on antecedents above and consequents below diagonal)

	A	G	I	J
A	...	.90[c]	.36	.76[c]
G	.64[c]	...	.36	.69[c]
I	.36	.22	...	−.10
J	.67[c]	.48[b]	−.04	...

Affective Meaning Indices of LAUGHTER

Z_E	0.84	0.43	0.61	2.00
Z_P	0.42	−0.77	−1.38	−0.89
Z_A	1.42	0.31	1.49	2.88
$C\eta$	0.35	0.24	0.63	0.12

[a] $p < .05$
[b] $p < .01$
[c] $p < .001$

it is rejected as an antecedent in Japan. A comical event is also not likely to lead to laughter in Japan. *Entertainment* is significantly high as an antecedent only in Greece; in America and Japan it is low.

For the Japanese LAUGHTER is highly valued and associated with what is considered most desirable and refined, such as *joy, happiness, humor,* and *satisfaction,* rather than with what is less refined, such as *tickling, comical events,* and *entertainment.*

The unique consequent of LAUGHTER for the Americans is *noise,* for the Greeks, *tears,* and for the Indians, *the stimulation of others to laugh;* for the Japanese these consequents are *joy, humor, happy feeling, health, love,* and *peace.*

The Indians tend to emphasize physical-tangible antecedents (chin reaction, tickling), but the Japanese and the Americans emphasize pleasant mental states and the unexpected. The consequences of LAUGHTER in India are again tangible (a chain reaction), whereas in Japan there is not only a pleasant but also a refined mental state.

Laughter in the semantic differentials is seen as good and active everywhere. Three of the four cultures (the exception is America) also see it as weak. India has the highest conflict index in these data, but this may be because the same word means both "smile" and "laughter."

It is notable that on the antecedents of LAUGHTER cultural similarities are substantial but cultural differences are minimal. On the other hand, this is not true of the consequences. The Indians are the most idiosyncratic.

Cultural Differences on Political-Individual Concepts

FREEDOM. In all cultures FREEDOM is valued but in Greece and Japan it is ranked more highly than in the United States, and in India the evaluation is relatively low. In all cultures except the Indian, in which it is seen as passive, it is considered potent and active.

The American and Japanese antecedents of freedom are quite similar ($r = .91$) and tend to emphasize individual freedom (e.g., *faith, equality, respect for human beings*). The Greek and Indian antecedents of freedom tend to be similar ($r = .44$) and to emphasize the social or collective aspects of the concept (e.g., *patriotism, discipline*).

In Japan a "democratic" interpretation of this concept was popularized by the Americans after World War II. Before the war FREEDOM connoted "dissoluteness" at the individual level and "anarchy" at the societal level. It was an undesirable concept. Only after the war did it become a positive concept. Thus it is not surprising that the Japanese youth's view of FREEDOM resembles that of the Americans. An older Japanese sample would probably have given different results.

Table 18 Frequencies of Antecedents and Consequents of FREEDOM

Antecedents	American	Greek	Indian	Japanese
American	10	20	34	4
Combat	2	39	34	9
Courage	78	51	48	100
Democracy	62	115	57	71
Discipline	33	64	73	4
Equality	111	73	40	108
Faith	115	57	49	151
Freedom of speech	18	38	47	18
God	58	71	47	40
Instinct	8	25	29	20
Liberation	85	67	57	104
Love	41	35	32	55
Love of freedom	39	76	62	54
Money	4	21	43	13
Patriotism	47	103	69	2
Peace	36	82	46	85
Peace of mind	105	38	68	124
Power	20	24	37	27
Quarrel	4	12	25	5
Respect for human beings	142	51	63	131
Respect for individual	154	79	52	137
Restriction	6	15	18	18
Rights	41	34	48	44
Servitude	4	29	43	10
Strength	72	23	66	48
Suppression	1	14	34	21
Tact	4	13	65	7
The constitution	32	79	47	65
Unity	16	28	69	12
War	2	11	34	4

Consequents	American	Greek	Indian	Japanese
Abuse	18	20	40	31
Civilization	59	134	60	35
Courage	39	34	50	11
Crime	14	8	35	31
Degradation	7	14	20	14
Democracy	50	75	79	30
Disorderly society	10	30	47	29
Duty	73	49	58	136
Educational facilities	10	47	43	14
Free speech	33	79	54	51
Growth of civilization	52	97	52	42
Happiness	102	75	39	151
Industrial production	2	24	55	9
Irresponsibility	9	19	57	41
Joy	88	32	46	131
Knowledge	27	15	34	9
Life	98	74	34	32
Love	29	39	36	33
Misuse	15	11	56	18
No restrictions	28	13	64	43
Peace	88	96	48	113
Progress	62	103	56	60
Public disorder	5	15	49	23
Respect	58	33	41	14
Responsibility	123	12	54	144
Rights	100	43	43	80
Satisfaction	41	20	40	79
Unity	32	40	56	13
Wealth	15	18	41	15
Well-being	72	107	45	29

Table 19   The Antecedents and Consequents of FREEDOM Presented According to the Rank Order of Their Frequencies

American	Greek	Indian	Japanese

The Top Antecedents

American	Greek	Indian	Japanese
Respect for individual	Democracy	Discipline	Faith
Respect for human beings	Patriotism	Patriotism	Respect for individual
Faith	Peace	Peace of mind	Respect for human beings
Equality	Respect for individual		Peace of mind
Peace of mind	The constitution		Equality
Liberation	Love of freedom		Liberation
Courage	Liberation		Courage
Strength			Peace

The Top Consequents

American	Greek	Indian	Japanese
Responsibility	Civilization	Democracy	Happiness
Happiness	Well-being		Responsibility
Rights	Progress		Duty
Life	Growth of civilization		Joy
Joy	Peace		Peace
Peace	Free speech		Rights
Duty	Democracy		Satisfaction
Well-being	Happiness		
	Life		

Correlations Among Cultures
(based on antecedents above and consequents below diagonal)

	A	G	I	J
A	...	.51[b]	.42[a]	.91[c]
G	.46[b]	...	.44[a]	.46[b]
I	.06	.28	...	.25
J	.75[c]	.16	.09	...

Affective Meaning Indices of FREEDOM

	A	G	I	J
Z_E	1.07	1.49	0.41	1.59
Z_P	1.17	1.23	1.58	0.34
Z_A	0.89	1.16	−0.76	0.88
$C\eta$	0.57	0.27	0.66	0.48

[a] $p < .05$
[b] $p < .01$
[c] $p < .001$

DISCIPLINE is an important antecedent in India and Greece, but is significantly low in Japan. This reflects the notion that to achieve freedom a society requires discipline but to achieve individual freedom this is not quite so important. Wealth is *not* seen as an antecedent of freedom in any culture. In other words, FREEDOM cannot be bought.

Consistent with the above interpretation of the differences in the meaning of FREEDOM are the consequents of this concept. The American and Japanese consequents are similar ($r = .75$) and emphasize individual states (*joy, happiness, responsibility, well-being*), whereas the Greek and Indian consequents emphasize social and political aspects of the concept, such as *democracy, civilization,* and *growth of civilization.* The Greeks are intermediate in this respect between the Indians and the other two cultures. Another important contrast can be seen in the American and Japanese emphasis on *responsibility* as a major consequent of FREEDOM, but the Greeks and the Indians see no significant connection between these concepts. To the extent that "freedom is accompanied by responsibility" both the Americans and the Japanese appear to have adopted a concept of social responsibility of self-regulated individual freedom. The fact that the Japanese sample sees *disorderly society* as significantly dissociated from FREEDOM indicates that they have departed from the traditional view of FREEDOM.

PEACE. This is a universl value, though it is rated much more highly in Japan and much less highly in Greece than it is in the United States or India. It is a potent but passive concept.

There is a striking resemblance between the pattern of results obtained for FREEDOM and that obtained for PEACE. Again, Americans and Japanese generally ($r = .64$) agree with one another in that they both emphasize *individualistic* antecedents and consequents ($r = .39$) of PEACE, whereas the Greeks and the Indians emphasize *societal* consequents ($r = .45$). Specifically, the Americans and Japanese emphasize antecedents that suggest the existence of appropriate psychological states (*kidness, cooperation, understanding,* and *trust*) and consequents that suggest serenity (*tranquility, happiness, joy,* etc.). The Greeks and the Indians give antecedents that suggest political and societal well-being (*democracy, brotherhood, equality, no war, disarmament,* and *unity*) and consequents that suggest states of general social well-being (*concordance, civilization, progress, increased standard of living, development,* and *well-being*).

All cultures consider FREEDOM an antecedent of PEACE, and this may be an explanation of the noticeable similarity in the patterns of results obtained with these two concepts. In addition, both the Greeks and the Japanese see FREEDOM as a consequent of PEACE. Going back to

Table 20 Frequencies of Antecedents and Consequents of PEACE

Antecedents	American	Greek	Indian	Japanese
Brotherhood	83	75	44	10
Contentment	92	25	41	58
Cooperation	121	47	28	110
Democracy	14	96	68	35
Disarmament	11	45	110	27
Equality	54	73	46	53
Fear of death	8	12	16	15
Freedom	69	134	85	98
Free mind	32	62	50	42
Friends	10	21	36	12
Good conduct	28	39	44	39
Good relations	40	48	50	18
Good will	77	48	34	40
Happiness	57	55	66	104
Honesty	61	54	15	63
Justice	74	76	37	100
Kindness	142	50	59	78
Knowledge	19	18	34	22
Logic	20	59	17	12
Love	49	57	36	125
No war	28	58	117	36
Observing non-violence	23	30	56	22
Patience	35	27	75	52
Self-determination	12	38	58	12
Tranquility	39	19	40	16
Trust	52	28	25	110
Understanding	117	35	53	124
Unity	45	63	89	25
War	10	14	11	23

Consequents	American	Greek	Indian	Japanese
Aloneness	5	13	23	20
Brightness	32	17	42	112
Civilization	42	128	73	61
Concordance	58	144	37	109
Development	72	80	55	32
Enjoyment	55	27	44	37
Equality	36	39	28	39
Freedom	46	79	43	87
Friendship	81	53	35	32
Good job	2	25	26	4
Happiness	70	53	76	136
Honor	25	27	28	5
Increase in standard of living	21	99	96	43
Joy	46	35	71	100
Love	48	52	40	91
No worry	39	22	51	37
Pleasantness	26	17	38	11
Progress	44	102	60	39
Quietness	47	52	95	39
Relief	29	21	39	15
Security	107	39	64	52
Serenity	56	41	38	60
Stable life	42	36	52	58
Tedium	2	8	18	29
Tolerance	78	5	46	34
Tranquility	127	49	60	91
Understanding	65	16	38	47
Unity	81	27	40	22
Well-being	54	65	40	41
Work success	1	31	29	3

Table 21   The Antecedents and Consequents of PEACE According to the Rank Order of Their Frequencies

American	Greek	Indian	Japanese

The Top Antecedents

American	Greek	Indian	Japanese
Kindness	Freedom	No war	Love
Cooperation	Democracy	Disarmament	Understanding
Understanding	Justice	Unity	Cooperation
Contentment	Brotherhood	Freedom	Trust
Brotherhood	Equality	Patience	Happiness
Goodwill		Democracy	Justice
Justice			Freedom
Freedom			

The Top Consequents

American	Greek	Indian	Japanese
Tranquility	Concordance	Increase in standard	Happiness
Security	Civilization	of living	Brightness
Friendship	Progress	Quietness	Concordance
Unity	Increase in	Happiness	Joy
Tolerance	standard of living	Civilization	Love
Development	Development	Joy	Tranquility
Happiness	Freedom		Freedom
	Well-being		

Correlations Among Cultures
(based on antecedents above and consequents below diagonal)

	A	G	I	J
A	...	.22	−.06	+.64[c]
G	.15	...	.38	.27
I	.33	.45[b]	...	−.03
J	.39[a]	.36[a]	.36[a]	...

Affective Meaning Indices of PEACE

Z_E	1.44	0.93	1.27	2.01
Z_P	0.75	0.96	0.43	1.43
Z_A	−0.12	−0.06	0.89	−0.47
C_η	0.46	0.28	0.92	0.66

[a] $p < .05$
[b] $p < .01$
[c] $p < .001$

Table 19, we note that PEACE or PEACE OF MIND was given by all cultures as an antecedent of FREEDOM and that PEACE was given significantly often as a consequent of FREEDOM in three out of four cultures. Thus there is much evidence that the two concepts are seen as being closely interrelated in all cultures.

Turning to Table 20 we note that for certain antecedents the cultures give a number of unique patterns. Specifically, "brotherhood" is an antecedent in the United States and Greece but *not* in Japan. Perhaps the dominantly nonreligious Japanese see PEACE as unrelated to a concept such as *brotherhood,* which has religious connotations. *Contentment* is *not* an antecedent in Greece, although it is relatively high in the other cultures. Perhaps the Greeks feel that contentment will lead to attacks by one's neighbors, hence to war. *Cooperation* is not an antecedent in India; *democracy* is not in the United States, nor is *disarmament. Patience* is irrelevant to the Greeks, but very important to the Indians, and *unity* is high among the Indians and low among the Japanese.

In summary, the Indians seem to stress a more pragmatic approach to the causes of peace (*disarmament, patience,* and *unity*), and, in contrast, the Americans and Japanese tend to emphasize a more idealistic approach to the same problem (*cooperation, justice,* and *understanding*). This may be a reaction to the Sino-Indian and Pakistan-India disputes. The Japanese are unique in stressing *love, trust,* and *happiness* as antecedents and *brightness, concordance,* and *love* as well as *joy* and *freedom* as consequents. It is as though the Japanese subjects were reacting to the preamble of the Japanese constitution:

"We desire peace for all time and are deeply conscious of the high ideals controlling human relationships and we have determined to preserve our security and existence trusting in the justice and faith of the peace-loving peoples of the world."

Thus the antecedent-consequent instrument, together with the semantic differential, reflects with some accuracy the bases of modern Japanese pacifism.

Philosophical Concepts

TRUTH. This concept is positively evaluated in all cultures, but more so in the two Eastern than in the two Western cultures. It is more potent and active in Greece and least potent as well as passive in Japan.

Subjects in all four cultures do not see this concept in its philosophic context (e.g., to understand correctly the nature of reality) but rather in its interpersonal context of "telling the truth." All cultures see personal morality (*integrity, honesty, sincerity,* and *trust*) as an antecedent of

Table 22 Frequencies of Antecedents and Consequents of TRUTH

Antecedents	American	Greek	Indian	Japanese	Consequents	American	Greek	Indian	Japanese
Beauty	34	45	36	92	Appreciation of God	51	103	82	24
Character	75	93	109	7	Beauty	79	42	34	130
Courage	85	51	48	145	Courage	97	74	73	107
Devotion to God	67	100	74	47	Fame	3	35	99	13
Expected conduct	16	60	81	24	Friends	69	50	60	53
Faith	89	62	72	108	Friendship	134	103	84	120
Fear	3	38	64	20	God	59	62	75	42
Friends	34	65	45	63	Hate	6	13	40	20
God	79	59	70	63	Honesty	151	106	83	104
Good companionship	20	57	88	49	Honor	61	64	87	10
Good man	61	126	63	45	Joy	11	101	77	95
Good upbringing	59	138	80	10	Justice	169	109	101	138
Habit	1	51	59	8	Knowledge	63	27	49	25
Honesty	197	123	103	167	Leadership	8	26	90	15
Integrity	224	47	122	119	Love	96	84	44	161
Intelligence	23	45	47	38	Morality	120	87	107	65
Justice	197	71	73	186	No hardship	9	64	78	13
Kindness	37	36	83	29	Peace	38	48	44	89
Knowledge	64	28	45	40	Profit	26	38	55	18
Love	86	58	58	143	Progress	34	98	71	96
Love of truth	66	143	95	148	Progress of society	87	143	111	112
Morality	83	112	100	92	Punishment	3	30	31	25
Peace	10	54	60	37	Relief	22	58	50	16
Reliance	45	34	76	49	Respect	160	85	99	109
Respect	154	88	62	48	Satisfaction	107	97	60	125
Scientific evidence	30	22	42	88	Self-confidence	96	78	71	105
Search	16	17	66	30	Sound thoughts	82	51	97	115
Sincerity	114	158	98	137	Success	69	114	76	66
Strength	5	31	53	27	Trust	183	78	80	209
Trust	129	75	98	139	Wealth	28	18	52	11

216

Table 23   The Antecedents and Consequents of TRUTH Presented
According to the Rank Order of Their Frequencies

American	Greek	Indian	Japanese

The Top Antecedents

American	Greek	Indian	Japanese
Integrity	Sincerity	Integrity	Justice
Honesty	Love of truth	Character	Honesty
Justice	Good upbringing	Honesty	Love of truth
Respect	Good man	Morality	Courage
Trust	Honesty	Sincerity	Love
Sincerity	Morality	Trust	Trust
	Devotion to God	Love of truth	Sincerity
	Character		Integrity
			Faith

The Top Consequents

American	Greek	Indian	Japanese
Trust	Progress of society	Progress of society	Trust
Justice	Success	Morality	Love
Respect	Justice	Justice	Justice
Honesty	Honesty	Fame	Beauty
Friendship	Appreciation of God	Respect	Satisfaction
Morality	Friendship	Sound thoughts	Friendship
Satisfaction	Joy		Sound thoughts
Courage	Progress		Progress of society
Love	Satisfaction		Respect
Self-confidence			Courage
			Self-confidence
			Honesty
			Peace

Correlations Among Cultures
(based on antecedents above and consequents below diagonal)

	A	G	I	J
A	...	.37[a]	.53[b]	.70[c]
G	.56[c]	...	.51[b]	.29
I	.40[a]	.54[b]	...	.24
J	.77[c]	.55[b]	.15	...

Affective Meaning Indices of TRUTH

	American	Greek	Indian	Japanese
Z_E	0.48	0.69	1.25	1.20
Z_P	1.52	2.27	1.18	0.91
Z_A	0.23	0.47	0.44	−0.57
C_η	0.37	0.40	0.77	0.32

[a] $p < .05$
[b] $p < .01$
[c] $p < .001$

217

TRUTH. The cultural differences in the antecedents are too subtle to be easily interpretable. They include *respect* among the Americans but not among the Japanese, *good upbringing* and *devotion to God* for the Greeks but not for the Japanese, and *courage* and *love* for the Japanese but not for the Indians. The Indians have no characteristic pattern.

The consequents of TRUTH in all cultures may be described as "individual uplifting" and satisfaction. The individual improvement is particularly strong in the United States, where almost all the consequents may be categorized as individual (courage, self-confidence, etc.). In the other three cultures the consequents include some social themes (progress of society and just plain progress, which, as shown earlier, is a societal concept in Greece). In all cultures there are themes of appreciation by others (respect, friendship, fame) and in Japan there is a suggestion of aesthetic satisfaction (beauty).

In general TRUTH appears to be a concept for which all cultures assign relatively similar meanings (most intercorrelations of Table 23 are significant) with variations in emphasis. The Japanese are unique in deemphasizing God-related antecedents and consequents and in their emphasis on *love* and *beauty*. Truth is linked with poetry, *courage,* and *scientific evidence* in a pattern not found in the other cultures.

Societal Control

PUNISHMENT. The unstandardized responses of the Greeks on the evaluative factor of the semantic differential show that they see this concept as good, whereas it is seen as bad in all other cultures. In the standardized scores it is clear that the two Eastern cultures consider it "more bad" than do the two Western cultures. It is "impotent" in Greece and most "potent" in India; it is passive all around the world, but most passive in Japan.

In all cultures "defiance of law," "illegal acts," and "lawlessness" are important antecedents and "regret" and "repentance" are important consequents.

The Americans are unique in emphasizing that "naughtiness" may lead to punishment. We suspect that this concept is not easily translatable into other languages to convey the same connotation in non-English cultures as the English word does to Americans. The Greeks are unique in their emphasis of "no God" as an antecedent, and the Indians, in emphasizing "theft." The Japanese are unique because they de-emphasize antecedents that are quite important in other cultures. Thus "bad conduct," "conscience," "disobedience," and "poverty" are significantly low in Japan but they have substantial frequencies in other cultures. The dissociation of *defiance of law* and *disobedience* from punishment may indicate some resis-

Table 24 Frequencies of Antecedents and Consequents of PUNISHMENT

Antecedents	American	Greek	Indian	Japanese	Consequents	American	Greek	Indian	Japanese
Bad conduct	93	56	75	18	Anger	57	27	42	41
Bad deeds	69	64	66	92	Change of behavior	66	83	58	58
Conscience	67	49	13	22	Compliance	40	103	35	12
Crime	149	52	59	96	Contempt	117	41	44	66
Deceit	41	35	55	42	Correction	126	54	38	104
Defeat	15	23	33	12	Crime	43	23	29	48
Defiance of law	173	83	77	68	Death	7	16	49	29
Disobedience	145	57	80	12	Dejection	71	19	46	45
Disturbance of peace	137	48	36	201	Dishonor	141	39	81	54
Evil	68	34	40	54	Exemplification	100	181	48	59
Exemplification	27	31	40	15	Fear	66	25	67	63
Hate	20	25	32	25	Guilt	132	28	64	103
Illegal acts	105	93	65	95	Hardship	68	26	80	67
Immoral acts	48	59	48	89	Hate	54	22	27	21
Imprisonment	74	20	31	4	Imprisonment	61	51	145	22
Injustice	84	70	38	114	Introspection	65	16	22	145
Law	32	25	38	55	Justice	81	92	23	66
Lawlessness	111	64	60	38	Pain	88	38	34	27
Lie	5	32	67	37	Poverty	7	25	54	9
Mistake	29	47	36	21	Reasonableness	7	88	35	6
Murder	83	41	87	68	Reform	92	55	45	64
Naughtiness	202	61	67	5	Regret	121	114	41	125
No God	20	69	54	14	Repentance	67	90	71	72
Pain	14	14	15	1	Repetition of error	19	23	54	21
Poverty	45	26	48	14	Resentment	111	19	61	20
Sin	74	43	19	80	Resistance	105	84	32	54
Theft	14	21	71	17	Revenge	53	43	48	19
Transgression	55	55	16	22	Sin	23	19	32	42
Unfair acts	28	69	53	98	Wronged	24	23	29	42
Wrong	62	40	36	63					

Table 25 The Antecedents and Consequents of PUNISHMENT Presented According to the Rank Order of Their Frequencies

American	Greek	Indian	Japanese

The Top Antecedents

American	Greek	Indian	Japanese
Naughtiness	Illegal acts	Murder	Disturbance of peace
Defiance of law	Defiance of law	Disobedience	Injustice
Crime	Injustice	Defiance of law	Unfair acts
Disobedience	No God	Bad conduct	Crime
Disturbance of peace	Unfair acts	Theft	Illegal acts
Lawlessness			Bad deeds
Illegal acts			Immoral acts
Bad conduct			Sin

The Top Consequents

American	Greek	Indian	Japanese
Dishonor	Exemplification	Imprisonment	Introspection
Guilt	Regret	Dishonor	Regret
Correction	Compliance	Hardship	Correction
Regret	Justice	Repentance	Guilt
Contempt	Repentance		Repentance
Resentment	Reasonableness		
Resistance	Change of		
Exemplification	behavior		
Reform			

Correlations Among Cultures
(based on antecedents above and consequents below diagonal)

	A	G	I	J
A	...	.55[b]	.39[a]	.30
G	.20	...	.39[a]	.41[a]
I	.13	−.01	...	.06
J	.57[c]	.13	−.13	...

Affective Meaning Indices of PUNISHMENT

	A	G	I	J
Z_E	−1.26	−0.51	−1.54	−1.68
Z_P	−0.17	−0.43	0.87	0.16
Z_A	−0.29	−0.08	−0.57	−0.85
C_η	0.77	0.65	1.03	0.85

[a] $p < .05$
[b] $p < .01$
[c] $p < .001$

tence among Japanese youth to tradition and the status quo. Students, who are the subjects of this study, often engage in militant student activities which defy law and constitute disobedience to established authority. Most of the participants in such movements may not accept the fact that they are "disturbing the peace," even though they are quite aware that they are defying the law and disobeying authority. It is probable that they would not accept any punishment that resulted from such defiance and disobedience.

The consequents of PUNISHMENT tend to be correlated ($r = .57$) in America and Japan and suggest guilt (*guilt, introspection*); shame appears to be the dominant theme in Greece and India (*exemplification, dishonor*), though both types of theme are present in all cultures. Greece is unique in that it emphasizes positive outcomes of PUNISHMENT (*justice, reasonableness*) and America is unique in emphasizing the non-acceptance of PUNISHMENT (*resentment, resistance*). The positive outcomes emphasized by the Greeks are consistent with their positive evaluation of this concept on the semantic differential, whereas the non-acceptance theme of the Americans appears to be unrelated to their semantic differential judgements. The Greek acceptance of PUNISHMENT is consistent with their evaluation of the imposition of societal controls on the individual and their acceptance of ingroup authorty figures (see Chapter 9). The Japanese also accept punishment, but this is related more to the concepts of *correction* and *introspection*. The Greek acceptance is closer to the conept of the individual needing to be controlled by punishment.

Social Disruption

CRIME. This concept is a disvalue or negative value in all cultures, particularly in Greece. It is seen as potent everywhere but in that country, as active in the United States and Japan, and as passive in Greece and India.

The American and the Indian antecedents are correlated .59 and involve specific crimes (*murder, stealing*); the other two cultures emphasize heredity (*criminal instinct*) and environment (*bad company*). The Greeks and Indians are negatively correlated ($-.42$) because of disagreement on the importance of *criminal instinct, lack of food, murder,* and *poverty*. All cultures except the Indian see a flaw in the personality (*loss of control, anger, hate*) as relevant. *Poverty* is seen as an antecedent of crime only in the United States and India. The Greeks are significantly low, thus emphasizing the existing environmental pattern in which there is widespread poverty but a low crime rate. Finally, the Indians emphasize the impor-

Table 26 Frequencies of Antecedents and Consequents of CRIME

Antecedents	American	Greek	Indian	Japanese	Consequents	American	Greek	Indian	Japanese
Anger	64	75	41	56	Anger	13	26	19	77
Bad company	59	91	73	91	Bad name	25	58	95	16
Character	9	39	31	29	Banishment	11	42	21	16
Cheating	59	34	90	57	Contempt	51	64	35	48
Criminal instinct	60	90	16	87	Criminals	58	33	32	46
Desire	58	23	58	103	Criminal is made an example of	8	40	40	12
Disobedience	51	20	64	13	Death	3	25	25	10
Fear	29	23	41	51	Destruction of criminal	7	56	15	6
Hate	83	57	26	127	Dishonesty	98	92	19	27
Heredity	4	30	25	3	Dishonor	119	36	99	54
Honor	6	25	8	20	Execution	6	37	101	9
Immortality	53	36	40	105	Fear	56	36	18	73
Inadequate education	53	43	42	45	Fine	4	16	91	5
Lack of food	14	21	68	25	Guilt	76	41	63	48
Lie	44	29	60	71	Hate	29	37	33	65
Loss of control	127	72	33	81	Imprisonment	57	47	166	37
Low intelligence	27	48	25	46	Insanity	0	31	17	16
Mental disease	9	46	10	12	Justice	31	53	12	26
Money	8	46	31	53	Lack of respect	72	32	48	16
Murder	125	27	121	64	Misery	64	68	35	89
Need	74	48	62	25	Pain	48	34	17	22
Perversity	32	47	18	3	Police	19	24	29	30
Poverty	69	29	77	39	Punishment	105	78	139	112
Poverty of politics	8	49	18	71	Repentance	21	55	25	100
Revenge	75	73	44	55	Sadness	38	24	60	88
Robbery	113	26	94	33	Sin	113	69	62	143
Sex	6	53	50	29	Social disorder	140	39	23	117
Speed	4	31	49	1	Spoiling of life	55	108	45	78
Stealing	110	27	97	42	Unhappiness	106	59	46	110
Uneasiness	17	77	38	51					

Table 27 The Antecedents and Consequents of CRIME Presented
According to the Rank Order of Their Frequencies

American	Greek	Indian	Japanese

The Top Antecedents

American	Greek	Indian	Japanese
Loss of control	Bad company	Murder	Hate
Murder	Criminal instinct	Stealing	Immorality
Robbery	Uneasiness	Robbery	Desire
Stealing	Anger	Cheating	Bad company
Hate	Revenge	Poverty	Criminal instinct
Revenge	Loss of control	Bad company	Loss of control
Need		Lack of food	Lie
Poverty			Poverty of politics

The Top Consequents

American	Greek	Indian	Japanese
Social disorder	Spoiling of life	Imprisonment	Sin
Dishonor	Dishonesty	Punishment	Social disorder
Unhappiness	Punishment	Execution	Punishment
Punishment	Sin	Dishonor	Unhappiness
Dishonesty	Misery	Bad name	Repentance
Guilt		Fine	Misery
Lack of respect			Sadness
			Spoiling of life
			Anger
			Fear

Correlations Among Cultures
(based on antecedents above and consequents below diagonal)

	A	G	I	J
A	...	.06	.59[c]	.42[a]
G	.40[a]	...	−.42[a]	.34
I	.22	.07	...	.04
J	.64[c]	.35	.06	...

Affective Meaning Indices of CRIME

Z_E	−2.83	−3.02	−2.42	−2.54
Z_P	0.51	−0.55	0.11	0.65
Z_A	0.09	−0.61	−0.64	0.41
C_η	0.50	0.69	0.92	0.59

[a] $p < .05$
[b] $p < .01$
[c] $p < .001$

tance of *lack of food* which is never seen as important by the other cultures. Significantly, none of the other cultures currently has serious food problems. It is also notable that in Japan a *lie* is seen as a crime; in Greece it is not. Greeks believe that face-saving lies are highly desirable and at any rate most acceptable. Significantly, also in Greece, *murder* is not necessarily seen as a crime. This is a culture in which killing "for honor" is still a cultural value and such murders would not be considered crimes. Although *desire,* which is usually negatively evaluated in Japan with regard to sexual activities as well as material desires, is associated with CRIME only in Japan, *need* is not related to it. This view appears to be consistent with the Japanese version of Buddhist stoicism.

Poverty of politics, a Japanese-generated antecedent, was chosen frequently only in Japan, as expected. It is an idiomatic expression suggesting the inadequacy of politics to improve the country. *Robbery* and *stealing* are not necessarily seen as crimes in Greece. This probably reflects the tradition of guerrilla fighters who for 300 years opposed the Turkish occupation. These guerrillas were called *kleftai kai armatoloi* which means literally "arms-carrying thieves," a definition close to that of the robber. They were instrumental in liberating the country from the Turks, hence are popular heroes.

All four cultures see crime followed by *punishment.* The Americans and the Japanese generally view the consequents in personal terms (*unhappiness, guilt, sadness, anger, fear*) and also emphasize social disorganization. The Americans and the Indians emphasize social retaliation (*dishonor, imprisonment, execution, bad name*). The Greeks and the Japanese also emphasize the dark side of individual life (*sin, misery,* and the *spoiling of life*) which results from crime.

Achievement

KNOWLEDGE. This concept is a universal value and is considered potent, particularly in Greece. On the other hand, although the Greeks see it as active, the Indians see it as rather passive.

The Indian semantic differential judgments on the active-passive dimension are reflected in the Indian antecedents. Only *schooling,* a *clear mind,* and *necessity* are listed as the Indian antecedents. They are rather passive. According to Shanmugam, *clear mind* means lack of confusion, no emotion, or "noise in the system." This constrasts with an *inquiring mind* emphasized by the other three cultures. We also note the emphasis on individual motivation (*curiosity, will, desire, willpower*) in the other three cultures. It is as though the Americans, Greeks, and Japanese emphasize what the individual has to do or the kind of a psychological state he must

Table 28 Frequencies of Antecedents and Consequents of KNOWLEDGE

Antecedents	American	Greek	Indian	Japanese	Consequents	American	Greek	Indian	Japanese
Ability	60	12	42	48	Ability	108	39	58	45
Aloneness	5	11	40	9	Advancement	78	9	60	92
Attention	18	51	23	19	Aloneness	3	13	30	9
Books	21	46	55	33	Brains	13	60	14	21
Brains	21	51	23	52	Calm judgment	53	30	32	133
Clear mind	22	49	72	6	Character	31	46	30	7
Common sense	56	9	65	37	Culture	33	55	15	82
Curiosity	92	43	50	88	Easy adjustment	138	59	50	109
Desire	105	79	52	67	Education	57	78	33	19
Effort	55	56	51	76	Erudition	13	65	17	33
Endeavor	41	52	51	22	Fame	1	35	76	17
Experience	88	29	49	134	Good job	4	49	75	9
Good companions	3	61	40	7	Good judgment	55	67	48	138
Good conduct	2	32	41	1	Intelligence	58	41	29	56
Inquiring mind	123	81	62	160	Joy	41	37	76	82
Intelligence	85	59	64	65	Learning	65	32	32	30
Memory	20	59	32	40	Peace	44	68	42	33
Motivation	164	12	24	34	Power	26	24	82	14
Necessity	18	11	68	91	Prestige	8	36	77	24
Peace	8	61	18	1	Progress	90	92	66	91
Reading	23	58	43	48	Religiosity	11	63	20	1
Schooling	25	37	76	2	Respect	36	54	63	13
Science	18	36	58	42	Ruin	4	9	52	21
Study	76	84	52	111	Self-confidence	112	74	39	121
Teaching	20	34	31	12	Sense of superiority	6	32	83	32
Travel	14	42	64	12	Success	65	73	40	32
Understanding	115	30	49	69	Understanding	132	42	50	125
Will	24	84	43	72	Well-being	43	42	55	17
Willpower	34	104	66	109	Wide knowledge	12	27	9	67
Wisdom	81	20	37	34	Wisdom	95	56	32	44

Table 29　The Antecedents and Consequents of KNOWLEDGE Presented According to the Rank Order of Their Frequencies

American	Greek	Indian	Japanese
		The Top Antecedents	
Motivation	Willpower	Schooling	Inquiring mind
Inquiring mind	Study	Clear mind	Experience
Understanding	Will	Necessity	Study
Desire	Inquiring mind		Willpower
Curiosity	Desire		Necessity
Experience			Curiosity
Intelligence			Effort
Wisdom			Will
Study			Understanding
		The Top Consequents	
Easy adjustment	Progress	Sense of superiority	Good judgment
Understanding	Education	Power	Calm judgment
Self-confidence	Self-confidence	Prestige	Understanding
Ability	Success	Fame	Self-confidence
Wisdom	Peace	Joy	Easy adjustment
Progress		Good job	Advancement
Advancement			Progress
			Culture
			Joy

Correlations Among Cultures
(based on antecedents above and consequents below diagonal)

	A	G	I	J
A	...	.00	.04	.55[c]
G	.32	...	.09	.46[b]
I	$-.01$	$-.21$	...	.28
J	.63[c]	.13	$-.03$	...

Affective Meaning Indices of KNOWLEDGE

Z_E	1.17	1.20	1.01	0.52
Z_P	1.55	2.46	1.63	1.00
Z_A	-0.26	0.51	-0.36	-0.14
C_η	0.42	0.35	0.80	0.50

[a] $p < .05$
[b] $p < .01$
[c] $p < .001$

actively seek in order to acquire knowledge, whereas the Indians emphasize that all that is needed is opportunity (schooling) and an open mind. We note further that the American and Japanese antecedents are much more differentiated than the Indian. The introspective attainment of knowledge is apparently seen as possible in India but definitely not in the other three cultures (see responses to *aloneness,* Table 28). *Experience* is an important antecedent in America and Japan but not in Greece, and *memory* is an antecedent of average importance in all cultures except the American. Possibly American emphasis on creativity rather than memorization of materials is behind this response pattern. *Necessity* leads to KNOWLEDGE in the two Eastern cultures but not in the two Western cultures. *Travel* is an antecedent of average importance in Greece and India but of no importance in the United States and Japan. This could reflect the fact that one can learn much without traveling abroad in the latter two countries, but in the former the accepted pattern of completion of one's education requires a trip.

For the Japanese the various achievement motives (*effort, experience,* and *study*) and the closely relevant internal (*curiosity, inquring mind, will,* and *willpower*) and external (*necessity*) factors are the major antecedents of acquiring knowledge. The Japanese appear to be strongly motivated to acquire knowledge and to "catch up with the West."

The consequents of KNOWLEDGE show substantial cultural differences. Only the Americans and the Japanese agree ($r = .63$). The Indians see KNOWLEDGE as leading to the acquisition of status (*sense of superiority, power, prestige, fame, a good job*), but the other three cultures see it as leading to personal improvement (*easy adjustment, self-confidence, good judgment,* and *calm judgment, progress,* and *advancement*). The Greeks see a substantial societal benefit (*progress, peace, success,* and *education*).

For the Japanese KNOWLEDGE as a cause of personal status and well-being is totally rejected, as can be seen from the significantly low frequencies of *power, prestige, respect, fame,* a *good job,* and *well-being.* Instead they place the major emphasis on *progress* and *advancement* and the factors leading to them (*calm judgment, good judgment, easy adjustment, self-confidence,* and *understanding*). Both antecedents and consequents taken together suggest that the Japanese appear to maintain the traditional values of hard work to achieve progress by the acquisition of knowledge.

POWER. This concept is a strong value in the two Western countries but not in the two Eastern countries, particularly Japan. On the other hand, it is potent in all cultures (this is, of course, tautological). Finally, it is active in all cultures except the Indian.

Table 30 Frequencies of Antecedents and Consequents of POWER

Antecedents	American	Greek	Indian	Japanese	Consequents	American	Greek	Indian	Japanese
Ability	65	63	39	82	Control	154	29	43	127
Competition	48	71	34	83	Courage	53	84	64	26
Desire to rule	23	54	42	118	Cruelty	5	33	40	17
Dictatorship	32	11	58	114	Destruction	8	12	41	31
Eating eggs	2	13	45	1	Dictatorship	11	11	55	103
Endeavor	35	104	29	27	Egotism	24	51	42	51
Exercise	5	84	51	5	Enemies	42	42	80	74
Friends	17	69	40	2	Fear	56	27	66	59
Force	59	50	53	88	Freedom	10	82	22	12
Guns	15	47	76	14	Glory	17	76	61	31
Hard work	52	58	57	5	Good job	4	42	29	6
Heredity	2	15	23	0	Government	14	15	30	59
Influence	64	27	61	23	Imposing will	95	76	26	52
Instinct	9	32	32	41	Influence	154	49	104	74
Intelligence	96	67	40	50	Money	13	10	52	22
Knowledge	134	56	35	57	Pressure	43	11	64	121
Leadership	178	75	34	118	Pride	102	101	52	70
Money	37	27	55	84	Respect	71	65	51	22
Muscles	18	44	55	52	Self-confidence	60	100	38	41
Nutritious food	7	43	82	1	Selfishness	10	18	45	64
Organization	65	55	39	111	Strength	138	76	87	87
Play	0	30	32	3	Struggle	30	38	35	63
Preparation	33	15	38	3	Subserviance	46	26	39	36
Respect	98	40	53	49	Success	76	100	51	19
Running	1	25	31	34	Superiority	131	85	72	83
Self-confidence	60	67	27	63	Vanity	19	18	52	38
Strength	175	62	90	114	Victory	33	96	40	29
Unity	54	43	71	35	War	8	20	20	57
Wealth	54	22	68	101	Wealth	31	15	39	33
Wrestling	12	36	50	23					

228

Table 31   The Antecedents and Consequents of POWER
Presented According to the Rank Order of Their Frequencies

American	Greek	Indian	Japanese

The Top Antecedents

American	Greek	Indian	Japanese
Leadership	Endeavor	Strength	Desire to rule
Strength	Exercise	Nutritious food	Leadership
Knowledge	Leadership	Guns	Dictatorship
Respect	Competition	Unity	Strength
Intelligence	Friends	Wealth	Organization
	Intelligence		Wealth
	Self-confidence		Force
			Money
			Competition
			Ability

The Top Consequents

American	Greek	Indian	Japanese
Control	Pride	Influence	Control
Influence	Self-confidence	Strength	Pressure
Strength	Success	Enemies	Dictatorship
Superiority	Victory	Superiority	Strength
Pride	Superiority		Superiority
Imposing will	Courage		Enemies
Success	Freedom		Influence
Respect	Glory		Pride
	Imposing will		
	Strength		

Correlations Among Cultures
(based on antecedents above and consequents below diagonal)

	A	G	I	J
A	...	.36	.15	.57[c]
G	.42[a]	...	−.14	.14
I	.55[c]	.11	...	.08
J	.50[b]	−.23	.40[a]	...

Affective Meaning Indices of POWER

	A	G	I	J
Z_E	0.73	0.69	0.11	−0.94
Z_P	1.81	1.67	1.24	0.69
Z_A	0.98	1.03	−0.01	0.79
C_n	0.25	0.18	0.91	0.68

[a] $p < .05$
[b] $p < .01$
[c] $p < .001$

Intelligence, knowledge, leadership, and *strength* are seen as important antecedents of power in all cultures. The Greeks see POWER as acquired by competition with members of one's outgroup and the help of one's friends. The Indians are unique in their emphasis of physical as well as psychological power. This difference in points of view results in a large conflict index on the semantic differential judgments, as it should. The negative evaluation of POWER by the Japanese is reflected both in the antecedents *(desire to rule, dictatorship)* and the consequents *(enemies, dictatorship).*

Both Eastern cultures emphasize some negative consequents of POWER *(enemies, dictatorship, pressure).* All four cultures emphasize some positive consequents such as *influence, pride, strength,* and *superiority.* The Greeks contrast with the Japanese in emphasizing *courage, glory, success,* and *victory* whereas the Japanese de-emphasize them as consequents of POWER. The Greeks are unique in their emphasis of *freedom, glory, self-confidence,* and *victory* as consequents of POWER, but the other three cultures see weak connections between POWER and these consequents. The Japanese responses seem to have been conditioned by a disillusionment with Japanese involvement in World War II, as shown by the responses to *war* as a consequent of POWER but not seen as such in the other three cultures, and the weak relation between the concepts POWER and *success* for the Japanese sample.

It appears clear that, as the dominant source of power, the Japanese perceive organization *(organization, leadership),* wealth *(wealth, money),* and collective action *(dictatorship, desire to rule, force),* whereas as the major results of power they consider, regimentation *(control, influence, pressure* and *dictatorship)* and conflict *(enemies, struggle, war).* Note also that the Japanese dissociate power from *respect, success, victory, freedom,* and *glory,* which are frequently mentioned consequents in other cultures. Although the Americans and the Japanese agree on many concepts, on the concept of power there is considerable disagreement. Whereas Americans see it positively, as a source of *control, influence, superiority,* and *pride,* derived from *knowledge, leadership* and *strength,* the Japanese reject it as a source of conflict and regimentation resulting from dictatorship and plutocracy.

PROGRESS. All cultures consider this concept highly desirable, potent, and active. The Indians who do not see it as potent are the only exception.

All cultures emphasize the importance of having the proper social conditions for PROGRESS *(cooperation)* and the appropriate individual characteristics. However, what is considered as an appropriate individual characteristic that might lead to PROGRESS differs from culture to culture.

Table 32 Frequencies of Antecedents and Consequents of PROGRESS

Antecedents	American	Greek	Indian	Japanese	Consequents	American	Greek	Indian	Japanese
Ability	76	67	51	58	Ability	29	36	48	48
Ambition	174	43	65	90	Achievement	250	19	68	92
Cooperation	209	105	79	209	Affluence	29	24	54	55
Courage	10	63	150	60	Automation	26	20	56	15
Diligence	92	135	16	116	Civilization	44	193	59	158
Drive	195	42	42	26	Convenience	11	30	67	63
Education	67	103	57	28	Courage	10	69	50	23
Endeavor	54	73	63	52	Development	279	93	69	213
Enthusiasm	89	69	143	261	Expansion	114	18	70	167
Friends	2	16	57	14	Friends	17	36	67	11
Foresight	114	31	70	107	Glory	8	49	124	108
Good conduct	3	82	100	22	Good name	3	99	63	18
Hard work	116	87	108	33	Happiness	36	133	66	114
Help from others	13	16	73	5	Improvement	288	135	48	151
Honesty	14	183	81	41	Increasing	37	21	70	39
Improvement	131	25	64	143	Inventions	31	45	75	27
Initiative	198	56	54	53	Knowledge	101	116	104	65
Interested learning	35	123	17	131	Money	15	46	74	7
Invention	79	36	56	49	Moral decline	4	11	61	27
Knowledge	83	52	62	32	Power	18	79	103	21
Luck	6	63	35	21	Respect	16	89	60	23
Money	10	46	114	11	Satisfaction	154	111	64	183
Peace	16	122	17	23	Scientific development	263	191	85	224
Research	68	34	47	150	Sorrow	1	14	54	15
Seriousness	22	70	45	70	Speed	17	23	71	20
Strength	17	17	161	31	Success	133	69	90	116
Study	36	50	65	32	Thrill of deeds	52	91	71	91
Thinking	64	60	43	216	Unfolding of intelligence	54	76	64	65
Unity	47	67	200	67	Wealth	33	29	98	61
Willpower	80	178	19	118	Well-being	50	152	72	34

Table 33 The Antecedents and Consequents of PROGRESS Presented
According to the Rank Order of Their Frequencies

American	Greek	Indian	Japanese

The Top Antecedents

American	Greek	Indian	Japanese
Cooperation	Honesty	Unity	Enthusiasm
Initiative	Willpower	Strength	Thinking
Drive	Diligence	Courage	Cooperation
Ambition	Interested learning	Enthusiasm	Research
Improvement	Peace	Money	Improvement
Hard work	Cooperation	Hard work	Interested learning
Foresight	Education	Good conduct	Willpower
			Diligence
			Foresight

The Top Consequents

American	Greek	Indian	Japanese
Improvement	Civilization	Glory	Scientific development
Development	Scientific development	Knowledge	Development
Scientific	Well-being	Power	Satisfaction
Development	Improvement	Wealth	Expansion
Achievement	Happiness		Civilization
Satisfaction	Knowledge		Improvement
Success	Satisfaction		Success
Expansion	Good name		Happiness
Knowledge			

Correlations Among Cultures
(based on antecedents above and consequents below diagonal)

	A	G	I	J
A	...	$-.05$	$-.17$	$.38^a$
G	$.38^a$	...	$-.26$	$.15$
I	$-.01$	$.05$	...	$-.05$
J	$.77$	$.53^b$	$.11$	...

Affective Meaning Indices of PROGRESS

	A	G	I	J
Z_E	0.80	0.96	0.82	1.06
Z_P	1.23	1.07	-0.33	1.12
Z_A	1.27	0.43	0.94	0.09
C_η	0.36	0.27	0.82	0.53

[a] $p < .05$
[b] $p < .01$
[c] $p < .001$

Thus the Americans emphasize *ambition, drive, foresight, hard work,* and *initiative;* the Greeks *diligence, honesty,* and *willpower;* the Indians *courage, enthusiasm,* and *hard work;* the Japanese *enthusiasm, willpower, diligence,* and *foresight.* In addition, there are cultural differences in the emphases on the proper social conditions; the Greeks emphasize *peace,* the Indians, *unity,* and the Japanese, *research.*

The Japanese consider certain qualities of the mind (*thinking, interested learning, foresight, research*) and *willpower* as important factors that, in addition to *cooperation, diligence* and *enthusiasm,* lead to PROGRESS. The Americans, on the other hand, emphasize motivational concepts (*drive, ambition, leadership*) as necessary to progress. In both the Japanese and American cultures chance factors (*luck, money*) are discarded as irrelevant to progress.

The consequents of PROGRESS are again either social (*scientific development*) or individual (*satisfaction*). All four cultures emphasize that *knowledge* is a consequent. The Americans differ with the Greeks in seeing a connection between PROGRESS and *achievement* and *expansion,* which the Greeks do not; the Greeks consider *civilization, good name,* and *well-being* as consequents; the Americans do not. The Indians are characterized by emphasis on *glory, power,* and *wealth.* Thus they see PROGRESS as leading to the achievement of high societal status. The Japanese are unique in their balanced emphasis on a variety of themes and their de-emphasis on *money* and *well-being.* It is interesting to note the contrast between the American and the Japanese emphasis on *happiness, glory,* and *civilization* as consequents of progress. The Americans appear disillusioned and cynical. The Japanese resemble the Americans in their emphasis on growth (*development, expansion, improvement, scientific development*) and de-emphasis on mechanical innovations (*automation, inventions*) and social conventions (*good name*). Thus, although both countries are similar in their positive orientation toward progress, the Japanese are more introspective and stoic than the Americans.

All in all, the Americans, who presumably have more of what is assumed to be PROGRESS, see the least connection of this concept to positive consequences such as *affluence, convenience, glory, good name, happiness, power, respect,* and *wealth.* The Indians, with the least PROGRESS, have the most positive outlook in that they see a connection with *glory, power,* and *wealth.*

SUCCESS. This is a value all over the world. It is potent and relatively active.

All cultures see *ability, cooperation, courage, effort, patience, planning, preparation,* and *willpower* either strongly or somewhat related to

Table 34 Frequencies of Antecedents and Consequents of SUCCESS

Antecedents	American	Greek	Indian	Japanese
Ability	104	81	51	118
Cooperation	68	69	62	76
Courage	33	72	50	71
Devotion	88	30	54	3
Discipline	35	46	70	35
Effort	96	81	54	191
Endeavor	34	33	60	42
Failure	1	12	42	51
Fortune	13	18	41	7
Friends	12	26	16	5
Happiness	48	40	23	4
Hard work	108	58	61	16
Huge army	5	12	73	8
Inquiring mind	36	55	28	108
Knowledge	61	44	15	23
Leadership	36	13	77	25
Love	28	25	16	23
Luck	10	39	43	44
Money	18	29	38	4
Patience	84	103	59	126
Peace	19	56	33	3
Planning	82	65	73	49
Preparation	75	49	61	53
Progress	55	66	31	63
Research	37	32	52	67
Sincerity	55	59	40	50
Tact	19	18	83	41
Unity	28	42	72	45
Wealth	22	13	22	12
Willpower	61	94	40	141

Consequents	American	Greek	Indian	Japanese
Achievement	161	27	48	72
Admiration	20	59	54	34
Courage	12	31	30	21
Egotism	13	32	41	12
Envy	14	19	36	24
False pride	3	22	41	18
Fame	8	59	83	36
Freedom	10	51	23	8
Friends	9	29	20	5
Gladness	29	55	56	88
Happiness	95	75	59	105
Increased aspiration level	70	74	56	75
Job	10	25	28	1
Job success	8	63	52	4
Joy	94	63	56	179
Knowledge	32	31	27	15
Love	30	76	34	8
Peace	19	45	22	14
Power	9	24	49	14
Praise	28	41	54	35
Pride	83	34	57	75
Progress	104	59	42	101
Respect	65	49	69	15
Satisfaction	147	74	55	169
Self-confidence	101	67	51	124
Social distinction	20	64	80	8
Social prominence	57	57	73	16
Vanity	4	9	58	15
Wealth	18	31	30	17

Table 35 The Antecedents and Consequents of SUCCESS Presented According to the Rank Order of Their Frequencies

American	Greek	Indian	Japanese
		The Top Antecedents	
Hard work	Patience	Tact	Effort
Ability	Willpower	Leadership	Willpower
Effort	Ability	Hugh army	Patience
Devotion	Effort	Planning	Ability
Patience	Courage	Unity	Inquiring mind
Planning	Cooperation	Discipline	Cooperation
Preparation	Progress		Courage
		The Top Consequents	
Achievement	Love	Fame	Joy
Satisfaction	Happiness	Social distinction	Satisfaction
Progress	Increased	Social prominence	Self-confidence
Self-confidence	Aspiration level	Respect	Happiness
Happiness	Satisfaction		Progress
Joy			Gladness
Pride			Increased
Increased aspiration			Increased aspiration
Level			Level
Respect			Pride
			Achievement

Correlations Among Cultures
(based on antecedents above and consequents below diagonal)

	A	G	I	J
A	...	.69[c]	.19	.48[b]
G	.40[a]	...	.04	.74[c]
I	.25	.41[a]	...	.14
J	.79[c]	.49[b]	.28	...

Affective Meaning Indices of SUCCESS

Z_E	1.05	0.99	0.42	1.77
Z_P	0.97	1.17	1.19	1.61
Z_A	0.09	0.18	−0.27	0.61
$C\eta$	0.37	0.21	0.86	0.44

[a] $p < .05$
[b] $p < .01$
[c] $p < .001$

SUCCESS. The Americans contrast with the Japanese in that they mention *devotion* and *hard work*. In terms of the over-all rankings, the Americans see *hard work* and *ability* as most important, whereas the Greeks see *patience* and *willpower,* the Indians, *tact* and *leadership,* and the Japanese, *effort* and *willpower.* Thus the Americans and the Japanese find a greater connection between individual effort, on the one hand, and success, on the other, than the other cultures; the Greeks see a relationship between persistence (*patience, willpower*) and success, the Indians, between effective social relations (*tact, leadership, planning*) and success.

On this concept the Indians appear to be different from the other cultures. They emphasize social factors that promote SUCCESS as well as a *huge army, leadership,* and *unity.* The other three cultures see SUCCESS as dependent on appropriate individual qualities.

In all cultures the consequences of SUCCESS are *happiness, increased aspiration level, joy, satisfaction,* and *self-confidence.* The Americans are high in their emphasis on *achievement, pride,* and *respect,* on which some cultures disagree. The Greeks emphasize *love.* In other words, in Greece SUCCESS leads to greater acceptance by the ingroup (see Chapter 9). The Indians emphasize the achievement of status (*fame, social distinction, prominence, respect*). The Japanese are quite similar to the Americans ($r = .79$), except that they disregard status (*social prominence* and *respect*) as consequents of success. The similarities between the Americans and the Japanese may reflect similar achievement orientations in industrialized free-enterprise societies.

WEALTH. This concept is a value in America and Japan but not in Greece and India. It is potent in all cultures. The two Western cultures regard it as active and the two Eastern, as passive.

We note that the concept is highly differentiated in America and to some extent in Japan. In India, however, it is not differentiated (note the small number of significant *C*s).

In all cultures *savings* and *success* are antecedents of WEALTH. In America *drive, education, happiness, knowledge,* and *money* are important antecedents. It is the individual's characteristics (*drive, education*) that are the primary determinants of WEALTH. In Greece the emphasis is on *courage, hard work, intelligence,* and *patience.* Again individual characteristics are important, but they are a different set from those used by the Americans. On the other hand, the Indians emphasize *ancestral property,* the *capitalist system, earnings, good fortune,* and *inheritance* as determinants of WEALTH. The Japanese emphasize the *capitalist system, fortune,* and *luck. Health* is not seen as an antecedent of WEALTH by the Indians, but it is in the two highly industrialized countries.

Table 36 Frequencies of Antecedents and Consequents of WEALTH

Antecedents	American	Greek	Indian	Japanese	Consequents	American	Greek	Indian	Japanese
Ancestral property	10	21	67	19	Abundance	100	50	51	135
Business profit	31	41	53	66	Affluence	79	12	37	61
Capitalist system	41	14	84	94	Arrogance	14	32	73	18
Courage	47	82	36	68	Benevolence	31	63	32	10
Crime	4	14	49	10	Comfort	101	89	38	19
Deceit	4	21	42	7	Decadence	9	17	54	19
Drive	90	17	32	9	Desire	33	30	46	112
Earnings	63	18	88	65	Destruction	6	19	36	18
Education	80	62	33	17	Enjoyment	84	81	42	86
Endeavor	24	51	30	42	Evil thoughts	4	17	66	50
Fortune	58	25	47	107	Fear of thieves	20	38	80	22
Good fortune	72	65	74	62	Friends	20	25	32	10
Happiness	85	30	29	67	Gorgeousness	6	27	35	78
Hard work	52	87	32	12	Happiness	75	63	44	72
Health	66	60	25	94	Health	15	60	30	20
High interest charges	4	15	60	12	Knowledge	27	37	34	8
Inheritance	24	51	86	30	Love	15	29	24	18
Inquiring mind	66	84	26	33	Luxury	93	100	39	138
Intelligence	42	107	31	33	Misery	11	22	50	29
Knowledge	82	47	28	50	Philanthropy	30	68	46	24
Love	58	28	24	54	Power	71	63	78	79
Luck	31	60	59	90	Prestige	65	37	72	32
Marriage	13	27	43	5	Respect	29	28	47	4
Money	65	37	80	62	Satisfaction	119	62	37	99
Patience	46	104	39	66	Selfishness	22	67	56	38
Power	42	28	29	57	Stability	49	39	41	106
Savings	68	85	70	104	Success	112	83	50	49
Stinginess	2	21	59	12	Unhappiness	9	25	62	23
Success	93	75	45	131	Vanity	19	34	66	81
Theft	5	17	40	9	Well-being	97	85	45	35

Table 37   The Antecedents and Consequents of WEALTH Presented According to the Rank Order of Their Frequencies

American	Greek	Indian	Japanese

The Top Antecedents

American	Greek	Indian	Japanese
Success	Intelligence	Earnings	Success
Drive	Patience	Inheritance	Fortune
Happiness	Hard work	Capitalist system	Savings
Knowledge	Savings	Money	Capitalist system
Education	Inquiring mind	Good fortune	Health
Good fortune	Courage	Savings	Luck
Savings	Success	Ancestral property	
Inquiring mind			
Health			
Money			

The Top Consequents

American	Greek	Indian	Japanese
Satisfaction	Luxury	Fear of thieves	Luxury
Success	Comfort	Power	Abundance
Comfort	Well-being	Arrogance	Desire
Abundance	Success	Prestige	Stability
Well-being	Philanthropy		Satisfaction
Luxury	Selfishness		Vanity
Enjoyment			Enjoyment
Affluence			Power
Happiness			Gorgeousness
Power			Happiness
Prestige			

Correlations Among Cultures
(based on antecedents above and consequents below diagonal)

	A	G	I	J
A	...	.37[a]	−.20	.52
G	.69[c]	...	−.25	.28
I	−.11	−.13	...	.17
J	.51[b]	.27	.01	...

Affective Meaning Indices of WEALTH

Z_E	0.81	−0.30	−0.27	0.80
Z_P	1.11	0.82	0.60	1.28
Z_A	−0.13	−0.91	0.66	1.05
C_η	0.41	0.41	0.92	0.51

[a] $p < .05$
[b] $p < .01$
[c] $p < .001$

Generally the Americans stress the importance of individual education (*education, inquiring mind, knowledge*) and the influence of chance (*good fortune*) and previous wealth (*money, savings*). The Greeks emphasize psychological conditions (*courage, inquiring mind, intelligence, patience*) and the Indians, private (*earnings, savings, money*) and institutional (*ancestral property, capitalist system, inheritance*) sources of wealth coupled with chance factors (*good fortune, luck*). The Japanese de-emphasize *education* and *hard work* and focus on the chance factors and the money-saving effort. This reflects some unique economic conditions in Japan, in which inheritance tax rates are extremely high and both education and hard work show little relation to the accumulation of wealth. Education and hard work, according to the Japanese, may enrich one's spiritual wealth but certainly not one's material wealth. Thus wealth depends on chance.

The slightly negative evaluation of WEALTH by the Greeks and the Indians is reflected in the high importance of consequents, such as *selfishness, fear of thieves,* and *arrogance,* in these cultures. By contrast the Americans give only good consequents and the Japanese give mostly good (with the exception of *vanity*). The Americans and Greeks and also the Americans and the Japanese share many *A*s and *C*s.

Abundance, enjoyment, happiness, luxury, power, success, and *well-being* tend to be high as consequents of WEALTH in all four cultures. The Americans also emphasize *affluence* but the Greeks de-emphasize it. The Americans and the Greeks emphasize *comfort,* but the Japanese de-emphasize it. The Greeks emphasize both *philanthropy* and *selfishness* as consequents of WEALTH. The Indians are unique in their emphasis on *fear of thieves* and *arrogance,* and the Japanese are unique in their emphasis on *stability* and *gorgeousness.*

Examination of the Japanese responses to WEALTH gives the impression that this is an ambivalent concept. On the one hand, it leads to *abundance, enjoyment, happiness, luxury, satisfaction,* and *stability* and, on the other, to *desire, power* (both negative concepts), *vanity* and *evil thoughts.* It is also dissociated from *comfort, prestige, success* and *well-being.* It is likely that WEALTH conflicts with the Japanese traditional positive evaluation of stoicism.

Nonachievement

DEATH. All cultures see this concept as "bad" and passive. The two Western cultures also see it as weak, whereas the two Eastern cultures see it as potent.

The antecedents of DEATH show much similarity across cultures, except that the Indians agree very little with the other cultures. All cultures

Table 38 Frequencies of Antecedents and Consequents of DEATH

Antecedents	American	Greek	Indian	Japanese	Consequents	American	Greek	Indian	Japanese
Accident	**79**	**85**	64	**71**	Burial	**64**	51	**81**	63
Bad luck	*19*	50	53	**78**	Crying	50	61	42	*8*
Carelessness	*17*	**69**	*26*	48	Decrease in population	**61**	53	47	37
Crime	50	61	*22*	57	Dejection	*9*	*18*	**69**	49
Decrepitude	*12*	**68**	32	**78**	Deliverance	40	49	42	*9*
Despair	*16*	54	*28*	**81**	Disgust	*8*	*18*	39	*21*
Disgust with life	38	46	**73**	47	Eternal life	38	56	34	66
Drunkenness	*3*	*20*	30	*5*	Extinction	**62**	30	40	**68**
Exhaustion	*17*	60	32	56	Family breakdown	*13*	**72**	44	*16*
External wound	*8*	32	*20*	*3*	Fear	24	*20*	**50**	**100**
Failure	31	*24*	**78**	*30*	Funeral	**68**	**76**	67	58
Fear	*17*	31	34	*17*	Going to heaven	*22*	*25*	40	*29*
Gun	*9*	*28*	**73**	*6*	Going to hell	*10*	*15*	34	*4*
Hardship	*14*	51	**89**	31	Grave	54	46	42	52
Hate	33	*29*	*26*	*28*	Hardship	*16*	*28*	64	*25*
Hunger	*10*	30	55	51	Joy of enemies	*12*	**72**	42	*3*
Illness	34	**73**	**86**	54	Loneliness	**69**	54	38	**101**
Incident	26	**71**	*29*	*21*	Loss of loved ones	**67**	60	59	47
Length of life	51	30	36	**136**	New birth	27	*29*	39	64
Life	**67**	35	31	52	Nothingness	54	42	32	48
Murder	**135**	**66**	**86**	**100**	Oblivion	**82**	59	60	**127**
No religion	47	34	38	*11*	Pain	*19*	39	44	*17*
No will	43	*28*	*19*	36	Peace	31	31	*15*	*15*
Old age	54	**79**	**67**	57	Rebirth	29	*25*	57	43
Quarrel	*1*	*22*	54	*1*	Ruin	*7*	65	49	48
Sin	38	*24*	44	*25*	Separation of body and soul	50	62	**82**	**72**
Sorrow	*11*	*29*	*25*	32	Sorrow	55	57	51	**132**
Suicide	**115**	47	**88**	**100**	Suffering	52	**81**	**90**	55
Thirst	*2*	*12*	42	*9*	Sympathy	32	50	*21*	*19*
War	**146**	**99**	59	**162**	Vacant mood	*25*	50	41	**84**

240

Table 39   The Antecedents and Consequents of DEATH Presented
According to the Rank Order of Their Frequencies

American	Greek	Indian	Japanese
The Top Antecedents			
War	War	Hardship	War
Murder	Accident	Suicide	Length of life
Suicide	Old age	Illness	Murder
Accident	Illness	Murder	Suicide
Life	Incident	Failure	Despair
	Carelessness	Disgust with life	Bad luck
	Decrepitude	Gun	Decrepitude
	Murder	Old age	Accident
The Top Consequents			
Oblivion	Suffering	Suffering	Sorrow
Loneliness	Funeral	Separation of body	Oblivion
Funeral	Family breakdown	and soul	Loneliness
Loss of loved	Joy of enemies	Burial	Fear
Ones		Dejection	Vacant mood
Burial		Funeral	Separation of body
Extinction			and soul
Decrease in			Extinction
population			

Correlations Among Cultures
(based on antecedents above and consequents below diagonal)

	A	G	I	J
A	. . .	.52[b]	.39[a]	.71[c]
G	.43[a]	. . .	.24	.60[c]
I	.27	.32	. . .	.23
J	.53[c]	.13	.30	. . .

Affective Meaning Indices of DEATH

Z_E	-1.93	-2.25	-1.65	-1.64
Z_P	-0.47	-0.59	0.74	0.37
Z_A	-2.87	-1.66	-1.19	-1.89
$C\eta$	0.67	0.48	1.05	0.79

[a] $p < .05$
[b] $p < .01$
[c] $p < .001$

find a substantial connection between *accident, illness, murder, old age, suicide,* and *war* on the one hand and DEATH on the other. However, there are also some cultural differences. Thus affluent Americans emphasize *life* but de-emphasize *hunger, dispair,* and *decrepitude* as an antecedent of death, the Greeks emphasize *carelessness* and *decrepitude* and the Indians *old age, hardship, disgust with life,* and *gun.* The Japanese stress *length of life, bad luck,* and *decrepitude.*

Again the Japanese display their neglect of religion-related antecedents (*no religion, sin*) and emphasize not only the common antecedents of death (*murder, accident, war*) but also self-produced causes (*despair, suicide*) and causes beyond one's control (*bad luck, length of life*). The latter antecedent is clearly Japanese and equivalent to "living out the whole of one's alloted span of life under the Heaven's will," which is traceable to the ancient Chinese concept of the "lifespan."

The consequents of DEATH also show some cross-cultural similarities. *Burial, funeral, loss of loved ones, oblivion, sorrow,* and *suffering* are given by the samples of all four cultures in substantial frequencies, although the required significance levels are not always reached in all cultures. On the other hand, *loneliness* and *extinction* are particularly high in the two industrialized societies, *family breakdown* and *joy of enemies* are emphasized by the Greeks, and *dejection,* by the Indians.

The Americans are unique in their emphasis on *decrease in population.* The Greeks are unique in their emphasis on *family breakdown* and *joy of enemies.* To understand the Greek responses it is necessary to know about the importance of the struggle between ingroups and outgroups in Greece (see Chapter 9) which suggests that out-group members may be pleased by the death of a member of an ingroup.

Although the Japanese are nonreligious, the pattern of their responses seem to conform to their version of Buddhist tradition which emphasizes the shift from "existence" to "nothingness" (*separation of body and soul, extinction, oblivion*). Consequently, various psychological states (*fear, loneliness, vacant mood, sorrow*) become important and indicate an unretrievable loss to those who stay behind.

Death is a universal phenomenon, but even such a fundamental concept reflects the unique social, economic, and religious conditions prevailing in the four societies under study.

DEFEAT. This concept is negatively evaluated in all cultures. It is seen as impotent and passive in the two Western cultures, as well as in Japan, and potent and passive in India.

Lack of confidence and motivation (*no desire, giving up, apathy*), as well as *weaknesses* and *mismanagement,* are important antecedents in

Table 40 Frequencies of Antecedents and Consequents of DEFEAT

Antecedents	American	Greek	Indian	Japanese	Consequents	American	Greek	Indian	Japanese
Accident	5	19	26	31	Anger	36	24	38	30
Apathy	110	14	25	15	Courage	20	41	28	30
Bad luck	21	36	55	36	Death	10	23	23	18
Cowardice	22	63	58	45	Deformation	17	29	104	7
Failure	73	38	48	40	Degradation	71	51	77	33
Faithfulness	4	75	18	7	Depression	78	28	97	35
Fear	17	38	61	49	Despair	99	57	42	54
Giving up	121	38	29	121	Destruction	43	86	48	27
Guilt	7	25	22	19	Difficulty	44	56	65	39
Hate	9	16	31	17	Disappointment	130	83	43	100
Illness	38	20	38	126	Discouragement	108	73	61	64
Ineptitude	53	80	25	55	Dishonor	66	53	103	34
Inferiority	86	74	36	26	Driving force for progress	42	46	30	91
Lack of arms	10	27	68	18	Failure	111	70	45	15
Lack of confidence	103	44	58	92	Fear	15	25	22	18
Lack of endeavor	41	52	53	63	Fight	13	62	54	11
Lack of power	35	48	45	17	Hate	12	32	27	29
Lack of unity	57	69	53	44	Inferiority complex	17	56	62	69
Mismanagement	84	41	84	38	Introspection	45	18	19	160
No desire	127	35	29	52	Misery	51	48	58	108
No enthusiasm	56	63	51	89	Nothing	34	15	16	30
No perseverance	79	80	53	73	Remorse	35	48	34	96
No plan	57	74	85	96	Revenge	32	57	30	49
No preparation	39	35	73	61	Ridicule	31	45	93	15
Powerlessness	55	52	43	60	Sadness	76	40	68	79
Small army	3	23	93	1	Servitude	10	54	23	21
Stopping	24	8	15	8	Shock	7	54	21	26
Superficiality	28	85	26	79	Sorrow	89	42	50	120
Treason	14	70	89	84	Stagnation	12	45	26	13
Weakness	76	37	60	41	Trying again	99	55	33	94

Table 41 The Antecedents and Consequents of DEFEAT Presented
According to the Rank Order of Their Frequencies

American	Greek	Indian	Japanese
		The Top Antecedents	
No desire	Superficiality	Small army	Illness
Giving up	Illness	Treason	Giving up
Apathy	No perseverance	No plan	No plan
Lack of confidence	Faithfulness	Mismanagement	Lack of confidence
Inferiority	Ineptitude	No preparation	No enthusiasm
Mismanagement	No plan	Lack of arms	Treason
No Perseverance	Treason		Superficiality
Weakness	Lack of unity		No perseverance
Failure			
		The Top Consequents	
Disappointment	Destruction	Deformation	Introspection
Failure	Disappointment	Dishonor	Sorrow
Discouragement	Discouragement	Depression	Misery
Despair	Failure	Ridicule	Disappointment
Trying again		Degradation	Remorse
Sorrow		Sadness	Trying again
Depression			Driving force
Sadness			For progress
Degradation			Sadness
			Inferiority
			Complex

Correlations Among Cultures
(based on antecedents above and consequents below diagonal)

	A	G	I	J
A	...	.00	− .09	.37[a]
G	.44[a]	...	.13	.51[b]
I	.23	.12	...	.15
J	.43[a]	.02	− .14	...

Affective Meaning Indices of DEFEAT

Z_E	−1.62	−2.24	−1.78	−1.95
Z_P	−0.30	−0.71	0.35	−0.56
Z_A	−0.39	−1.51	−1.17	−1.21
$C\eta$	1.01	0.74	0.87	0.67

[a] $p < .05$
[b] $p < .01$
[c] $p < .001$

America. All cultures agree that either *no preparation* or *no planning* may lead to DEFEAT. *Treason* is not an antecedent in the United States, as it is in the other three cultures. The Greeks emphasize *superficiality* and *ineptitude,* as well as *illness.* These are flaws of the individual but not of individual motivation. The Indians see DEFEAT in its political-societal context—*small army, lack of arms,* etc.

The Japanese emphasize both physiological and psychological causes of defeat (*illness, giving up, lack of confidence, no enthusiasm,* and *no perseverance*), but they underemphasize indications of insufficient ability (*lack of power, inferiority*). The Americans contrast with the Japanese in their emphasis on *inferiority.* The Japanese educational system is highly competitive and gives young people much opportunity to experience defeat. It is in this context that the meaning of the word can best be seen and explains the reason why *illness* is such an important antecedent.

The consequents in all four cultures are *disappointment* and *discouragement.* The Americans also emphasize *failure, sorrow,* and *trying again.* The Greeks emphasize *destruction* (so often experienced in their turbulent history as a consequence of defeat). The Indians emphasize *defamation* and *ridicule.*

The American view of DEFEAT may reflect the fact that the United States has not been defeated in war. This view is different from that of the other three cultures in that *treason* is underemphasized. It is known that after a defeat the most "popular" explanation which reduces cognitive dissonance is treason. It may be that a country that has not gone through such an experience does not develop the cognitive norms typical of those that have. The consequents of DEFEAT in America seem to be characterized by the fact that they are not devastating. There is a note of optimism. The Greeks see *destruction*—a more devastating consequent; the Indians, *loss of status.* The Japanese emphasize not only the consequents of defeat (*disappointment, sadness, sorrow*) but also *introspection, trying again,* and *driving force for progress.* It is clear that they see defeat as a temporary state of affairs a natural event in the ever-present process of trial and error, and an important basis for future progress. Quick recovery after World War II and the "great leap forward" in economic activity may have conditioned this meaning of DEFEAT.

Social Relations

LOVE. This is positively evaluated, potent, and active in all four cultures. The only exception is a low value on potency in India.

In all cultures affection and trust are antecedents of LOVE. The United States and Japan have a number of common antecedents: *beauty, happi-*

Table 42 Frequencies of Antecedents and Consequents of LOVE

Antecedents	American	Greek	Indian	Japanese	Consequents	American	Greek	Indian	Japanese
Admiration	62	54	64	13	Bad workmanship	0	39	23	1
Affection	161	70	93	119	Calamity	2	11	53	6
Beauty	67	37	78	98	Children	21	68	56	24
Cooperation	28	24	46	23	Companionship	121	65	62	72
Devotion to God	48	74	24	27	Concern for others	102	22	33	27
Education	0	28	37	7	Concordance	40	87	33	56
Emotions	57	51	33	111	Crime	0	17	30	7
Faith	86	69	44	8	Disappointment	52	43	59	71
Family	50	56	34	79	Emptiness	1	15	18	34
Friends	27	25	55	49	Eternity	18	18	46	23
Girl	40	49	92	24	Friends	186	135	76	145
Good conduct	6	82	65	29	Gain	19	27	22	4
Goodness	54	65	37	22	Goodness	69	51	43	31
Goodwill	27	24	38	110	Happiness	185	121	58	168
Happiness	104	53	48	97	Hatred	2	15	46	16
Instinct	15	15	21	51	Joy	105	79	61	170
Joy	91	30	40	77	Lust	6	24	59	39
Kindness	126	32	46	77	Madness	1	16	51	14
Leniency	6	17	23	61	Marriage	43	79	76	53
Loveliness	14	14	57	30	Painfulness	4	15	55	42
Morality	24	68	49	16	Peace	44	70	62	104
Niceness	27	77	28	18	Progress	23	71	50	51
Obedience	6	39	54	5	Prostitution	1	19	53	3
Presence of mate	18	6	49	51	Respect	111	47	30	41
Politeness	2	73	30	14	Sacrifice	81	47	54	27
Respect	101	51	43	65	Sex	32	44	94	39
Sex love	30	84	49	30	Sorrow	4	9	68	21
Sexual drive	18	23	46	12	Suicide	1	18	24	6
Trust	138	76	63	170	Trust	106	57	29	127
Wealth	3	15	56	3	Truth	56	68	60	71

246

Table 43   The Antecedents and Consequents of LOVE Presented
According to the Rank Order of Their Frequencies

American	Greek	Indian	Japanese

The Top Antecedents

American	Greek	Indian	Japanese
Affection	Sex love	Affection	Trust
Trust	Good conduct	Girl	Affection
Kindness	Niceness	Beauty	Emotions
Happiness	Trust		Good will
Respect	Devotion to God		Beauty
Joy	Politeness		Happiness
Faith	Affection		Family
Beauty	Faith		Joy
	Morality		Kindness

The Top Consequents

American	Greek	Indian	Japanese
Friends	Friends	Sex	Joy
Happiness	Happiness	Friends	Happiness
Companionship	Joy	Marriage	Friends
Respect	Marriage	Sorrow	Trust
Trust	Progress		Peace
Joy	Children		Companionship
Concern for others	Truth		Disappointment
Sacrifice			Truth
Goodness			

Correlations Among Cultures
(based on antecedents above and consequents below diagonal)

	A	G	I	J
A	...	.33	.34	.67[c]
G	.76[c]	...	.09	.06
I	.22	.37	...	.17
	.78[c]	.79[c]	.35	...

Affective Meaning of Indices of LOVE

	A	G	I	J
Z_E	1.38	1.13	0.37	1.32
Z_P	1.93	2.02	−0.31	0.72
Z_A	0.89	1.64	0.14	0.84
C_η	0.34	0.39	0.94	0.35

[a] $p < .05$
[b] $p < .01$
[c] $p < .001$

ness, joy, and *kindness* are emphasized by both cultures. The Greeks are unique in emphasizing *devotion to God, good conduct, morality, niceness,* and *sex love.* The Indians are unique in emphasizing the connection between *girl* and LOVE. *Devotion to God* has nothing to do with love in Japan, where love is associated with positive interpersonal emotions (*affection, goodwill, kindness, joy, happiness, trust*) and is rather nonsexual; emphasis is on *family,* and de-emphasis on *sexual drive, sex love,* and *girl.*

The consequents of LOVE include *friends, happiness,* and *joy* in most cultures. For the Americans and the Japanese they are highly intercorrelated ($r = .78$) and include an emphasis on *companionship* and *trust.* *Concern for others, sacrifice,* and *goodness* are mentioned by the Americans, *marriage,* by the Greeks and Indians, *children,* by the Greeks. The Indians are unique in emphasizing that sorrow is a consequent of LOVE. The Japanese emphasize the connection between LOVE and desirable states (*happiness, joy, trust, companionship, friends*), but they see it as a state that is short-lived and frail, as suggested by the emphasis on *disappointment and emptiness* and de-emphasis on *eternity.*

RESPECT. With the exception of the Greeks who see it as active, this concept is good, strong, and passive in all cultures.

All cultures see *morality* as an antecedent of RESPECT. The Greeks, Indians, and Japanese differ from the Americans in that they emphasize rather ordinary behavior or characteristics as leading to RESPECT. Thus *behavior with decorum* and *sincerity* lead to RESPECT in those three cultures. The Americans are unique in their overemphasis of extraordinary behavior or characteristics as antecedents of RESPECT. Thus *loyalty, admiration, courage,* and *honor* are important. The Greeks are unique in their overemphasis on *behavior with decorum, good breeding,* and *good conduct.* They emphasize that if one behaves properly he will be respected by his ingroup. The Indians are unique in emphasizing that *respect for leaders* is an antecedent of RESPECT. The Japanese are unique in emphasizing the importance of *good deeds* and *personality* in gaining RESPECT. Old age is an antecedent of RESPECT only in the less industrialized societies (Greece and India).

All four cultures have similar consequents of RESPECT. *Honor* is a universal consequent of RESPECT and *status* and *trust* are generally given. The Americans and Japanese also emphasize *friendship;* the Americans and Greeks emphasize the *return of respect.* RESPECT leads to *success* and *trust* in Greece, to *fame* and *power* in India, and to *worship* and *love* in Japan.

The major cultural difference appears to be the rather exalted view of RESPECT in the United States, which is not shared by the other three

Table 44 Frequencies of Antecedents and Consequents of RESPECT

Antecedents	American	Greek	Indian	Japanese
Admiration	**94**	*27*	56	*28*
Behavior with decorum	33	**147**	**70**	**81**
Brains	*16*	32	38	38
Courage	**126**	*22*	**76**	**71**
Endeavor	*7*	*18*	36	*25*
Excellence	53	*18*	41	56
Fear	*21*	*11*	*13*	8
Friendship	**93**	31	37	38
Good breeding	8	**105**	*22*	5
Good character	**93**	83	**72**	33
Good conduct	*14*	**82**	53	48
Good deed	*7*	49	57	**98**
Greatness	**71**	*20*	**73**	**98**
Honor	**92**	44	51	*27*
Knowledge	47	*24*	32	50
Love	**95**	**68**	52	**81**
Loyalty	**121**	34	45	57
Money	*4*	*10*	*25*	*4*
Morality	**98**	**114**	**144**	**132**
Old age	*14*	**74**	**97**	*25*
Personality	19	38	35	**114**
Power	46	38	39	61
Respect for leaders	*30*	49	**82**	*24*
Self-respect	**121**	**97**	58	41
Sincerity	56	**73**	**74**	**104**
Superiority	*16*	50	*22*	*20*
Trust	**110**	40	45	**122**

Consequents	American	Greek	Indian	Japanese
Admiration	**110**	34	67	67
A pupil	*5*	*25*	*10*	*20*
Disappointment	*9*	*12*	*19*	*20*
Endeavor	*13*	*19*	51	*25*
Envy	*19*	*16*	45	69
Fame	*12*	31	**79**	69
Friendship	**93**	62	40	**81**
Good character	48	**68**	49	*28*
Good name	42	**80**	61	*28*
Help	*26*	37	*23*	53
Honor	**255**	**110**	**123**	**129**
Knowledge	31	*17*	53	*20*
Liking	62	56	48	59
Love	60	63	54	84
Money	*3*	*20*	*26*	*2*
Obedience	37	59	54	*2*
Peace	33	51	*22*	62
Politeness	*27*	63	53	53
Position	*23*	55	66	44
Power	*17*	*14*	**72**	*22*
Progress	61	65	53	35
Recognition of superiority	65	55	52	48
Return of respect	**74**	**92**	51	63
Self-satisfaction	33	48	*17*	27
Status	**75**	**73**	**91**	31
Success	49	**66**	46	47
Trust	**130**	**66**	54	**152**
Vanity	*12*	*13*	*21*	*16*
Worship	*11*	*21*	40	**113**

Table 45   The Antecedents and Consequents of RESPECT Presented According to the Rank Order of Their Frequencies

American	Greek	Indian	Japanese

The Top Antecedents

American	Greek	Indian	Japanese
Loyalty	Behavior with	Morality	Morality
Self-respect	decorum	Old age	Trust
Trust	Morality	Respect for leaders	Personality
Morality	Good breeding	Courage	Sincerity
Love	Self-respect	Sincerity	Good deed
Admiration	Old age	Greatness	Greatness
Friendship	Sincerity	Good character	Behavior with
Good character	Love	Behavior with	decorum
Honor		decorum	Love
Greatness			Courage

The Top Consequents

American	Greek	Indian	Japanese
Honor	Honor	Honor	Trust
Trust	Return of respect	Status	Honor
Admiration	Good name	Fame	Worship
Friendship	Status	Power	Love
Status	Good character		Friendship
Return of respect	Success		
	Trust		

Correlations Among Cultures
(based on antecedents above and consequents below diagonal)

	A	G	I	J
A	. . .	.04	.34	.32
G	.70[c]	. . .	.49[a]	.21
I	.65[c]	.51[b]	. . .	.47[a]
J	.67[c]	.39[b]	.42[a]	. . .

Affective Meaning Indices of RESPECT

Z_E	1.00	0.81	0.98	0.97
Z_P	1.36	1.14	0.32	0.98
Z_A	−0.49	0.66	−0.27	−0.82
$C\eta$	0.21	0.37	0.85	0.59

[a] $p < .05$
[b] $p < .01$
[c] $p < .001$

cultures. Americans treat other people *fairly,* but RESPECT requires some extraordinary achievement, unusual courage, or the presence of some other basis of honor. The other three cultures see RESPECT as an ordinary consequent of normal living. As long as a person does what he is expected to do he receives respect and *then* is treated fairly. The consequents of RESPECT are similar across the four cultures.

SYMPATHY. This concept is a universal value, particularly in the East. It is seen as potent and active in all cultures except the United States, where it is considered weak and passive.

There is a distinction between the *common* American meaning of sympathy, which connotes *pity,* and the primary meaning of this concept, which is defined as the "quality of being affected by the state of the other with feelings correspondent in kind" (*Britannica Dictionary*). In spite of the fact that the *Britannica Dictionary* gives pity as a third choice and the above definition as the first, it appears that Americans think of *pity* and *compassion* rather than similarity of affect when defining SYMPATHY. *Care, compassion, pity, concern, love,* and *emotion* are the important American antecedents of SYMPATHY. The Greeks, on the other hand, clearly favor the primary definition, since *goodness, good character, trust, good behavior,* and *admiration* are their preferred antecedents. The Indians think of tangible objects of pity (*beggars, poverty, hardship, deplorable conditions, illness*), but they also feel that it is particularly appropriate to show sympathy toward those who follow the principles of *nonviolence.* Among the Japanese *compassion* and *pity* are indicated by the same word. Both definitions of the concept are present, however, as represented by *pity, deplorable conditions,* and *care* on the one hand and *same experience* on the other.

The consequents of SYMPATHY universally include *bonds, help,* and *offer of help.* As expected from the analysis of the antecedents, in which the Greeks are different from the other three cultures, we see a more reciprocal set of consequents in the case of the Greeks (*friendship, trust, love, respect,* and *admiration*) and more unilateral consequents among the other cultures (*compassion, care, sorrow, pity,* and *charity*).

TRUST. This concept is good, strong, and passive in the United States and Japan, bad, weak, and active in India, and good, strong, and active in Greece. Thus the semantic differential profiles of this concept in the four cultures tend to differ.

The antecedents of this concept (*honesty, sincerity, truth, truthfulness,* and *understanding*) have considerable cross-cultural generality. In addition, "good character" and fairness seems to be an important theme in

Table 46 Frequencies of Antecedents and Consequents of SYMPATHY

Antecedents	American	Greek	Indian	Japanese	Consequents	American	Greek	Indian	Japanese
Admiration	13	92	20	7	Admiration	22	66	53	39
Agreement	15	35	17	19	Bonds	81	92	91	146
Beauty	2	50	11	9	Care	119	38	45	72
Beggary	38	7	142	62	Charity	41	28	137	53
Care	136	30	41	91	Compassion	137	55	28	64
Compassion	131	54	39	147	Conduct according	12	61	53	7
Concern	91	66	70	39	to expectations				
Death	51	14	79	30	Cooperation	26	44	33	96
Defeat	20	6	25	64	Coquetry	5	17	23	13
Deplorable con-	24	19	113	101	Crying	35	16	30	13
ditions					Feeling	184	43	59	65
Emotion	69	44	17	54	Friendship	24	104	27	89
Feeling	129	57	27	63	Help	70	46	94	99
Good behavior	4	111	32	18	Joy	2	43	37	20
Good character	48	124	27	63	Kindness	158	20	82	112
Good looks	1	35	13	6	Love	29	76	41	53
Goodness	46	164	67	36	Lovers' suicide	4	39	18	5
Hardship	52	18	91	66	Marriage	1	52	14	1
Illness	42	9	78	16	Offer of help	95	79	112	74
Inferior others	8	7	15	44	Peace	14	44	75	36
Kindness	50	68	71	43	Pity	112	10	58	112
Love	71	103	20	72	Praise	8	33	55	14
Nonviolence	1	23	79	7	Respect	93	68	26	32
Pity	104	22	31	93	Satisfaction	10	41	21	22
Poverty	14	23	110	18	Saved life	5	44	79	18
Sadness	61	10	75	77	Self-respect	4	40	34	23
Same experience	44	13	53	94	Sense of superiority	6	39	26	55
Sense of superiority	5	17	6	35	Sex love	1	54	9	5
Trust	13	112	16	22	Sorrow	118	26	39	79
Understanding	129	58	55	90	Trust	23	82	32	60

Table 47   The Antecedents and Consequents of SYMPATHY Presented
According to the Rank Order of Their Frequencies

American	Greek	Indian	Japanese

The Top Antecedents

American	Greek	Indian	Japanese
Care	Goodness	Beggary	Compassion
Compassion	Good character	Deplorable conditions	Deplorable conditions
Feeling	Trust	Poverty	Same experience
Understanding	Good behavior	Hardship	Pity
Pity	Love	Nonviolence	Care
Concern	Admiration	Death	Understanding
Love	Kindness	Illness	Sadness
Emotion	Concern	Sadness	Love
		Concern	

The Top Consequents

American	Greek	Indian	Japanese
Feeling	Friendship	Charity	Bonds
Kindness	Bonds	Offer of help	Kindness
Compassion	Trust	Help	Pity
Care	Offer of help	Bonds	Help
Sorrow	Love	Kindness	Cooperation
Pity	Respect	Saved life	Friendship
Offer of help	Admiration	Peace	Sorrow
Respect			Offer of help
Bonds			Care
Help			

Correlations Among Cultures
(based on antecedents above and consequents below diagonal)

	A	G	I	J
A	...	.04	.03	.71[c]
G	−.11	...	−.29	−.16
I	.31	.00	...	.13
J	.63[c]	.19	.45[a]	...

Affective Meaning Indices of SYMPATHY

Z_E	0.12	0.90	1.35	1.25
Z_P	−0.29	0.78	0.06	0.86
Z_A	−0.75	0.48	0.72	−0.01
$C\eta$	0.65	0.24	0.78	0.52

[a] $p < .05$
[b] $p < .01$
[c] $p < .001$

Table 48 Frequencies of Antecedents and Consequents of TRUST

Antecedents	American	Greek	Indian	Japanese
Ability to keep secrets	7	40	87	18
Admiration	43	22	38	3
Companionship	24	22	34	39
Confidence	88	58	52	28
Cooperation	50	37	25	56
Diligence	11	27	57	16
Fair dealing	35	68	70	10
Faith	102	40	29	43
Friendship	58	48	45	111
High social position	1	54	72	14
Honesty	117	98	56	84
Humbleness	6	26	67	5
Joy	4	13	34	17
Justice	52	65	43	55
Keeping of promises	34	61	67	57
Knowledge	22	18	14	16
Love	76	61	16	141
Loyalty	97	41	69	65
Money	2	4	19	7
Morality	26	63	82	37
Peace	5	28	16	24
Reliance	67	48	71	30
Respect	92	41	51	89
Sincerity	77	82	78	132
Sympathy	5	34	24	8
Tolerance	7	10	13	23
Truth	117	96	65	113
Truthfulness	70	95	63	23
Understanding	158	111	84	233

Consequents	American	Greek	Indian	Japanese
Admiration	46	107	76	17
Confidence	130	52	64	83
Confiding	111	32	61	58
Cooperation	78	88	52	95
Courage	25	32	57	59
Deceit	1	17	61	6
Delegation of responsibility	24	55	50	49
Devotion	45	52	24	66
Faith	109	43	53	36
Friendship	76	84	66	145
Good conduct	8	31	58	14
Happiness	46	50	27	106
Hardship	2	11	35	11
Honesty	78	55	68	45
Honor	76	29	76	10
Knowledge	18	16	31	8
Love	67	85	29	135
Loyalty	167	64	68	75
Marriage	6	22	19	30
Peace	28	39	23	59
Progress	36	79	40	36
Reciprocal trust	80	89	57	92
Relief	7	26	16	15
Respect	119	59	68	95
Satisfaction	40	22	24	77
Sex love	10	38	20	15
Status	2	53	68	14
Success	24	53	32	43
Sympathy	3	32	33	6
Treachery	1	8	74	9

Table 49 The Antecedents and Consequents of TRUST Presented
According to the Rank Order of Their Frequencies

American	Greek	Indian	Japanese

The Top Antecedents

American	Greek	Indian	Japanese
Understanding	Understanding	Ability to keep secrets	Understanding
Honesty	Honesty	Morality	Love
Truth	Truth	Sincerity	Sincerity
Faith	Truthfulness	High social position	Truth
Loyalty	Sincerity	Reliance	Friendship
Respect	Fair dealing	Fair dealing	Respect
Confidence		Loyalty	Honesty
Sincerity			
Love			
Truthfulness			

The Top Consequents

American	Greek	Indian	Japanese
Loyalty	Admiration	Admiration	Friendship
Confidence	Reciprocal trust	Honor	Love
Respect	Cooperation	Treachery	Happiness
Confiding	Love	Honesty	Cooperation
Faith	Friendship	Loyalty	Respect
Reciprocal trust	Progress	Respect	Reciprocal trust
Cooperation		Status	Confidence
Honesty		Friendship	Satisfaction
Friendship			Loyalty
Honor			
Love			

Correlations Among Cultures
(based on antecedents above and consequents below diagonal)

	A	G	I	J
A	...	.72^c	.30	.76^c
G	.45^a	...	.60^c	.65^c
I	.44^a	.26	...	.24
J	.57^c	.58^c	.01	...

Affective Meaning Indices of TRUST

Z_E	0.83	0.76	−0.10	1.28
Z_P	0.92	0.78	−0.47	1.66
Z_A	−0.12	0.13	0.25	−0.68
$C\eta$	0.24	0.27	0.84	0.55

[a] $p < .05$
[b] $p < .01$
[c] $p < .001$

the United States (*faith, loyalty*), in Greece (*fair dealing*), and in India (*morality, ability to keep secrets, reliance, fair dealings,* and *loyalty*). Friendship is important in the two industrialized societies; that is, in Japan (*friendship, love, respect*) and the United States (*respect, love*). In status-oriented India a unique theme is concerned with *high social position.*

The consequents of TRUST include *friendship, cooperation, reciprocal trust,* and *respect* in all four cultures. In addition, in the United States strong emphasis is placed on *confidence, loyalty, honesty, honor* and *love,* in India, *admiration, honor, treachery, honesty, loyalty* and *status,* and in Japan, *love, happiness, confidence, satisfaction,* and *loyalty.*

It is also noted that TRUST is associated with the same antecedents and consequents and thus forms a "causation loop"; for example, *friendship, love, loyalty,* and *respect* are involved in such a loop for both the Americans and the Japanese. It is quite possible that certain phenomena are connected with each other in reciprocal ways, so that A causes B which in turn causes A. This may or may not be true, but at least it appears to be so in the subjective reasoning of our subjects.

We conclude that the meaning of this concept is similar across cultures, even though India is somewhat unusual in that apparently high social position leads to TRUST, which in turn leads to *honor, respect,* and *status,* symbolic of *high social position.* This reciprocal relationship between social status and TRUST is not found in the other three cultures.

Summary

The Relationship Between the Antecedent-Consequent Data and Semantic Differential Data. The information obtained by the antecedent-consequent procedure is different from that obtained from the semantic differential. Whereas the new procedure explores the cognitive component of attitudes, the semantic differential explores the affective component. The two components are often interrelated, but there are many cases in which the results obtained with one are unrelated to the results obtained with the other. Consider, as an example, the responses of the various cultures to the concept KNOWLEDGE. We note that the semantic differential profiles of the Americans and the Indians are quite similar but that those of the Americans and the Japanese are much less so. Yet there is no significant tendency for the American antecedents to be the same as the Indian, whereas there is a significant tendency (determined by the Fisher exact test) for the American antecedents to be the same as the Japanese. We inspected such similarities on the semantic differential and the antecedent-consequent method across cultures, but no systematic relationship was found.

On the other hand, there was a slight systematic relationship between semantic differential judgments and the consequents given by certain cultures. We noted five occasions on which the semantic differential profiles could be understood by examination of the antecedent-consequent results. Five occasions out of 20 is not an impressive overlap, but it suggests that the two methods are not entirely unrelated.

The examples are as follows:

1. The Indian semantic differential judgments of the concept COURAGE are distinguished by the fact that they are low in evaluation, potency, and activity. In other cultures this is not the case. Examination of the Indian consequents reveals that the Indians are significantly low in their frequency of seeing "self-confidence" as a consequent of COURAGE.

2. In Greece the concept PUNISHMENT is positively evaluated. The Greeks are unique in emphasizing positive consequents, such as "justice" and "reasonableness," for this concept.

3. The concept POWER is positively evaluated in the United States and Greece and negatively in the other two cultures. Consistent with these evaluations is a variety of negative consequents, such as "enemies" and "dictatorship," given by the Indians and Japanese.

4. The concept WEALTH is negatively evaluated in Greece and India. The consequents of WEALTH, according to the Greeks, include "selfishness"; according to the Indians they include "fear of thieves" and "arrogance."

5. The concept KNOWLEDGE is passive in India, whereas the other three cultures see it as active. The important antecedents of KNOWLEDGE in India include a "clear mind" (i.e., open, without noise); in the other three cultures an "inquiring mind" is a much more active concept. Furthermore, the consequents in the other cultures include "self-confidence," "progress," and "advancement," which are rather active concepts. In India these consequents do not occur. The Indian consequents "sense of superiority," "prestige," and "fame" are clearly less dynamic than in the other cultures.

One major purpose of the development of the antecedent-consequent method was to provide a procedure that would distinguish reliably between concepts with the same semantic differential profiles. This appears to have been achieved; for example, the concepts FREEDOM and POWER have similar profiles for Americans (about one standard deviation unit above average in evaluation, about 1.5 units above average in potency, and about one unit above average in activity). Yet the top antecedents of the two concepts do not overlap at all; nor do the consequents.

COURAGE with a profile of 1.9, 2.0, and .7 is similar to FREEDOM, which has a profile of 2.0, 1.8 and .6 non-standardized semantic differential scores (American data); yet the antecedents and consequents of these terms are entirely different. TRUST and WEALTH also have similar profiles (1.8, 1.6, —.01 versus 1.7, 1.7, —.02); yet again there is no overlap in either their antecedents or their consequents. Thus the antecedent-consequent procedure provides new information not available from semantic differential measurement. Specifically, the semantic differential profiles indicate the affective meanings, or "feeling tones," of a given concept. The antecedent-consequent procedure explores the perceived implicative relationships among concepts which include the concept under investigation. There is no reason for the two kinds of data to be interrelated; for example, it is logically possible for two events to have similar causes and different affective tones (war may lead to peace and also destruction) or for two concepts to have similar feeling tones but different antecedents or consequents (both CUCUMBER and FROG are affectively cold but one comes from seeds and the other from eggs).

One over-all observation is possible: the work with the semantic differential is striking because of the large variance accounted for by cross culturally common factors. The work with the antecedent-consequent method is impressive because of the large number of cultural differences obtained. It appears that the "learned biases" unique to each culture are reflected more readily in the antecedents and consequents than in the structure of affective meaning.

The Study of Values Through the Antecedent-Consequent Method. What kinds of antecedent and consequent are associated with concepts that are highly evaluated in each culture? Common themes found among such *A*s and *C*s would reveal underlying values, that is, cultural patterns of preferences for certain outcomes.

Such an analysis revealed that there were certain "universal themes" associated with "good outcomes"; for example, in all cultures "morality," "proper behavior," and "good characteristics of the individual" were antecedents of valued concepts. The cultures did differ, however, in the kinds of characteristic they considered good.

The ideal person, according to the Americans, would be highly motivated (achievement-oriented with drive, hard-working), seeking to improve himself, a good planner, easily adjusted to others, courageous, faithful, showing respect for the rights of others, intelligent, curious, and experienced. According to the Greeks, the important characteristics are patience and willpower, followed by diligence, honesty, ability, motivation, and courage. There are no strong achievement or planning themes among the Greeks. According to the Indians, the important characteristics are discipline, tact, openness to experience, courage, enthusiasm, and luck. Finally, according to the Japanese, the ideal individual is achievement-oriented, concerned with "being right," highly motivated, enthusiastic, courageous, faithful; he also has a pleasant personality and shows respect for others.

Each culture has some additional themes as antecedents of good concepts. The Americans repeatedly mention "respect"; the Greeks, "competition" and the "need of social control over the individual"; the Indians, "encouragement" and "inheritance"; the Japanese, "peace" and "cooperation."

The consequents that follow from "good" concepts emphasize the following themes:

AMERICAN. Individual progress, self-confidence, good adjustment, status, serenity (peace of mind), and satisfaction (achievement, joy).

GREEK. Societal well being (civilization, glory, victory) and individual success (more love, more appreciation by others).

INDIAN. Increased status of the individual; glory; societal well-being.

JAPANESE. Serenity; aesthetic satisfaction; satisfaction; self-confidence, responsibility, peace, advancement, good adjustment.

Thus, although all groups emphasize satisfaction as a major consequent, the Americans and the Japanese are unusual in emphasizing serenity, good adjustment, and achievement, with the Japanese, in addition, emphasizing aesthetic satisfaction. The Greeks are unusual in emphasizing the increased acceptance of the individual by others. The Indians are unusual in emphasizing increases in individual status more than the other cultures. At the risk of oversimplification it appears that the Americans are hoping to reach a state in which they have achieved much and can relax and admire their own self-development. The image of the self-made man enjoying his vacation-retirement suggests itself. The Greeks are hoping to reach a state in which they are greatly loved by others. The image of the adored central ingroup member is suggested. The Indians hope for a state in which they will have status, glory, and fame. The image of a Maharaja on top of an elephant in a glorious procession suggests itself. Perhaps such images are the distillations of the values of these cultures.

We turn now to those concepts that were evaluated negatively.

For the Americans great disvalues are ignorance, loneliness, and injury to self-esteem. A consequent of unfortunate events is likely to be guilt. For the Greeks injury to self-esteem (dishonor), superficiality, and loss of friends are likely to lead to destruction. For the Indians frustration, bad spirits (demons), and dishonor are disvalues which may lead to loss of status. For the Japanese deviation from the proper conditions, ignorance, and loneliness are disvalues and may lead either to guilt or to introspection and correction.

Such themes fit the analyses of values presented above. The American concern with achievement and self-development is clearly inconsistent with ignorance and injury to self-esteem. The Greek concern with being loved is inconsistent with dishonor and loss of friends. The Indian concern for status comes through in all analyses. The Japanese concern for achievement and self-development is inconsistent with ignorance.

A Word of Caution Concerning Interpretations. We have suggested that the antecedent-consequent method is effective in the exploration of implicit norms and values. It must be remembered, however, that much depends on the "meaningful" interpretation of the obtained results. The data are not meaningful in themselves without outside information concerning the economic, political, religious, and other cultural characteristics of the samples that provided the responses. To understand, for example, the American underemphasis of *hunger* as a cause of DEATH one needs to know about the availability of food in North America; to understand the Japanese emphasis on *length of life* as an antecedent of DEATH one must know some Japanese philosophy and history.

Applications to Research on Conflict Resolution. To study conflict resolution in the laboratory it is necessary to develop materials in relation to the subjects from different cultures that are likely to show substantial disagreements. The present method, by revealing both cultural similarities and differences in the perception of implicative relationships among concepts, allows us to select concepts on which members of different cultures are likely to disagree. By examining the overlap in the antecedents and consequents of each of our 20 concepts across our four cultural groups we can specify that particular pairs of cultures will experience conflict concerning particular issues; for example, we can predict that Americans and Greeks will disagree about issues centered around the concept of PUNISHMENT. Thus, if we were to give a negotiation team consisting of Americans and Greeks a problem involving the inappropriate behavior of an employee, whether he should be punished by his supervisor, the kind of punishment that would be appropriate, etc., we would expect the Greeks to take a much "tougher" position on PUNISHMENT, since "it is good for a man to be punished." We can even predict the kinds of argument that the Greeks would present in the negotiations—"the man will become more reasonable after he is punished," "it is just that he be punished," and so on.

Our data suggest that in a negotiation situation between Americans and

Japanese there would be much agreement on the meaning of FREEDOM; but what if the Americans propose to use POWER to achieve FREEDOM? This is a more complex case because POWER is a negative concept for the Japanese but not for the Americans. Cognitive interaction would probably change the evaluation of FREEDOM and make it a less positive concept for the Japanese. If the Americans insisted on the use of POWER to achieve FREEDOM, the Japanese would be likely to see some of the words connected with POWER become connected with FREEDOM. Thus *dictatorship* and *force* and even *war* might become connected with FREEDOM: Thus we might expect the Japanese to be most reluctant to accept the American proposal. The Americans would be at a loss to explain the Japanese reactions and would tend to think that the Japanese lacked intelligence, knowledge, and respect, since for the Americans, but not the Japanese, these are concepts connected with POWER. The Japanese, on their side, would deny that *success, control,* and *influence* would result from the use of POWER. Thus each side, assuming that the other had the same image of key terms such as POWER, would be likely to find it more and more difficult to understand the reactions of the other. The disagreements would lead to further deterioration of the relationship. The Japanese would see the Americans as evil, power-hungry, would-be dictators, and the Americans would see the Japanese as stupid and ignorant.

Of course, it is necessary to validate these hypotheses. If, however, such validation supports our predictions, the present method could become a powerful procedure for the determination of appropriate experimental materials for studies of negotiations across cultures. Furthermore, the method would provide a kind of "map" of the negotiations, predicting some of the arguments that would be used by each of the sides.

Concluding Comment

The antecedent-consequent procedure described in this chapter has been found to have high reliability and validity (Haried, 1969) and to provide a useful approach to the study of the cognitive structures of individuals representing various cultural groups. This method yields a rich harvest of cultural differences and is most promising for further cross-cultural research.

CHAPTER EIGHT

A Cross-Cultural Study of Role Perceptions

HARRY C. TRIANDIS, HOWARD MCGUIRE,
TULSI B. SARAL, KUO-SHU YANG, WALLACE LOH,
AND VASSO VASSILIOU

One of the most important concepts of the scheme described in Part I is *role*. This concept is central to much anthropological, social psychological, and sociological thinking. In fact, some social scientists believe that a large proportion of the variance in human social behavior is determined by social roles.

The literature on role theory is vast (e.g., Biddle and Thomas, 1966), but most of the theoretical literature is concerned with problems of conceptualization and has no connection with empirical work. This chapter is part of a series that has followed the reverse process; that is, empirical work resulted in theoretical formulations that led to particular theoretical deductions which were then tested with new empirical studies. Specifically, this chapter reports the latter empirical studies.

Triandis, Vassiliou, and Nassiakou (1968) have presented a procedure for the cross-cultural measurement of role perceptions. An instrument, called the role differential, which is an adaptation of the behavioral differential (Triandis, 1964b), provides an opportunity for subjects from different cultures to indicate the behaviors they believe are appropriate between persons holding particular roles in their cultures. In the first study 100 role pairs, such as father-son, male-female, and prostitute-client, were judged by American and Greek subjects against a set of 60 scales defined by interpersonal behaviors. A typical item is the following

Male-Female

would   ′ X ′ ′ ′ ′ ′ ′   would not
let go first through a door

263

The subjects were instructed to consider the first member of a role pair as the actor and the second as the person acted on. The behaviors were obtained from pretest samples of subjects from each culture who indicated what behaviors are likely to occur between persons holding the various roles. In each culture the most frequently elicited behaviors constitute that culture's role differential.

In this chapter we refer to *role* rather than *role pair*. Actually this is a more specific definition of role, since it considers the relationship explicitly; for instance, the role son-father is not the same as the role son-mother, yet when we say the role of *son* we do not make this distinction. Our definition of role as a relationship seems clearer.

The data obtained, with any differential, form a cube with three sides: concepts (in this case, roles), scales (behaviors), and subjects. A variety of factor analyses may be employed to reduce the complexity of the data. In the Triandis et al. (1968) study the responses of the subjects in each culture were summed, the correlations of the scales were factor-analyzed, and four culture-common (possibly pancultural) factors were identified. Two of these factors were bipolar, the other two unipolar.

1. *Association-dissociation* (defined by behaviors such as help, reward, advise, stand up for, be interested in, be eager to see, and respect versus grow impatient with, be indignant with, argue with, infuriate, fear, be prejudiced against, and exclude from the neighborhood).

2. *Superordination-subordination* (defined by behavior such as to command, advise, treat as a subordinate, inspect work of, and feel superior to versus apologize to, ask for help of, be dependent on and accept commands of).

3. *Intimacy* (defined by kiss, cuddle, love, marry, pet, and cry for).

4. *Hostility* (defined by throw rocks at, fight with, quarrel with, exploit, cheat, and so on).

In addition to the culture-common factors, each culture yielded culture specific factors. The American data yielded six additional culture specific factors (*contempt, tutoring, kinship acceptance, high intensity behaviors, envy,* and *work acceptance*). The Greek data yielded three more factors labeled *ingroup concern for consensus* (adore the same God with, be saddened by attitude of, desire good attitude of), *suspicion* (be cautious, be discriminating), and *overt aggression* (hit).

To compare role perceptions cross-culturally it is essential to obtain some equivalent dimensions in each culture. It is then possible to express any role by a set of coordinates on these common dimensions; for example, it is possible to state that a particular role involves moderate association, high superordination, a slight amount of intimacy, and no hostility. By noting the location of the role in the mathematical space defined by the common dimensions it is possible to make cross-cultural comparisons.

Unfortunately the culture-common factors obtained in any study of this sort depend in part on the sample of roles employed by the investigator; for example, an investigator who sampled only family roles could not have obtained the intimacy dimension becuse his roles would not differ in this dimension.

Triandis et al. (1968) present role comparisons between American and Greek samples on the association, superordination, intimacy, and hostility dimensions. They argue that these culture-common dimensions may be truly fundamental and other dimensions emerging from factor analyses may be due to accidents of sampling. It is conceivable that further studies might reveal additional fundamental dimensions, but for the time being we may assume that these four are *the* basic dimensions of role perception. These authors also selected 60 American- and 60 Greek-generated behaviors and asked samples of American and Greek students to judge the behaviors on the four culture-common dimensions, using standard Thurstone equal-appearing interval procedures; for example, the behavior "to hit" was judged on the intimacy dimension to be quite intimate. The scale values of the 120 behaviors obtained from each culture on each of the four culture-common dimensions were intercorrelated, and it was determined that *association* is highly positively correlated with *giving status* and negatively correlated with *hostility,* whereas *intimacy* is an independent factor. From this finding they concluded that positive versus negative affect and intimacy versus formality are *the* basic dimensions of social behavior.

Finally, Triandis et al. (1968) have presented a theoretical scheme in which roles are to be described by their coordinates in a space defined by association, status, and intimacy. They argue that since both behaviors and roles can be placed in the affect-status-intimacy space it is possible to determine the behaviors that are appropriate for each role by considering the coordinates of any role and all behaviors in this space.

The authors also define *general intentions* (e.g., to be helpful) and *behavioral intentions* (e.g., to wash the dishes) and argue that the latter are expressed in behavior. They stated that behavioral intentions and behavior are largely situationally determined; for example, behavior depends on the person's *knowledge* (does he know how to wash dishses), previous *habits* (does he usually wash dishes), *intrinsic satisfaction with the behavior* (does he enjoy washing dishes), as well as on the behavioral *norms* defined by the person's role (male-female, husband-wife, guest-host, etc.). On the other hand, general intentions are less situationally determined and may therefore be an appropriate focus for theory. The responses made by subjects to a particular behavioral differential *scale* are behavioral intentions;

the sums of these responses reflected in a role's *factor* scores are general intentions. They finally define a correspondence between the general intentions and the behavioral intentions obtained with the role differential, on the one hand, and the *general behavioral norms* and the *behavioral norms* obtained with the behavioral differential, on the other, and show that empirically such correspondence is justified.

Triandis et al. also argue that the basic dimensions common to both general intentions and general behavioral norms may be three: (a) giving versus denying affect, (b) giving versus denying status, and (c) intimacy versus formality. They propose to use these three dimensions in future theory building. They suggest that a number of variables determine the extent to which a person will give affect, status, or desire intimacy and may include the length of acquaintance, the history of interpersonal reinforcements, and the power of one to reinforce the other.

Finally, looking at the high correlations between the coordinates of the behaviors used in one of their studies on the affect, status, and hostility (negative) scales and the independence of the intimacy scale from these three scales, they suggest that perhaps both roles and behaviors might be expressed in this most fundamental affect-intimacy space.

Oncken (1968) tested this speculation and found that it is oversimplified. By having samples of behaviors and roles judged by Thurstone equal-interval procedure scaling on the four culture-common factors isolated by Triandis et al. (1968) he obtained scale values for each behavior and each role on four dimensions. He correlated the Thurstone scale values of the *behaviors* on the four factors and replicated the Triandis et al. results; that is, he found that affect and intimacy are indeed the basic independent dimensions of perception of social behavior. However, the corresponding correlations of the scale values of the *roles* yielded a two-dimensional space consisting not of affect and intimacy but of affect and status. Oncken then developed a mathematical model that permits the "translation" of data obtained from the role space to the behavior space. The model assumes that coordinates of a role in the role space can be mathematically transformed to coordinates in the behavior space. It assumes that affect in the role space has the same dimension and the same units of measurement as affect in the behavior space; similarly, the status in the role space can be transferred to the status dimension in the behavior space. With this model he was able to test Triandis' speculations that the appropriateness of a behavior in a given role is an inverse function of the distance between the coordinates of the behavior and the role in the behavior space; for example, roles judged as intimate and subordinate would require behaviors judged as intimate and involving the giving of affect. Oncken's test of this theoretical speculation resulted in strong support of the Triandis argument.

Specifically, Oncken used the Thurstone scale values of the roles and behaviors he obtained from his subjects to predict the role differential judgments of the subjects tested two years earlier by Triandis. He found that for 29 of 50 roles he was able to predict the judgments of Triandis' subjects at a statistically significant level.

The usefulness of such a model can be made apparent if we consider the following: the adequate description of social behavior in a culture may require the investigation of 250 roles and 100 social behaviors. Such an investigation with the role differential would require 25,000 judgments. On the other hand, if there were only two fundamental dimensions of perception of roles and two dimensions of perception of behaviors, we should need only 500 plus 200, or 700, judgments to describe all important roles in the culture. Assuming that 1000 subjects are required to obtain a complete picture of role perception in a complex culture such as the United States, and since most people can make 700 judgments in less than one and one-half hours, the total subject time with this approach would be 1500 hours. The role differential would require 53,500 hours of subject time. Thus, if the Triandis-Oncken model can be made to work adequately, a tremendous saving in subject time in studies of role perception would be possible.

It is now possible to restate our cross-cultural understanding of role perception in terms of the following assumptions and hypotheses:

AXIOM I. *Any role pair can be defined by a set of coordinates on behavior factors.*

AXIOM II. *Any interpersonal behavior can be defined by a set of coordinates on behavior factors.*

From considerations of theories of cognitive consistency, these axioms lead to the following:

THEOREM I. *The distance between a role pair, defined as a point in the behavior factor space, and any behavior, defined also as a point in the behavior factor space, is inversely proportional to the judged appropriateness of the behavior taking place between persons occupying that role.*

Support for Theorem I was obtained by Oncken (1968).

Correspondence of General Behavior Norms and Factors Obtained in Other Studies. The argument that emerges from a review of the above studies may be restated. There are three fundamental general behavioral norm dimensions: giving versus denying affect, giving versus denying status, and intimacy versus formality. Any role can be expressed by a set of coordinates in this three-dimensional space; any behavior can be expressed by a set of coordinates in the *same* space. A behavior is appropriate, within a given role, if it has similar coordinates in the common role-behavior space with this role.

There remains the empirical fact that in different studies we do not obtain these three dimensions but some other dimensions that appear similar to them. It is argued here, however, that specific factor analytic results depend on sampling, not only of roles but also of scales (behaviors) and subjects. Variations are to be expected and these are not necessarily accidental but simply involve distortions due to interaction between the general behavioral norms and situational factors; for example, the early work with the behavioral differential (Triandis, 1964b) had extracted five factors: formal social acceptance (to admire, to vote for), marital acceptance (to marry, to date), friendship (to gossip with, to play with), social distance (to exclude from the neighborhood, to reject as kin by marriage), and superordination-subordination. It can be argued that formal social acceptance is a phenotype of the basic genotypes of positive affect and formality, with giving of status; marital acceptance is the phenotype of the basic genotypes of positive affect, intimacy, and giving of status; and friendship involves positive affect, intermediate intimacy and some giving of status. Social distance is a phenotype that depends on the genotypes of negative affect, intimacy, and denying status. Finally, superordination-subordination is probably a clear manifestation of the denying-giving status genotype. In other words, although Triandis (1964b) obtained five phenotypic dimensions, they can be reduced to only three genotypic dimensions.

In cross-cultural replications (America-Japan-India) of the behavioral differential (Triandis, Tanaka, & Shanmugam, 1967), we obtained factors that closely correspond to the formal social acceptance, friendship, and marital acceptance factors. The separation of the formal social acceptance or respect factor from the friendship factor was also obtained from a representative sample of the population of urban Greece (Triandis, Vassiliou, & Thomanek, 1966).

The role differential replications also appear to extract factors that are phenotypic but clearly related to the more fundamental genotypic factors. Thus Loh and Triandis (1968), in two separate analyses of Peruvian data, obtained factors which they labeled rejection (insult, ignore), respect (admire, trust), formal friendship (treat as equal, accept as intimate friend), subordination (not treat as subordinate, envy), and marital acceptance (marry, accept marriage to own sister). These factors obviously correspond to the earlier Triandis (1964b) factors.

Yang (1970) obtained from Taiwan students a set of factors which he labeled *nurturance* (help, love, respect, protect), *hostility* (be angry with, hate, and laugh at), *superordination* (punish, command), and a separate *subordination* (fear, obey, apologize to) factor. These factors again resemble the earlier American factors, although Yang also obtained two additional factors (*acquiescence* and *dependency*) which did not appear in the American data. Yang also showed that highly authoritarian subjects, as measured by a specially standardized balanced *F*-scale, tended to see more nurturance, acquiescence, subordination, and dependency as appropriate in subordinate-to-superordinate and in equal-status roles than did subjects low in authoritarianism. Furthermore, the highly authoritarian subjects considered *superordination* as more appropriate in superordinate-subordinate roles than did the nonauthoritarian. Personality consistencies in the judgment of role constructs have also been obtained by Messick and Kogan (1966).

Using a somewhat different format of the role differential, Osgood (1970) tested students in Japan, Hawaii, and Illinois. All possible combinations of 20 interpersonal verbs and 40 roles [drawn from the Triandis et al. (1968) pool of roles] were rated by the following format:

FATHER to defy SON
never   seldom   sometimes   depends   often   usually   always

The correlations among the subjects' responses to the verbs were subjected to factor analysis and four factors were extracted. Osgood calls two of these factors association-dissociation, with suggestions of formality in the first case and intimacy in the second case. Actually, these factors are phenotypes that appear to be very similar to those found in previous work. The first factor grouped "cooperate with" with "show respect for," on the one hand, and "defy," "criticize," and "hinder," on the other. It is quite close in meaning to the respect factor (Triandis, Vassiliou, & Thomanek, 1966). The second factor contrasted "display affection to," "console," and "protect" with "keep distance," which suggests a similarity to the intimacy-formality factor of Triandis, Vassiliou, and Nassiakou (1968). The third factor was clearly superordination-subordination. The last, which was not clearly present in all three samples, suggested the hostility ("corrupt," "deceive," "hinder," "compete with") factor.

Thus, using a different technique, but a similar set of roles, Osgood found factors that appear to be generated from various combinations of affect, intimacy, and status.

Triandis et al. (1968) reviewed the close relationship of the commonly obtained, culture-common dimensions of social behavior and the work of other investigators (e.g., Foa, Longabaugh). They conclude that association-dissociation, superordination-subordination, and intimacy are the fundamental dimensions of human social behavior and are obtained with different methods of investigation.

At the lowest level of social behavior animal studies reveal the phenomena of *solidarity* (grooming, helping, cooperating among primates), *dominance* (pecking orders for food, sex), and *territoriality* (attack of "outsiders" getting into animal's territory). The correspondence with giving affect, denying status, and hostility is striking. Furthermore, primates do change their behavior toward one another and toward humans, over time, which suggests the dimension of intimacy. In short, solidarity, status, and intimacy are probably the basic dimensions of ingroup behavior and hostility, the basic ingroup/outgroup dimension of social behavior.

If we view these three dimensions as genotypes and the obtained factor analytic results as phenotypes, we may be able to simplify an otherwise most complex problem. In this chapter we examine the extent to which this is possible.

The Hypotheses. If the theory sketched out in the preceding section has some validity, there should be similar factors employed to describe roles in many different cultures. These factors should be phenotypes of the hypothesized culture-common genotypes—solidarity (or giving positive effect), status, intimacy, and hostility. A few phenotypic factors should be sufficient to describe the majority of the variance of role perceptions; some of them should be quite similar from culture-to-culture. On the other hand, the way the members of various cultures respond to the roles does not necessarily have to be identical. The members of each culture when tested with role differentials may provide different coordinates for each role on the culture-common factors. Finally, we expect shifts in the size of these coordinates to be systematically related to the nature of the role relationship. Roles may differ in the degree of cooperation required between the members of the role in that some involve common goals and require cooperation, whereas others involve incompatible goals and result in conflict. We will call the former type ingroup roles, the latter type, conflict roles. There are also other roles that involve a mixture of cooperation and conflict. Probably most roles are of a mixed kind. We will call these outgroup roles, using the definition of ingroup-outgroup provided by the Greeks (Chapter 9), since it involves the most precise discrimination between the various types of role.

These expectations may be stated slightly more formally. A limited set of phenotypic behavior factors will suffice to account for the majority of the variance of role perceptions in each culture. It is expected that more than 50% of the variance of role perceptions will be determined by a limited set of five or six factors, as we examine different roles in each culture.

HYPOTHESIS I. *Across cultures there will be some invariance in the nature of the phenotypic factors employed in role perception.*

Specifically, it is expected from previous work that three or four of the five or six factors necessary to account for 50% of the variance of role perceptions will be equivalent (or similar) as we examine the factor structures across cultures.

HYPOTHESIS II. *The coordinates of a role on the culture-common (or equivalent) behavior factors will be different from culture to culture.*

Specifically, it is expected that, for the three or four culture-common factors, the coordinates of a particular role in one culture will not necessarily be the same as the coordinates of this role in another culture. Nevertheless, the data will conform to Theorem I, for when the coordinates of a role change there will be a corresponding change of the coordinates of the behaviors that are appropriate in that role.

HYPOTHESIS III. *The largest changes in the coordinates of roles on behavior factors will be observed when roles are examined that differ in status or the ingroup-outgroup dimension.*

Specifically, this hypothesis is a deduction from Oncken's finding that status and affect are the most important dimensions of role perception. The hypothesis leads us to expect large changes in the coordinates of roles on behavior factors when we examine roles that involve high status individuals interacting with low status individuals and compare them with roles in which low status individuals interact with high status individuals. Similarly, in examining roles involving the exchange of positive affect (e.g., ingroup roles) or those involving the exchange of negative affect (e.g., conflict roles) we should obtain large differences in the coordinates of roles on the behavior factors. If Hypothesis III is supported, and since Theorem I has already been supported, it will be possible to predict the behaviors that will be appropriate within a particular role in a particular culture by simply knowing the amount of status in the relationship and the affective bond within that role. Such information is easy to obtain from informants.

Method

The basic instrument of this study was the role differential (Triandis et al., 1968) described above. A sample of 24 culture-common roles was selected from the Triandis et al. study. The sample (see Table 5 for the actual roles) consisted of roles that were quite heterogeneous, as determined in the previous study, and represented the basic *types* of role found in that study. Specifically, there was at least one role in each of the cells of a 3 × 3 design which consisted of (a) high-low status, (b) equal status, and (c) low-high status roles and (a) ingroup, (b) outgroup, and (c) conflict roles; for example, the high-low status ingroup cell was represented by the roles father-son, father-daughter, and mother-son. The high-low status outgroup cell (as defined in Triandis et al., 1968, for the Greek sample) included foreman-worker and boss-secretary. A high-low conflict role was client-prostitute. Equal status roles included brother-brother, low-high status roles son-father, etc. In addition to these roles, which are easy to classify in the 3 × 3 design, there were some that were labeled "general roles." Specifically, these roles were the roles woman-man, man-woman and young man-old man.

The sample of behaviors employed to define the behavior scales of the role differential was also selected to be maximally heterogeneous and to represent all important factors found by Triandis et al. (1968). Twenty scales were used in each culture. (Table 4 includes examples of the particular behaviors).

The original study was designed to include three cultures: Illinois Americans, several samples of Greeks, and northern Indians from the area of Uttar Pradesh. However, since the data of Loh and Triandis (1968) and Yang (1970) were amenable to similar analyses and the generality of findings from five cultures provides more confirmation of a theory than findings from only three cultures, it was decided to include in the present chapter the equivalent analyses of a Peruvian data of Loh and Triandis and the Taiwan Chinese data of Yang. Thus the present report presents data from five cultures. The Peruvian and Taiwan data were collected for a different purpose and have already been reported in another form. The present report provides a re-analysis of these data.

Since the Peruvian and Taiwan data were collected for different purposes, the samples of roles and behaviors of these studies overlap very little with the samples of roles used in the three main cultures. Nevertheless the data conform sufficiently to our requirements to be useful.

A total of about 1800 subjects responded to the role differential. More specifically, the samples of subjects can be described as follows:

AMERICANS. Three hundred and fifty introductory male psychology students at the University of Illinois.

GREEKS. (a) The first Greek sample consisted of 322 new recruits for officer candidate school. They came from all parts of the country, all had at least a high school education, and the majority had several years of college. (b) A representative sample of the population of the city of Thessaloniki, in northern Greece, constituted the second sample, which also included females. This city has a population of approximately 350,000. A procedure described earlier by Triandis, Vassiliou, and Thomanek (1966) for interview work with the behavioral differential was employed in door-to-door calls. A total of 400 persons was interviewed but usable data were obtained from only 287.

INDIANS. A sample of 300 undergraduate (male and female) students from Lucknow University was equally representative of the urban and rural student populations of Uttar Pradesh. Of the 300 students tested 253 usable questionnaires were obtained.

PERUVIANS. A sample of 161 males who were high school students in Lima, Peru was interviewed.

TAIWAN, CHINESE. This sample consisted of 227 students from the National University of Taiwan and Taiwan Normal University, in Taipei, enrolled in introductory courses.

Analyses

The data consist of n roles, judged on m scales, by N subjects. In the past we summed the responses of the N subjects and obtained an n by m matrix of scores, which consisted of the sums of the judgments of the N subjects. The $m \times m$ matrix of intercorrelations (based on n observations per variable) of the behavior descriptive scales was subjected to factor analysis; for example, in the main study by Triandis et al. (1968) 100 roles and 60 behaviors were utilized in the analysis. The result was 60×60 matrices of intercorrelations in each culture. These matrices were based on 100 observations per variable (behavior scale).

In this study we adopted a different strategy; that is, we performed separate analyses for each role. Thus the $m \times m$ matrices of intercorrelations among the behaviors were based on N observations (the number of subjects). Since we employed a small number of behaviors (20) and a large number of subjects (depending on the sample, anywhere from 161 to 350), our results are much more stable than those in our previous study (Humphreys et al., 1968). The ratio of observations to variables is much larger than five, which both Tucker and Humphreys suggest as a rule of thumb for stable factor analytic results.

The disadvantage of the present approach is that it requires a large number of factor analyses. In our case we performed 178. To understand why we performed so many it is necessary to describe the exact nature of these samples. Thus in Illinois 350 males judged 24 roles on 20 behavior-descriptive scales. In Greece we had three samples: (a) 322 subjects judged 24 roles on 20 scales, (b) 143 judged 24 roles on 20 scales in one order of presentation of the scales, and (c) 145 subjects judged 24 roles on 20 scales but with a different order of presentation of the scales. In India there were 253 satisfactory subjects who judged 24 roles on 20 scales. In Peru 77 subjects judged 25 roles on 17 scales and 84 subjects judged 25 roles on a different set of 18 scales. In Taiwan 227 subjects judged 15 roles on 20 scales, but only 8 of the 15 roles overlapped sufficiently with the American-Greek-Indian study to be included in the present analysis.

Now it should be clear that there are 24 American factor analyses, 72 Greek, 24 Indian, 50 Peruvian, and only 8 Taiwan-Chinese. This sums to 178 analyses. Each analysis was done on a 20×20 matrix of correlations (except in Peru, where the matrices had 17 or 18 variables) and 161 to 350 observations per variable were utilized in the computation of the intercorrelations. We performed principal axes factor analyses with unities in the communalities and iterative communality estimates which were used in the final factor analytic solution. Inspection of the drop in the size of the eigenvalues determined the number of factors to be extracted and rotated. The typical solution involved from four to six factors. The most frequent solution involved five. Thus a role can be expressed as a set of factor scores on these five factors. Since the mean scores of the subjects' judgments on each scale were available, the factor scores were obtained by averaging the mean judgments of the subjects on those scales with high loadings on a particular factor. These averages were rounded off to the nearest half-point, since considerations of reliability suggested that the accuracy of these scores is no greater than half a scale unit. These procedures provided a "profile" for each role (see Table 5); for example, for the father-son role and from the American data we see that low hostility, low intimacy, high respect, and high superordination are seen as appropriate behaviors for this role by American male students.

The Within-Culture Homogeneity of the Data

In previous reports of role perception in different cultures (e.g., Triandis et al., 1968) it is assumed that the role perceptions within culture are relatively homogeneous, so that the between-culture variance will be much larger than the within-culture variance. This assumption needs to be tested. If we define a culture-group as one sharing the same language, race, religion, and nationality and we can show that there is the kind of homogeneity required to permit us to make statements about "role perception with this culture," we will know the limits of generalization of the above hypotheses. Accordingly, since Greece is a case in which a group of people share a language, race, religion, and nationality, it was decided to attempt a systematic sampling of Greeks and an examination of the variability of role perception in that culture.

The variability of role perceptions can be examined in various ways. One method determines whether there are systematic relationships between demographic variables and role perceptions. The three Greek samples were analyzed. The first was representative of high school graduates from the whole country and the other two representative of one of the two largest cities. Our first approach was to use Tucker-Messick (1963) two-mode factor analysis. This method results in "subject factors" that indicate inter-subject consistencies in response patterns. The factor scores of the subjects on these subject factors were then correlated with the demographic variables we had collected in our interviews. The demographic variables included age, sex, region of the country (birth), urban-rural information, number of years the subject has lived in an urban environment, region of the country in which subject went to school, population of the town in which he grew up, and social-class indices based on father's education, mother's education, father's occupation, and family income. The subjects were also asked to answer a number of questions concerning the appropriate ways in which to bring up children.

The results obtained with the sample of high school graduates from all parts of the country showed no significant trends with any of the demographic variables. In other words, this is an extremely homogeneous sample. Whatever significant results were obtained can easily be attributed to chance, since a large number of significance tests was performed.

Some trends could be determined between the subject-types obtained from the factor analysis and the demographic characteristics.

SUBJECT-TYPE I. These subjects tended to give extreme judgments to obviously taboo behaviors, such as sex-love between family members, showing no contempt in the guest-to-host role, and emphasized nurturance within the ingroup. We might call these subjects *stereotypic*. There were more of them from the Ionian Islands and Thrace and from the large cities whose parents tended to have less education. Most probably, the under-educated parents in other parts of the country and the nonurban environments did not send their children to high school (high schools are more accessible in the Ionian Islands and large cities); hence these data are probably not meaningful in terms of regions of the country but rather reflect the difference in parental education. It is well known (Triandis & Triandis, 1962) that low education is cross-culturally associated with stereotypic responses.

SUBJECT-TYPE II. These subjects are characterized by low hostility in outgroup roles and extremely low hostility in low-high and equal status roles. They tended to have more highly educated parents.

SUBJECT-TYPE III. These subjects are characterized by more hostility, more superordination, less nurturance in high-low status roles, and extreme inhibition of hostility in ingroup roles. No demographic variables were related to this subject type, but these subjects tended to answer a number of opinion questions concerning how to raise children by emphasizing the use of ridicule in socialization and by not punishing an angry child when it is making a scene.

SUBJECT-TYPE IV. These subjects emphasized intimacy in heterosexual relations and did not approve of intimacy in conflict group relations. Again no demographic variables were related to this type, and on the child-rearing opinion questionnaire there was only an indication of low severity in socialization.

SUBJECT-TYPE V. These subjects emphasized that there should be no hostility in equal-status roles but that there should be high nurturance. Again there was no relation with the demographic characteristics, but the child-rearing opinion questionnaire indicated a tendency to be consistent in rewarding children and a willingness to play (spend time) with children.

SUBJECT-TYPE VI. These subjects were extreme in showing superordination in high-low status roles and avoided intimacy in them. There were no demographic relationships but the preferred child-rearing procedures suggested authoritatianism (end justifies the means; acceptable to threaten children; it is good for a child to have the same opinions as his parents).

The results of this analysis can be summarized by stating that only education had some dependable relation to differences in role perception. The relationships between role perception and child-rearing opinions cannot be considered as established, since a very large number of tests was performed and statistical theory would lead to the expectation that several of the observed correlations would be significant by chance. We conclude that this is an exceptionally homogeneous population.

The responses of the samples representing the cities of Greece were first analyzed by selecting a few representative roles and doing separate factor analyses of the scales. After these factor analyses, we summed the responses of each subject to the scales, with high loadings on each factor. These composite scores were placed in analyses of variance in which the sex, age, and social status of the subjects were the independent treatments. The results of these analyses again show no relation between the demographic variables and role perceptions; most of the significant results were at the 5% level and could have been obtained by chance. A few results, however, reached significance at the .001 level and should be considered as reliable.

The sex variable had a small number of highly significant ($p < .001$) effects, mainly in responses to the hostility factor involving outgroup or conflict roles. In such roles females tended to see less hostility as appropriate than males. The age variable had an effect on the hostility factor in conflict roles, with older subjects seeing more hostility as appropriate than the younger subjects. Social status had an effect only in increasing the cognitive complexity of the judgments, since we found a highly significant tendency for high-social-status subjects to see more friendship behavior as appropriate in conflict roles.

A few of the interactions between the independent variables also reached highly significant levels. Thus high-social-status males differed from other males and also from females in seeing greater admiration as appropriate in the mother-son role. In the wife-husband role a rather complex triple interaction (sex by age by social class) appeared twice, suggesting that older high-status females had a rather cynical view of this role, older low-status females, a rather idealistic view, and men showed no such trend. Specifically, the older high-status females saw less friendship and less admiration in the wife role, and the older low-status females saw more friendship and more admiration in the role than was the case in all other samples. High-status males saw more hostility in conflict roles than did other samples; otherwise most of the other interactions were not significant.

An additional analysis of the representative samples utilized the discriminant-function analysis technique. Since our previously mentioned analyses indicated that differences in role perceptions could be obtained only from family roles and were mostly related to social-status differences (which are highly correlated with education), the discriminant-function analyses were performed only on the nine family roles which were available in our sample and were attempts to discriminate between the subjects who belonged to the categories of social status. The analyses utilized both Greek representative samples and discriminated five social status groups having the following Ns: low status, N of 100; upper-lower, N of 54; lower-middle, 94; middle-middle, 38, upper-middle, 12.

Of the nine discriminant-function analyses only three resulted in significant ($p < .01$) Wilks *lambdas*. These were for the father-son, son-father, and mother-son roles.

FATHER-SON. The first discriminant function, which accounted for 75% of the discrimination between social-status groups, has a positive loading on control (reprimand, quarrel with, and scold) and a negative loading on dependence (ask for advice and help). The relation with social status was curvilinear, with the very low and very high status groups showing low control and high dependence and the middle social status groups showing high control and low dependence.

The second discriminant function accounted for 12% of the discrimination and had a loading on the *no hostility* factor. Again the relationship was curvilinear, with the middle-social-status groups showing a less extreme lack of hositility than the other groups. The remaining discriminant functions did not give clear results.

SON-FATHER. The first discriminant function accounted for 43% of the discrimination and reflected the *no hostility* factor. The middle social-status groups showed more extreme *lack* of hostility in this role than did the others.

The second discriminant function accounted for 35% of the discriminatory power and had high loadings on *subordination* and *informality*. The high-social-status group was different from the remaining groups in that it indicated that less *subordination* (accept orders, ask for advice and help) and less *informality* (have fun with, pet) were more appropriate in the son-to-father role than in other groups.

The third discriminant function accounted for 20% and was loaded on *control,* (quarrel with, scold). The lowest status group differed from the other groups in that it indicated that control of the father by the son would be less appropriate.

The fourth discriminant function accounted for only 2% of the discrimination and was loaded on *nurturance* (take care of, love). It discriminated the lower-middle-social-status groups from the others in that these groups report relatively less nurturance as appropriate to this role. The most nurturance was shown by the two high-social-status groups.

MOTHER-SON. The first discriminant function accounted for 79% of the discrimination and was loaded on *control* and *intimacy*. The major contrast occurred between the lowest social-status and middle-status groups. Specifically, the lowest status groups saw less control and less intimacy as appropriate to this role.

The second discriminant function accounted for 10% of the discrimination and was loaded on *no hostility* and *nuturance;* that is, it was related to the giving of affect. The relationship was again curvilinear, with the middle-middle-status group being extremely high on the giving of affect compared with the other groups.

The third function accounted for 9% of the discrimination and was loaded on *control* and *intimacy*. The lowest social-status group contrasted with the middle-status groups who considered control and intimacy more appropriate than the lowest group.

The fourth function accounted for only 1% of the discrimination and was loaded on *subordination*. The middle-status groups considered that it was less appropriate for a mother to ask for the advice and help of her son than did the other social groups.

To summarize these analyses, it appears that the low-social-status groups make rather stereotypic responses, involving little control (scold, quarrel with) among family members and emphasizing the lack of hostility and the interdependence of these members. The high-social-status group is characterized by more equalitarian relationships with the family and more nurturance between son and father. The middle-status groups are high in control and superordination of high-status family members but also very high in the giving of affect. This group appears to be similar to the Greek samples we tested earlier (e.g., Triandis, Vassiliou and Nassiakou, 1968), as it should be, since we had tested college students who came mostly from the middle group.

A final test of within-culture consistency proved more sensitive. This analysis was done separately for each role, and for the three Greek samples. It will be recalled that sample (a) consisted of 322 high school graduates; sample (b) was a representative sample of one large city, which responded to the role differential in one random order, and sample (c) responded in another random order. We would therefore expect the differences between samples (b) and (c) to indicate the degree of accuracy of the measurement (since it is a kind of parallel form scale reliability).

We expected the comparisons of samples (a) and (b) or (a) and (c) to show some differences, since sample (a) is a student sample and the other samples are representative of one large city. On the other hand, we expected to obtain no differences between samples (b) and (c), since these two samples represented the same population and the only differences between them were that they consisted of different individuals who responded to the role-differential items in two different random orders.

Table 1 tends to support our expectations. The two similar Greek samples [(b) and (c)] had on the average 3.3 common factors, whereas the students and the two representative samples had only 2.2 or 2.4 common factors. For a comparison of these results with the cross-cultural results we also include in Table 1 the same statistics for the three samples of American, Greek, and Indian students. We note that the Greeks are

Table 1   Number of Common Factors and Average Discrepancies in the Factor Sources When Comparing all Possible Pairs in the Three Greek Samples, the Student Samples, and Samples from America, Greece, and India

	Average Number of Common Factors[a]	Average Discrepancies in Factor Scores[a]
Greek students, Greek sample (a) versus Greek sample (b)	2.2	0.6
Greek students, Greek sample (a) versus Greek sample (c)	2.4	0.9
Greek samples (b) and (c)	3.3	0.7
American and Greek students	1.6	0.8
American and Indian students	1.9	0.8
Greek and Indian students	2.2	0.7

[a] Computed over 24 roles.

similar to the Indians but that the Americans are quite different from the other two groups, having only 1.6 and 1.9 common factors with them. In other words, the samples that are expected to be similar have more than three common factors in each role; the sample that are different have, on the average, only two common factors.

We also examined the average discrepancies on the factor scores of the roles on the sample-common factors. These discrepancies tend to average around 0.7 scale units on a nine-point scale for all comparisons.

Finally, by means of matched t-tests of the discrepancies of the factor scores we examined the extent of the differences between the various samples. These analyses indicated that there were no statistically significant differences between the two Greek representatives samples (b) and (c) but that there were differences between the students and one of the two representative samples ($p < .01$). Furthermore, the over-all role perceptions of Greeks did not differ significantly from those of either the

Americans or the Indians, but the Americans and the Indians were different from one another (p < .05). In short, the 24 roles are seen to be similar across cultures, but, as we shall learn, specific roles do show differences in role perception.

Results of Main Study

Our first expectation was that the factors extracted in each factor analysis would account for at least half the variances in role differential judgments. Table 2 shows that this is indeed the case. The data show that

Table 2   Percentages of Variance Accounted for by Factor Analytic Results

Culture	Number of Roles Analyzed	Mean Percentage of Variance	Range of Percentages	Median Number of Factors Accounting for Variance	Range in Number of Factors Extracted
Greece	24[a]	59	47–69	5	4–6
India	24	63	54–70	5	4–6
Peru	50	63	54–69	5	4–6
Taiwan	8	57	53–59	4	3–5
United States	24	57	54–61	5	4–6

[a] Only sample (a) was computed.

on the average five factors were extracted from each factor analysis; in some roles only four factors were extracted, whereas in others as many as six were extracted. The mean variance accounted for by the extracted factors ranged from 57 to 63, with the actual variance ranging from 47 to 70. In other words, about five factors are usually extracted and they account for more than half the variance.

HYPOTHESIS I. *There will be some invariance across cultures in the phenotypic factors employed in role perception; that is, similar factors will emerge in different cultures.*

Support for this hypothesis requires that the factors emerging in the various cultures should be similar. Similarity here has to be determined judgmentally, since the behavior scales employed in each culture were suitable for that culture and not necessarily the same across cultures. Since our analyses were done separately for each role, a pancultural factor analysis, such as Osgood's in his semantic differential work, was not feasible. Table 3 summarizes our judgments of the number of factors that were similar

Table 3   Number of Culture-Common Phenotypical Factors Across the Five Cultures

	Greece	India	Peru	United States
Greece	...			
India	7	...		
Peru	6	5	...	
U.S.A.	5	4	7	...
Taiwan	6	6	5	5

across the various cultures.[1] The reader does not have to depend on our judgments, since Table 4 presents a summary of the phenotypic factors obtained in each culture. The names given to the phenotypic factors are not necessarily the best and the reader may perfer to name them differently. In Table 4 the phenotypic factors were grouped according to our judgments of the underlying genotypic factors. Again the reader may disagree with our judgments. The word (no) precedes some phenotypic factors to make their meaning consistent with the genotypic, but the tables refer to the phenotypic factor without this inversion; for example, hostility is indexed with "throw rocks at" and "be enemy of," and in Table 5 there are negative signs on hostility for ingroup roles which indicate that hostility is seen as inappropriate. Table 5 presents the factor scores of the role-pairs on the various phenotypic factors. The reader who uses Tables 4 and 5 simultaneously can obtain much information about role perception in the various cultures. Consider, for example, the father-son role. The love *factor* appears in connection with this role only in India. We can examine Table 4 and see that in India the love-behavior *scale* is correlated with appoint and have fun with to form the love factor. The factor score is

[1] The number of typical culture-common factors of Tables 1 and 3 refer to different data. In Table 1 we examine each role separately and the data refer to whether two cultures employed the same or different factors when judging each role. The scores are averaged over 24 roles. In Table 3 we examine the factors extracted, regardless of role. Since on the average each of the 24 roles yielded five factors, we looked at 120 factors. These factors tended to be quite similar to one another. In Table 4 we show what these factors actually were, how frequently they were observed, and how important they were. Table 3, then, is a summary of our judgments concerning Table 4.

2.0, which means that the average judgment of the Indian subjects was around 2.0 on a scale that ranged from —4 to +4. We note in Table 4 that the Greeks have a love factor, but it is not employed for the father-son role (Table 5). This means that the behavior love correlated with some other behaviors in the Greek father-son role. Examination of Table 4 tells us that the love scale in Greece is associated with "advise, take care of, and discuss with," which we called nurturance. Hence in the father-son role the Greeks group the behavior scales differently from the Indians, and indeed we note that they see extreme nurturance as appropriate but define it a little differently, grouping together the behaviors of "advise, take care of, admire, and pet."

The reader can judge for himself whether there is invariance in the phenotypic factors across cultures. In our judgment there is considerable invariance (summarized in Table 3), and we find the data consistent with Hypothesis I.

HYPOTHESIS II. *The coordinates of a role in a behavior space will be different from culture to culture.*

Table 5, which we have already discussed, is relevant to this hypothesis. Examination of this table shows numerous differences; for example, in the United States it is inappropriate for the father to show hostility toward the son (factor score: —1.5), but in Greece it is *extremely* inappropriate to do so (—3.0), whereas in India and Taiwan the responses are intermediate (—2.0). From considerations of reliability we expect that differences in factor scores greater than 0.7 are statistically significant at $p < .01$. Thus Hypothesis II receives much support.

HYPOTHESIS III. *Large changes in the coordinates of role pairs will be observed when we examine roles that differ in status or the ingroup-outgroup dimension.*

Support for this hypothesis requires that roles differing in status or the ingroup/outgroup dimension have different factor-score profiles in Table 5. Careful examination of this table confirms this prediction for each culture. Specifically, on the genotypic factor called solidarity (giving affect), which is manifested in such phenotypic factors as love, cooperation, nurturance, respect, no hostility, and formality, we note the following trends: On love, 18 of 19 ingroup roles show positive factor scores; by contrast four out of five conflict roles show negative scores on Love. On nurturance we note high scores in ingroup roles, lower in outgroup roles, and lower still in conflict roles. Nurturance is also high in low-high status

Table 4 Definition for Factors That Appear to be Culture Common (Equivalence to be Established by Reader)

Genotypic Factor	Phenotypic Factors	Scales Loading on Factors				
		Greece	India	Peru	Taiwan	United States
Solidarity	Love	Love Appoint Fall in love with (4–13)[a]	Love Appoint Have fun with (17–10)[a]		Help Respect Love (12–29)[a]	
	Cooperate with				Cooperate with (37–4)	Work with Respect (12–10)
	Nurturance	Advise Take care of Love Discuss with (71–16)	Advise Take care of Admire Pet (41–25)	Help in difficulty Admire (24–20)	Help Love Cooperate with Forgive Protect (63–17)	
(NO)	Hostility	Be enemy of Ignore Consider inferior (58–13)	Throw rocks at Be enemy of Ignore Be indignant with (87–20)	Make fun of Ignore Not trust (32–15)	Fear Laugh at Hate (50–9)	Throw rocks at Be enemy of Fear Laugh at Fight with (100–11)
	Formal acceptance			Invite to movie Have relations with Not ignore (58–11)		Buy gift for Mourn for Kiss (54–11)
Mixture of solidarity and status	Respect	Not advise Not scold Not appoint (16–15)		Trust word of Obey Admire Not insult (62–14)	Respect Apologize to Obey Admire Protect (50–14)	Admire ideas of Respect Depend on Learn with help of Ask for help of (62–13)

284

Mixture of solidarity and status					
Submission	Scold / Quarrel with / Castigate / Be indignant toward (83-13)	Scold / Castigate / Quarrel with (50-10)	Accept orders of Love / Ask for advice / Ask for help (41-16)	Apologize to / Agree with / Fear (12-8)	
Denying status Control					
(NO) Envy			Envy (14-8)		Fear / Envy / Be enemy of (16-8)
(NO) Subordination	Accept orders / Ask for advice / Ask for help (54-14)	Accept orders / Ask for advice / Ask for help (62-10)	Obey / Trust word / Believe / Accept as commander (58-11)	Ask for help / Fear / Depend on (12-17)	Depend on / Learn with help / Ask for help (54-14)
Superordination	Advise / Be indignant toward (21-7)	Appoint / Consider inferior / Castigate (67-7)	Treat as subordinate / Not treat as equal / Not obey (76-11)	Command / Punish (62-11)	Command / Teach / Inspect work (83-9)
Intimacy	Have fun with Pet (41-9)	Have fun with Pet (16-8)	Marry / Have confidence (16-12)		Kiss / Cuddle (87-9)

a The first number refers to the percentage of all the roles studied in a particular culture that yielded this factor. The second number refers to the median percentage of variance accounted for by this factor in those roles in which the factor appeared (it is a measure of the relative importance of the factor).

Table 5 Factor Scores of Roles on Phenotypic Factors in Five Cultures: Ingroup Roles in Which Actor is of High Status

Genotypic Factors	Phenotypic Factors	Father-Son					Mother-Son				Father-Daughter				Husband-Wife			
		Greece	India	Peru	Taiwan	United States	Greece	India	Peru	United States	Greece	India	Peru	United States	Greece	Peru	India	United States
Solidarity	Love		2.0					0.5				1.0						
	Cooperate																	
	Nurturance	3.0	2.0	3.0			3.5	2.0	3.2		3.0	2.0	3.0			3.0	2.5	
	Hostility[a] (No)	-3.0	-2.0	-2.0		-1.5	-3.0	-1.0		-0.5	-2.5	-2.5		-1.0		-2.0	0.0	-2.0
Mixture of solidarity and status	Formal acceptance				0.5	1.0			2.5				3.0					3.5
	Respect			0.5	0.5					2.5			2.5					
	Submission															2.0	2.0	
Denying status	(No) Envy[a] Control					-1.0				-1.0	0.5	-0.5		-1.0	0.0	-0.5		-1.0
	(No) Subordination[a]	0.5	0.5		0.0		0.5	-0.5			0.5	-0.5		0.0	-0.5		1.0	
	Superordination	-0.5	1.0	2.0	2.0	2.5	1.0	1.5	1.4	2.0			1.5	2.0	2.0		1.0	2.0
Intimacy	Intimacy	1.0				-1.5	2.0			2.0	1.0			1.5	3.0	0.5	0.5	1.5

286

Table 5 (Continued) Ingroup Roles in Which the Actor is of Equal Status

Genotypic Factors	Phenotypic Factors	Brother-Brother					Student-Roommate				Guest-Host			Host-Guest		
		Greece	India	Peru	Taiwan	United States	Greece	India	Taiwan	United States	Greece	India	United States	Greece	India	United States
Solidarity	Love		1.5		2.5				2.5	+1.0			1.0			
	Cooperate															
	Nurturance	2.5	-0.5	3.0	3.0	-2.0	1.5	1.0			0.5			1.5	1.0	1.0
	(No) Hostility[a]	-2.0		-1.0	-1.0		-1.5	-1.5	-0.5	-1.0	-2.0	-2.5	-2.5	-2.0	-2.0	-2.0
Mixture of Solidarity and status	Formal acceptance			2.0		3.0				-0.5						1.0
	Respect		2.5	2.5		2.0										
	Submission							1.0								
	(No) Envy[a]												-1.0		1.0	
Denying status	Control	0.0	0.0				-1.0									
	(No) subordination[a]						-1.0	1.5		1.0	1.0		1.0		-1.5	0.5
	Superordination		-1.0	1.0				-0.5				0.0	-2.0	-1.0	0.0	
Intimacy	Intimacy					-3.0				-4.0						-1.5

287

Table 5 (*Continued*) Ingroup Roles in Which the Actor is of Low Status

Genotypic Factors	Phenotypic Factors	Son-Father					Daughter-Father				Son-Mother					Wife-Husband			
		Greece	India	Peru	Taiwan	United States	Greece	India	Peru	United States	Greece	India	Peru	Taiwan	United States	Greece	India	Peru	United States
Solidarity	Love		1.0					1.5				0.5							
	Cooperation				2.5														
	Nurturance	3.0					0.5				3.0						3.0		
	(No) Hostility[a]	-2.0	-3.0	-2.0		-2.5	-2.5	-2.5	-3.0	-1.5	-3.0	-2.5		-0.5	-2.5	-2.5	-2.5		-2.0
Mixture of solidarity and status	Formal acceptance		2.4	3.0	2.5	3.0	1.5	2.5	0.5	3.5			3.0	2.5	3.0			1.0	4.0
	Respect		3.0		2.5				1.5	3.0			3.0	1.0				1.0	
	Submission	2.0		2.0									2.0					3.0	
Denying status	(No) Envy[a]	2.0					-0.5				-1.0	-2.5				-0.5	-1.5		-1.0
	Control (No) Subordination[a]	2.0	1.0	3.0	3.0	3.0		2.5	2.5	3.0	2.5		3.5			2.5		2.2	2.0
	Superordination	-1.0		-2.0	-1.5				-2.0	-1.0	-1.0		2.0		-1.5	0.5	-1.5	-1.5	
Intimacy	Intimacy	1.0		-2.0		-2.0	0.5			2.0	-1.0		2.0		1.5	3.0			3.0

288

Table 5 (*Continued*) Outgroup Roles in Which Actor is of High Status

Genotypic Factors	Phenotypic Factors	Foreman-Laborer					Boss-Secretary				Client-Prostitute		
		Greece	India	Peru[b]	Taiwan[b]	United States	Greece	India	Peru[c]	United States	Greece	India	United States
Solidarity	Love										−2.0		
	Cooperate		0.5		+1.0	+1.0				+1.0			
	Nurturance	+0.5	−1.5	−0.5	+2.0	−2.0		+0.5	2.0				
	(No) Hostility[a]	−1.0		+0.5	−0.5		−1.0	−2.0	1.0	−3.5	−1.0		−1.5
Mixture of solidarity and status	Formal acceptance												
	Respect					+1.0				+2.0			
	Submission												
Denying status	(No) Envy[a]												
	Control	+1.0	0.5				+0.5	+1.0			−0.5	−1.5	
	(No) Subordination[a]	−1.5	−1.0	−1.5			−0.5	−0.5	−2.0		−2.0	−1.0	
	Superordination				+2.0	+3.0	+2.0	+2.0	+1.0	+3.0	+0.5	+0.5	
Intimacy	Intimacy					−3.5				−0.5			−1.0

Table 5 (*Continued*) Outgroup Roles in Which the Actor Is of Equal Status

Genotypic Factors	Phenotypic Factors	Salesman-Client				Lawyer-Client		
		Greece	India	Peru[d]	United States	Greece	India	United States
Solidarity	Love		0.5				0.5	
	Cooperate							
	Nurturance							
Mixture of solidarity and status	(No) Hostility[a]	−1.0	−1.5		−2.0		−1.5	−3.0
	Formal acceptance			2.0	−2.0			0.0
	Respect			+1.5	+0.5			0.5
	Submission							
Denying Status	(No) Envy[a]							
	Control	−0.5	−1.5	1.0	−1.0	+1.0	0.0	
	(No) Subordination		0.0			−0.5	0.5	1.5
	Superordination		−1.0					
Intimacy	Intimacy	−2.0			−3.5		−2.0	−3.0

290

Table 5 (Continued) Outgroup Roles in Which the Actor Is of Lower Status

Genotypic Factors	Phenotypic Factors	Secretary-Boss					Prostitute-Client		
		Greece	India	Peru[e]	Taiwan[e]	United States[f]	Greece	India	United States
Solidarity	Love		+1.0					0.5	
	Cooperate								
	Nurturance	+1.0	+0.5		+1.5		-0.5	-1.5	-1.5
	(No) Hostility[a]	-1.0	-2.0		-0.0	-1.0	-0.5		-1.5
Mixture of solidarity and status	Formal acceptance			2.0					
	Respect	+2.5		2.0					
	Submission					+1.5			
Denying status	(No) Envy[a]								
	Control							-1.0	-1.0
	(No) Subordination[a]	+2.0	+1.0		+2.0	+2.0		-1.0	-0.5
	Superordination	-0.5	-0.5	-1.0	-2.0	-1.0			
Intimacy	Intimacy			-1.0		-1.0		+2.0	-2.5

Table 5 (*Continued*)   Conflict Roles in Which the Actor Is of High Status

Genotypic Factors	Phenotypic Factors	Liman-Andean Indian Peru
Solidarity	Love	
	Cooperate	
	Nurturance	
	(No) Hostility[a]	
Mixture of solidarity and status	Formal acceptance	
	Respect	−1.5
	Submission	
Denying status	(No) Envy[a]	−1.0
	Control	
	(No) Subordination[a]	
	Superordination	1.0
Intimacy	Intimacy	−2.0

Table 5 (*Continued*)   Conflict Roles in Which the Actor Is of Equal Status

Genotypic Factors	Phenotypic Factors	Diplomat-Diplomat			Jew-Catholic Catholic-Jew
		Greece	India	United States	Peru
Solidarity	Love		−1.0		
	Cooperate				
	Nurturance				
	(No) Hostility[a]	0.0	−1.0	0.5	
Mixture of solidarity and status	Formal acceptance				0.5
	Respect			1.5	1.0
	Submission		−0.5		
Denying status	(No) Envy[a]				−1.0
	Control				
	(No) Subordination[a]			0.0	+0.5
	Superordination		−1.0		
Intimacy	Intimacy	−3.0		−3.5	−0.5

Table 5 (*Continued*)   Conflict Roles in Which the Actor Is of Lower Status

Genotypic Factors	Phenotypic Factors	Labor Leader-Factory Manager			Andean Indian-Liman
		Greece	India	United States	Peru
Solidarity	Love				
	Cooperate				
	Nurturance	0.0	−0.5		
	(No) Hostility[a]	0.5	−1.0	−2.0	
Mixture of solidarity and status	Formal acceptance				0.5
	Respect			+0.5	1.0
	Submission		0.5		
Denying status	(No) Envy[a]				0.5
	Control	0.5	−0.5		
	(No) Subordination[a]	0.5		0.0	
	Superordination		−1.0	0.5	
Intimacy	Intimacy			−3.5	

[a] The original sign of the factor score is entered in this table, but the meaning of the phenotypic factor has to be reversed to be consistent with the other phenotypic factors listed as corresponding to the particular genotypic factor.

[b] Architect-house construction worker was used in Peru; employer-employee was used in Taiwan.

[c] Boss-employee was used in Peru.

[d] Grocer-customer was used in Peru.

[e] Office employee-boss in Peru; employee-employer in Taiwan.

roles. In this case we must consider the respect dimension as a mixture of the solidarity and status genotypic factors, since an additional trend shows a reduction in respect as we examine low-status roles and compare them with high-status roles. Specifically, as we move away from the "ingroup, low-high status roles" cell, respect drops systematically. Similarly, we note that this happens to the submission factor, which must therefore have much in common with the respect factor. Hostility is low for all roles but extremely low in ingroup roles.

Turning now to the genotypic factor giving-denying status, we find as expected, the tendency in the control factor for most of the high-low roles to be positive and all the low-high roles to be negative. This indicates that changes in the status dimension of roles produce most of the changes in the coordinates of roles on the control dimension. A similar trend can be seen for the superordination factor, for which a maximum is found in the "outgroup, high-low" status cell and a minimum in the "low-high roles," regardless of the nature of the group. Finally, on subordination we note a maximum for the "ingroup, low-high status roles" and a minimum in the "conflict, high-low status" cell. These trends are not completely consistent across the various manifestations of the genotypic status factor but they are almost consistent.

Intimacy is high in ingroup roles, low in all other roles. It is clear that the coordinates of roles in all the culture-common factors show systematic relation to the solidarity and status classification of Table 5. Thus Hypothesis III is strongly supported. The empirical data are summarized in Table 6.

Table 6 is essentially a summary of Table 5 and was constructed by averaging all the phenotypic factors that correspond to each genotypic factor, for each kind of role, and further averaging these scores across all roles of the same type; for example, in the high-low status roles we averaged the factor scores of the phenotypic fatcors that imply solidarity (love, cooperation, nurturance, no hostility, and formal acceptance) across the father-son, mother-son, father-daughter, and husband-wife roles. This required that we average the American scores: 1.5, 0.5, 1.0, 2.0 and 3.5 (from Table 5). The average of these scores is 1.7.

Examination of Table 6 shows clearly that Hypothesis III is supported. The profiles of the nine *types* of role differ considerably but the cultures agree among themselves in the way they perceive each type of role.

Some obvious exceptions can be seen but can be explained as peculiarities of the samples; for example, in the ingroup high-to-low status roles the Indians are rather low in denying the status genotypic factor. The reason is that they have some negative scores on this factor because the fathers are not supposed to control or subordinate their daughters—this is the job of the mothers in that culture. To take another example, although

Table 6 Mean Factor Score Profiles of Nine Kinds of Roles in Five Cultures on Four Genotypic Factors

Genotypic Factor	Status of Roles	Ingroup Roles					Outgroup Roles					Conflict Roles				
		Greece	India	Peru	Taiwan	United States	Greece	India	Peru	Taiwan	United States	Greece	India	Peru	Taiwan	United States
Solidarity		3.0	1.5	2.5	2.5	1.7	0.4	1.1	1.0	1.2	1.4	...	...	...	...	...
Solidarity and status	High to low	...	1.0	1.3	0.5	1.7	...	0.0	...	...	1.5	...	...	1.5	...	...
Denying status		0.9	0.4	1.1	1.0	0.8	0.8	0.6	1.5	1.7	1.6	...	...	0.0	...	...
Intimacy		1.3	...	2.0	...	0.7	...	...	...	...	-2.0	...	...	-2.0	...	...
Solidarity		1.0	1.3	2.3	1.9	1.5	1.0	0.7	2.0	...	0.7	0.0	-1.0	0.5	...	0.5
Solidarity and status	Equal	...	1.9	1.9	...	2.0	...	...	1.5	...	0.5	...	-0.5	0.0	...	1.5
Denying status		-0.3	-0.5	-1.4	...	0.0	0.7	-0.4	-1.0	...	1.2	...	-0.6	...	...	-0.5
Intimacy		...	...	...	...	-2.6	-2.0	-2.0	...	...	-3.2	-3.0	...	0.5	...	-3.5
Solidarity		2.8	1.6	2.2	1.2	2.8	0.9	1.1	2.0	0.7	0.6	-0.2	+0.2	1.5	...	0.8
Solidarity and status	Low to high	1.2	1.7	1.6	2.4	2.2	2.5	-1.0	2.0	...	1.5	...	0.0	0.0	...	1.0
Denying status		-1.2	-1.8	-2.9	-2.0	-1.6	-2.0	-0.1	-1.0	-2.0	-1.1	0.0	-0.2	...	...	0.0
Intimacy		1.5	...	...	...	1.1	-0.5	2.0	...	...	-1.6	-3.0	...	0.5	...	-3.5

... means no information available.

294

ingroup roles are characterized by great intimacy, the Americans show a negative score of —2.6 in ingroup equal status roles. This is because intimacy (kiss and cuddle) is appropriate only in heterosexual roles in America, whereas in other cultures this is not the case. Since the sample of equal status roles included brother-brother and student-roommate, the American results deviated from expectation. Another exception in that table involves the Indian low-to-high status outgroup roles on the intimacy factor. This deviant score is because the role that represented this cell was prostitute-client. Therefore, if we ignore these understable abberations of the data, the scores in Table 6 are strikingly consistent across cultures.

Some striking cultural differences can be seen as "epiphenomena" of the general regularities just mentioned; for example, Greeks are quite extreme in showing solidarity in ingroup roles, but they also show a large drop in the factor scores on this genotypic factor in outgroup roles (from 3.0 to 0.4, from 1.6 to 1.0, and from 2.8 to 0.9). On the other hand, Americans do not show such a large drop in these roles (1.7 to 1.4 and 1.5 to 0.7) except in the low-high status roles, in which the Americans behave just like the Greeks (2.8 to 0.6). In other words, there is a kind of *noblesse oblige* view of American role behavior when the person holds a high-status position which disappears when he holds a low-status position. In conflict roles the Greeks again seem to "go all out" with extremely negative factor scores on solidarity and intimacy; the Americans are extremely low in intimacy (—3.5) but not in solidarity (0.5 to 0.8). The Indians are low on solidarity in equal-status conflict roles but not in low-to-high-status conflict roles. The American-Greek findings are replications of the results of Triandis, Vassiliou, and Nassiakou (1968) and have already been discussed in detail in that publication.

A more detailed examination of cultural differences requires a careful study of Table 5. Two kinds of judgment can be made about cultural differences: (a) in some cultures a particular phenotypic factor does not even emerge, whereas in other cultures it does emerge; (b) the coordinates of roles on the phenotypic factors are often quite different. Even a glance at Table 5 suggests numerous cultural differences in both the kinds of factor that emerge and the coordinates of the roles on the factors. The reader may wish to study Table 5 to examine some of the details of the obtained cultural differences but discussion of these differences is beyond the scope of this chapter.

Summary

The data are generally consistent with the expectations derived from the theoretical statements presented in the introduction of this chapter.

Role perceptions are quite homogeneous within cultures, although slight variations due to personality and education or social status can be found. By contrast, there are large differences in role perception across cultures. The measurement procedures developed to study role perceptions appear to identify cultural differences with sensitivity and to provide data consistent with other cultural information. Role perceptions can be described by a few (typically five) phenotypic role-behavior factors, which account for more than half the variance in the judgments. Of these five factors, two or three are typically equivalent, cross-culturally, and allow for cross-cultural comparisons to be made on equivalent dimensions. Cultures differ not only in the kinds of social-behavior dimensions they employ but also in the coordinates of the roles on the culture-common behavior factors. Some of these differences are understandable from existing knowledge of customs.

The usefulness of examining role perceptions by studying the judgments of roles on specific behavior factors seems strongly supported by these data. Specifically, it was shown that the coordinates of a role on the behavior factors vary systematically, depending on whether the roles are (a) ingroup, (b) outgroup, or (c) conflict roles and (a) high-low, (b) equal, or (c) low-high status roles. It seems quite certain, then, that in analyses of role perceptions we must examine these nine major types of role. In addition, general versus specific roles and other kinds of role dimension which have not been considered in the present analysis may exist, but the data suggest that a satisfactory first approximation can be provided by consideration of these nine kinds of role.

The behavior dimensions appear to include the genotypic factors *solidarity* (love, cooperation, nurturance, no hostility, formal acceptance) *giving versus denying status* (control, envy, no subordination, superordination), and *intimacy*. A mixture of solidarity and status (dependence, respect, submission) was also found. The three genotypic dimensions identified by Triandis et al. (1968) as the basic culture-common dimensions of role perception appear adequate in the present study.

The nine kinds of role and three genotypic kinds of behaviors, which have been extracted in previous work, appear to be culture-common and provide a basis for cross-cultural comparisons. The specific manifestations of the genotypic behavior factors may differ from role-to-role and from culture-to-culture. Nevertheless, enough cultural invariance remains to allow for meaningful cross-cultural comparisons.

PART THREE

An Example of the Integrated Use of these Approaches

CHAPTER NINE

A Comparative Analysis of Subjective Culture

HARRY C. TRIANDIS AND VASSO VASSILIOU

The conceptual scheme of Part I suggests various "probes" into subjective culture. There is now a legitimate question whether the information one obtains from such probes is consistent. Since we have studies involving all our methods from Greece and the United States, this chapter reviews these studies and attempts to answer the question.

One major advantage of consistencies across methods of gathering subjective culture data is that it provides concurrent validation of the instruments. We can anticipate the conclusions of the review presented in this chapter by stating that we did find a good deal of consistency across methods. Much of the information, however, is complementary rather than overlapping. In the next chapter we review two studies of predictive validity of our methods of measurement, which will give us even more confidence that what we are getting when we measure subjective culture is valuable.

In this chapter we review data obtained with various instruments. We show that in each culture the kinds of answers given by our respondents can be described most parsimoniously by certain basic themes and that these themes emerge consistently from all instruments. More specifically, in our work on Greek and American stereotyping, attitudes toward key concepts, implications of various concepts, and role perceptions the basic theme of a strong ingroup-outgroup contrast can be detected in all Greek data. Reality in Greece is impregnated with social considerations, whereas in America it is focused on the individual. The Greek seems to define his universe in terms of the triumphs of the ingroup over the outgroup and his social behavior is strongly dependent on whether "the other person" is a member of his ingroup. Key concepts are judged according to their relevance to this social reality. Relations with authority figures, with persons with whom one is in conflict, etc., are also conditioned by the ingroup-outgroup contrast.

In addition, this chapter attempts to place the data from our analysis of subjective culture in historical and ecological perspective. This suggests hypotheses for further work on how different ecologies determine the subjective culture of groups of people.

The majority of the readers of the present chapter will be familiar with American culture and will have a "subjective culture" similar to that found in our studies to be typical of Americans. Our findings are therefore presented as *explanations of Greek subjective culture from an American point of view*.

This chapter illustrates consistencies in the response of subjects to different kinds of instrument. Thus it is concerned with substantive findings rather than the methodology that led to the finding and attempts to summarize these substantive findings rather than give the details discovered with each instrument.

Stereotypes as Hypotheses of National Character

When members of Culture A perceive members of Culture B, they make judgments about the probable characteristics of members of Culture B. Such judgments are related to the difference in the mean values of the corresponding traits of the two groups. Specifically, on trait X the mean value of this trait in Culture A is designated by $\bar{X}_A$, in Culture B by $\bar{X}_B$. The probability that members of Culture A will mention trait X when they give their stereotypes of members of Culture B is proportional to $\bar{X}_A - \bar{X}_B$ (Campbell, 1967); for example, if members of Culture A wash their hands three times an hour and those of Culture B wash only once an hour, there is a high probability that members of Culture A will call members of Culture B "filthy." In fact, in terms of the total distribution around the world of the characteristic "filthy" both cultures are excessively clean.

Our view is that we can employ the stereotypes of different culture groups as *estimates* of the probable differences in the mean values of their traits.

We can then ask if the trait differences are consistent with historical and ecological analyses of the experiences of subjects in different cultures. Following this line of thought, we discuss first the stereotypes of Americans and Greeks and then present a historical-ecological analysis. The point here is that when a person is stereotyping a group he is not only responding to characteristics of the group being stereotyped but is also revealing the way he perceives himself. It is the contrast between his perceptions of $\bar{X}_A$ and $\bar{X}_B$ that is reflected in the stereotype.

Since much of this chapter discusses differences between Americans and Greeks in their perception of subjective culture, it is appropriate to begin with a discussion of how these groups see each other and themselves.

Stereotypes of Americans and Greeks

Triandis and Vassiliou (1967b) have shown that each of the two cultural groups has a much more positive opinion of itself than it has of the other group but each group also recognizes that the other group has some "good" traits. By and large, the Americans see the Greeks as *inefficient, competitive,* and *suspicious* but at the same time *charming* and *witty.* The Greeks see the Americans in exactly the opposite fashion; that is, they see them as *efficient* but rather *dull* and not particularly *charming.*

The method employed to obtain these results involved the presentation of semantic differential scales that utilized characteristics elicited from open-ended interviews of Americans and Greeks (Triandis, 1967a). The concepts "Americans tend to be" and "Greeks tend to be" were utilized. Characteristics such as *dull-witty* defined the scales. The study found specifically that Americans see Greeks as *emotional, competitive, egotistic, suspicious, rigid,* and *with poor working habits.* At the same time they see them as *witty* and *sociable.*

Furthermore, we asked 400 Americans how they perceive Greeks (see Chapter 5). These subjects were also asked how much contact they had with Greeks. Four groups of Americans were formed. Group 1 had very little contact; Group 2 had some contact; Group 3 had considerable contact, and Group 4 had daily contact. The perceptions of Greeks by these four groups of Americans were analyzed. It was found that the greater the reported contact, the more the Americans considered the Greeks as *emotionally uncontrolled, competitive, suspicious, egotistic, unsystematic, inexact in following procedures, undecisive, sly,* and *rigid.* The greater the contact, however, the more they also saw them as *witty, honest,* and *obliging.* Americans see themselves as less *sly* and more *rational, trusting, modest, flexible, emotionally controlled, decisive, systematic, exact in following procedures, honest,* and *unselfish* than the Greeks.

In contrast, in a study of 800 Greeks from a representative sample of the population of Athens and Thessalonica the Greeks saw the Americans quite differently from the way the Americans saw themselves. They found the Americans to be *arrogant, suspicious, sly,* and *competitive,* although *systematic, emotionally controlled,* and *flexible* as well. The Greeks in this sample perceived themselves as *modest, honest, witty, flexible, obliging,* and *emotionally controlled,* but they also saw themselves as *suspicious, competitive,* and *go-getting.*

When such discrepancies in the perception of social groups are observed, it is likely that (a) there is some truth in what is seen and (b) the differences between the two groups are exaggerated. Americans may find Greeks "exasperating" because of their *inefficiency, competitiveness,* and *suspiciousness.* On the other hand, Americans may like the Greek *warmth* and *charm.* Greeks may find Americans "exasperating," because of their *arrogance, coldness,* and overwhelming stress on *efficiency,* but at the same time admire American *efficiency.*

Our evidence suggests that there is a kernal of truth in the stereotypes under discussion. It is well to remember, however, that there are "inefficient," "competitive," and "suspicious" Americans also. Furthermore, the Greeks are aware that they themselves have such traits.

In any event, the Greek traits under discussion are consistent with analyses of the ecology and history of that country, as the following argument will indicate. Furthermore, after describing the ecology we discuss some characteristic patterns of thought concerning interpersonal relations which constitute the bases for understanding Greek subjective culture.

Geography and History

Greece is a predominantly mountainous country (80%), cut up by the sea into a large peninsula and hundreds of scattered islands. Two basic geographic characteristics, the mountains and the sea, have brought about a considerable isolation of many segments of the population. As a result the social environment of the average Greek is limited and he is most powerfully identified with his island, his valley, or his small town. Greece is also low on natural resources. Four-fifths of the country is so mountainous that cultivation is extremely difficult. Today it is hard to raise crops except in two or three fertile valleys, among which is Thessaly. Although the country lacks resources, it has simultaneoulsy experienced considerable pressures from an expanding population. The extensive use of the sea (fishing and the merchant marine) plus the emigration of a large number of Greeks have prevented the standard of living from falling. Major influences on modern Greek culture have come from Byzantium and the 350-year-long Ottoman occupation. The Byzantines had several Christian and nationalistic concepts still to be found in modern Greece. At the same time there are unmistakable remnants of Turkish influence in the popular music, the food, and in certain social customs.

Among the most significant historical events that have probably been influential in molding the Greek national character is the fall of Constantinople in 1453, which placed the Balkans under the domination of the Ottoman Empire. The Ottomans used the Greek intellectuals as their clerks. This had the effect of preserving some of the values of Byzantine culture. In addition, the Greek Orthodox Church facilitated the continued study of the Greek language, and local priests ran clandestine schools in which some of the Greek values and traditions were taught.

During the 350 following the fall of Constantinople the relationship between Greeks and Ottomans was hostile. The mountainous environment allowed autonomous Greek fighting units which never submitted to the Ottoman occupation to operate; the Ottomans retaliated against their attacks by executing the village leaders. The threat of these executions kept the best of the Greeks constantly in the mountains and away from the villages, so that the modern Greek view of the ideal man is strongly influenced by the image of the guerrilla.

This incomplete and sketchy analysis of early modern Greek ecology leads to the speculation that the period was characterized by child-rearing practices that reflect the fact that women were the only adults physically present in the home. The father was psychologically present, but the mother was the chief agent who perpetuated the values of the culture. The mother's task was extremely difficult. On the one hand she had to prevent assimilation of her children into Ottoman culture and on the other she had to rear them in the image of a hero. Such a difficult task demanded strong maternal control which in turn fostered great dependency among the children.

Moreover, one can speculate that the Ottoman practice of kidnapping male children further contributed to the development of the overprotectiveness of Greek mothers. As early as 1330 the Ottoman Empire undertook a program of recruiting an independent military force by abducting 7-to-11-year-old male Christian children and placing them in specially formed schools for soldiers, the so-called Janissaries. Between 1330 and 1826, when the Janissaries were disbanded, the threat of Turkish abduction of male children was real and relevant. This threat probably had a significant impact on Greek child-rearing practices, which have in turn determined certain aspects of modern Greek national character.

An organized revolution began against the Ottoman rule in 1821. It led to a series of wars which continued intermittently for the next hundred years. During this period the modern Greek state was formed by importing political institutions (e.g., government ministries, parliaments) from Western Europe. The first Greek king was Bavarian, and the second, a Danish prince, was the founder of the current dynasty.

Modern Greece (1821 to the present) has been characterized by political instability. Several revolutions erupted during this period. World War II was especially damaging and was followed by several years of conflict.

The significance of these events from a psychological point of view is that in the last 150 years the Greeks have had little control over their personal life. Much of their behavior has been directed toward meeting crises created by war or revolution and survival has often been the major concern. As a result they have developed exceedingly effective procedures for meeting crises but have neglected skills for long-term planning. Clearly one cannot plan when one does not know the outcome of next month's events.

In summary, this introduction to Greek geography and history suggests that modern Greek culture was influenced by six important factors: (a) scarce resources and keen competition for them, (b) reaction to the domination by autocratic rulers, (c) dependence on the "male hero" for survival of the cultural values, (d) increased dangers for boys resulting in increased protectiveness of mothers, (e) the unadapted importation of foreign institutions, and (f) low control over the environment. These characteristics provide an explanatory base for our empirical exploration of Greek "subjective culture."

Greek National Character

The Importance of the Ingroup. The foregoing six factors have probably had an important bearing on the molding of Greek national character. The competition for scarce resources and the struggle for survival created an extremely tightly knit family and an "ingroup" that provides protection, social insurance, and a warm and relaxing environment; in short, a haven from the larger world. The Ottoman domination led to a division between established authority and informally accepted authority. Thus the behavior toward a person in authority *depends* on whether he is perceived as a member of the ingroup or of the outgroup. If the authority figure is accepted, then the response is one of submission and self-sacrifice; if it is rejected (i.e., belongs to an outgroup), the response is one of defiance, resentment, and undermining. A regulation imposed by a policeman (member of the outgroup) may be violated "just for fun," if the probability of punishment for breaking the law is not too great.[1]

---

[1] One aspect of the ingroup concept of particular interest is the fact that different ingroups have different leaders. A threat from the external environment (as in war with neighboring countries) often makes these leaders cooperate. On the other hand, when there is no outside danger, the leaders are likely to pursue individualistic goals and to behave competitively toward one another. The size of the ingroup depends on the type of the threat. If a member's life is threatened by illness, the immediate ingroup will be mobilized. If the threat is relevant to a widely shared characteristic such as nationality or religion the ingroup expands to include all members having this characteristic. Thus effective cooperation characterizes Greek behavior in wartime, whereas internal competitiveness is typical during peace.

The definition of the "ingroup" is somewhat different for Greeks than it is for Western Europeans or Americans. The ingroup may be defined as "my family, relatives, friends, and friends of friends." In addition, guests and people who are perceived as "showing concern for me" are seen as members of the ingroup. Within the ingroup the appropriate behaviors are characterized by cooperation, protection, and help. Not only are these "warm" behaviors appropriate, but the concept of the *philotimo* (discussed later) demands that a person sacrifice himself to help members of his ingroup.

The functional significance of such ties among members of the ingroup is clear. It is easier to survive in a highly competitive world as a member of a group of people who cooperate and help one another. In contrast to the ingroup the "outgroup" consists of anyone who is not perceived at least as an acquaintance or as a person who is concerned with one's welfare. Acquaintances are somewhat ambiguously classified more frequently in the ingroup than in the outgroup.

Relations with members of the outgroup are essentially competitive. The Greek language has at least three synonyms equivalent to the word *competition*. Amilla is "benovolent competition" appropriate for the ingroup. *Synagonismos* is equivalent to the American word. *Antagonismos* means "hostile competition" appropriate to members of the outgroup in which success requires the other's failure.

The existence of these clear distinctions between ingroup and outgroup makes the Greeks appear to be extremely suspicious when they first meet strangers. The newcomer has to be classified and until this happens he remains in limbo. If he is classified in the outgroup, all kinds of competition and unfair play are "par for the course." If he is classified in the ingroup, all kinds of help are likely to come his way.

Differences between the American and Greek relationships within the ingroup are substantial. One way of describing them is to discuss the perceptions of *appropriate behavior* of Greeks and Americans in certain roles. Triandis, Vassiliou, and Nassiakou (1968) have shown that such perceptions can be described in terms of the two dimensions: (a) the degree of affect and kind of emotion that is perceived to be appropriate (e.g., the intensity of love) and (b) the degree of intimacy that is appropriate. The basic instrument used in these studies is the "role differential." It utilizes a format exemplified by the following items:

father-son

would not ------------------------------------- would

hit

would not ------------------------------------- would

obey

The subjects are asked to indicate whether in their culture it is appropriate for a father to hit, obey, etc. his son. In a typical study 100 roles such as father-son and son-father are judged against a set of 50 behavior-descriptive scales selected by facet and factor analysis. The factors "associative versus dissociative" and "intimate versus formal" behaviors are both culture-common and completely independent of one another.

These studies have shown some rather interesting results when we compared the way Americans and Greeks perceive relationships between people; for example, Americans and Greeks see the relationship between parents and children and wives and husbands as involving about the same amount of positive emotion, but they are quite different in the degree of intimacy they consider appropriate. Americans consider the appropriate intimacy between husbands and wives to be greater than the appropriate intimacy between parents and children. The Greeks reverse this perception so that they see less intimacy between husbands and wives than Americans see between parents and children. Thus the central role in the American family is husband-wife; the central roles in the Greek family are parents-children. Of special importance is the mother-son role. In Greece a strong bond between mother and son is considered highly commendable.[2]

Turning now to relationships with relatives, friends, and acquaintances, we find that the Greeks consider it appropriate to show more love and more intimacy with relatives or friends than do Americans. In the case of acquaintances they do not differ from Americans on the amount of love appropriate but they differ on the amount of intimacy: Here again the Greeks see more intimacy as appropriate between acquaintances.

These results do not suggest that Greeks, compared with Americans, see more intimacy as appropriate in *all* human relationships. There are a number of roles in which the reverse is true. Broadly speaking, roles in which Greeks perceive conflict are seen by them as involving less intimacy than is the case in America; for example, they see less intimacy in the roles of landlord-tenant and boss-subordinate.

To restate an important point that must always be kept in mind, there is a big difference in the way the Greeks behave toward their ingroup as opposed to the way they behave toward their outgroup. Within the ingroup they cooperate and show great intimacy. Within the outgroup they compete and behave most formally. Bosses belong to the outgroup *unless* they are extremely fatherly, warm, and helpful, in which case they are classified as

[2] For example, in an opening speech to the Greek parliament, a new M.P. began his remarks while looking at the spectator's gallery, where his proud mother was seated, with the words: "Mother, Your Majesty, Distinguished Members of this House, Ladies and Gentlemen." This was most favorably reported in the Greek press.

members of the ingroup. Guests and tourist are also likely to be classified
as members of the ingroup, provided they have behaved in a warm and
accepting manner.

The Greek Self-Concept. At an earlier point we referred to the
importance of the guerrilla in the formation of the image of the Greek
male and to the lesser importance of the community as a social milieu
for the development of child-rearing standards. We also mentioned that
fear of having the boys abducted required Greek mothers to become unusually strong in control and often overprotective. This also led to an over-
evaluation of boys. Consequently in rural Greece it is common to hear
the word "children" applied only to boys. When a parent says, "I have
three children and three girls," he means that he has three of each.

The need for high control of the child results in a number of cases in
which mothers tend (a) to be too helpful to their sons, taking every conceivable opportunity to assist and protect them,[3] (b) to confine them in
an area in which they can always see them, and (c) make most of the
decisions for both boys and girls. Even 18-year-olds are often treated like
small children. The result is that 12-year-old Greek children see achievement related to the help they receive from others.

The above point was confirmed by a study of the motivational patterns
of Greek adolescents. Vassiliou and Kataki[4] have asked normal adolescents
to make up stories in response to TAT (ambiguous) pictures. When these
stories were analyzed, the investigators found a considerable emphasis on
the idea that achievement requires both one's personal effort and the help
of authority figures. They perceive ingroup authority figures as monitoring
their efforts, as giving good advice and assistance, as restricting them in
order to protect them from others as well as from themselves, and as
restricting them because they love them. These adolescents are also apprehensive about deviating from the advice they receive. They are especially
apprehensive about the future and their efficiency when it comes to self-
initiated action. By the time they are 18 these young people feel grateful
for the help they have received, express appreciation for the sacrifices of
authority figures, and feel the need to pay them back by their own achievement. At the same time this study revealed a good deal of conflict: on
the one hand, these young people recognized that to achieve they must
break away from their dependency on their family; on the other hand,
this breaking away was seen as painful to the authority figures as well as

---

[3] Mothers study with their boys while they do their homework (help) and check
the boys memorization of the lesson (protect them from the criticism of the teacher).

[4] V. Vassiliou and Harikilia Kataki. Motivational patterns of Greek adolescents
(in preparation).

to themselves. The achievers among them considered breaking away. They felt that if they did they would find someone to help them to achieve. If they failed, they could return to their family, where they would always be warmly consoled.

Thus the self-concept of normal achieving Greek adolescents is characterized by dependency on others and by questions concerning their own effectiveness. At the same time the ideal of the hero, as molded by the image of the guerrilla, requires achievement, fame, and immortality. Furthermore, the social status of the Greek woman is very low unless and until she is the mother of an achiever. Thus there are great pressures on mothers to "push" their sons to achieve. As a result most Greek mothers are prone to make unrealistic efforts to increase their sons' self-esteem. Greek mothers tend to tell their children that they expect them to become important and to consider them unique. This leads to a facade of self-confidence which could increase exaggerated inner insecurity and lower the self-esteem.

This speculation about the self-esteem of some Greek males allows us to understand certain characteristics of the Greek national character which Americans find difficult to work with. A low self-esteem implies, of course, that the Greek is easily hurt.

1. Greeks are oversensitive to criticism; that is, the slightest critical remark is likely to be reacted to as a major threat.

2. They tend to blame their own mistakes on others.

On the other hand, the facade of an overcompensating high self-confidence can be seen in characteristics that an American will interpret as *arrogance, dogmatism,* and *attempts to appear all-knowing and all-powerful.*

It is, we feel, relevant and revealing that in a study by Vassiliou and Osgood (in preparation) a number of concepts including MYSELF were rated on a number of semantic differential (Osgood et al., 1957) scales. The ratings of Americans and Greeks were compared. The concept MYSELF was rated as stronger by the Americans than by the Greeks. On the other hand, the concept MY RELATIVES was rated stronger by the Greeks than by the Americans.

In other words, the Greeks attribute less strength to themselves and more strength to their relatives than the Americans do.

The most important element of the Greek self-concept is the *philotimo.* When a representative sample of Greeks was asked to describe themselves, 74% used *this* word to describe themselves. The only other characteristic they used as frequently was the word *diligent.* The meaning of *philotimo* is not easy to define. A person who has this characteristic is polite, virtu-

ous, reliable, proud, has "a good soul," behaves correctly, meets his obligations, does his duty, is truthful, generous, self-sacrificing, tactful, respectful,
and grateful (Vassiliou and Vassiliou, 1966). The best way to summarize
what is meant by this concept is to say that a person who is *philotimous*
behaves toward members of his ingroup the way they expect him to
behave.

As an example, some Americans complained, in interviews with
Triandis, that they get little cooperation from their Greek maids and other
servants. On the other hand, some other Americans were enthusiastic
about the cooperation, honesty, and devotion of their servants. What
seemed to be the difference between these two kinds of American was
whether they included the servants in their "extended family" or simply
treated them as belonging to "another group." When the servant was made
part of the family, the *philotimo* principle required sacrifice to help the
family. Under such conditions stealing never occurred, but when the family
was in the servant's "outgroup" stealing was quite likely.

A true story from the experiences of an American archaeologist will
further illustrate this point. He had accepted his servant and she felt accepted. During a trip his boat ran aground on a rock. When several American crews, with the help of heavy equipment, failed to dislodge it, the
servant on her own initiative mobilized her ingroup, which consisted of
brothers-in-law, cousins, etc. These men abandoned their normal pursuits
to help in the rescue of the boat, and accomplished the task at considerable
risk.

Another way to explain the *philotimo* is to consider the concept of *fairness* as used by Americans. Americans consider it important to behave
fairly toward other people, but note that, at least among prejudiced Americans, "other people" do not include Negroes, or Jews. In fact, for many
Americans the ingroup is "other people like me" (white, protestant,
Anglo-Saxon, middle class, etc.). The concept of fairness operates inten-
sively within *this* ingroup and rather weakly among members of the outgroup. The more a person deviates from the white, Anglo-Saxon,
protestant characteristics, the more unlikely it is that the principle of fairness will operate.

With the Greeks the principle of the *philotimo* applies to members of
the ingroup. One must sacrifice himself to help ingroup members. The less
concern shown by a person, the less likely it is that the Greek will use
the *philotimo* principle in relating to him. The principle of fairness and
the principle of the *philotimo* are equivalent, although different in the two
cultures. Fairness does not require self-sacrifice. Furthermore, the two
ingroups are not the same: the American ingroup is large and less
salient, whereas the Greek ingroup is small (family, friends, and friendly

guests) and more important. Thus the way Greeks classify other people and the principles that guide their actions are different from the way Americans classify and behave, but the equivalence of the principles of fairness and *philotimo* may lead to an understanding of Greek behavior.

Relations with Others

Kinship. The relationships of Greeks with members of their extended families are much closer than is typical among Americans. To provide an intuitive feeling for this difference it may be stated that roughly speaking the relationships among first cousins in Greece are approximately as close as the relationships among brothers in America. With this "translation," it is possible to look at the total pattern of family relationships in Greece with some increased understanding. The word BROTHER is seen by the Greeks as more "good" and "powerful" than it is seen by Americans (Vassiliou and Osgood). There is also much more conflict among brothers in the United States than in Greece, which shows that Americans disagree in their perception of this concept to a larger extent than do the Greeks.

The general trend in the results of the Triandis, Vassiliou, and Nassiakou (1968) studies is that Greeks show more positive affect (to love, to help, to stand up for) and more intimacy (to pet, to caress, to kiss) within family roles than do Americans. The one exception can be found in the bride-groom and husband-wife relationships. This is the only family relationship in which the Americans are closer than the Greeks, not so much because Americans are exceptionally close but because Greeks are more distant. Vassiliou[5] has found that a successful and happy marriage is seen by Greeks as dependent on mutual understanding, agreement of character, and mutual concessions rather than on love. Within this type of marriage the channeling of emotions is found most strongly in the parent-child relationship—especially in the mother-son relationship, which is characterized by extreme interdependence. Furthermore, the whole family exists in a difficult environment and makes success, in the *present, very* difficult. Thus the *future* is the only bright spot for the family and this future can be brightened by the achievement of a son. Achievement, however, demands independence; therefore there is conflict between dependence and achievement. The conflict can be resolved by underemphasizing one or the other. For the healthy majority who eventually achieves there is usually some evidence of a rational break in dependence which has originated with the parents, children, or both (Vassiliou and Kataki, *op. cit.*).

---

[5] In preparation.

Authority Figures. The relationship of Greeks with authority figures depends on whether the authority figure belongs to the ingroup or the outgroup. In the ingroup it is seen as concerned and benevolent, in the outgroup, as competitive. If it is benevolent, the responses of subordinates are characterized by submissive acceptance and warmth. If it is competitive, the responses of subordinates are avoidance and hostility. The typical response of Greeks to authority figures can be characterized as authoritarian submission (and warm acceptance) within the ingroup and nonacceptance and defiance in the outgroup. If an outgroup member has little power, the typical Greek response will be one of indifference. The greater the power of the outgroup authority, the greater the perceived threat, which means that if somebody has power it automatically makes him a competitor. For this reason groups of Greeks find it difficult to cooperate among themselves and group leaders would rather have stagnation or even deterioration of the existing situation than see their competitors acquire more power. It further means that the sympathies of the Greeks are with the underdog in any kind of intergroup struggle. Therefore as long as a particular group is out of power it tends to become more popular, but as soon as it gets into power it tends to lose popularity. Such fluctuations of popular support affect the struggles between all kinds of power groups.

The worst thing anyone can do in Greece is to boast or to show that he has power before he proves that he has concern; that is, before he becomes a member of the ingroup. This immediately produces a reaction of hostility which is likely to undermine his power at the earliest opportunity. This is somewhat different from the American "bandwagon" effect, which causes people to join and support those most "successful" in politics. Greek defiance of authority can also be seen in the complete distrust of Greeks who are "experts."

To understand this phenomenon it is important to consider the ease with which Greek self-esteem can be threatened. If a consultant is an expert who is trying to help in ingroup situations, his power is welcomed. However, if the situation is such that the expert is not helpful to the person involved, he is perceived as a member of the outgroup and therefore a competitor. An American expert is more likely to be perceived as a guest, that is, an ingroup member, than a Greek expert.[6]

Another matter of relevance to the Greek relationship with authority figures concerns the ease with which Greeks work in organizations managed mostly by ingroup members. By contrast, they find it difficult to adjust to large impersonal organizations. This phenomenon may contribute to the success of small Greek businesses as contrasted to the underdevelopment

---

[6] When a Greek professor at M.I.T. was suggested to the Greek government as a consultant, they answered, "We do not want a Greek; we want an expert."

of large-scale industry. Certain kinds of relations with others are likely to be of particular interest as illustrative of the differences between Americans and Greeks.

BOSS-SECRETARY. Both cultures see much positive affect in this relationship but Americans see somewhat more than Greeks. There is no difference between the two cultures on the intimacy dimension. Greeks see more superordination as being appropriate in this relationship than Americans do.

SECRETARY-BOSS. The relationship between secretary and boss is seen as affectively neutral in Greece, whereas it is positive in America. Greeks tend to see the relationship as somewhat formal; Americans tend to see it as somewhat intimate. Finally both groups see subordination in this relationship but the Greeks place more emphasis on it than the Americans.

FOREMAN-LABORER. There is no difference in the amount of affect seen by the two cultures. Both see some positive affect. There is a substantial difference in the amount of intimacy. Greeks expect more intimacy in this relationship than the Americans. They also expect considerably more superordination than do Americans.

LABORER-FOREMAN. Between laborer and foreman the Greeks see affective neutrality; whereas Americans see positive affect; the Greeks see formality, Americans see slight intimacy, and the Greeks see more subordination than do the Americans.

SALES PERSON-CUSTOMER. There is no difference in the amount of affect perceived between sales persons and customers in the two cultures, but the Greeks see considerably greater intimacy in that relationship than the Americans. They also see more superordination in the customer-sales person relationship than do Americans. The same pattern of greater intimacy in Greece is seen in other relationships with customers; for example, beautician-customer involves greater intimacy in Greece. In the relationship between clients and professionals Americans perceive more affect than the Greeks, but Greeks see considerably more intimacy than do Americans. Finally, Greeks perceive considerably more superordination on the part of the professional (lawyer, physician, etc.) and more subordination on the part of the client than do Americans.

TENANT-LANDLORD. There is no difference between the two cultures in the amount of affect seen in this role. The Greeks, however, see more intimacy in the tenant-landlord relationship and more formality in the land-lord-tenant relationship than do Americans. Greeks see more superordination in both the tenant-landlord and the landlord-tenant relationships than do Americans.

BUSINESS PARTNER-BUSINESS PARTNER. There is a great difference in the amount of affect perceived as appropriate by Americans and Greeks in this relationship. Americans consider it appropriate to show a great deal of positive affect in this relationship, whereas Greeks are almost affectively neutral. Furthermore, Americans see more intimacy in this relationship than do the Greeks. Since Greeks in general tend to see most relationships as being more intimate, the reversal on the intimacy dimension for this particular role is especially significant. There is no difference in the amount of superordination-subordination perceived in the two cultures.

We now turn to a number of general roles and their perception in the two cultures.

OLD PEOPLE VERSUS YOUNG PEOPLE. There is a slight tendency for Greeks to perceive greater affect on the part of old people toward younger people than do Americans and for the reverse to be true for younger people toward older people. On the other hand, there is more intimacy seen in these relationships by Greeks than by Americans. On the super-ordination-subordination dimension older people are perceived as showing more superordination in Greece than in America and younger people are seen as showing more subordination in Greece than in America.

Both Americans and Greeks see a CHILD as *weak* but Americans see him as weaker. ADOLESCENCE and MATURITY are seen as being more *good, powerful,* and *active* in Greece than in America. This is because Greeks lack the horror of old age that characterizes Americans. OLD PEOPLE are seen much more negatively in the United States than in Greece. This is particularly so on the dimension of *power*.

GUEST-HOST. There is no difference in the amount of affect in either culture; however, the Greeks see more intimacy in the guest-host relationship than do Americans. The Greeks also see more subordination of the guest to the host than do Americans.

TOURIST-NATIVE. Both cultures see positive affect in this relationship, but the Greeks see more positive affect in the native-to-tourist role than do Americans. The Greeks also see more intimacy as appropriate in this relationship than do Americans. There is no difference between the two cultures on the amount of perceived subordination.

PRESIDENT-CLUB MEMBER. Both cultures see about the same amount of affect in this relationship but Greeks see more intimacy in the president-to-club-member role than do Americans. There is no difference between the cultures on the subordination dimension.

MEMBER OF THE AUDIENCE-MUSICIAN. Greeks see greater positive affect as well as greater intimacy in this relationship than do Americans.

SINGING STAR-FAN. There are no significant differences in the amount of affect seen by the two cultures; but again the Greeks see more intimacy as appropriate in these relationships than do Americans. They also see more superordination in both the singing-star-to-fan and fan-to-singing-star relationships than do Americans. In other words, the singing star can make demands on the fans and the fans can make demands on the singing star that would seem inappropriate to Americans.

CONFLICT ROLES. Greeks see more negative affect in conflict roles than do Americans. This is true for roles such as Protestant minister-Catholic priest, administrator-university student, university student-administrator, diplomat-diplomat, player of game-opponent, and politician-follow politician. In some cases, as in the diplomat opposing diplomat, the Greeks perceive that it is appropriate to show a great deal of negative affect, whereas in other cases they are closer to a neutral point on affect. In all of these conflict roles Greeks tend to be higher in intimacy than is true of Americans. Finally, Greeks see more superordination than do Americans.

Prejudices. All groups have some targets of prejudice. Just as the Americans show prejudice towards Negroes, Jews, and Catholics, some Greeks show prejudice towards gypsies, Jews, and Turks. Religious prejudice is manifested at the point of entrance into the ingroup (Triandis and Triandis, 1962). Naturalistic observations show that non-Christians are called "nonbelievers" and are not accepted as intimate friends or as kin by marriage. On the other hand, they are accepted as acquaintances, business partners, etc. These observations agree with the questionnaire responses obtained in our research program.

Differences of the Perception of Social Behavior

In the preceding section we have shown differences in the way Greeks and Americans perceive relationships between kinds of people. In the present section we describe differences in their perception of social behaviors. It is a frequent observation among persons who have engaged in social relations with persons from other cultures that their behaviors are sometimes "misinterpreted" and their intentions "misunderstood"; for example, a person from one culture may provide what he considers to be "friendly criticism" to a person from another culture only to discover that the other person interprets it as "hatred." A person from Culture *A* behaves in a manner he considers extremely "positive" toward a person from Culture *B*. The individual from Culture *B*, however, perceives the behavior as "neutral" and the individual from Culture *A* feels that he has been "given the cold shoulder." His negative reaction is perceived in turn as negative, and a vicious circle of mutual punishment takes place. One possible explanation of such misinterpretation is that the meaning of the social behavior is not the same across cultures.

We have investigated such differences in the perception of social behavior with rather rigorous procedures involving Thurstone scaling of the social behavior descriptions (Triandis, Vassiliou, & Nassiakou, 1968). We found differences that correspond rather closely to the differences we have already discussed concerning behaviors in ingroups and outgroups.

Specifically, the behaviors *to help, to advise,* and *to feel sorry for,* which are most appropriate in the ingroup, as well as *to thank, to praise,* and *to appreciate* are seen by the Greeks as related to the "giving of love" to a much greater extent than do Americans. This may be due to the context of these behaviors, which is typically the ingroup, and therefore in Greece they are more frequently associated with positive emotional states such as love than they are in America. On the other hand, the behavior *to compete with* is associated with negative emotions in Greece, whereas it is emotionally neutral among Americans. Again, it must be remembered that competition occurs with members of the outgroup in Greece, and for this reason this behavior has a different meaning for Greeks than it has for Americans.

Greeks see more positive emotion in the behavior *to enjoy working for* than do Americans. This behavior in Greece has the connotation that the employee feels loyal to the employer and therefore is required to do "extra things" to please him. Thus *to enjoy working for* a boss is likely to imply "going out of your way to help him," even when you are not asked to do so, if a difficult moment requires additional effort. On the other hand employees are likely to enjoy working for an employer only if he is responsive to their idiosyncratic needs and special requests for exemption from general rules.

Greeks see more negative emotion associated with the behaviors *to be indifferent to* and *to punish* than do Americans. Indifference is a real insult and is somewhat related to the notion, which we have already discussed, that most Greek social relations are characterized by greater intimacy. To be indifferent is *not* neutral; it is essentially hostile. One of the reasons Americans are considered *arrogant* and *cold* by Greeks is exactly that; Americans believe it is perfectly proper to be indifferent to somebody; indifference has no negative implications, but exactly the same behavior would be interpreted by a Greek as involving coldness, arrogance, and hostility.

Another example in which differences in the interpretation of the meaning of behavior could lead to a misunderstanding involves certain behaviors perceived by Greeks as involving "denying of status" to a greater extent than is true of Americans. It is appropriate for a high-status person to behave in ways that "deny status" to his subordinate, but Greeks are quite sensitive to such implications and react quite negatively when a person denies status to them. The following behaviors are seen by the Greeks as denying status to a larger extent than is the case of Americans: *to be impatient with, to be indifferent to, to inspect work of, to accuse,* and *to protect.* Clearly *to be impatient with* involves denying status but the Greeks exaggerate the significance of this behavior and react much more negatively than do Americans. We have already mentioned that *to be indifference to* involves hostility; it also involves denying status. *To accuse* and *to inspect work of* are obviously related to denying status, but again for the Greeks the meaning is more exaggerated than it is for Americans.

We have already discussed the differences between the two cultures in the perception of intimacy. Greeks perceive many social behaviors as much

Table 1

Behaviors Greeks Perceive as More *Intimate*

To annoy	To be a friend of
To quarrel with	To learn with help of
To scold	To laugh at jokes of
To complain to	To enjoy company of
To hit	To kiss
To correct	To go to movies with
To protect	To wish good luck to
To ask for advice of	To share responsibility with
To study with	To be loyal to
To advise	To date
To be grateful to	

Behaviors Greeks Perceive as More *Formal*

To despise	To mourn for
To ask for forgiveness	To follow instructions of
To invite for dinner	To be commanded by
To congratulate	

more intimate than do Americans and therefore much more appropriate for roles that are more intimate. Table 1 shows the behaviors that are perceived as more intimate. The implication of these facts can be stated as follows: if an American engages in such behaviors before he has established sufficient intimacy with the Greek, the Greek will be offended.

We now turn to certain behaviors that the Greeks see as more formal than do Americans and therefore much more appropriate in roles involving formal relations. Table 1 also lists these behaviors. One can state that Americans will find Greek social relations much more informal than they are used to *within the ingroup* and much more formal between *ingroup* and *outgroup* members. This means in effect that Americans will find all Greek social relations either too informal or too formal.

Greek Work Habits

In our earlier discussion we hypothesized that Greeks have had little opportunity to control their environment. They have not been able to plan successfully for hundreds of years because their plans have typically been foiled by wars and revolutions. The responses that helped survival, for hundreds of years, were global and fast and left little time for analysis, integration, and precision. The result is that much of Greek work behavior appears to be unsystematic. Little attention to detail, rather careless execution of work, and little evidence of careful planning are characteristics of Greek behavior. Estimates of time to complete a job are likely to be inaccurate, and there is little concern with the actual time it takes to finish a job.

Attitudes Toward Significant Aspects of the Environment

In this section we discuss the way Greeks think and feel about a large number of issues and objects in their environment. Consistent with the work of Osgood et al. (1957) and as reviewed in Chapter 4, we use three dimensions for the description of these attitudes:

1. The evaluation of an attitude object; in other words whether it is good or bad.
2. The *power* of the attitude object.
3. The amount of *activity* in the attitude object.

These three dimensions are common to all humans and therefore they can be used in comparing cultures (Osgood, 1965); for example, a person may consider his father good or bad, powerful or weak, and active or passive. Any attitude object can be seen as high or low on these three dimensions.

The results that we discuss come from extensive studies of the way Greeks and Americans perceive and react to various stimuli in their environments. We have organized our discussion under four headings:

1. The human body.
2. Religious concepts.
3. Institutions and social processes.
4. Relationships with the environment.

The Human Body

Body Parts. Americans and Greeks perceive body parts, such as FEET, HAIR, HEAD, HANDS, STOMACH, and LIPS in extremely similar ways. The only major difference is that the LEFT HAND is considered much *weaker* by the Greeks than by Americans. The Greeks feel that left-handedness in a person implies that he has been neglected by his parents and teachers. They therefore feel pity for the lefthanded person.

There is a value in righthandedness that is somewhat exaggerated in Greece as compared with United States; for example, good luck is associated with the right hand. Thus giving with the right hand and entering a house with the right foot are associated with correctness of behavior and fortunate events.

Body Characteristics. In general the meaning attributed to these characteristics is rather similar in these two cultures. However, Greeks have a horror of dismembered bodies. They react much more negatively than do Americans to CRIPPLES and to people who are "physically different."

Life and Health. Greeks are realistic and down to earth about concepts such as PAIN, PUNISHMENT, and DUTY, for they have a rather Spartan view of the world. They see them as less *bad* and more *potent* than do Americans on semantic differential scales. They consider these concepts as part of life and therefore not unacceptable. Americans tend to romanticize life (Triandis & Osgood, 1958), hence reject such concepts as completely unacceptable.

DRUNKENNESS is seen as more *potent* by Americans than by Greeks. Greeks drink more frequently than Americans but with considerable moderation (Vassiliou, Seferi, & Koukouridou, 1968). On the other hand, they almost never drink to knock themselves out. They also drink wine rather than hard liquor and eat while drinking. Hence they seldom get drunk, and when they do (as in a tavern) they are likely to sing and dance rather than vomit or pass out. Thus drunkenness is "less controlling" for them.

Emotions. Greeks differentiate among emotions more finely than do Americans, focusing among specific rather than general feelings. They think of emotions more in terms of how they are expressed rather than how they are felt. Greeks have a more explicit set of norms for expressing emotions and they focus on these norms more than on the specific stimuli that produce the emotions. Similarly, on other occasions a Greek may appear to be angrier than he really is.

As a result Greeks may seem emotionally more active. There is less of a cultural norm to "hold your temper"; in fact there are specific cultural norms that direct a person to express his emotions. Greeks also perceive a bigger difference between pleasant and unpleasant emotions.

In one of our studies (see Chapter 8) we obtained the causal links perceived by Americans, Greeks, Indians, and Japanese between certain concepts. We obtained the major causes of ANGER as well as the major consequences of this concept as seen by subjects in various cultures.

The Greeks consider that the major causes of ANGER are *insults, bad manners,* the use of *nicknames, lying,* and *jealosy.* Americans consider *contempt, bad temper,* and *jealousy* as the major causes of ANGER. Note that there is a suggestion of a direct "injury to self-esteem" in the basic theme of the causes of Greek ANGER and an indirect "injury to self-esteem" in the American ANGER theme.

The consequences of ANGER are seen by the Greeks as *crime, murder,* and *"no friends,"* whereas for Americans the major consequences are *displeasure, violence,* and *pain.* Thus the Greek reaction to ANGER is specific, whereas the American reaction is general.

FEAR is seen by the Greeks as caused by *lack of manliness, past life,* and *fantasies;* Americans frequently mention *pain* and the *unknown.*

The lack of manliness is reminiscent of the image of the hero which is important to the Greeks. The connection between past life and fear is due to the painful experiences of the past which enhance the hopefulness of the future. Fantasies lead to fear because they are likely to be worrisome rather than pleasant anticipations. The consequences of FEAR for the Greeks are *failure,* an *inferiority complex,* and *defeat;* for Americans, *mental worry* and *trouble.* Thus for Greeks FEAR is a threat to self-esteem; for Americans it is a specific unpleasant emotional state.

SYMPATHY is an ingroup behavior for Greeks. It is a powerful emotion exchanged frequently among ingroup members. This is perhaps the reason Vassiliou and Osgood[7] found that in Greece sympathy is related more to *potency* and *activity* than it is in the United States. In Greece you show SYMPATHY toward those you are concerned with. Therefore it is seen as being determined by the other person's *good behavior, good character, goodness, kindness,* and *love*. The person who feels admiration and trust will also feel SYMPATHY. In contrast to the Greeks who see little relation between SYMPATHY and pity the Americans find a definite relationship between SYMPATHY and *compassion, care, understanding,* and *pity*. For the Greek showing SYMPATHY to members of the ingroup is one of his obligations under the *philotimo rules*. It occurs in the context of trust. For the American it is a means of enhancing his self-esteem; it is a way to prove to himself that he is a "good person."

The consequences of SYMPATHY determined in our study are consistent with this interpretation. The Greek consequences are *admiration, friendship, love,* and *trust*. The American consequences are *care, compassion, help, kindness, pity, sorrow,* and *charity*.

There is also a strong cultural difference in the reaction to PASSION: Greeks see it as *bad;* Americans see it as *good*. Greeks see it as uncontrolled emotion, hence unacceptable. Acceptable emotions are those under the control of social norms. Americans see it as an expression of one's individuality, hence good.

Consequently, as expected, we found in our studies that Greeks perceive less *power* in the emotions of ANGER, FEAR, and GUILT than do Americans.

Finally, Greeks see more activity in *HOPE* because their unfavorable environment has forced the Greeks to underemphasize the here and now and to focus on the hopeful future.

Religious-Philosophical Concepts

Religion. Americans and Greeks agree in their responses to religious concepts. The only major difference is that the concept NONBELIEVER is seen as "more bad" and "weaker" in Greece than in the United States and Americans disagree among themselves much more than do Greeks when they judge the concept ATHEIST; that is, Greeks are quite definite in their rejection of nonbelievers and atheists, whereas Americans show a variety of responses to these concepts. These results are understandable in view of the fact that 92% of all Greeks are at least nominally Greek Orthodox but in America a variety of religions coexists.

[7] V. Vassiliou and C. E. Osgood. Data on Greek Atlas of meaning (in preparation).

Ethical Concepts. In all cultures there are two basic ways in which behavior is controlled: internally (a person does not do something because his "conscience" does not allow him to do it) and externally (a person does not do something because others prevent him). Control by the conscience is essentially control by guilt; control by others is essentially control by shame.[8]

In Greece control by guilt is primarily relevant to behavior in the ingroup. Since the principle of the ingroup involves mutual "concern for the other," anything associated with disregard for the other is likely to produce a guilt response; for example, a son leaving his mother for an acceptable cause but against her will (e.g., to go to the city to study) will feel guilty. On the other hand, behavior involving interaction with outgroup members is only externally controlled, primarily by enforcing authorities.

CHEATING is more acceptable in Greece than in the United States when it is directed toward members of the outgroup. It is completely unacceptable within the ingroup. This is not dishonesty in the way an American will understand this concept. Rather, when there is competition, such as exists between a Greek and members of his outgroup, the social norms permit (from an American point of view) or require (from a Greek point of view) that the outgroup member be taken advantage of if he is weak. It is "up to" the outgroup member to defend himself against CHEATING, and if he does not he is simply stupid. There is no change in the Greek's self-esteem when he cheats an outgroup member. Furthermore, when the outgroup member can be cheated his prestige drops; when he cannot be cheated, his prestige rises. As a result Greeks perceive CHEATING as relatively more powerful and more active (Vassiliou and Osgood).

Furthermore, Greeks are suspicious about any communication they receive from an outgroup member; therefore LYING does not "work so well"; hence they judge it as less powerful than do Americans (Vassiliou and Osgood).

CRIME is seen as more *powerful* by Americans than by Greeks, probably because, statistically, American crimes involve more money. The causes of CRIME according to Greeks include *bad company* (i.e., bad ingroup), *criminal instinct* (inability of the ingroup to control), and *psychic turmoil* (related to mental illness). The causes of CRIME according to Americans are *previous crimes* (bad habits), such as *murder, stealing,* and *robbery,* as well as *needs* and *loss* of *control* (ineffectiveness of guilt). Thus Greeks see crime as due to factors unrelated to the person

[8] This formulation should be assumed to be equivalent to Riesman's. Riesman's formulation refers to the sources of norms, ours, to the sources of enforcement of norms.

himself, whereas Americans see it as caused by previous actions and internal weaknesses of the individual.

In other words, the Greek sees less personal responsibility and more justification for CRIMES. The latter point is illustrated by the predominance of "crimes of honor" and the acquittal of the defendants by juries in such cases. Although this is typical of rural Greece, it almost never occurs in the United States.

The consequences of CRIME according to Greeks are *justice, dishonor,* and the *spoiling of life.* According to Americans, they are *lack of respect, guilt, misery, uneasiness, social disorder,* and *dishonor.* It is notable that the Greek consequences of crime emphasize the theme of punishment and interference with one's life, whereas the American consequences emphasize the theme of guilt and social disorganization.

The perceived causes of PUNISHMENT in Greece were found to be *injustice* and *illegal acts* as well as "no God." In other words, when somebody does "something wrong," he is punished. The consequences of PUNISHMENT are *compliance, exemplification, justice, repentance,* and *no resentment* or *resistance* (to the punishing authority). Thus for the Greeks PUNISHMENT is fully accepted, a result consistent with the *positive* evaluation of this concept, as found by Vassiliou and Osgood, *op. cit.* In all other cultures PUNISHMENT is rated *bad,* but in Greece it is rated *good.* Americans see the consequences of PUNISHMENT as *dishonor, guilt, resentment, resistances* (presumably to authorities), and *correction.* Thus, although Americans see some correction (presumably forced compliance) as a result of punishment, they also associate this concept with resentment, resistance, and guilt.

Institutions and Social Processes

Institutions. The ARMY is seen as "more good" by Greeks than by Americans. Army life is considered an exceptionally good influence on young people. These results may reflect "authoritarian submission," but they may also be explained by acknowledging the fact that many Greeks realize that the exceptionally strong bond established in the typical Greek family between mother and son needs to be weakened so that the son may mature. There are special designations for those who have not served in the armed forces that can be translated into "he is his mama's son." Army life forces a separation of the son from the mother which weakens this bond and allows for new experiences and greater independence. Furthermore, for most Greeks, experience in the army involves an increase in their standard of living, including education and travel, which they could not otherwise afford. Even those aspects of army life to which some Americans object, such as the rigid control of the individual by an institution, are perfectly consistent with the Greek value pattern. The high evaluation of social control is also seen by Greeks in the more extreme positive evaluation of the word LAW.

The Greeks love to discuss, to argue, and to match their wits with other debaters. This can be seen in the more extreme agreement by Greeks with the statements, "I enjoy a good rousing argument" and "I like arguing with an instructor or supervisor." It can also be observed in their positive evaluation of the concept POLITICS.

Both Americans and Greeks see education as a positive value. An educated person in Greece has more prestige than a rich person, even though education does not necessarily lead to material advantages. The association of the concept SCHOOL with education explains why Greeks see SCHOOLS as "more good," and Americans see them as more *powerful*. The very concept of EDUCATION is seen as more *powerful* by Americans than by Greeks.

Vassiliou and Osgood found that the concept REVOLUTION is seen by Greeks as *good* and by Americans as *bad*. This can be understood in the context of our previous discussion. First it should be recalled that the Greeks reject useless and unjustified authority. Second, morality is a focal concern and Greeks are willing to adopt extreme measures to enforce it. Third, we found that the Greeks would use any available means to achieve highly desirable ends. Thus a revolution is considered part of life and under many conditions perfectly justifiable from the Greek point of view. On the other hand, Americans with their tradition of political stability naturally find the idea of a revolution highly distasteful.

LABOR UNIONS are seen as more powerful by Americans than by Greeks. This simply reflects the actual relative power of labor unions in the two countries.

MARRIAGE is seen as more powerful by Americans than by Greeks. This is consistent with the central position of the husband-wife relationship in America and the focus on the parent-child relationship in Greece.

In connection with the present discussion of the way Greeks and Americans view institutions it should also be remembered that there are differences between the way Greeks and Americans are rewarded by the large-scale institutions for which they work. In Greece they are generally rewarded (promoted) if they have reached a certain age, have been loyal to the organization, and have made no mistakes during their careers. Americans are rewarded not only because they make no mistakes but also because they have accomplished something in their jobs. This means, in effect, that a Greek is not likely to take a chance on a decision if success is not almost certain; an American has to take more risks. Furthermore,

Greeks tend to "play it safe" to a larger extent than is true of Americans, and as a result they appear more inflexible, rigid, and unwilling to adapt to change than Americans.

Occupations. Greeks in general tend to see more activity in most occupations than do Americans, which probably reflects differential unemployment rates. In addition, they value ARTISTS, AUTHORS, and PROFESSORS more than do Americans. This is consistent with the great emphasis on education and a very old cultural tradition.

Political Concepts. CAPITALISM, DEMOCRACY, NATIONALISM, and SOCIALISM are seen as more *powerful* by Americans than by Greeks. NATIONALISM on the other hand is seen as "more good" by Greeks than by Americans. Finally, NEUTRALITY is seen as "more good" by Greeks than by Americans.

Such differences can readily be related to the histories of the two countries.

Social Attitudes

A sample of about 600 American male students was compared with a sample of about 400 male Athenians. They were asked to indicate their agreement with a number of statements relevant to a variety of social attitudes (Triandis, Davis, and Vassiliou).[9]

The Greeks emphasized the need for social control to a much larger extent than did the Americans. They also approved of corrective punishment, no matter how severe. However, they disapproved of capital punishment and hostility in exercising control within the ingroup. They were also opposed to the use of violence in settling international disputes to a larger extent than Americans.

Specifically, the agreement on the need for social control is evident at three levels: the personal, the interpersonal, and the governmental. At the personal level it was manifested by agreement on 10 items such as "I try to keep a tight rein on myself at all times" with which the Greeks strongly agreed, whereas Americans were uncertain.

At the interpersonal level it can be seen in the Greek responses to statements such as the following: "As long as so many of our teachers are afraid to administer physical punishment our schools will probably continue to decline." The Greeks agreed with this statement; the Americans

[9] H. C. Triandis, E. E. Davis, and Vasso Vassiliou. Social attitudes in cross-cultural perspective (unpublished study).

disagreed with it. In the matter of the societal (state) control we see the Greeks agreeing with and the Americans disagreeing with the following statement: "We will probably be a lot better off if some of the bigots in favor of racial and religious discrimination were expelled from the country." In 22 statements, such as the above, which referred to social control, Greeks approved of control to a larger extent than did Americans. Particularly characteristic was approval of control on moral issues; for example, "sex crimes, such as rape and attacks on children, deserve more than mere imprisonment; such criminals ought to be publicly whipped or worse." Greeks strongly agreed with that statement; Americans disagreed.

As a specific illustration of the Greek agreement with items involving corrective punishment, we can mention that Greeks strongly agreed with the statement "it would probably provide a good example for this entire nation if people who refused to salute our flag were imprisoned." Americans strongly disagreed.

Such results suggest that the Greeks are high on the *F*-scale. Empirically this is so. It is not certain, however, that the theory of the authoritarian personality, as developed in America, applies to them without modification. In particular, the importance of the ingroup-outgroup distinction, and the definition of the ingroup which implies a face-to-face group, modifies the character of Greek authoritarianism. It should be recalled that authoritarian submission is typical within the ingroup but *not* in response to outgroup authority figures.

A final point concerning Greeks who agreed with the statement about imprisoning those who refuse to salute the flag. It is most probable that they have in mind members of their outgroup. It is most likely that they consider that members of their ingroup "would behave correctly" and therefore would not be affected by the situation described in the statement. If a member of the ingroup behaved "incorrectly," he would be pressured to change his behavior, but if he were imprisoned the members of the ingroup would be upset and would consider the imprisonment unfair. In other words, in responding to such items the Greeks probably are thinking of outgroup members, and in view of the competitiveness between ingroups and outgroups their threshold for imprisoning people who do not behave correctly may well be much lower than it is in America; hence the difference in the Greek and American responses.

Finally, to illustrate Greek disapproval of the use of violence for the settlement of international disputes we may examine their responses to the item: "Politicians who actively support the arms race should be thrown out of office." Greeks agreed and Americans disagreed.

In this study our data also suggests that Greeks have a much clearer system of values. They agree among themselves to a much greater extent than Americans. Furthermore, on moral issues Greeks tended to agree or disagree strongly with our statements, whereas Americans used more moderate responses, such as "slightly agree"; for example, in responses to the statement, "We cannot know for sure whether or not there is a God" Americans either slightly agreed or slightly disagreed! Greeks only slightly disagreed. The majority of the Greeks strongly agreed and the Americans slightly disagreed with the statement, "No person who would ever think of hurting his parents should be permitted in a society of normal decent people."

Greek values are not only clearer but are openly proclaimed and expressed in unhesitating action. Thus Greeks agreed with the statements, "I am generally spontaneous in my speech or actions" and "I do not mind having others judge me by the organizations to which I belong"; Americans showed uncertainty. These trends were observed in seven other statements in which Americans and Greeks had different responses.

Greeks show a clear hierarchy of values. The success of the ingroup (both survival and growth) is more important than the success of the individual. The size of the ingroup depends on the situation. In moments of national crises the whole country is the ingroup and national survival becomes the predominant value. At other times the ingroup is the family, friends, and people with mutual concerns. The collective achievement of this group is central. In the United States the individual is at the center of the value system; his own survival and self-actualization are central values. The individual's success even at the expense of his family is sometimes acceptable in America, whereas it is inconceivable in Greece.

In the ingroup, of whatever size, depending on the situation, authority figures are blindly accepted in Greece; for example, Greeks disagreed and Americans agreed with the statement, "Almost everyone has at some time hated his parents." On five other statements of this type the results obtained from the two countries supported this generalization.

Furthermore, in response to eight statements referring to acceptance of the ingroup the Greeks are much more extreme; for example, they strongly disagreed with the statement, "I have sometimes wanted to run away from home," but strongly agreed with the statement, "I often find it difficult to break with familiar and pleasant surroundings."

Not only do the Greeks show exceptional acceptance of the ingroup but they also reject influence and pressure from the outgroup; for example, they agreed with the statement "I usually do not care very much about what people think about me." Americans disagreed with this statement. On the other hand, when authorities are seen as useless or ineffective, they are strongly rejected; for example, Greeks strongly agreed with the statements, "It is the duty of the citizen to criticize or censure his country whenever he considers it to be wrong" and "Disobedience to the government is sometimes justified."

Other values of great importance to Greeks are the *inviolability of personal honor* (e.g., they agreed with the statement, "An insult to our honor should always be punished"), *the belief in the effectiveness of will power* (e.g., they strongly agreed with the statement, "Few difficulties can hold us back if we have enough will power"), and *rejection of human passions* (e.g., "Human passions cause most of the evil in the world" was strongly agreed with by almost all our Greek respondents).

Strong emphasis is also given to *concern for others* and to *kindness* as being significant in one's life. On 13 items which referred to kindness and concern for others the Greeks indicated more concern than did our American respondents; for example, to the statement, "It upsets me very much to see another person suffer," the Greeks overwhelmingly responded with "strongly agree," whereas the Americans only agreed. Even practical jokes are perceived by Greeks as unkind to other people. Most Greeks strongly agreed and most Americans slightly disagreed with the statement, "I don't enjoy playing practical jokes on people."

The Greeks also value *personal dependability,* as seen in their strong agreement with items such as, "I would rather be a steady and dependable worker than a brilliant but unstable one," "Once I have my mind made up I seldom change it," and "I take great pride in being an orderly person." On five such items the Greeks agreed and the Americans were uncertain. Finally, the Greeks were more extreme than the Americans in their belief in God and in man's ability to control the environment.

The latter point can be seen in the strong agreement of Greeks with fundamentalist statements such as, "If the world continues on its present wicked course, God will probably have to destroy it." The majority of Greeks agreed and the majority of Americans disagreed with this statement. We observed the same kind of response from the two cultural groups on four similar statements.

The American value of fairness is incompatible with the Greek value system which changes when one moves from the ingroup to the outgroup. Thus the Greeks agreed and the Americans disagreed with the items, "I do not blame a person for taking advantage of someone who leaves himself open to it" and "I treat people according to their just deserves."

Greeks are reality-oriented and nonromantic and by adequate testing of reality avoid becoming too inflexible. Since the Greeks live in a difficult and crises-laden environment, it is reality-oriented for them to agree strongly with the statement, "It is better never to expect too much; in that way you are rarely disappointed." Their flexibility can be seen in their agreement with the statement, "The findings of science may some day show that many of our most cherished beliefs are wrong." On 20 items on which it was possible for the Greeks to show either rigidity or reality orientation they tended to respond in the direction of reality orientation showing a good deal of reality testing.

Interpretation of these results is difficult. On the one hand, there is in our new data, just as there was in the older data (Triandis & Triandis, 1962), an extremely reliable tendency for the Greeks to display an extreme checking style and an acquiescence response set. Such response tendencies normally indicate rigidity. On the other hand, it is not certain that the relationship between checking style and rigidity holds cross-culturally. If the checking style is statistically controlled, the highly reliable differences between Americans and Greeks on the Gough-Sanford Rigidity Scale are eliminated (Triandis & Triandis, 1962, p. 10). Perhaps a distinction must be made between rigidity in style and rigidity in content. The Greeks are certainly rigid in style, but they appear to be no different from Americans in their responses to the content of rigidity items.

Consistent with our interpretation that they are reality-oriented is their unwillingness to take risks in their uncertain environment. Greeks disagreed with the item, "I enjoy taking risks in games and in life," and with the item, "I like walking along a dark street in the rain," but Americans slightly agreed.

Values and Disvalues

In Chapter 7 we examined the perceived "antecedents" and "consequents" of certain concepts by Americans, Greeks, and others. We abstract some of these results that are relevant to the present discussion.

Freedom. The Greek perception of the causes of FREEDOM emphasizes the relevance of this concept to national freedom. The American perception emphasizes individual freedom. Thus the Greeks see *democracy, peace, patriotism,* and the *Constitution* as the determinants of FREEDOM; Americans emphasize *respect for human beings* and the *individual, strength, equality,* and *faith.*

Consistent with this interpretation, the consequents of FREEDOM given to us by Greeks include *civilization, growth of civilization, progress,* and *well-being.* On the other hand, for Americans FREEDOM connotes *happiness, joy, life, well-being,* and *responsibilities* as well as *rights.* Thus the consequents of FREEDOM, according to the Greeks, can be seen in the well-being of the collectivity, whereas for the Americans they are seen in the well-being of the individual. Furthermore, the American recognizes the responsibilities associated with FREEDOM; the Greek does not.

Peace. Consistent with the cultural differences in the meaning of FREEDOM, the Greeks emphasize societal causes and the Americans, individual causes, for PEACE. The major causes of PEACE perceived by Greeks are *freedom, brotherhood, democracy,* and *equality.* Our Americans gave as the major causes *cooperation, understanding, contentment, goodwill,* and *kindness.*

The same trend is seen in the consequents of PEACE, where again the emphasis in Greece is societal rather than individualistic. PEACE leads to *concordance, freedom, a higher standard of living, progress,* and *well-being* according to the Greeks and to *security, tranquility, tolerance, unity, friendship,* and *happiness* according to the Americans.

Since the focus of Greek life is the ingroup, little value is placed on personal freedom or individualized peace. In fact, a member of the ingroup would feel left out and unhappy if he were given much personal freedom and if ingroup members left him in peace by not allowing him to be concerned with their problems. Thus the central meaning of these words for the Greek is societal, often at the level of the total body politic, whereas Americans focus more on the individual meanings of these concepts and less on the political meanings. Furthermore, it is likely that Americans take freedom at the political level for granted; for the Greeks it is a big issue for which they have often struggled under various historical circumstances.

Truth. The responses of both Americans and Greeks to this concept suggest that they do not see it in its philosophical context but primarily as the opposite of lying. The major difference between the two cultures is that although both see TRUTH determined by the "good quality of the individual" the Greeks also assign much responsibility to others in the individual's environment. Thus, although both mention *honesty, respect,* and *sincerity* as causes of truth, the Greeks also mention good *upbringing, devotion to God,* and *good companionship.* Furthermore, the Greek perception of the causes of TRUTH is more global (e.g., a good man) and the American is more specific (e.g., justice, trust).

Although both Americans and Greeks feel better about telling the truth because they experience themselves as better human beings, the Greeks in addition feel satisfaction for telling the truth because this implies acceptance by ingroup authority figures.

Specifically, the Greeks see the *progress of the society* and the *individual, joy,* and *success* as consequents of TRUTH. In addition, they feel that TRUTH results in "appreciation of God," presumably because TRUTH involves following the directions of ingroup authorities, which in turn implies acceptance of these authority figures, including God. The

Americans see the gains of TRUTH at the individual level as *trust, respect, self-confidence, morality, love,* and *courage.*

Courage and Defeat. The causes of COURAGE are seen quite similarly in both cultures. The Greeks, however, associate COURAGE with everyday experiences; the Americans see it as enhancing *self-confidence* and leading to greater *respect, honor,* and *strength.*

DEFEAT is seen by both cultural groups as resulting from personal weaknesses. The Greeks emphasize *ineptitude, superficiality, lack of planning,* and *lack of perseverence.* The Americans emphasize *apathy, no desire, giving up,* as well as *lack of confidence,* and *lack of perseverence.* The Greeks, in addition, focus on factors that are beyond their control. Thus they mention *illness, treason,* and *lack of unity.*

The consequents of DEFEAT are seen similarly by the two cultures. They include *disappointment, discouragement, depression,* and *sorrow.* The Greeks also mention *destruction, servitude,* and *shock* which the Americans almost never mention. The Americans also emphasize *trying again.* The Greeks see greater finality in defeat (e.g., destruction) and associate in with the fate of the collectivity (e.g., servitude).

Achievement Concepts. The essential difference between Americans and Greeks in the perception of KNOWLEDGE is that Greeks react to this concept in a global way. As a prerequisite they see the will to learn, coupled with an inquiring mind. As a process they only see *studying* in order to learn. As a consequence of learning they see general positive values such as *progress, success, peace,* and *self-confidence.*

By contrast, Americans have a more differentiated response to this concept. As prerequisites they mention *motivation* and *an inquiring mind,* as do the Greeks. They also mention *curiosity, intelligence,* and *wisdom.* As a process they mention *understanding* and *experience,* and as consequents they mention *easy adjustment, understanding, ability, wisdom, advancement, progress,* and *self-confidence.* Thus there appears more differentiation in the American responses, particularly at the point of the "payoff" of KNOWLEDGE.

The major cause of PROGRESS seen by the Greeks relates to the individual who has characteristics that make him acceptable to his ingroup in an environment that permits progress. Thus *diligence, honesty, willingness to learn, willpower, cooperation, education,* and *peace* result in PROGRESS. Americans mention *cooperation, initiative, ambition, foresight, drive,* and *hard work.* In other words, the Greeks describe the person who progresses in terms of his traits; the Americans, in addition to the traits, emphasize the behaviors that lead to PROGRESS.

PROGRESS is seen by the Greeks as resulting in gains to the collectivity (e.g., *civilization, scientific development,* and *well-being*). The American emphasis is spectacularly high on individual achievement (e.g., *achievement, development, expansion, knowledge,* and *success*), although the improvement in the status of the collectivity is also mentioned. The Greek sees his personal progress as a consequent of the improvement of the collectivity, whereas the American sees his personal progress as leading to the improvement of the collectivity.

Power, Success and Wealth. The Greeks see power as being acquired by struggle with their outgroups with the help of their friends. The Americans see it as being acquired by cooperative processes, such as an increase in knowledge and the organization of activities by good leadership. Specifically, *competition, endeavor, exercise, self-confidence,* and *friends* are the causes of POWER mentioned by Greeks; *knowledge, respect, strength,* and *leadership* are emphasized by Americans.

As a consequent of POWER the Greeks see *self-confidence, courage, freedom, glory,* and *victory;* the Americans, *control, influence,* and *respect.* Thus the Greeks see it in terms of struggle with others and the Americans in terms of influence on others.

As causes of SUCCESS the Greeks mention *cooperation, courage,* and *willpower.* The Americans mention *devotion, planning, preparation,* and *hard work.* Thus the Greeks see it again in terms of a struggle, whereas the Americans see it in terms of careful planning and hard work.

As a consequent of SUCCESS the Greeks report *happiness* and *love,* that is, more intensive acceptance by the ingroup. The Americans mention *achievement, pride, satisfaction, self-confidence, joy,* and *progress,* which appear to be qualities or attributes of the individual.

As a cause of WEALTH Greeks mention *courage, hard work, intelligence,* and *patience;* the American respondents mention *drive, knowledge and education, good fortune, money, happiness,* and *health.* In contrast to the way the Greeks see the causes of SUCCESS, which do not involve hard work and are conceived as enhancing the values of the ingroup, they see WEALTH in more specific terms involving inborn skills, *hard work,* and *patience.* The Americans emphasize the health of the individual (*drive, happiness*), his acquired skills (*knowledge, education*), and luck (*good fortune, money*).

The consequents of WEALTH are perceived by both Americans and Greeks to be *enjoyment, comfort,* and *luxury.* The Greeks also see *selfishness* and *philanthropy;* the Americans see *abundance, affluence,* and *further satisfaction.*

When the Greek has money, he shares it with his ingroup. If he has more than the amount needed by his immediate ingroup, he shares it with the community (i.e., he expands his ingroup). There is a considerable record of philanthropy by wealthy Greeks in their own towns. Some of the major national monuments were donated to the Greek state by wealthy Greeks. This is somewhat similar to philanthropy in America; however, our evidence suggests that the Greek experiences more gratification by giving because he satisfies his basic needs. Although Americans satisfy prestige and superiority (reflected in feelings of pity) needs, the Greeks satisfy their needs for acceptance by the ingroup. The Greek pattern of giving produces no resentment because the giver receives as much basic gratification as the receiver. On the other hand, the American pattern of giving emphasizes the giver's superiority and the receiver's subordinate position. The receiver experiences gratitude for what is given and resentment for the feelings that are associated with the way it is given.

Death. We can conceive of DEATH as the opposite of actualization implied in the achievement themes discussed in the preceding section. The major causes of DEATH perceived by the Greeks are natural—*old age* and *illness.* By contrast the major causes of DEATH perceived by Americans are unnatural—*murder, suicide,* and *war.* This is consistent with the more matter-of-fact attitude toward life and death characteristic of the Greeks and the more romantic attitude that characterizes Americans (Triandis & Osgood, 1958). It may also reflect the violence that is frequent in both real life and American television.

The consequents of DEATH according to the Greeks are matter-of-fact but also suggest the struggle with the outgroup—they include *family breakdown* and the *joy of enemies.* Americans mention *oblivion* and *extinction,* which are individual states, and *loss of loved ones* and *loneliness* at the social level.

In summary, the contrast between Americans and Greeks on achievement and death themes suggest that for the Greeks achievement leads to the strengthening of the ingroup and the weakening of the power of the outgroup, and death involves the weakening of the ingroup and the satisfaction of the outgroup. By contrast the American view of both achievement and death focuses more on the individual.

Relations with Others

Three concepts are considered in connection with relationships among people—LOVE, TRUST, and RESPECT. The major difference between Americans and Greeks in the way they perceive these three concepts is that the Greeks see good behavior appropriately guided by ingroup norms as leading to all three. The Americans relate these concepts to general feelings, such as loyalty, admiration, and honor.

Love. The major cause of LOVE perceived by Greeks is appropriate behavior within the ingroup. The emphasis is on *good conduct.* In our studies Greeks mention good conduct as a cause significantly more frequently than Americans. In addition, they specify what it means to behave correctly by mentioning *niceness, politeness, devotion to God, faith,* and *morality.* The Americans see the cause of LOVE in terms of emotional states—*affection, trust, kindness, happiness,* and *respect.* Thus love is seen as dependent on a person's adherence to ingroup norms in Greece.

The consequents of LOVE in Greece include marriage and children; that is, they are more matter of fact. They also include *progress,* which suggests that the person is improving because of his greater acceptance by the ingroup. The American consequents of LOVE, which are similar to the Greek, emphasize only slightly more social relationships such as *friends, companionship,* and *concern for others. Intense social behavior* is perceived by Americans as a consequent of love; in Greece they are not necessarily related.

The causes of TRUST are essentially the same in the two cultures. The Greek, however, sees TRUST in the context of personal relationships as a consequence of the other person's *good behavior* and *character.* The American sees it as a personal feeling toward someone, hence is related to *faith, love,* and *loyalty.*

For the Greeks TRUST is a prerequisite of effective cooperation within the ingroup. They emphasize *admiration, reciprocal trust, cooperation,* and *progress* as consequences of TRUST. For the Greek, then, TRUST leads to a better working group. By contrast the American sees TRUST as leading to a better face-to-face interpersonal relationship. The American emphasizes *loyalty, confidence,* and *respect* as consequents of TRUST.

Respect. Appropriate behavior is the most frequently mentioned theme as a cause of RESPECT by Greeks. Americans mention the achievement of specific values—*loyalty, self-respect, trust, admiration,* and *honor*—as leading to RESPECT. The contrast here is between the relatively limited connotation of this word for Greeks and the relatively rich connotation for Americans.

Consistent with this analysis of the way the two cultures perceive the causes of respect is the way they perceive its consequences. The Greeks mention *good character, good name,* and *success;* the Americans mention *honor, trust, admiration,* and *friendship.* Thus the Greek sees RESPECT as acquired by ordinary good behavior and leading to nothing particularly extraordinary; the American sees it as a result of extraordinary behavior and leading to extraordinary states such as honor.

Summary and Conclusions

In this chapter we have presented an intensive comparative analysis of the subjective cultures of Americans and Greeks. We summarized results obtained with several instruments and noted an emphasis on achievement and efficiency in the American data and interpersonal relations and social control in the Greek data.

In the first part of the essay we presented the stereotypes Americans and Greeks hold about each other. Basically the Americans perceive the Greeks as *inefficient, competitive, suspicious, emotional,* and *rigid* but also as *charming, witty, obliging,* and *honest.* The Greeks perceive the Americans as *efficient* but *cold, arrogant, suspicious, dull, competitive,* and *sly.* These stereotypes are veridical from the perspective of each culture as well as from our own analysis of the way each culture looks at its social environment.

Specifically, the Greeks have lived in an environment in which planning, efficiency, and smooth working habits had little opportunity to be rewarded. In an environment of constant political unrest and resources that were unavailable because of wars and revolutions long-term planning and smooth working habits were less likely to lead to survival; spontaneous activity and crisis behavior were more likely to be rewarding. Thus the contrast between Greek *inefficiency* and American efficiency is real; the perceptions of the two groups reflect reality.

Greek behavior is very different in the ingroup than it is in the outgroup. In the ingroup it is cooperative and characterized by self-sacrifice; in the outgroup it is competitive and hostile. When an American comes to Greece he is likely to be perceived as a guest, hence a member of the ingroup. However, the Greek's commitment to an "ingroup relationship" with the American requires much intimacy, concern of the American for the Greek's welfare, and self-sacrifice. The American is unprepared for such a relationship. He cannot accept either the degree of intimacy or the self-sacrifice required by the Greeks. Hence he recoils from them. His behavior is seen by the Greek as indifference, interpreted as hostility. A vicious circle of mutual recrimination then takes place.

The Americans see the Greeks as *emotional* because the Greeks consider the expression of emotion as perfectly healthy and desirable, whereas Americans feel guilty when they are unable to control their feelings and exteriorize them. Greeks follow social convention, are influenced by the ingroup authority figures, and behave in traditional ways to a larger extent than do Americans. For this reason Americans see them as *rigid*. If the Greek perceives the American as belonging in his outgroup, he behaves *competitively* and *suspiciously*. This is the way he behaves toward outgroup Greeks and is therefore perfectly "normal" behavior. On the other hand, if the Greek accept the American as one of his ingroup, he behaves cooperatively and with self-sacrifice. Then he is seen by the Americans as *charming, witty, obliging,* and *honest*.

The American rejection of the Greek's concept of proper ingroup interpersonal behavior—great intimacy and self-sacrifice—leads Greeks to perceive Americans as *cold, dull, arrogant, suspicious,* and *competitive*. The Greek is simply saying that the American is an outgroup member. The fact that the American claims that he is friendly, yet behaves in such a nonintimate fashion, implies to the Greek that the American is *sly*. Of course, the Greek admits the American's *efficiency*, but he sees the American as a cold and arrogant human being with few traces of charm.

The above analysis has the merit of illustrating the relationship between the subjective culture of two cultural groups and the stereotypes they hold about each other. Our empirical studies have shown that the views of social life that govern the interpersonal behaviors of Americans and Greeks are quite different. For the Americans, in the American-Greek confrontation, the primary purpose of life is to achieve and secondarily to have a good interpersonal relationship with his spouse, to bring into the world useful citizens who will in their turn achieve, and so on. For the Greeks the basic unit of concern is the ingroup. The survival of the ingroup is enhanced by the achievement of its members, but achievement is not the primary focus of concern. Rather, the important issue is the creation of a happy ingroup.

Since these two cultures have subjective cultures that are different in these important characteristics, it is not surprising that when they come in contact they achieve limited interpersonal success and insufficient admiration. The implications of the present analysis is that the two subjective cultures are indeed so different that it is unlikely that "unmodified" Americans and Greeks could have a successful relationship.

This chaper has presented a comparative analysis of American and Greek subjective cultures which is consistent across instruments and fits naturalistic observations of the two cultures, the stereotypes that each group has of the other, field experiments (Feldman, 1968b), and anthropological and sociological analyses of Greek culture (see Triandis, Vassiliou, and Nassiakou, 1968, for a review of the correspondence between our own analysis and the work of Friedl, Gouldner, and others). Our review suggests that our procedures are reliable, valid, internally coherent, and useful.

PART FOUR

Conclusions

CHAPTER TEN

Summary and Implications

Subjective culture is defined as a group's characteristic way of perceiving its social environment. It includes attitudes, roles, values, and other constructs defined and discussed in Part I of this book. In that part of the book we also examined the methodological problems we need to solve when measuring subjective culture, and we suggested some solutions.

An important part of this book consists of the presentation of some basic tools for the analysis of subjective culture. In Part I we suggested a whole range of tools and in Part II we illustrated the use of some of them. In Chapter 9 we showed that the information obtained with each instrument is consistent, suggesting that the instruments have concurrent validity. Other studies suggest that the instruments also have a good deal of predictive validity.

Before we turn to the implications of the analysis of subjective culture we shall review two studies that suggest how subjective culture information can be used to predict behavior.

The first of these studies (Davis & Triandis, 1965, in press) was concerned with the prediction of the negotiatary behavior of blacks and whites. The study was done in 1963 while the civil rights laws of 1964 was being debated in the United States Congress. This law had provisions that outlawed various forms of discrimination toward blacks. We constructed a set of positions concerning laws that a City Council might pass, dealing with various aspects of discrimination; for example, one set of positions dealt with discrimination in the area of housing. The most liberal position was worded as follows: "The City Council should pass a law prohibiting discrimination on the basis of race, religion, or ethnic background in any and all housing." The most conservative position was worded as follows: "Discrimination in housing is strictly a private affair and no action should be taken by the City Council or other government body which would interfere with private property rights in any way." Ten positions, ranging from the most liberal to the most conservative, were scaled by standard Thurstone successive interval methods, so that each position was one unit away from the next; for example, a middle position was, "The City Council should recommend non-discriminatory practices in the renting or selling of housing."

Three hundred naïve white students were given a broad range of instruments concerning interpersonal attitudes toward Negroes and civil rights issues. Respondents who were homogeneous in their attitudes toward these issues were brought together in caucus groups, in which they decided which of the positions on each issue they would adopt. They were told that they would role-play the representatives of a City Council and some black students would role-play representatives of civil rights organizations. After one hour's discussion the caucus groups were divided into teams of two persons. These teams negotiated three civil rights issues with two-man teams of black confederates of the experimenters. After one hour of negotiation the outcomes were recorded, whether there was agreement or not, and if there was no agreement the position up to which the respondents were willing to move in order to reach agreement. After the negotiations the subjects returned to their original caucus groups, in which their negotiation agreements were evaluated by the caucus members. They also responded to instruments that measured their postnegotiation attitudes.

The results were analyzed by examining the relationships of the subjective culture variables (predictors), the caucus outcomes, and the outcomes of the negotiations. Significant relationship between a large number of our predictors and both kinds of outcome were obtained, suggesting that the (a) affect toward the issues, (b) persons involved in the negotiation, and (c) behavioral intentions toward Negroes predict negotiation agreements.

The second predictive study (Triandis & Vassiliou, 1968, in press) started with the evidence reported in Chapter 9 concerning American and Greek subjective culture. It predicted that a Greek employer, faced with an employment decision, will give *more* weight to the opinions (recommendation) of his close friends and *less* weight to the recommendations of "unknown neighbors" or "unknown persons" than will an American employer. In short, the prediction is that when the recommendation comes from the ingroup (as defined in Greece) it will receive more weight and when it comes from the outgroup it will receive less weight in Greece than in America.

The data were personnel decisions made by Americans and Greeks working in Greece, when presented with descriptions of 16 hypothetical job applicants. Highly significant interactions between culture and relative weights were obtained which were consistent with the predictions. Specifically, when the applicant was recommended by a friend, the Greeks gave an average rating of 5.4, on a 7-point scale, where 7 was, "I would strongly recommend that we hire him." The Americans averaged 4.7. When the person was recommended by complete unknowns, the Greeks averaged 3.5, the Americans, 4.4. Since 4.0 is the neutral point, these data show that the Americans would hire people recommended by persons whom they do not know. The Greeks would not do so.

The two prediction studies taken together are encouraging. They suggest that subjective culture data can be used to make relatively precise predictions of behavior. Of course, much more work needs to be done in this general area (for a review see Triandis, 1971, Chapter 1) but the evidence reviewed so far suggests enough concurrent and predictive validity for our instruments to encourage further major research efforts.

To summarize, then, the evidence we have so far suggests that our methods of analysis of subjective culture give us information that has both predictive and concurrent validity, is consistent with anthropological analyses and useful in understanding the way groups of people perceive their social environment.

The extent to which this approach in the analysis of subjective culture has practical implications is still unclear, since we have not yet taken our tools to the field to solve any social problems. However, it has obvious implications concerning the data-gathering phase before social problems can really be solved, since they must first be understood.

The implications of this analysis are so numerous that we can only suggest the most obvious. Understanding the subjective culture of a particular cultural group is much like learning its language. In fact, when we learn the language of a cultural group we learn part of its subjective culture, but there is more to subjective culture than mere language. People can be experts in the language of a cultural group, yet have a limited understanding of its subjective culture. In fact, as we look around any country and observe failures in political action, in the effectiveness of new legislation, in educational policy, and in the control of environmental pollution we can easily see that these failures are in part due to our lack of understanding of the subjective cultures of significant, relevant groups—ghetto dwellers, educators, industrialists, politicians, and students—a lack of understanding that occurs in spite of a common language. If we knew more about the way these groups of people typically "cut the pie of experience," give priorities to various goals, behave in different kinds of situation, and see connections between their behavior and various outcomes, we would be in a much better position to understand these failures.

A major area of future research concerns the relationship of subjective culture variables to behaviors that cause overpopulation—in our judgment the most important problem of the world. It is simply unthinkable for us to continue at our present rate of population growth, since it is estimated that in less than five centuries we will have no more room to stand on than people at a cocktail party. The earth cannot support a world-wide cocktail party. Something drastic will have to be done soon. Since procreation is in part dependent on the behavioral intentions, norms, and habits of various cultural groups, it is essential that we discover the relationships among subjective culture variables and procreation behavior in different cultural contexts.

Related to this problem is pollution and research on the adoption of a variety of new habits both in eating and social life and in life styles generally. A particularly important phenomenon involves differences in the perception of what is important. An industrialist who uses the waters of a lake to discharge his effluents finds the convenience of eliminating his wastes infinitely greater than the inconvenience of a few people who, on certain occasions, cannot swim in that lake. For the swimmers, however, it is the *idea* that the lake is sometimes polluted that really matters; once it is polluted, even for one minute, it is no longer aesthetically the same. Similarly, what appears trivial to a person from an industrialized society may have major emotional significance to a person from another society. Modern highway technology, for instance, considers the earth as mere material, whereas the traditional villager considers it sacred. When the engineers dynamite a hill, cut down trees, and upset the topography to build a modern highway, they may appear to the villagers like the barbarians who blew up the Acropolis.

Take any act that pollutes the environment. Consider, for example, the use of paper towels instead of cloth (washable) ones. In developed countries the cost of paper towels is so small and the convenience of not having to launder them so great that they are widely used. Thus more paper than is necessary is dumped into municipal disposal systems. This action is determined by the habits, behavioral intentions, and expectations of reinforcement (no washing) as described by our theoretical framework. Changes in this behavior might be obtained by means of cognitive inputs (e.g., messages such as "the cost of paper towels has increased by $X\%$," "do not use paper towels"), affective inputs (e.g., unpleasant associations), normative inputs (e.g., friends who disapprove of your using paper towels), as well as sheer changes in the expectations of reinforcement (e.g., the government may put a 100% tax on paper towels). By multiplying this analysis by the number of specific polluting acts and doing something about changing each of them it would be possible to have a substantial reduction in pollution.

To change habits it is necessary to provide a schedule of reinforcements that will reward new behaviors; to change norms it is necessary to introduce new group members who have different norms in a social environment. To change attitudes, including behavioral intentions, it is necessary to provide new information and social situations in which people behave inconsistently with their attitudes and are reinforced for doing so. All these considerations point to the fact that the most effective way to change people is to put them in contact with other people—teachers, community developers, and extension workers. The mass media simply will not do enough. They may expose the population to new ideas but they will not change their behavior. In short, one of the most important ways to solve the problems of overpopulation, pollution, etc., is to introduce appropriate "change agents" at all levels of social life, all around the world. In every developing country there are many people who could function as change agents, but these people need logistic and emotional support for this work. One source of support for such change agents could come from the relatively developed world (Europe, North America, Australia, New Zealand, and Japan). The developed world has the resources to pay the salaries of the change agents. If such an arrangement did evolve, however, some of the bureaucrats of the developed world would come in frequent contact with the change agents of the less developed.

Mercury pollution of the ocean seems to have relevance to the way certain fish-eating people (e.g., the Japanese) are likely to see their environment. For many Americans such pollution has less impact than it must have for the Japanese for whom fish is a more central element of their diet. If Americans are to develop joint methods for control of mercury pollution, they may need to "understand" the Japanese viewpoint, for if the American representatives on such joint commissions act insensitively, not realizing how important the issue really is to the Japanese, they may antagonize their Japanese colleagues. One way to increase such empathy is to study the affective and implicative meaning of various foods in the two countries and discover which American foods have the same central position in the American diet that fish has in the Japanese diet. We can *guess* that beef has this role in America, but we have no data. At any rate, if an American representative were to substitute "polluted beef" for "polluted fish" when thinking about the way the Japanese react to these foods, he might be able to experience some of the emotions that a people surrounded by water and depending on fish for their diet must feel when they confront mercury pollution and be more sensitive to their viewpoints.

As mentioned earlier, it will be necessary to introduce people from the developed countries to less developed settings in large numbers. However, this immediately exposes both sides to intensive conflict *caused by differing subjective cultures*. Furthermore, the subjective culture of the change agents themselves is quite different from the subjective culture of their other countrymen and thus introduces further conflict. The major social psychological problem of the next century, then, is to learn how people with different subjective cultures can respect one another, cooperate together, and live in harmony.

The applications of the analysis of subjective culture to international behavior are numerous. It is obvious that intercultural contact can be a failure or a success, depending on the extent to which each person understands and appreciates the subjective culture of the other. In international relations diplomats too often look at the world from within a framework that is limited by their own cultural and cross-cultural experiences and corresponds poorly to the frameworks of the diplomats from the cultures with whom they are negotiating. Much time in any negotiation is devoted to the gradual learning by each side of the framework of assumptions and patterns of thought of the other. If diplomats or international civil servants who live in a kind of culture of their own have trouble, consider the difficulties of a Western teacher in an African or Asian village.

In intercultural encounters it often happens that a "signal," verbal or nonverbal, coming from one group has positive connotations, but when it comes from another group it has negative implications; for example, Americans unwrap the gifts they receive in the presence of the givers; Greeks consider that such behavior indicates that one is so starved and in such great need that he cannot wait. In short, Greeks would lose face if they unwrapped their presents the way Americans do. This difference in the meaning of "unwrapping" in the two cultures produces easy misunderstandings in which the American feels that his gifts are not wanted or appreciated. A vicious circle is generated when the hurt American does something negative to the Greek who then reacts negatively. George Vassiliou reports that while attending international meetings or observing intercultural encounters it is quite easy to detect, if one is sensitive to this phenomenon, a repeated and frequent exchange of such ambiguous signals.

A major form of intercultural contact involves technical assistance. There are literally thousands of examples that can be found in the literature of such assistance which show that equipment is often misused, its functions are poorly understood, and the training for its operation and use is completely inadequate. Even in relatively developed countries such as Greece machinery is often put to some strange use, as, for instance, in the case of electric stoves on which villagers burned wood or a washing machine whose spinning cycle was used to tenderize octopus! In India refrigerators have been used to store money!

Technical assistance can be related to industrial, educational, health, agricultural, or economic policy. The typical perspective of the technician is, "If it works back home in Michigan, it will work anywhere." Although this perspective simplifies the world of the technician and makes his job appear easier to him, it leads to countless disappointments and frustrations. An understanding of how cultural factors interact with industrial, educational, agricultural, or economic factors is greatly needed. It is time that people who prepare themselves for work outside their own culture learn that they must acquire special skills in analyzing those aspects of the subjective culture of the people with whom they will work that are likely to be relevant to their speciality.

A more subtle form of cultural insensitivity equates the experience in one foreign culture with that in another. A typical development expert who found a successful formula in one culture applies it to an entirely different setting often with disastrous results. This error is not limited to engineers and physical scientists but is often also made by social scientists who ignore the "milieu-specificity" (Vassiliou & Vassiliou, 1968) of their findings.

It often happens, as discussed in Chapter 3, that the research procedures which were found to be successful in one culture are "translated" into another without awareness of the way they interact with cultural variables. Often cross-cultural investigators are satisfied when they meet formal criteria, such as the same number of people studied, similar sizes of community in which they live, and similar distances of their community from urban centers. Such investigators fail to consider how the meaning of their data changes in different contexts. They also ignore cultural differences in the importance of a phenomenon, assuming that the same categories that are important in one culture will be important in another. Cultural differences can be so extreme that data collected in another culture sometimes look completely reversed, as if a "clerical error" were involved. The staff of the Athenian Institute of Anthropos, which has been involved in several cross-cultural investigations in collaboration with numerous European and American researchers, has repeatedly observed such "surprises." Particularly embarrassing are problems of diagnosis and treatment.

A frequent error is the diagnosis of a phenomenon in terms of the criteria of one culture—the assumption that it is the same phenomenon in another culture. The Vassilious, for instance, describe a pattern of Greek child rearing which most Western-trained psychologists and psychiatrists identify as "overprotection." This pattern, however, has different antecedents and consequents in the Greek setting than it has in Western Europe or the United States. In short, "Greek overprotection" is a unique phenomenon with dissimilar antecedents and consequents from American or French overprotection. It would be an error to "diagnose" it and then expect that some particular behaviors of the therapists will be beneficial to the patient. For a practitioner to be fully effective in another culture he must be aware of such phenomena. It is difficult to develop effective prevention, diagnosis, or therapy skills directed at individuals, families, or groups without considerable awareness of the interaction between culture and the phenomena under study. The concept of "milieu-specificity" is of considerable importance in understanding such interactions.

Vast areas of research are opened when we consider the implications of the present analysis for psychotherapy in situations in which the therapist and the patient belong to different cultures. Such situations are still common in some underdeveloped regions in which the only medical persons are Europeans, or Western trained and will become more frequent as people do more traveling and "break down" under the influence of culture shock. Not much is known yet about the interactions of subjective culture variables and various strategies for effective psychotherapy, although this is an important area, regardless of the theoretical perspective of the psychotherapist. Whether he adopts an approach that requires insight or one involving behavior modification by reinforcement, he needs to know much about the culture of his patient in order to understand the course of psychological change and the meaning of various reinforcements in various contexts.

The world is getting smaller as communications become easier, faster, and more effective. It will not be long before people in advertising, marketing, and industry will have global policies. Yet such policies will be deficient if they ignore the cultural dimensions of these fields. Already in the areas of agricultural innovation and population control the major obstacles appear to be caused by human factors. Thus we need a major breakthrough in our ability to utilize relevant information about the subjective cultures of the people we are going to be dealing with and major research programs to explore the interface between the analysis of subjective culture and other disciplines.

Since facilitation of intercultural contact is one of the central areas of application in the analysis of subjective culture, we are concentrating on this implication of our analysis for the rest of this chapter.

Subjective Culture and Intercultural Interaction

It will be useful to begin with a discussion of some of the characteristics of intercultural interaction. The best model is that of speaking a foreign language. Those who are perfect bilinguals can slip from one set of language behaviors into another without experiencing the slightest discomfort. Similarly, intercultural interaction can be extremely easy for those who know the subjective culture of the other cultural group and have the proper skills for emitting the proper behaviors in each social situation.

Normally, however, this is not the case. Most people encounter difficulty in intercultural contacts.

The problem can be analyzed in terms of the differentiations between social situations on the one hand and emitting the proper responses on the other. The simplest condition occurs when the social situations in the host and the subject's culture are similar and require similar behaviors. Here no special learning is required, since one behaves abroad exactly the way he does at home. The most difficult situation occurs when the same social situations require different responses. Here all the cues one has learned will call out inappropriate responses, so that this is the most difficult situation to master. In foreign-language speaking it corresponds to saying a word that is written the same way in two languages but is pronounced differently. It is well known that even perfect bilinguals slip when they are faced with such situations. When the social situations in the two cultures are very different, the intercultural encounter is intermediate in difficulty. Cultures differ from one another in degrees, along several dimensions. Anthropologists have shown us that the world is divided into cultural areas. Within these areas interaction should be easier, provided the same response is appropriate. If the same situation calls for a different response, the fact that two cultures belong to the same cultural area may lead to difficulties, as, for example, in the case of interactions among Americans and British when the response concerns the use of first names.

The same laws described above can apply to the difficulty of various kinds of intercultural contact, namely, the greater the similarity between two cultures, the easier the contact when the same response is required and the more difficult the contact when a different response is required. When the cultures are very different, contact is always difficult but probably at an intermediate level between the extreme levels of difficulty found in contact among similar cultural groups. This argument suggests that the same laws that apply to positive and negative transfer of motor skills may apply to the ease or difficulty of intercultural contact. It also makes sense in the context of impressionistic statements by American businessmen with wide intercultural experience, who claim, for instance, that dealing with southern Europeans or Latin Americans is more difficult than dealing with the Chinese or Japanese.

A further implication of this argument leads to the hypothesis that intercultural training is specific. One has to learn anew the subjective culture of each cultural group with which he comes into contact. Though some general sensitivity to interpersonal relations may facilitate cross-cultural interaction, it is not sufficient to overcome the communication barriers and intercultural misunderstandings.

Analyses of subjective culture can be used to develop maps of the cultural areas of the world. Such maps will correspond to those developed by anthropologists but may also show some differences, since subjective culture maps will ignore nonpsychological elements. Research is needed to test the hypotheses just described concerning the similarity in the subjective cultures between two groups and its effect on the difficulty of cross-cultural interaction. If the hypotheses are supported, we will have a simple rule for computing the difficulty of intercultural contact. Sending people to one post or another might then be determined in part by the relations between their abilities, attitudes, and preparation on the one hand and the difficulty of the post on the other. It is obvious that much more research is needed to clarify these relations. How is modernization changing the subjective culture of groups of people in less developed countries? More specifically, we might examine some common elements in the subjective cultures of people in developed and less developed countries and explore the role of environmental changes on the changes in subjective culture. Even more specifically, we might ask how ingroups are formed in different cultural environments, how they function to improve or impede cooperation in industrial activities, and how they influence technological change.

Some research relating subjective culture variables to the adoption of innovation is already available. Thus Tully, Wilkening, and Presser (1964) present a convincing argument that the major focus in introducing change in farming methods must be directed toward changing the norms, values, and aspirations of the farmers. They show that such factors have a direct influence on the adoption process. Nonadopters put more value on ease and convenience and have lower aspirations and less need for money than adopters. The way the innovation is perceived, its cost, convenience, and risk, is directly related to adoption (Kivlin & Fliegel, 1967). The relative advantage of the new idea, as perceived by members of a social system affects its rate of adoption (Rogers, 1962). Individual values are a good predictor of innovation behavior (Cohen, 1962). The attitudes toward the proposed innovation are also relevant in predicting adoption behavior (Moulik, Hrabovzky & Rao, 1966; Fliegel, 1956).

There is already a fair amount of evidence suggesting that the subjective culture of modern man is different from the subjective culture of traditional man. Here, then, is a situation in which certain subcultures within a modern nation may look at their social environment differently from the way their fellow-countrymen do. The major determinant of the subjective culture of modern man seems to be education. In study after study the amount of education received by an individual is the best predictor of whether or not he will adopt the point of view of modern industrial man. Inkeles (1969) found a pattern of values and attitudes characteristic of modern man which has a number of elements in common with the pattern found by Dawson (1963, 1967, 1969b, 1969c) and Dobb (1967). In all cases education is the best predictor of this syndrome.

In a study not yet completed Inkeles (1969) sampled 6000 persons in six diverse countries (Argentina, Chile, India, Israel, Nigeria, and East Pakistan). He found a pattern of values and attitudes that he described as involving, among other things, (a) openness to new experience, (b) independence from parental authority, (c) involvement in civic affairs, and (d) concern with time (characterized by being on time, planning, and keeping up with the news). He argued that these qualities are present across occupations, urban-rural breakdowns of the samples, and several other variables. In short, here is some evidence of the psychic unity of mankind in that it shows that modern men have a number of characteristics in common, no matter where they are studied. Of course, both individual and cultural differences probably increase the variance on these attributes but what is presented here is an average profile. Smith and Inkeles (1966) have published a scale of individual modernity, which asks the person such questions as, "Do you read a newspaper?" and obtains responses on the frequency or likelihood of events (daily, weekly, monthly, etc.). This scale correlated with level of education in all the countries studied.

Dawson (1963, 1967, 1969b) examined traditional versus Western attitudes in samples from Africa, Asia and Australia. He used a Likert-type scale which samples 18 types of attitudes, such as attitudes toward parental authority, ethical obligations, and the giving of gifts. He scored his data to obtain four subscales which he labeled traditional, semitraditional, semi-Western, and Western. He showed good validities, with Western samples high on the Western and low on the traditional scales, and other samples, of known modernity, showing corresponding patterns. Both Dawson and Inkeles found that the amount of education received by a person is the best predictor of his modernity; for example, Inkeles reports that every year of schooling raises a person's modernity score by about three points on a 100-point scale.

Dawson (1963) sampled several African tribes and examined the work effectiveness of members of these tribes in various industrial and mining environments. He found that the more traditional the attitudes of the tribesmen, the *less* likely they were to be considered effective workers and the *more* likely they were to quit their jobs. In fact, some tribes do not even attempt to gain employment in industrial enterprises, since they find such activities beneath their dignity. Typically, Dawson's subjects developed cognitive compartmentalization; that is, they allowed logically inconsistent ideas to coexist. In such cases their scores were highest on the semitraditional or semi-Western scales.

Another use of Likert-type scales to measure psychological modernization was made by Doob (1967) who surveyed substantial numbers of
Africans. Here is a typical item from his survey, which gives a person a
high modernization score if he agrees: "Worthwhile goals are never obtained immediately; you must work hard to reach them in the future."
The item stresses deferred gratification, which is essential for success in
a modern society. Doob's scale focuses on the following: (a) time—emphasis on the future; (b) positive attitude toward government activities;
(c) sense of optimism and control over one's destiny; (d) patriotism; (e)
belief in determinism and scientific knowledge; (f) a trusting conception
of people; (g) positive attitude toward the leaders of the country; and
(h) de-emphasis of traditional beliefs.

It is clear from what has been said so far that there is a core of agreement among those who have studied the psychological correlates of
modernization. One can find a number of areas of agreement, for instance,
between Inkeles, Dawson, and Doob. However, reviews of the literature,
such as McKendry, McKendry, & Guthrie (1967), show a variety of points
of view concerning which elements in the total modernization syndrome
are fundamental and important. One view, for instance, is that existing
social norms and reinforcement contingencies prevent modernization in
spite of the existence of positive attitudes (Guthrie, 1970). Another view
stresses the individual's breadth of perspective, in time and place, and
claims that modernity means, among other things, a cosmopolitan perspective (Rogers, 1962). Still another (Foster, 1965) argues that in traditional
societies life is seen as a stochastic zero sum game guided by chance; that
is, there is the view of limited good and the notion that chance or fate
is the major determiner of one's share of this good. Another emphasis is
on the value orientation which Kluckhohn and Strodtbeck (1961)
described as man's mastery over nature, accompanied with a sense of
potency that the individual is in fact able to control his reinforcements
from the environment. This suggests Rotter's (1966) generalized expectancies for internal versus external control of reinforcement. The in-
ternals believe that what they *do* changes the probability that they will
be reinforced, whereas the externals consider external factors, such as luck
or fate, to be primarily responsible for the determination of the probability
of reinforcement. Perhaps it is a central characteristic of modern man that
he is likely to perceive more internal than external control of
reinforcement.

McClelland (1961) presented the argument that the large differences
in per capita income that characterize various regions of the world are
primarily due to differences in the need for achievement that characterize
those who inhabit these regions. The argument is rather complex, and here

we can present it only in an oversimplified form. Basically, McClelland argues that high training of the child in self-reliance and high achievement standards used by the mother lead to a personality type characterized by high need achievement. Winterbottom (1958) showed that mothers of high need-achievement boys make early demands on them; for instance, they expect them to learn to put their clothes on by themselves at an earlier age and expect greater accomplishment and also reward accomplishment more frequently than mothers of boys who are low in need achievement. Those high in need achievement, according to McClelland, work harder, choose experts over friends as work partners, are more resistant to social pressures, and are more likely to compete with a standard of excellence than are those low in need achievement.

He presented data on the distribution of need achievement in different parts of the world, and at different historical times, which are consistent with his argument that need achievement is a mediating variable in economic development. He finds high need achievement in societies that are less tradition directed, in which the authority of the father has been challenged, and in which child-rearing practices are warm but firm and demanding of excellence. He argues that those high in need achievement are characterized by willingness to take reasonable risks, individual responsibility, and delay immediate gratification.

A number of American studies (e.g., Littig & Yeracaris, 1965; Rosen & D'Andrade, 1959) have supported McClelland's contentions, and several cross-cultural studies (e.g., Danzinger, 1960; LeVine, 1966; Rogers & Neill, 1966) are also supportive. Pareek (1968) proposed that economic development requires persons who are high in the need for achievement and extension and low in the need for dependence. Need for extension is characterized by concern for the common good or concern for others. Need for dependence reflects a need for guidance and direction by other people. People high in this need avoid taking initiatives, find arguing with others most unpleasant, and look for others to supply leadership.

Each of these viewpoints probably has some validity. In fact, there is no good way, at this time, to pit one against the other, since it is only in a study involving a giant regression equation that we can decide which of these elements is most important. The discussion in Chapter 9, however, suggests that the most important element is the way a person looks at social relations, which can be described by the size of his ingroup and the kinds of behavioral intentions he has toward members of his ingroups and outgroups.

In a more general sense we might define the ingroup as the set of people with whom a person believes that it is appropriate to cooperate to achieve a particular goal. This means that for every group goal there may be a different ingroup. However, if we count the number of people a given person includes in each ingroup, we will find that in traditional societies most respondents include *few* people in their ingroups. These people are typically chosen from among the person's extended family or tribe. In modern societies ingroups are much broader; for example, modern psychologists would probably cooperate with psychologists in any part of the world to promote the development of psychological knowledge; it would be unthinkable to limit cooperation only to members of one's extended family or tribe. The traditional viewpoint would be consistent with such limitations, and the justification can be found in Foster's argument that, according to the traditional conception, the world is a place where *good* is limited and should not be shared with others.

Whyte (1969) has reviewed evidence that in less developed countries, such as Peru, industrial workers, students, and others have low faith in people, have trouble developing collateral (same level) bonds with colleagues, and show several behavioral patterns suggestive of a narrow ingroup.

Now it is obvious that if a person brings to an industrial organization a conception of social relations which involves narrow ingroups economic development is difficult (Triandis & Triandis, 1969) because, among other things, most effective economic enterprises involve more than one family. On the other hand, although a narrow ingroup may not be conducive to economic development, it leads to many gratifications, including the development of high self-esteem (Ziller et al., 1968). Although, on the one hand, it tends to promote identification with the parents (Long et al., 1967), which makes traditionalism more likely and innovation less likely, on the other hand it provides the individual with a sense of belonging to a social order, a sense of security. In short, narrow ingroups can gratify the individual but they are not compatible with economic development. This argument agrees with Pareek's point that the need for extension is conducive to economic development and the need for direction is not, since broad ingroups imply a high need for extension and narrow ingroups imply identification with parental authority and the development of a need for direction.

To summarize, modern man is apparently open to new experiences, relatively independent of parental authority, and concerned with time and planning and willing to defer gratification; he feels that man can be the master over nature and that he controls the reinforcements he receives from his environment; he believes in determinism and science, has a wide, cosmopolitan perspective, and uses broad ingroups; he competes with standards of excellence and is optimistic about controlling his environment. Traditional man has narrow ingroups, looks at the world with suspicion, believes that good is limited, and that one obtains a share of it by chance or by pleasing the gods; he identifies with his parents and receives direction from them; he considers planning a waste of time and does not defer gratification; he feels at the mercy of obscure environmental forces and is prone to mysticism; he sees interpersonal relations as an end, rarely as means to an end, and does not believe that he can control his environment but rather sees himself under the influence of external, mystical powers.

It has been argued by many that modernization puts people in stressful social environments that result in poor mental health; Inkeles (1969), however, presents data that are contrary to this argument. He finds that modern people report the same number of psychosomatic symptoms as people living in less modern environments. Some caution, however, is needed in interpreting this finding. It is clear that modernization is associated with better physical health and symptoms of every kind are probably more prevalent among persons whose general health is poorer. Hence the lack of a difference in the rates of psychosomatic symptoms between less and more developed environments might suggest that indeed there is more stress in the modern environment, but it is not revealed by an examination of psychosomatic symptoms because of the better physical health of persons living in environments with better public health facilities.

Modernization seems to have consequences that are both desirable and undesirable. Since the desirable are rather obvious, it is more interesting to discuss the undesirable. First, they seem to be associated with a weakening of the traditional social units. This happens because the traditional family breaks down and is replaced by the nuclear family living in urban, industrialized centers. However, when an individual's social ties are weakened, there is a higher incidence of suicide (Krauss & Krauss, 1968). During the period of transition from traditional to modern social organization many peoople are likely to feel left out of the opportunity structure, a condition associated with problem drinking (Jessor et al., 1968; Robbins & Pollnac, 1969), riots (Allen, 1970), and other forms of social disorganization. The creation of large urban centers is associated with a condition that Zimbardo (1969) described as de-individuation. According to his analysis, anonymity, the large size of social units, and diffusion of responsibility are among the antecedents of individuation, whereas irrational, high amplitude impulsive behaviors are among the consequences. In experiments in which subjects who were either anonymous or not were asked to shock various kinds of victims, who were confederates of the experimentor, he showed that the anonymous subjects administered more shock to their helpless victims. Second, modernization has the effect of changing the level of aspirations (Dawson, 1969a; Lerner, 1958). As Diaz-Guerrero (1967a) has pointed out in his comparative studies of Americans and Mexicans, Americans expect life to be great fun and almost invariably feel frustrated; Mexicans expect life to be endured and almost invariably find it more fun than they expected. Morse (1953) has pointed out that satisfaction depends not only on how much a person realizes but also on his aspirations. Thus satisfaction with life may be negatively correlated with level of aspiration. Unreasonably high aspirations lead to frustrations and a predisposition to aggression. In short, some rates of economic development are likely to lead to low satisfaction and social disorganization. We need to study this question quite carefully.

Third, development is associated with excessive rates of use of the world's resources, pollution, unequal distributions of the population over the earth's surface, and many other problems that are only too well known.

We need to do many studies to examine the total relationship of development to mental health, ecological adjustment, satisfaction with life, and social harmony. After such studies we will arrive at a more complex and more realistic view of what it does to the total quality of human life. Such studies will also help us understand the details of how one achieves development and what precisely one gets from it.

Implications for Further Research

This book is only a beginning. Its function was to define the elements of subjective culture, to suggest appropriate approaches for their measurement, to suggest the utility of some specific approaches, and to indicate that the analysis of subjective culture can lead to the prediction of behavior. As we close this book, something should be said about the major trends in theoretical research.

The major theoretical developments needed in this area must focus on three types of concern: (a) the antecedents of subjective culture; (b) the relationships among the elements of subjective culture, and (c) the consequents of subjective culture. A variety of studies is needed in each of these areas, but the first priority concerns the development of a theory of the interrelations of the major elements of subjective culture with their consequents. Such a theory will need to be tested by means of path analysis (Wright, 1931; Simon, 1954; Duncan, 1966; Werts & Linn, 1970) or some such statistical approach, and it should incorporate the feedback loops of the system; hence it cannot employ an ordinary multiple correlation approach.

A Concluding Comment

In this book we avoided many of the issues and controversies that have occupied some psychologists for a long time. We did not touch, for instance, on those issues that have philosophical implications such as the relative importance of biological versus environmental factors on the determination of subjective culture, whether studying subjective experience is reducible to the basic studies suggested by behaviorists of the Skinnerian variety, or the relative merits of phenomenology, behaviorism, and so on. We find such arguments less productive than the development of reliable and valid measures of subjective experience and the discovery of the laws relating such measures to behavior. Many of the philosophical problems appear to be in the same category as some of the medieval discussions about the number of angels that can stand on the tip of a needle. On more detailed analysis they turn out to be the wrong questions or issues; for example, the relative importance of biological versus environmental factors is probably an issue whose answer differs from one measure of subjective culture to another. Most probably for some measures the interactions between these two broad classes of factor are much more important than any of the main effects. Our present work can be characterized by an inductive, data-related, development of concepts and the study of the interrelationships of these concepts. Our only theoretical bias is the Brunswikian notion (e.g., Hammond, 1966) of adequate representation of the events occurring naturally in a human environment. Indeed, probabilistic functionalism is a broader psychological theory than the one we sketched in our theoretical chapter. It seems, however, that our effort is a *social* psychological elaboration of the "central states" described by Brunswik. The correspondence should be obvious, since the cognitive structures we employ as elements of subjective culture are the results of the pairings of events in the organism's environment and result in patterns of action and experience that determine the meaning of these events. Our system, too, is probabilistic, and much of the language of Brunswik would be useful in an analysis of the antecedents of subjective culture. This work remains to be done.

References

Adler, L. L. A note on cross-cultural preferences: fruit-tree preferences in children's drawings. *J. Psychol.*, 1967, **65**, 15–22.

Adler, L. L. A note on the cross-cultural fruit-tree study: a test-retest procedure. *J. Psychol*, 1968, **69**, 53–61.

Adorno, T. W., Frenkel-Brunswik, E., Levinson, D. J., & Sanford, R. N. *The authoritarian personality.* New York: Harper, 1950.

Albert, E. M. The classification of values: a method and illustration. *Amer. Anthropologist,* 1956, **58**, 221–248.

Albert, E. M., & Kluckhohn, C., with LeVine, R., Seulowitz, W., & Gallaher, M. *Values, ethics and esthetics.* Glencoe, Ill.: Free Press, 1959.

Allen, V. L. Ghetto riots. *J. soc. Issues,* 1970, **26**, No. 1 (whole issue).

Allport, G. W., & Kramer, B. M. Some roots of prejudice. *J. Psychol.,* 1946, **22**, 9–39.

Almond, G. A., & Verba, S. *The civic culture.* Princeton, N.J.: Princeton University Press, 1963.

Amir, Y. Contact hypothesis in ethnic relations. *Psychol. Bull.,* 1969, **71**, 319–342.

Anderson, N. H. Averaging versus adding as stimulus combination rule in impression formation. *J. exp. Psychol.,* 1965, **70**, 394–400.

Anderson, R. B. On the comparability of meaningful stimuli in cross-cultural research. *Sociometry,* 1967, **30**, 124–136.

Ardrey, R. *African genesis.* New York: Delta, 1961.

Aronoff, J. *Psychological needs and cultural systems.* Princeton, N.J.: Van Nostrand, 1967.

Ayal, E. B. Value systems and economic development in Japan and Thailand. *J. soc. Issues,* 1963, **19**, 35–51.

Bales, R. F. *Interaction process analysis.* Cambridge, Mass.: Addison-Wesley, 1950.

Banfield, E. C. *The moral basis of a backward society.* Glencoe, Ill.: Free Press, 1958.

Barry, H., Child, I., & Bacon, M. Relation of child training to susistence economy. *Amer. Anthropologist,* 1959, **61**, 51–63.

Bastide, R., & Von Den Berghe, P. Stereotypes, norms and inter-racial behavior in São Paulo, Brazil. *Amer. sociol. Rev.,* 1957, **22**, 689–694.

Beg, M. A. Value orientation of Indian and American students: A cross-cultural study. *Psychologie,* 1966, **9**, 111–119.

Berrien, F. K. Japanese vs. American values. *J. soc. Psychol.,* 1965, **65,** 181–191.

Berrien, F. K. Cross-cultural equivalence of personality measures. *J. soc. Psychol.,* 1968, **75,** 3–9.

Berrien, F. K. A super-ego for cross-cultural research. *Int. J. Psychol.,* 1970, **5,** 33–39.

Berry, J. W. Temne and Eskimo perceptual skills. *Int. J. Psychol.,* 1966, **1,** 207–229.

Berry, J. W. On cross-cultural comparability. *Int. J. Psychol.,* 1969, **4,** 119–128.

Biddle, B. J., & Thomas, E. J. *Role theory: concepts and research.* New York: Wiley, 1966.

Biesheuvel, S. Some comments on the application of vocational guidance in West Africa. In A. Taylor (Ed.), *Educational and occupational selection in West Africa.* London: Oxford University Press, 1962.

Biesheuvel, S. Personnel selection. *Ann. Rev. Psychol.,* 1965, **16,** 295–324.

Black, M. Some questions about Parsons' theories. In M. Black (Ed.), *The social theories of Talcott Parsons.* Englewood, N.J.: Prentice-Hall, 1961, 268–288.

Blood, M., & Hulin, C. L. Alienation, environmental characteristics and worker responses. *J. appl. Psychol.,* 1967, **51,** 284–290.

Bogardus, E. S. *Immigration and race attitudes.* Boston: Heath, 1928.

Brewer, M. B. Determinants of social distance among East African tribal groups. *J. pers. soc. Psychol.,* 1968, **10,** 279–289.

Brislin, R. W. Back-translation for cross-cultural research. *J. cross-cultural Psychol.,* 1970, **1,** 185–216.

Brown, R. *Words and things.* Glencoe, Ill.: Free Press, 1958.

Brown, R. *Social psychology.* New York: The Free Press, 1965.

Brown, R. W., & Lenneberg, E. H. A study in language and cognition. *J. abnorm. soc. Psychol.,* 1954, **49,** 454–462.

Buchanan, W., & Cantrill, H. *How nations see each other.* Urbana, Ill.: University of Illinois Press, 1953.

Buhler, C. *Values in psychotherapy.* Glencoe, Ill.: Free Press, 1962. (a)

Buhler, C. Goal-structure of human life: model and project. *Psychol. Reps.,* 1962, **10,** 445–446. (b)

Campbell, D. T. From description to experimentation: interpreting trends as quasi-experiments. In C. W. Harris (Ed.), *Problems in measuring change.* Madison: University of Wisconsin Press, 1963. (a)

Campbell, D. T. Social attitudes and other acquired behavioral dispositions. In S. Koch (Ed.), *Psychology: a study of a science.* New York: McGraw-Hill, 1963. (b)

Campbell, D. T. Distinguishing differences of perception from failures of communication in cross-cultural studies. In F. S. C. Northrop and H. H. Livingston (Eds.), *Cross-cultural understanding: Epistemology in anthropology.* New York: Harper and Row, 1964.

Campbell, D. T. Stereotypes and the perception of group differences. *Amer. Psychol.,* 1967, **22,** 817–829.

Campbell, D. T. A cooperative multinational opinion sample exchange. *J. soc. Issues,* 1968, **24,** 245–258.

Campbell, D. T. Reforms as experiments. *Amer. Psychologist,* 1969, **24,** 409–429.

Campbell, D. T., & Fiske, D. W. Convergent and discriminant validation by the multitrait-multimethod matrix. *Psychol. Bull.,* 1959, **56,** 81–85.

Campbell, D. T., & LeVine, R. A. Field-manual anthropology. In R. Naroll and R. Cohen (Eds.), *A handbook of method in cultural anthropology.* New York: American Museum of Natural History, 1970.

Campbell, D. T., & Stanley, J. C. Experimental and quasi-experimental designs for research on teaching. In N. L. Gage (Ed.), *Handbook of research on teaching.* Chicago: Rand McNally, 1963.

Cantril, H. *The pattern of human concerns.* New Brunswick, N.J.: Rutgers University Press, 1965.

Cappon, D., Banks, R. and Ramsey, C. Improvement of recognition on a multi-model pattern discrimination. *Perc. Mot. Skills,* 1968, **26,** 431–441.

Cattell, R. B. The dimensions of culture patterns by factorization of national characters, *J. abnorm. soc. Psychol.,* 1949, **44,** 443–469.

Coch, L., & French, J. R. P., Jr. Overcoming resistance to change. *Human relations,* 1948, **1,** 512–532.

Cohen, R. A. A theoretical model for consumer market production. *Sociol. Inquiry,* 1962, **32,** 43–50.

Conklin, H. C. The ethnoecological approach to shifting agriculture. *Trans. N.Y. Acad. Sci.,* 1954, **17,** 133–142.

Couch, A., & Keniston, K. Yeasayers and naysayers: agreeing response set as a personality variable. *J. abnorm. soc. Psychol.,* 1960, **60,** 151–174.

Danzinger, K. Parental demands and social class in Java, Indonesia. *J. soc. Psychol.,* 1960, **51,** 75–86.

Davis, E. E. Validity studies of the behavioral differential. I. Negotiations between white and Negro students on civil rights issues. Paper read at the American Psychological Association, Los Angeles, 1964.

Davis, E. E. A methodological study of behavioral and semantic differential scales relevant to intercultural negotiations. Technical Report No. 32. Urbana, Ill.: Department of Psychology, University of Illinois, 1966.

Davis, E. E., & Triandis, H. C. An exploratory study of intercultural negotiation. Technical Report No. 26. Urbana, Ill.: Department of Psychology, University of Illinois, 1965. Also, in *J. Appl. Soc. Psychol.* (in press).

Dawson, J. L. M. Traditional values and work efficiency in a West African mine labor force. *Occup. Psychol.,* 1963, **37,** 209–218.

Dawson, J. L. M. Kwashiorkor, gynaecomastia and feminization processes. *J. trop. Med. Hyg.,* 1966, **69,** 175–179.

Dawson, J. L. M. Traditional versus western attitudes in West Africa: the construction, validation, and application of a measuring device. *Brit. J. soc. clin. Psychol.,* 1967, **6,** 81–96.

Dawson, J. L. M. Exchange theory and comparison level changes among Australian aborigines. *Brit. J. soc. clin. Psychol.,* 1969, **8,** 133–140. (a)

Dawson, J. L. M. Attitudinal consistency and conflict in West Africa. *Int. J. Psychol.,* 1969, **4,** 39–53. (b)

Dawson, J. L. M. Theoretical and research bases of bio-social psychology. *University of Hong Kong Supplement to the Gazette,* 1969, **16,** No. 3, 1–10. (c)

Dearborn, D. C., & Simon, H. A. Selective perception: a note on the departmental identifications of executives. *Sociometry,* 1958, **21,** 140–144.

Deese, J. On the structure of associative meaning. *Psychol. Rev.,* 1962, **69,** 161–175.

Deese, J. *The structure of associations in language and thought.* Baltimore: Johns Hopkins Press, 1966.

Dennis, W. *Group values through children's drawings.* New York: Wiley, 1966.

Deutsch, K. *Nationalism and social communication.* Cambridge, Mass.: Technology Press of M.I.T., 1953.

Deutsch, M., & Collins, M. E. *Interracial housing: a psychological evaluation of social experiment.* Minneapolis: University of Minnesota Press, 1951.

Devereux, E. C., Jr. Parsons' sociological theory. In Max Black (Ed.), *The social theories of Talcott Parsons.* Englewood Cliffs, N.J.: Prentice-Hall, 1961, 1–63.

Diaz-Guerrero, R. Exploring dimensions in socio-economic development. Paper presented to the International Conference on the Cross-Cultural Generality of Affective Meaning Systems, Tehran, Iran, 1967. (a)

Diaz-Guerrero, R. The active and the passive syndromes. *Rev. Interamer. Psicol.,* 1967, **1**, 263–272. (b)

Doob, L. W. Scales for assaying psychological modernization in Africa. *Publ. Opin. Quart.,* 1967, **31**, 414–421.

Dukes, W. F. Psychological studies of values. *Psychol. Bull.,* 1955, **51**, 24–50.

Dulany, D. E. Awareness, rules and propositional control: a confrontation with S-R behavior theory. In T. R. Dixon and D. L. Horton (Eds.), *Verbal behavior and general behavior theory.* Englewood Cliffs, N.J.: Prentice-Hall, 1967, 340–387.

Duncan, O. D. Path analysis: sociological examples. *Amer. J. Sociol.,* 1966, **72**, 1–16.

England, G. W. Personal value systems of American managers. *Acad. Mgmt. J.,* 1967, **10**, 53–68.

Fallding, H. A proposal for the empirical study of values. *Amer. Sociol. Rev.,* 1965, **30**, 223–233.

Farrell, J. C., & Smith, A. P. *Image and reality in world politics.* New York: Columbia University Press, 1967.

Fehling, M. R., & Triandis, H. C. Implied attitude structure (submitted for publication), 1970.

Feldman, J. M. Stimulus characterstics and subject prejudice as determinants of stereotype attribution. Unpublished M. A. thesis. Urbana, Ill: University of Illinois, 1968. (a)

Feldman, R. E. Response to compatriot and foreigner who seek assistance. *J. pers. soc. Psych.,* 1968, **10**, 202–214. (b)

Ferguson, G. A. *Statistical analysis in psychology and education.* New York: McGraw-Hill, 1966.

Finley, D. J., Holsti, O. R., & Fagen, R. R. *Enemies in politics.* Chicago: Rand McNally, 1967.

Fishbein, M. An investigation of the relationship between beliefs about an object and attitude towards that object. Technical Report No. 6, Los Angeles, California: Department of Psychology, University of California, 1961.

Fishbein, M. The relationship of the behavioral differential to other attitude instruments. Paper read at the American Psychological Association, Los Angeles, 1964.

Fishbein, M. A consideration of beliefs, attitudes, and their relationships. In

I. D. Steiner & M. Fishbein (Eds.), *Current studies in social psychology.* New York: Holt, Rinehart, and Winston, 1965, 107–120.

Fliegel, F. C. A multiple correlation analysis of factors associated with adoption of farm practices. *Rur. Sociol.,* 1956, **21,** 284–292.

Foa, U. G. Cross-cultural similarity and difference in interpersonal behavior. *J. Abnorm. Soc. Psychol.,* 1964, **68,** 517–522.

Foa, U. G. New developments in facet design and analysis. *Psychol. Rev.,* 1965, **72,** 262–274.

Foa, U. G. Perception in behavior in reciprocal roles: the Ringex model. *Psychol. Monogr.,* 1966, **80,** No. 15.

Foa, U. G., & Chemers, M. M. The significance of role behavior differentiation for cross-cultural interaction training. *Int. J. Psychol.,* 1967, **2,** 45–57.

Forster, K. I., Triandis, H. C., & Osgood, C. E. An analysis of the method of triads in research on the measurement of meaning. Technical Report No. 17. Urbana, Ill.: Department of Psychology, University of Illinois, 1964.

Foster, G. M. Peasant society and the image of limited good. *Amer. Anthropol.,* 1965, **67,** 293–315.

Fouraker, L. E., & Siegel, S. *Bargaining behavior.* New York: McGraw-Hill, 1963.

Frake, C. O. The diagnosis of disease among the Subanun of Mindanao. *Amer. Anthropologist,* 1961, **63,** 113–132.

Frake, C. O. Cultural ecology and ethnography. *Amer. Anthropologist,* 1962, **64,** 53–59. (a)

Frake, C. O. The ethnographic study of cognitive systems. In *Anthropology and human behavior.* Washington: The Anthropological Society of Washington, 1962. (b)

French, J. R. O., Jr., Israel, J., & As, D. An experiment on participation in a Norwegian factory. *Human Relations,* 1960, **13,** 3–19.

Friedman, G. *The anatomy of work.* (Translated by W. Rawson.) Glencoe, Ill.: Free Press, 1961.

Frijda, N. H., & Geer, J. P. van de. Codability-recognition: an experiment with facial expressions. *Acta Psychol.,* 1961, **18,** 360–367.

Frijda, N., & Jahoda, G. On the scope and methods of cross-cultural research. *Int. J. Psychol.,* 1966, **1,** 109–128.

Gardner, R. W. Cognitive styles in categorizing behavior. *J. Pers.,* 1953, **22,** 214–233.

Gardner, R. W., Jackson, D. N., & Messick, S. J. Personality organization in cognitive controls and intellectual abilities. *Psychol. Issues,* 1960, **2,** No. 4.

Gay, J., & Cole, M. *The new mathematics and an old culture.* New York: Holt, Rinehart and Winston, 1967.

Gibbs, J. P. Norms: the problem of definition and classification. *Amer. J. Sociol.,* 1965, **70,** 586–594.

Gibson, J. J. *The senses considered as perceptual systems.* Boston: Houghton Mifflin, 1966.

Gillespie, J. M., & Allport, G. W. *Youth's outlook on the future: a cross-national study.* Garden City: Doubleday, 1955.

Glenn, E. Learning theory and theory of social organization. Paper presented at a conference on cross-cultural interaction, Washington, D.C., 1968.

Glixman, A. F. Categorizing behavior as a function of meaning domain. *J. pers. soc. Psychol.,* 1965, **2,** 370–377.

Glixman, A. F., & Wolfe, J. C. Category membership and interitem semantic space distances. *J. Pers.,* 1967, **35,** 133–144.

Goldberg, G. N. Visual behavior and face-to-face distance during interaction. Unpublished Master's thesis, Yale University, 1968.

Goodman, M. E. Values, attitudes and social concepts of Japanese and American children. *Amer. Anthropologist,* 1957, **59,** 979–999.

Gordon, L. V. Comments on "Cross-cultural equivalence of personality measures." *J. soc. Psychol.,* 1968, **75,** 11–19.

Gordon, L. V., & Kikuchi, A. American personality tests in cross-cultural research—a caution. *J. soc. Psychol.,* 1966, **69,** 179–183.

Gordon, L. V., & Kikuchi, A. The comparability of the forced-choice and *Q*-sort measurement approaches: another culture study. *J. soc. Psychol.,* 1970, **81,** 137–144.

Gorlow, L., & Noll, G. A. A study of empirically derived values. *J. soc. Psychol.,* 1967, **73,** 261–269. (a)

Gorlow, L., & Noll, G. A. The measurement of empirically determined values. *Educ. psychol. Measmt.,* 1967, **27,** 1115–1118. (b)

Guetzkow, H., Alger, C. F., Brody, R. A., Noel, R. C., & Snyder, R. C. *Simulation in international relations: development for research and teaching.* Englewood Cliffs, N.J.: Prentice-Hall, 1963.

Guilford, J. P. *The nature of human intelligence.* New York: McGraw-Hill, 1967.

Guilford, J. P. Intelligence has three facets. *Science,* 1968, **160,** 615–620.

Gulliksen, H. Methods for determining equivalence of measures. *Psychol. Bull.,* 1968, **70,** 534–544.

Guthrie, G. M. *The psychology of modernization in the rural Phillipines.* Quezon City, Phillipines: Ateno de Manila University Press, 1970.

Guttman, L. A structural theory of intergroup beliefs and action. *Amer. sociol. Rev.,* 1959, **24,** 318–328.

Hall, E. T. *The silent language.* Garden City, N.Y.: Doubleday, 1959.

Hall, E. T. *The hidden dimension.* Garden City, N.Y.: Doubleday, 1966.

Hallowell, A. I. *Culture and experience.* Philadelphia: University of Pennsylvania Press, 1955.

Hammer, M. Some comments on formal analysis of grammatical and semantic systems. *Amer. Anthropologist,* 1966, **68,** 362–373.

Hammond, K. R. *The psychology of Egon Brunswik.* New York: Holt, Rinehart and Winston, 1966.

Harding, J., Kutner, B., Proshansky, H., & Chein, I. Prejudice and ethnic relations. In G. Lindzey (Ed.), *Handbook of social psychology,* Vol. II. Reading, Mass.: Addison Wesley, 1954.

Hare, A. P. *Handbook of small group research.* New York: Free Press, 1961.

Haried, A. The semantic problem of external accounting communication. Ph.D. dissertation, University of Illinois, 1969.

Hebb, D. O., & Thompson, W. R. The social significance of animal studies. In G. Lindzey (Ed.), *Handbook of social psychology.* Reading, Mass.: Addison-Wesley, 1954.

Heise, D. R. Sensitization of verbal response-dispositions by *n* Affiliation and *n* Achievement. *J. Verbal Learning Verbal Behav.,* 1966, **5,** 522–525.

Helson, H. *Adaptation level theory.* New York: Harper & Row, 1964.

Herskovits, M. J. *Cultural anthropology*. New York: Knopf, 1955.

Hockett, C. F. Chinese versus English: an exploration of the Whorfian thesis. In H. Hoijer (Ed.), *Language in culture*. American Anthropological Association, 1954, No. 79.

Holtzman, W. H. Cross-cultural studies in psychology. *Int. J. Psychol.*, 1968, **3**, 83–92.

Homans, G. C. *The human group*. New York: Harcourt, Brace, 1950.

Homans, G. C. *Social behavior: its elementary forms*. New York: Harcourt, Brace and World, 1961.

Horst, P. *Factor analysis of data matrices*. New York: Holt, Rinehart, and Winston, 1965.

Hudson, W. Pictorial depth perception in sub-cultural groups in Africa. *J. soc. Psychol.*, 1960, **52**, 183–208.

Humphreys, L. G., & Ilgen, D. Note on a criterion for the number of common factors. Urbana, Ill.: Department of Psychology, University of Illinois, 1968. (Mimeo)

Hyman, H. Studying expert informants by survey methods: A cross national inquiry. *Publ. Opin. Quart.*, 1967, **31**, 9–26.

Iacono, G. An affiliative society facing innovations. *J. soc. Issues*, 1968, **24**, No. 2, 125–130.

IED (Information and Education Division, United States War Department). Opinion about Negro infantry platoons in white companies of seven divisions. In C. E. Swanson, T. M. Newcomb, and E. L. Hartley (Eds.), *Readings and social psychology*. New York: Holt, Rinehart and Winston, 1952.

Ikle, F. C. Political negotiation as a process of modifying utilities. *J. Conflict Resolution*, 1962, **6**, 19–28.

Inkeles, A. Making men modern: On the causes and consequences of individual change in six developing countries. *Amer. J. Sociol.*, 1969, **75**, 208–225.

Irvine, S. H. Factor analyses of African abilities and attainments: constructs across cultures. *Psychol. Bull.*, 1969, **71**, 20–32.

Jacob, P. E., Teune, H., & Watts, T. Values, leadership and development: a four-nation study. *Soc. Sci. Inf.*, 1968, **7/2**, 49–92.

Jahoda, G. Geometric illusions and environment: A study in Ghana. *Brit. J. Psychol.*, 1966, **57**, 193–199.

Jakobovits, L. A. Comparative psycholinguistics in the study of cultures. *Int. J. Psychol.*, 1966, **1**, 15–37.

Jakobovits, L. A. Some potential uses of the cross-cultural Atlas of affective meanings. Paper presented at the XI Interamerican Congress of Psychology, Mexico City, 1967.

Jessor, R., Graves, T. D., Hanson, R. C., & Jessor, S. L. *Society, personality and deviant behavior: a study of a tri-ethnic community*. New York: Holt, Rinehart and Winston, 1968.

Kahl, J. A. Some measurements of achievement orientation. *Amer. J. Sociol.*, 1965, **70**, 669–681.

Kahl, J. A. *The measurement of modernism: a study of values in Brazil and Mexico*. Austin: University of Texas Press, 1968.

Kaiser, H. F. The varimax criterion for analytic rotation in factor analysis. *Psychometrika*, 1958, **23**, 187–200.

Katz, D. The functional approach to the study of attitudes. *Publ. Opin. Quart.*, 1960, **24**, 163–204.

Katz, D., & Braly, K. W. Racial stereotypes of 100 college students. *J. abnorm. and soc. Psychol.*, 1933, **48,** 327–335.

Kelly, G. A. *The psychology of personal constructs.* New York: Norton, 1955.

Kelman, H. C. *International behavior: a social psychological analysis.* New York: Holt, Rinehart and Winston, 1965.

Kerlinger, F. N. Social attitudes and their criterial referents: a structural theory. *Psycholog. Rev.*, 1967, **74,** 110–122.

Kiesler, C. A., & Goldberg, G. N. Multidimensional approach to the experimental study of interpersonal attraction: Effect of a blunder on the attractiveness of a competent other. *Psychol. Reps.* 1968, **22,** 693–705.

Kikuchi, A., & Gordon, L. V. Evaluation and cross-cultural application of a Japanese form of the Survey of Interpersonal Values. *J. soc. Psychol.*, 1966, **69,** 185–195.

Kilty, K. M. The methodological and theoretical consideration of the implicative meaning procedure. Technical Report No. 53. Urbana, Ill.: Department of Psychology, University of Illinois, 1967.

Kivlin, J. E., & Fliegel, F. C. Differential perceptions of innovations and rate of adoption. *Rur. Sociol.*, 1967, **32,** 78–91.

Klineberg, O. *The human dimension in international relations.* New York: Holt, Rinehart and Winston, 1964.

Kluckhohn, C. Culture and behavior. In Lindzey, G. (Ed.), *Handbook of social psychology.* Reading, Mass.: Addison-Wesley, 1954, 921–976.

Kluckhohn, C. Toward a comparison of value-emphases in different cultures. In L. D. White (Ed.), *The state of the social sciences.* Chicago: University of Chicago Press, 1956, 116–132.

Kluckhohn, C. The scientific study of values. In *University of Toronto Installation Lectures.* Toronto: University of Toronto Press, 1959.

Kluckhohn, F. R., & Strodtbeck, F. L. *Variations in value orientations.* New York: Harper and Row, 1961.

Kramer, B. M. Residential contract as a determinant of attitudes toward Negroes, Unpublished Ph.D. dissertation, Harvard University, 1951.

Krauss, H. H., & Krauss, B. J. Cross-cultural study of the thwarting-disorientation theory of suicide. *J. abnorm. Psychol.*, 1968, **73,** 353–357.

Kruskal, J. R. Multidimensional scaling optimizing goodness of fit to a nonmetric hypothesis. *Psychometrika,* 1964, **29,** 1–28.

Kuusinen, J. A. Affective and denotative structures of personality ratings. *J. pers. soc. Psychol.*, 1969, **12,** 181–188.

Lambert, W. E. Paper presented at a conference on subjective culture. Athens, Greece, 1968.

Lambert, W. E., Havelka, J., & Crosby, C. The influence of language-acquisition context on bilingualism. *J. abnorm. Soc. Psychol.*, 1958, **56,** 239–244.

Lambert, W. E., & Tucker, G. R. A social-psychological study of interpersonal modes of address: I. A French-Canadian illustration, 1969. (Mimeo)

Landar, H. J., Ervin, S. M., & Horowitz, A. E. Navaho color categories. *Language,* 1960, **36,** 368–382.

Landsberger, H. A. Interaction process analysis of the mediation of labor-management disputes. *J. abnorm. Soc. Psychol.*, 1955, **51,** 552–558.

LaPiere, R. T. Attitudes vs. action. *J. soc. Forces,* 1934, **14,** 230–237.

Lenneberg, E. H. *Biological foundation of language.* New York: Wiley, 1967.

Lenneberg, E. H., & Roberts, J. M. The language of experience: a study in methodology. *Int. J. Amer. Linguistics,* 1956, Supplement to Vol. 22, No. 2.

LeShan, L. L. Time orientation and social class. *J. abnorm. Soc. Psychol.,* 1952, **47,** 589–592.

Lerner, D. *The passing of traditional society.* Glencoe, Ill.: Free Press, 1958.

Lévi-Bruhl, L. *Les fonctions mentales dans les sociétés inféreures.* Paris: Alcan, 1910.

Levin, J. Three-mode factor analysis. Unpublished Ph.D. dissertation, University of Illinois, 1963.

LeVine, R. A. *Dreams and deeds: achievement motivation in Nigeria.* Chicago: University of Chicago Press, 1966.

Levi-Strauss, C. *The savage mind.* Chicago: University of Chicago Press, 1966.

Lewin, K. *Field theory in social science.* New York: Harper, 1951.

Lewis, O. Controls and experiments in field work. In A. Kroeber (Ed.), *Anthropology today.* Chicago: University of Chicago Press, 1953.

Lingoes, J. C. An IBM 7090 program for Guttman Lingoes smallest space analysis. *Behavl. Sci.,* 1965, **10,** 183–184.

Lippman, W. *Public opinion.* New York: Macmillan, 1922.

Littig, L. W., & Yeracaris, C. A. Achievement motivation and intergenerational occupational mobility. *J. pers. soc. Psychol.,* 1965, **1,** 386–389.

Little, K. B. Cultural variations in social schemata. *J. pers. soc. Psychol.,* 1968, **10,** 1–7.

Loh, W. D., & Triandis, H. C. Role perceptions in Peru. *Int. J. Psychol.,* 1968, **3,** 175–182.

Long, B. H., Henderson, E. H., & Ziller, R. C. Developmental changes in the self-concept during middle childhood. *Merrill-Palmer Quart.,* 1967, **13,** 201–215.

Lorr, M., & McNair, D. M. Expansion of the interpersonal behavior circle. *J. pers. soc. Psychol.,* 1965, **2,** 823–830.

Lund, F. H. The psychology of belief: IV. The law of primacy and persuasion. *J. abnorm. soc. Psychol.,* 1925, **20,** 174–196.

McClelland, D. C. *The achieving society.* Princeton, N.J.: Van Nostrand, 1961.

McGrath, J. E. A social psychologial approach to the study of negotiations. Technical Report #1, Contract AF-49-(638)-1291. Urbana, Ill.: University of Illinois, 1964.

McKendry, J. M., McKendry, M. S., & Guthrie, G. M. *The impact of social change in developing countries.* State College, Penn.: Singer, 1967.

McLeod, R. B. The phenomenological approach to social psychology. *Psychol. Rev.,* 1947, **54,** 193–210.

Marshall, G. R., & Cofer, C. N. Associative indices as measures of word relatedness: a summary and comparison of ten methods. *J. Verbal Learning Verbal Behav.,* 1963, **1,** 408–421.

Mercado, S. J., Diaz-Guerrero, R. D., & Gardner, R. W. Cognitive control in children of Mexico and the United States. *J. soc. Psychol.,* 1963, **59,** 199–208.

Messick, S., & Kogan, N. Personality consistencies in judgment: Dimensions of role constructs. *Multivariate Behav. Res.,* 1966, **1,** 165–175.

Metzger, D. G., & Williams, G. E. Some procedures and results in the study of native categories: Tzeltal "Firewood." *Amer. Anthropologist,* 1966, **68,** 389–407.

Miller, G. The magical number seven, plus or minus two. *Psychol. Rev.,* 1956, **63,** 81–97.

Miron, M., & Wolfe, S. A cross-linguistic analysis of the response distributions of restricted word associations. University of Illinois, 1962. (Mimeo)

Morgaut, M. E. *Cinq années de psychologies Africaines.* Paris: Presse en Universitaires, 1962.

Morris, C. G., & Fiedler, F. E. Application of a new system of interaction analysis to the relationships between leader attitudes and behavior in problem-solving groups. Technical Report No. 14, Contract NR 177-472, Nonr 1834(36). Urbana Ill.: Department of Psychology, University of Illinois, 1964.

Morris, C. W., and Jones, L. V. Values scales and dimensions. *J. abnorm. soc. Psychol.,* 1955, **51,** 523–535.

Morris, C. W. *Varieties of human value.* Chicago: University of Chicago Press, 1956.

Morse, N. *Satisfaction in the white-collar job.* Ann Arbor: University of Michigan, Institute of Social Research, 1953.

Moulik, T. K., Hrabovszky, J. P., & Roa, C. S. S. Predictive values of some factors of adoption of nitrogenous fertilizer by North Indian farmers. *Rur. Sociol.,* 1966, **3,** 467–477.

Naroll, R. *Data quality control—a new research technique.* New York: Macmillan, 1962.

Naroll, R. Some thoughts on comparative method in cultural anthropology. In H. M. Blalock, Jr., and A. B. Blalock (Eds.), *Methodology in social research.* New York: McGraw-Hill, 1968, 236–277.

Naroll, R., & Cohen, R. *A handbook on method in cultural anthropology.* New York: American Museum of Natural History, 1970.

Neisser, U. *Cognitive psychology.* New York: Appleton-Century-Crofts, 1967.

Newcomb, T. M. *The acquaintance process.* New York: Holt, 1961.

Niyekawa, A. M. A study of second language learning. Final report to Department of Health, Education and Welfare, 1968.

North, R. C., Holsti, O. R., Zaniovich, M. G., & Zinnes, D. A. *Content analysis: a handbook with application for the study of international crisis.* Evanston, Ill.: Northwestern University Press, 1963.

Northrup, F., & Livingston, E. *Cross-cultural understanding: epistemology in anthropology.* New York: Harper and Row, 1964.

Oncken, G. A predictive model of role behavior. Unpublished M. A. thesis, University of Illinois, 1968.

Opler, M. E. Themes as dynamic forces in culture. *Amer. J. Sociol.,* 1945, **51,** 198–206.

Osgood, C. E. *Method and theory in experimental psychology.* New York: Oxford University Press, 1953.

Osgood, C. E. Cognitive dynamics in the conduct of human affairs. *Publ. Opin. Quart.,* 1960, **34,** 341–365.

Osgood, C. E. *An alternative to war and surrender.* Urbana, Ill.: University of Illinois Press, 1962.

Osgood, C. E. Semantic differential technique in the comparative study of cultures. *Amer. Anthropologist,* 1964, **66,** 171–200.

Osgood, C. E. Cross-cultural comparability in attitude measurements via multilingual semantic differentials. In I. D. Steiner and M. Fishbein (Eds.),

Current studies in social psychology. Chicago: Holt, Rinehart and Winston, 1965, 95–107.

Osgood, C. E. *Perspective in foreign policy.* Palo Alto, Calif.: Pacific Books, 1966.

Osgood, C. E. On the strategy of cross-cultural research into subjective culture. *Soc. sci. Inf.,* 1967, **6,** 5–37.

Osgood, C. E. Speculation on the structure of interpersonal intentions. *Behav. Sci.,* 1970, **15,** 237–254.

Osgood, C. E., Archer, W. K., & Miron, M. S. The cross-cultural generality of meaning systems. Urbana, Ill.: Institute of Communications Research, University of Illinois, 1963. (Mimeo)

Osgood, C. E., Suci, G. J., & Tannenbaum, P. H. *The measurement of meaning.* Urbana, Ill.: University of Illinois Press, 1957.

Osgood, C. E., & Tannenbaum, T. H. The principle of congruity in the prediction of attitude change. *Psychol. Rev.,* 1955, **62,** 42–55.

Pareek, U. A motivational paradigm of development. *J. soc. Issues,* 1968, **26,** 115–124.

Peak, H. Attitudes and motivation. In M. Jones (Ed.), *Nebraska Symposium on Motivation.* Lincoln: University of Nebraska Press, 1955.

Pearlin, L. I., & Kohn, M. L. Social class, occupation and parental values: a cross-national study. *Amer. sociol. Rev.,* 1966, **31,** 466–479.

Peck, R. F. A comparison of the value systems of Mexican and American youth. *Rev. Interamer. Psicol.,* 1967, **1,** 41–50.

Pelto, P. J. Psychological anthropology. In B. J. Siegel and A. R. Beals (Eds.), *Biennial review of anthropology.* Stanford: Stanford Press, 1967, 140–208.

Pike, K. L. *Language in relation to a unified theory of the structure of human behavior.* The Hague: Mouton, 1966.

Porteus, S. D. Ethnic group differences. *Mankind Quart.,* 1961, **1,** 187–200.

Posavac, E. J., & Triandis, H. C. Personality characteristics, race, and grades as determinants of interpersonal attitudes. *J. soc. Psychol.,* 1968, **76,** 227–242.

Prezeworski, A., & Teune, H. Equivalence in cross-national research. *Publ. Opin. Quart.,* 1967, **30,** 551–568.

Przeworski, A., & Teune, H. *Logic of comparative social inquiry.* New York: Wiley, 1969.

Radin, P. *The world of primitive man.* Paris, Abelard-Schuman, 1953.

Rapoport, A. *Fights, games and debates.* Ann Arbor: University of Michigan Press, 1960.

Redfield, R. *The primitive world and its transformations.* Ithaca, New York: Cornell University Press, 1953.

Remmers, H. H. *Anti-democratic attitudes in American schools.* Evanston, Ill.: Northwestern University Press, 1963.

Riecken, H. W., & Homans, G. C. Psychological aspects of social structure. In G. Lindzey (Ed.), *Handbook of social psychology.* Reading, Mass.: Addison-Wesley, 1954, 786–832.

Riegel, K. F. A comparison of restricted associations among six languages. *J. soc. Psychol.,* 1968, **75,** 67–78.

Robbins, M. C., & Pollnac, R. B. Drinking patterns and acculturation in rural Buganda. *Amer. Anthropologist,* 1969, **71,** 276–284.

Roethlisberger, F., & Dickson, W. J. *Management and the worker.* Cambridge, Mass.: Harvard University Press, 1939.

Rogers, E. M. *Diffusion of innovations.* New York: The Free Press, 1962.

Rogers, E. M., & Neill, R. E. *Achievement motivation among Colombian farmers.* East Lansing, Mich.: Department of Communications, Michigan State University, 1966.

Rokeach, M. Belief versus race as determinants of social distance. Comment on Triandis' paper. *J. abnorm. soc. Psychol.,* 1961, **62,** 187–188.

Rokeach, M. *Beliefs, attitudes and values.* San Francisco: Jossey-Bass, 1968.

Rokeach, M., & Rothman, G. The principle of belief congruence and the congruity principle as models of cognitive interaction. *Psychol. Rev.,* 1965, **72,** 128–142.

Rokeach, M., Smith, P. W., & Evans, R. I. Two kinds of prejudice or one? In M. Rokeach (Ed.), *The open and closed mind.* New York: Basic Books, 1960, 132–168.

Rommetveit, R., & Israel, J. Notes of the standardization of experimental manipulations and measurements in cross-national research. *J. soc. Issues,* 1954, **10,** No. 4, 61–68.

Romney, A. K., & D'Andrade, R. D. Transcultural studies in cognition. *Amer. Anthropologist,* 1964, **66,** Special Issue, 1–253.

Rose, A M. *Studies in reduction of prejudice.* Chicago: American Council on Race Relations, 1948.

Rosen, B. C., & D'Andrade, R. The psychological origins of achievement motivation. *Sociometry,* 1959, **22,** 185–218.

Rosenberg, M. J. Cognitive structure and attitudinal affect. *J. abnorm. and soc. Psychol.,* 1956, **53,** 367–372.

Rosenberg, M. J. Inconsistency arousal and reduction in attitude change. In I. D. Steiner and M. Fishbein (Eds.), *Current studies in social psychology* New York: Holt, Rinehart and Winston, 1965, 121–134.

Rosenzweig, M. R. Etudes sur l'association des mots. *Année psychol.,* 1957, **57,** 23–32.

Rosenzweig, M. R. Comparison among word associations with responses in English, French, German and Italian. *Amer. J. Psychol.,* 1961, **74,** 347–360.

Rotter, J. B. Generalized expectancies for internal versus external control of reinforcement. *Psychol. Monogr.,* 1966, **80,** No. 1. (Whole No. 609)

Rozelle, R. M., & Campbell, D. T. More plausible hypotheses in the cross-lagged panel correlation technique. *Psychol. Bull.,* 1969, **71,** 74–79.

Rudin, S. A. National motives predict psychogenic death rates 25 years later. *Science,* 1968, **160,** 901–903.

Rummel, R. J., Sawyer, J., Guetzkow, H., & Tanter, R. *Dimensions of nations: A factor analysis of 236 social, political and economic characteristics* (in preparation).

Samuelson, B. The patterning of attitudes and beliefs regarding the American Negro: An analysis of public opinion. Unpublished Ph.D. dissertation, Radcliff College, 1945.

Sawyer, J. Dimensions of nations: Size, wealth, and politics. *Amer. J. Sociol.* 1967, **7,** 145–172.

Sawyer, J., & LeVine, R. A. Cultural dimensions: a factor analysis of the world ethnographic sample. *Amer. Anthropologist,* 1966, **68,** 708–731.

Schachter, S., Nuttin, J., de Monchaus, C., Maucorps, P. H., Osmer, D., Duijker, H., Rommetveit, R., & Israel, J. Cross-cultural experiments on threat and rejection. *Human Relations,* 1954, **7,** 403–439.

Schuman, H. The random probe: a technique for evaluating the validity of closed questions. *Amer. Sociol. Rev.,* 1966, **31,** 218–222. (a)

Schuman, H. Social change and the validity of regional stereotypes in East Pakistan. *Sociometry,* 1966, **29,** 426–440. (b)

Schwarz, P. A. Adapting tests to cultural setting. *Educ. psychol. Measmt.,* 1963, **23,** 672–686.

Scott, W. A. Cognitive complexity and cognitive flexibility. *Sociometry,* 1962, **25,** 404–414.

Scott, W. A. Cognitive complexity and cognitive balance. *Sociometry,* 1963, **26,** 66–74.

Scott, W. A. *Values and organizations: a study of fraternities and sororities.* Chicago: Rand McNally, 1965.

Scott, W. A. Brief report: Measures of cognitive structure. *Multivariate behavl. Res.,* 1966, **1,** 391–395.

Seashore, S. E. *Group cohesiveness in the industrial work group.* Ann Arbor: Survey Research Center, Institute of Social Research, University of Michigan, 1954.

Segall, M. H. Research by expatriates in Africa: Can it be "relevant?" *African Stud. Rev.,* 1970, **13,** 35–41.

Segall, M. H., Campbell, D. T., & Herskovits, M. J. *The influence of culture on visual perception.* Indianapolis, Ind.: Bobbs-Merrill, 1966.

Selekman, B. M., Selekman, S. K., & Fuller, S. H. *Problems in labor relations.* New York: McGraw-Hill, 1958.

Shartle, C. L., Brumback, G. B., & Rizzo, J. R. An approach to dimension of value. *J. Psychol.,* 1964, **51,** 101–111.

Shelling, T. C. *Arms and influence.* New Haven: Yale University Press, 1966.

Shepard, R. N. The analysis of proximities: multidimensional scaling with an unknown distance function, I and II. *Psychometrika,* 1962, **27,** 125–139, 219–246.

Sherif, C. W. Social categorization as a function of latitude of acceptance and series range. *J. abnorm. Soc. Psychol.,* 1963, **67,** 148–156.

Sherman, A. W. *The social psychology of bi-lateral negotiation.* Evanston, Ill.: Northwestern University, Department of Psychology, 1963.

Simon, H. A. Spurious correlation: a causal interpretation. *J. Amer. Statist. Ass.,* 1954, **49,** 467–479.

Singer, J. D. *Quantitative international politics: insight and evidence.* New York: The Free Press, 1968.

Singh, P. N., Huang, S. C., & Thompson, G. G. A comparative study of selected attitudes, values and personality characteristics of American, Chinese and Indian students. *J. soc. Psychol.,* 1962, **57,** 123–132.

Skinner, B. F. *Science and human behavior.* New York: Macmillan, 1953.

Slater, P. E. Contrasting correlates of group size. *Sociometry,* 1958, **21,** 129–139.

Smith, D. H., & Inkeles A. The OM scale: a comparative social-psychological measure of modernity. *Sociometry,* 1966, **29,** 353–377.

Snider, J. G., & Osgood, C. E. *Semantic differential technique: a sourcebook,* Chicago: Aldine, 1969.

Solomon, R. An extension of the control group design. *Psychol. Bull.,* 1949, **46,** 137–150.

Staats, C. K., Staats, A. W., & Heard, W. G. Attitude development and ratio of reinforcement. *Sociometry,* 1960, **23,** 338–350.

Staats, A. W. An outline of an integrated learning theory of attitude formation and function. In M. Fishbein (Ed.), *Readings in attitude theory and measurement.* New York: Wiley, 1967. Pp. 373–377.

Stagner, R. *Psychological aspects of international conflict.* Belmont, Calif.: Brooks/Cole, 1967.

Stefflre, V., Vales, C. C., & Morley, L. Language and cognition in Yucatan: a cross-cultural replication. *J. pers. soc. Psychol.,* 1966, **4,** 112–115.

Steiner, I. D. Perceived freedom. In L. Berkowitz (Ed.), *Advances in experimental social psychology.* New York: Academic, 1970. Pp. 187–249.

Steiner, I. D., & Rogers, E. D. Alternate responses to dissonance. *J. abnorm. soc. Psychol.,* 1963, **66,** 129–136.

Straus, M. A. Methodology of a laboratory experimental study of families in three societies. *Yearbook of the International Sociological Association,* 1966.

Strodtbeck, F. L. Husband-wife interaction over revealed differences. *Amer. sociol. Rev.,* 1951, **16,** 468–473.

Strodtbeck, F. L. Considerations of meta-method in cross-cultural studies. *Amer. Anthropologist,* 1964, **66** (special issue), 223–229.

Szalay, L. B., & Brent, J. E. The analysis of cultural meanings through free verbal associations. *J soc. Psychol.,* 1967, **72,** 161–187.

Szalay, L. B., Windle, C., & Lysne, D. A. Attitude measurement by free verbal associations. *J. soc. Psychol.,* 1970, **82,** 43–55.

Tajfel, H. Social and cultural factors in perception. In G. Lindzey and E. Aronson (Eds.), *The handbook of social psychology.* Reading, Mass.: Addison-Wesley, 1969.

Tanaka, Y. A cross-cultural study of the congruity hypothesis. Unpublished study at the Institute of Communications Research, University of Illinois. 1960.

Tanaka, Y. A cross-cultural study of national stereotypes held by American and Japanese college graduate subjects. *Jap. Psychol. Res.,* 1962, **4,** 65–78.

Tanaka, Y. A test of the congruity hypothesis across three language/culture communities. *Gakushuin University review of politics and economics,* Vol. 9. Tokyo, 1963.

Tanaka, Y. The use of the entropy measure, *H,* as an index of perceptual sign codability: a cross-cultural study. *Jap. Psychol. Res.,* 1964, **6,** 38–45.

Tanaka, Y. A political differential, or POLDI, for the measurement of national images. Unpublished research at the Gakushuin University, Tokyo, 1965. (a)

Tanaka, Y. A cross-cultural approach to the study of inter-nation perception: An application of the semantic differential method to automated content analysis. *Ann. Jap. soc. psychol. Ass.,* 1965, 100–124 (text in Japanese). (b)

Tanaka, Y. Cross-cultural comparability of the affective meaning systems (measured by means of multilingual semantic differentials). *J. soc. Issues,* 1967, **23,** 27–46. (a)

Tanaka, Y. Toward the literacy and semantics of nuclear proliferation. Regina, Canada: Division of Social Sciences, University of Sakatchewan, 1967. (Mimeo) (b)

Tanaka, Y. *The science of human communication.* Tokyo: Nihon Hyoron, 1969 (text in Japanese).

Tanaka, Y. Japanese attitudes toward nuclear arms. *Publ. Opin. Quart.,* 1970.

Tanaka, Y., & Iwamatsu, Y. An exploratory semantic differential study of the affective and the cognitive components of the attitudes held by Japanese college Ss toward nuclear testing and proliferation. *Peace Research in Japan, 1968,* 1968, 25–70. (a)

Tanaka, Y., & Iwamatsu, Y. Psycholinguistic studies on cross-cultural generality in cognitive interaction. *Jap. psychol. Res.,* 1968, **10,** 45–58. (b)

Tanaka, Y., Iwamatsu, Y., & May, W. A. Cross-cultural investigation of nation perception. Reported in Tanaka, May & Iwamatsu, 1968.

Tanaka, Y., May, W., & Iwamatsu, Y. Psycholinguistic studies on the cross-cultural generality of cognitive interaction. *Proceedings of the XI Inter-American Congress of Psychology,* 1968.

Tanaka, Y., & Osgood, C. E. Cross-culture, cross-concept, and cross-subject generality of affective meaning systems. *J. pers. soc. Psychol.,* 1965, **2,** 143–153.

Tanaka, Y., Oyama, T., & Osgood, C. E. A cross-culture and cross-concept study of the generality of semantic spaces. *J. Verbal Learning Verbal Behav.,* 1963, **2,** 392–405.

Thiabaut, J. W., & Kelley, H. H. *The social psychology of groups.* New York: Wiley, 1959.

Thomanek, E. K. The measurement of implicative meaning. Technical Report No. 63, Urbana, Illinois: Department of Psychology, University of Illinois, 1968.

Thurstone, L. L. Comment. *Amer. J. Sociol.,* 1946, **52,** 39–50.

Tolman, E. D. Cognitive maps in rats and men. *Psychol. Rev.,* 1948, **55,** 189–208.

Torgerson, W. S. *Theory and methods of scaling.* New York: Wiley, 1958, 247–297.

Triandis, H. C. Differential perception of certain jobs and people by managers, clerks and workers in industry. *J. appl. Psychol.,* 1959, **43,** 221–225. (a)

Triandis, H. C. Cognitive similarity and interpersonal communication in industry. *J. appl. Psychol.,* 1959, **43,** 321–326. (b)

Triandis, H. C. Categories of thought of managers, clerks and workers about jobs and people in industry. *J. appl. Psychol.,* 1959, **43,** 338–344. (c)

Triandis, H. C. A comparative factor analysis of job semantic structures of managers and workers. *J. appl. Psychol.,* 1960, **44,** 297–302.

Triandis, H. C. A note on Rokeach's theory of prejudice. *J. abnorm. soc. Psychol.,* 1961, **62,** 184–186.

Triandis, H. C. Factors affecting employee selection in two cultures. *J. appl. Psychol.,* 1963, **47,** 89–96.

Triandis, H. C. Cultural influences upon cognitive processes. In L. Berkowitz (Ed.), *Advances in experimental social psychology.* New York: Academic, 1964, 1–48. (a)

Triandis, H. C. Exploratory factor analyses of the behavioral component of social attitudes. *J. abnorm. soc. Psychol.,* 1964, **68,** 420–430. (b)

Triandis, H. C. Interpersonal relations in international organizations. *Organizational behavior and human performance,* 1967, **2,** 26–55. (a)

Triandis, H. C. Toward an analysis of the components of interpersonal attitudes. In C. Sherif and M. Sherif (Eds.), *Attitudes, ego involvement and change.* New York: Wiley, 1967, 227–270. (b)

Triandis, H. C. *Attitudes and attitude change.* New York: Wiley, 1971.

Triandis, H. C., & Davis, E. E. Race and belief as determinants of behavioral intentions. *J. pers. soc. Psychol.,* 1965, **2,** 715–725.

Triandis, H. C., Davis, E. E., & Takezawa, S. Some determinants of social distance among American, German and Japanese students. *J. pers. soc. Psychol.,* 1965, **2,** 540–551.

Triandis, H. C., Davis, E. E., Vassiliou, V., & Nassiakou, M. Some methodological problems concerning research on negotiations between monolinguals. Technical Report No. 28. Urbana, Ill.: Department of Psychology, University of Illinois, 1965.

Triandis, H. C. Feldman, J., & Harvey, W. Person perception among black and white adolescents and the hard-core unemployed. Technical Report No. 5, SRS No. RD 2841-G. Champaign, Ill.: Department of Psychology, University of Illinois, 1970.

Triandis, H. C., Feldman, J., & Harvey, W. Role perceptions among black and white adolescents and the hard-core unemployed. Report No. 6, SRS No. RD 2841-G. Champaign, Ill.: Department of Psychology, University of Illinois, 1971. (a)

Triandis, H. C., Feldman, J., & Harvey, W. Job perceptions among black and white adolescents and the hard-core unemployed. Report No. 7 SRS No. RD 2841-G. Champaign, Ill.: Department of Psychology, University of Illinois, 1971. (b)

Triandis, H. C., Feldman, J., & Harvey, W. The perceptions of implicative relationships among black and white adolescents and the hard-core unemployed. Report No. 8 SRS No. RD 2841-G. Champaign, Ill.: Department of Psychology, University of Illinois, 1971. (c)

Triandis, H. C., & Fishbein, M. Cognitive interaction in person perception. *J. abnorm. soc. Psychol.,* 1963, **67,** 446–453.

Triandis, H. C., Loh, W. D., & Levin, L. A. Race, status, quality of spoken English and opinions about civil rights as determinants of interpersonal attitudes. *J. pers. soc. Psychol.,* 1966, **3,** 468–472.

Triandis, H. C., & Malpass, R. S. Field guide for the study of aspects of subjective culture. Department of Psychology, University of Illinois, Technical Report No. 4, 1970.

Triandis, H. C., & Osgood, C. E. A comparative factor analysis of semantic structures in monolingual Greek and American college students. *J. abnorm. soc. Psychol.,* 1958, **57,** 187–196.

Triandis, H. C., Tanaka, Y., & Shanmugam, A. V. Interpersonal attitudes among American, Indian, and Japanese students. *Int. J. Psychol.,* 1966, **1,** 177–206.

Triandis, H. C., & Triandis, L. M. Race, social class, religion and nationality as determinants of social distance. *J. abnorm. soc. Psychol.,* 1960, **61,** 110–118.

Triandis, H. C., & Triandis, L. M. A cross-cultural study of social distance. *Psychol. Monogr.,* 1962, **76,** No. 21.

Triandis, H. C., & Triandis, P. F. The building of nations. *Psychol. Today,* 1969, **2,** 31–35.

Triandis, H. C., Tucker, L. R., Koo, P., & Stewart, T. Three-mode factor analysis of the behavioral component of interpersonal attitudes. Technical Report No. 50. Urbana, Ill.: Department of Psychology, University of Illinois, 1967.

Triandis, H. C., & Vassiliou, V. A comparative analysis of subjective culture,

Urbana, Ill.: Department of Psychology, University of Illinois, 1967. (a)

Triandis, H. C., & Vassiliou, V. Frequency of contact and stereotyping. *J. Pers. Soc. Psychol.,* 1967b, **7,** 316–328. (b)

Triandis, H. C., and Vassiliou, V. Interpersonal influence and employee selection in two cultures. Technical Report No. 60, Champaign-Urbana, Ill.: Department of Psychology, 1968. Also, in *J. Appl. Psychol.* (in press).

Triandis, H. C., Vassiliou, V., & Nassiakou, M. Some cross-cultural studies of subjective culture. Technical Report No. 45. Urbana, Ill.: Department of Psychology, University of Illinois, 1967.

Triandis, H. C., Vassiliou, V., & Nassiakou, M. Some cultural differences in the perception of social behavior. Technical Report No. 49. Urbana, Ill.: Department of Psychology, University of Illinois, 1967.

Triandis, H. C., Vassiliou, V., & Nassiakou, M. Three cross-cultural studies of subjective culture. *J. pers. soc. Psychol., Monogr. Suppl.,* 1968, **8,** No. 4, Part 2, 1–42.

Triandis, H. C., Vassiliou, V., & Thomanek, E. K. Social status as a determinant of respect and friendship acceptance. *Sociometry,* 1966, **29,** 396–405.

Tucker, G. R., Lambert, W. E., & Viera, S. A social-psychological study of interpersonal modes of address: II. A Puerto-Rican illustration, 1969. (Mimeo)

Tucker, L. R. The extension of factor analysis to three-dimensional matrices. In N. Frederiksen (Ed.), *Contributions to mathematical psychology.* New York: Holt, Rinehart and Winston, 1964.

Tucker, L. R. Some mathematical notes on three-mode factor analysis. *Psychometrika,* 1966, **31,** 279–311.

Tucker, L., & Messick, S. An individual difference model for multidimensional scaling. *Psychometrika,* 1963, **28,** 333–367.

Tully, J., Wilkening, E. A., & Presser, H. Factors in decision making in farming problems. *Human Relations,* 1964, **17,** 295–320.

Tumin, M., Barton, P., & Burrus, B. Education, prejudice and discrimination: A study in readiness for desegregation. *Amer. sociolog. Rev.,* 1958, **23,** 41–49.

Turner, A. N., & Lawrence, P. R. *Industrial jobs and the worker.* Boston: Harvard University Graduate School of Business Administration, 1965.

Vassiliou, G. Aspects of parent-adolescent transaction in the Greek family. In G. Kaplan and S. Levovici (Eds.), *Adolescence: Psychological perspectives.* New York: Basic Books, 1968. (a)

Vassiliou, G. An introduction to transactional group image therapy. In B. Riess (Ed.), *New directions in mental health.* New York: Grune and Stratton, 1968. (b)

Vassiliou, G. Milieu-specificity in family therapy. In J. Pearce and J. Lieb (Eds.), *Transactions in family psychotherapy.* New York: Little Brown, 1969.

Vassiliou, G., Seferi, M., & Koukouridou, E. Patterns of alcohol consumption in Greece. *Int. ment. Hlth Res.,* 1968, **10,** No. 2.

Vassiliou, G., & Vassiliou, V. Social values as a psychodynamic variable: Preliminary explorations of the semantics of philotimo. *Acta Neurol. Psychiat. Hellenika,* 1966, **5,** 121–135.

Vassiliou, G., & Vassiliou, V. A transactional approach to mental health.

In B. Riess (Ed.), *New directions in mental health*. New York: Grune and Stratton, 1968, 133–172.

Vassiliou, V., Triandis, H. C., Vassiliou, G., & McGuire, H. J. Reported amount of contact and stereotyping. Technical Report No. 59. Urbana, Ill.: Department of Psychology, University of Illinois, 1968.

Voegelin, C. F., & Voegelin, F. M. *Hopi domains: a lexical approach to the problem of selection*. Baltimore: Waverly, 1957.

Vogt, E. Z., & Albert, E. People of Rimrock: a study of values in five cultures. Cambridge, Mass.: Harvard University Press, 1966.

von Neumann, J., & Morgenstern, O. *Theory of games and economic behavior*. Princeton, N.J.: Princeton University Press, 1957.

Vroom, V. *Work and motivation*. New York: Wiley, 1964.

Vygotsky, L. S. *Thought and language*. New York: Wiley, 1962.

Wallace, A. F. C. *Culture and personality*. New York: Random House, 1962. (a)

Wallace, A. F. C. Culture and cognition. *Science*, 1962, **135,** 351–357. (b)

Walton, R. E., & McKersie, R. B. *Attitudes change in intergroup relations*. Lafayette, Ind.: Industrial Administration, No. 86, 1964.

Warr, P. B., & Haycock, V. Scales for a British personality differential, *Brit. J. soc. clin. Psychol.*, 1970.

Werner, O., & Campbell, D. T. Translating, working through interpreters and the problem of decentering. In R. Naroll and R. Cohen (Eds.), *A handbook of method in cultural anthropology*. New York: American Museum of Natural History, 1970.

Werts, C. E., & Linn, R. L. Path analysis: Psychological examples. *Psychol. Bull.*, 1970, **74,** 193–212.

Whitehead, A. M., Jr., & Takezawa, S. *The other worker*. Honolulu: East-West Center, 1968.

Whiting, J. W. M. The cross-cultural method. In G. Lindzey (Ed.), *Handbook of social psychology*. Reading, Mass.: Addison-Wesley, 1954.

Whiting, J. W. M. Socialization, process and personality. In F. L. K. Hsu (Ed.), *Psychological anthropology*. Homewood, Ill.: Dorsey, 1961.

Whiting, J. W. M. Effects of climate on certain cultural practices. In W. H. Goodenough (Ed.), *Explorations in cultural anthropology*. New York: McGraw-Hill, 1964, 496–544.

Whitehill, A. M., & Takezawa, S. *The other worker*. Honolulu: East-West Press, 1968.

Whyte, W. F. An interaction approach to the theory of organization. In M. Haire, (Ed.), *Modern organization theory*. New York: Wiley, 1959.

Whyte, W. F. *Organizational behavior: theory and applications*. Homewood, Ill.: Irwin, 1969.

Wickert, F. A test of personal goal values. *J. soc. Psychol.*, 1940, **11,** 259–274.

Wiggins, J. S. Strategic method and stylistic variance in MMPI. *Psychol. Bull.*, 1962, **59,** 224–242.

Williams, R. M., Jr. Racial and cultural relations. In J. B. Gittler (Ed.), *Review of sociology*. New York: Wiley, 1957.

Winterbottom, M. R. The relation of need for achievement to learning experience in independence and mastery. In J. W. Atkinson (Ed.), *Motives in fantasy, action and society*. Princeton, N.J.: Van Nostrand, 1958.

Witkin, H. A., et al. *Personality through perception*. New York: Harper, 1954.

Wober, M. Sensotypes. *J. soc. Psychol.,* 1966, **70,** 181–189.

Wober, M. Distinguishing centricultural from cross-cultural test and research. *Perc. Mot. Skills,* 1969, **28,** 488.

Wright, S. Statistical methods in biology. *J. Amer. Statist. Ass.,* 1931, **26,** 155–163.

Yang, K. Authoritarianism and evaluation of appropriateness of role behavior. *J. soc. Psychol.,* 1970, **80,** 171–181.

Yee, A. H., & Gage, N. L. Techniques for estimating the source and direction of casual influence in panel data. *Psychol. Bull.,* 1968, **70,** 115–126.

Ziller, R. C., Long, B. H., Ramana, K. V., & Reddy, V. E. Self-other orientations of Indian and American adolescents. *J. Pers.,* 1968, **36,** 315–330.

Zimbardo, P. G. The human choice: Individuation, reason and order versus deindividuation, impulse and chaos. In *Nebraska Symposium on Motivation,* 1969, 237–307.

Author Index

Index of Concepts